Wittgenstein

Rules, Grammar and Necessity

Also by the authors:

Frege: Logical Investigations
Language, Sense and Nonsense
Scepticism, Rules and Language
Wittgenstein: Meaning and Understanding

An analytical commentary
on the *Philosophical Investigations*

Volume 2

Wittgenstein

Rules, Grammar and Necessity

G. P. Baker & P. M. S. Hacker

Fellows of St John's College · Oxford

Basil Blackwell

First published 1985
First published in paperback 1988

Basil Blackwell Ltd
108 Cowley Road, Oxford OX4 1JF, UK

Basil Blackwell Inc.
432 Park Avenue South, Suite 1503
New York, NY 10016, USA

British Library Cataloguing in Publication Data

Baker, G.P.
An analytical commentary on the Philosophical investigations.
Vol. 2: Wittgenstein: rules, grammar and necessity
1. Wittgenstein, Ludwig. Philosophical investigations
I. Title   II. Hacker, P.M.S.   III. Wittgenstein.
Ludwig. Philisophische Untersuchungen
149'.943   B3376.W563P53

ISBN 0-631-13024-1
ISBN 0-631-16188-0 Pbk

Library of Congress Cataloging in Publication Data

Baker, Gordon P.
Wittgenstein, rules, grammar, and necessity.
(An analytical commentary on the Philosophical Investigations; v.2)
Includes index.
1. Wittgenstein, Ludwig, 1889–1951. Philosophische Untersuchungen.   2. Philosophy.   3. Languages—Philosophy.
4. Semantics (Philosophy)   I. Hacker, P.M.S. (Peter Michael Stephan)   II. Title.   III. Series: Baker, Gordon P.   Analytical commentary on the Philosophical Investigations; v.2.
B3376.W563P5323 1980 vol.2   192s[192]   85-11216

ISBN 0-631-13024-1
ISBN 0-631-16188-0 (pbk.)

Typeset by Freeman Graphic, Tonbridge, Kent
Printed in Great Britain by Billing & Sons Ltd, Worcester

For Anne and Sylvia

Contents

Contents

part of our enterprise to present this documentation. The extensive unpublished material is indispensable for arriving at an understanding of Wittgenstein's ideas, and it provides the background against which our exposition of his ideas must be judged to be illuminating or found to be wanting.

The essays too had an entelechy to grow and multiply. Little seems clear, or at least beyond dispute. The very concept of a rule needs to be clarified, and Wittgenstein's use of 'rule' to be explained. He calls things 'rules' which no one had ever thought of as rules. And his use of the terms 'grammar', 'technique' and 'practice' is, in more or less similar respects, problematic. Clouds of controversy shroud the concepts of acting in accord with a rule and of following a rule. Even denser clouds cluster around the discussion of agreement and forms of life. Moreover, each of these issues involves all the rest. If a rule is characterized by its role, then misconceptions about following rules cannot be put aside while attention is focused on making clear what rules are. *Pari passu*, confusions about rules ramify into muddles about following rules. Here, it seems, light will dawn simultaneously over this whole network of normative concepts – or else not at all. We came to realize that our essays had to cover more topics than we had originally envisaged, and that they had to be interwoven with care. Unlike the relatively self-contained essays of Volume 1, these essays are more closely integrated as parts of a single logical nexus, even though, as in Volume 1, we have deliberately allowed some overlap between the essays themselves and between the essays and the exegesis.

Finally, we became convinced that Wittgenstein's writings on the philosophy of mathematics not only are illuminated by, but also illuminate, his discussions of following rules. Some of this material constituted the second half of the 1937 version of the *Philosophical Investigations*. Hence it is *a priori* probable that it has direct relevance to the first half of that version (i.e. what is roughly §§1–189 of the final text). We think that this case can be demonstrated, and we came to the view that it was worth demonstrating, not only to clarify the ideas presented in §§185–242, but also to throw light upon a whole side of Wittgenstein's thought that has been relatively neglected, grossly misconstrued and often scorned. This unanticipated project greatly extended our task. Though trying not to double our commentary, we adopted two subsidiary aims. The first was to sketch a map of the invisible companion to the final version of the *Investigations*[1] and to analyse its relation to the reasoning of §§185–242. The second was to explore, if only in a preliminary manner, the relation

---

[1] As late as 1949 Wittgenstein wrote 'I want to call the enquiries into mathematics *that belong to* my Philosophical Investigations "Beginnings of Mathematics".' (MS 169, 37; our italics)

between Wittgenstein's discussion of rule-following and his account of propositions typically conceived as necessary truths.

The upshot of these developments was the decision to interpose between *Wittgenstein: Understanding and Meaning* and the projected *Wittgenstein: Meaning and Mind* a shorter separate volume concerned exclusively with *Investigations* §§185–242. It may well evoke a chorus of criticism: 'An exemplary case of more and more about less and less!' critics will exclaim, 'May we look forward to a third volume on §243?' In response, we should point out that these sections of the *Investigations* are not only part of the core of the book, but also the least understood and the most widely *mis*understood. (As in Volume 1 we have adopted an indirect approach to the extensive, and extensively confused, secondary writings on these themes.) If we have succeeded in establishing a sound conception of Wittgenstein's remarks on following rules, and perhaps also demonstrated its viability, then the narrowing of the scope of our endeavours in this volume will have been justified. For we would have cleared the ground of extensive weeds obscuring from view, and stunting the growth of, the seeds Wittgenstein planted. If, in addition, we succeed in persuading philosophers to take a fresh look at Wittgenstein's philosophy of mathematics from a perspective different from that adopted in most current secondary writings, then more and more on less and less may yield a greater and richer harvest.

Abbreviations

1. *Published works*

The following abbreviations are used to refer to Wittgenstein's published works, listed in chronological order (where possible; some works straddle many years). The list includes derivative primary sources and lecture notes taken by others.

NB *Notebooks 1914–16*, ed. G. H. von Wright and G. E. M. Anscombe, tr. G. E. M. Anscombe (Blackwell, Oxford, 1961).

TLP *Tractatus Logico-Philosophicus*, tr. D. F. Pears and B. F. McGuiness (Routledge and Kegan Paul, London, 1961).

RLF 'Some Remarks on Logical Form', *Proceedings of the Aristotelian Society*, suppl. vol. ix (1929), pp. 162–71.

WWK *Ludwig Wittgenstein und der Wiener Kreis*, shorthand notes recorded by F. Waismann, ed. B. F. McGuinness (Blackwell, Oxford, 1967). The English translation, *Wittgenstein and the Vienna Circle* (Blackwell, Oxford, 1979) matches the pagination of the original edition.

PR *Philosophical Remarks*, ed. R. Rhees, tr. R. Hargreaves and R. White (Blackwell, Oxford, 1975).

M 'Wittgenstein's Lectures in 1930–33', in G. E. Moore, *Philosophical Papers* (Allen and Unwin, London, 1959).

LWL *Wittgenstein's Lectures, Cambridge 1930–32, from the notes of John King and Desmond Lee*, ed. Desmond Lee (Blackwell, Oxford, 1980).

PG *Philosophical Grammar*, ed. R. Rhees, tr. A. J. P. Kenny (Blackwell, Oxford, 1974).

AWL *Wittgenstein's Lectures, Cambridge 1932–35, from the notes of Alice Ambrose and Margaret MacDonald*, ed. Alice Ambrose (Blackwell, Oxford, 1979).

BB *The Blue and Brown Books* (Blackwell, Oxford, 1958). Occasionally 'Bl.B.' and 'Br.B.' are used for special reference.

LPE   'Wittgenstein's Notes for Lectures on "Private Experience" and "Sense Data"', ed. R. Rhees, *Philosophical Review* 77 (1968), pp. 275–320.

LSD   'The Language of Sense Data and Private Experience', notes taken by R. Rhees of Wittgenstein's lectures, 1936, *Philosophical Investigations* 7 (1984) pp. 1–45, 101–40.

EPB   *Eine Philosophische Betrachtung*, ed. R. Rhees, in *Ludwig Wittgenstein: Schriften 5* (Suhrkamp, Frankfurt, 1970).

RR   'On Continuity; Wittgenstein's Ideas, 1938', in R. Rhees, *Discussions of Wittgenstein* (Routledge and Kegan Paul, London, 1970), pp. 104–57.

RFM   *Remarks on the Foundations of Mathematics*, ed. G. H. von Wright, R. Rhees, G. E. M. Anscombe, tr. G. E. M. Anscombe, revised edn (Blackwell, Oxford, 1978).

LA   *Lectures and Conversations on Aesthetics, Psychology and Religious Beliefs*, ed. C. Barrett (Blackwell, Oxford, 1970).

LFM   *Wittgenstein's Lectures on the Foundations of Mathematics, Cambridge 1939*, ed. C. Diamond (Harvester Press, Sussex, 1976).

PI   *Philosophical Investigations*, ed. G. E. M. Anscombe and R. Rhees, tr. G. E. M. Anscombe, 2nd edn (Blackwell, Oxford, 1958).

Z   *Zettel*, ed. G. E. M. Anscombe and G. H. von Wright, tr. G. E. M. Anscombe (Blackwell, Oxford, 1967)

RPP I *Remarks on the Philosophy of Psychology*, Volume I, ed. G. E. M. Anscombe and G. H. von Wright, tr. G. E. M. Anscombe (Blackwell, Oxford, 1980).

RPP II *Remarks on the Philosophy of Psychology*, Volume II, ed. G. H. von Wright and H. Nyman, tr. C. G. Luckhardt and M. A. E. Aue (Blackwell, Oxford, 1980).

LW   *Last Writings on the Philosophy of Psychology*, Volume I, ed. G. H. von Wright and H. Nyman, tr. C. G. Luckhardt and M. A. E. Aue (Blackwell, Oxford, 1982).

CV   *Culture and Value*, ed. G. H. von Wright in collaboration with H. Nyman, tr. P. Winch (Blackwell, Oxford, 1980).

C   *On Certainty*, ed. G. E. M. Anscombe and G. H. von Wright, tr. D. Paul and G. E. M. Anscombe (Blackwell, Oxford, 1969).

IMT   *Introduction to Mathematical Thinking*, F. Waismann, tr. T. J. Benac (Hafner, London, 1951).

PLP   *The Principles of Linguistic Philosophy*, F. Waismann, ed. R. Harré (Macmillan and St Martin's Press, London and New York, 1965).

LPM   *Lectures on the Philosophy of Mathematics*, F. Waismann, ed. with an introduction by W. Grassl (Rodopi, Amsterdam, 1982).

Reference style: all references to *Philosophical Investigations* Part I are to sections (e.g. PI §1), except those to notes below the line on various pages. References to Part II are to pages (e.g. PI p. 202). References to other printed works are either to numbered remarks (TLP) or to sections signified '§' (Z, RPP, LW); in all other cases references are to pages (e.g. LFM 21 refers to LFM page 21).

2. *Nachlass*

All references to unpublished material cited in the von Wright catalogue (G. H. von Wright, *Wittgenstein* (Blackwell, Oxford, 1982), pp. 35ff.) are by MS or TS number followed by page number. Wherever possible, we make use of the pagination or foliation entered in the original document (although these numerations follow no uniform pattern). For memorability, we have introduced the following special abbreviations.

Manuscripts

Vol. I	refer to the 18 large manuscript volumes (MSS 105–22) written
Vol. II	between 2 February 1929 and 1944. The reference style Vol. VI,
etc.	241 is to Volume VI, page 241.

C1	refer to eight notebooks (MSS 145–52) written between 1933 and
to	1936. The reference style C3, 42 is to C3, page 42.
C8	

Typescripts

EBT	'Early Big Typescript' (TS 211): a typescript composed from Vols. VI–X, 1932, 771 pp.
BT	The 'Big Typescript' (TS 213): a rearrangement, with modifications, written additions and deletions, of TS 211, 1933, vi pp. table of contents, 768 pp.
PPI	'Proto-Philosophical Investigations'[1] (TS 220): a typescript of the first half of the pre-war version of the *Philosophical Investigations* (up to §189 of the final version, but with many differences); 1937 or 1938, 137 pp. The shortened title form 'Proto-Investigations' is used freely. All references are to sections (§).
PPI(I)	The so-called 'Intermediate Version', reconstructed by von Wright; it consists of 300 numbered remarks; 1945, 195 pp. All references are to sections (§).
B i	*Bemerkungen I* (TS 228), 1945–6, 185 pp. All references are to sections (§).

---

[1] Our title.

3. Abbreviations for works by Frege

BG   *Begriffsschrift, eine der arithmetischen nachgebildete Formelsprache des reinen Denkens* (Halle a/S., 1879).
FA   *The Foundations of Arithmetic*, tr. J. L. Austin, 2nd edn (Blackwell, Oxford, 1959).
GA i, ii *Grundgesetze der Arithmetik, begriffsschriftlich abgeleitet*, Band I, 1893, Band II, 1903 (Hermann Pohle, Jena).
PW   *Posthumous Writings*, ed. H. Hermes, F. Kambartel, F. Kaulbach, tr. P. Long, R. White (Blackwell, Oxford, 1979).

4. Abbreviations for works by Russell

PrM   *The Principles of Mathematics*, 2nd edn (revised) (Allen and Unwin, London, 1937).
PM i *Principia Mathematica*, Vol. i (with A. N. Whitehead), 2nd edn (Cambridge University Press, Cambridge, 1927).

5. References to Volume 1

References to Volume 1 of this Analytical Commentary are flagged 'Volume 1' with a page number referring to the hardback edition. Where necessary the abbreviation 'MU' (with a page number) is used, referring to the paperback volume of *essays* entitled *Wittgenstein: Meaning and Understanding* (Blackwell, Oxford, 1983).

Analytical
Commentary

I

TWO FRUITS UPON ONE TREE

1. *The evolution of the* Philosophical Investigations

The constructional history of Part I of the *Philosophical Investigations* is not a matter of interest only to chroniclers of the history of ideas. It bears directly on features of Wittgenstein's thought. Indeed it raises a general question about his philosophy, namely how can two such disparate fruits as his philosophy of psychology and his philosophy of mathematics grow from the same trunk of *Investigations* §§1–189?

Genetically speaking, the printed text falls roughly into three parts.[1] The first (§§1–189(a)) stems from the 1937 typescript which we have called the 'Proto-Investigations'. This constituted the foundations upon which Wittgenstein strove over the next eight years to construct a complete edifice. The second (§§189–421) is primarily derived from a single polished manuscript compiled late in 1944. A typescript based on it was appended to the (somewhat revised) 'Proto-Investigations', which was then prefixed with a Preface dated January 1945. This constitutes the so-called 'Intermediate Version' of the *Investigations*.[2] The final part (§§422–693) is a selection from a compendium *(Bemerkungen I)* of remarks culled by Wittgenstein in 1945 from a thorough review of his notebooks dating back to 1930. Organized into relatively short sequences by thematic links, these remarks lack the overall integration into chains of argument which is characteristic of the first two thirds of the book.

The published text manifests few obvious traces of the various endeavours to compose the book. There were in fact four attempts to write continuations of the 'Proto-Investigations'. The first was contemporaneous with it, continuing without break into a further typescript (TS 221) of remarks on philosophy of mathematics and logic. These two typescripts comprise the 'Early Version' of the *Investigations*, which Wittgenstein offered for publication to Cambridge University Press in 1938. The second half of it is nearly identical in content with Part I of the *Remarks on the Foundations of Mathematics* but differently arranged.

A second attempt was probably made when he again offered the Press a text in 1943. This text cannot be reconstructed. Since his manuscripts between 1938 and 1944 concentrated on philosophy of mathematics, it is

---

[1] For detailed evidence see G. H. von Wright, 'The Origin and Composition of the *Philosophical Investigations*' in his *Wittgenstein* (Blackwell, Oxford, 1982).

[2] This text has been fully reconstructed and annotated under the direction of G. H. von Wright. (One copy is deposited in the Bodleian Library, Oxford.)

plausible to conjecture that this continuation of the 'Proto-Investigations', like the first one, focused on that subject. Conceivably the arrangement published as Part I of the *Remarks on the Foundations of Mathematics* derives from this revision.

A third continuation of the 'Proto-Investigations' is the 'Intermediate Version'. This was written towards the end of 1944, when the current of his thinking took a new direction. The earlier discussion of mathematics and logic is replaced by remarks about following a rule, 'private language', and the clarification of psychological concepts such as pain, hoping, expecting, thinking, calculating in the head, and consciousness. Although the 1945 Preface mentions philosophy of mathematics as one topic to be discussed, there is little trace of it in the 'Intermediate Version' and hence little thematic overlap between this continuation of the 'Proto-Investigations' and the two previous ones. This discontinuity marks a permanent shift in Wittgenstein's attention; he did no further work in philosophy of mathematics.

The fourth continuation is the published text. It evolved directly from the 'Intermediate Version' by the insertion and appending of selections from *Bemerkungen I*. Here too there is little trace of topics in the philosophy of mathematics. As in the 'Intermediate Version', different fruits are harvested from the same original stock.

One is prompted to speculate what motivated this metamorphosis, and also to wonder what were his longer term plans for a book on the philosophy of mathematics. What did he conceive to be the relationship between philosophy of mathematics and philosophy of psychology? Had he simply regrouped his forces in waging a single philosophical campaign? What can we learn from the remarkable possibility of such a realignment about his tactics, strategy and grand-strategy? Clearly a host of issues can be probed. Our ambitions here are strictly limited. Biographical questions are left aside; we shall explore a textual and a methodological question. The textual issue concerns the integration of the remarks and structure of the chain of reasoning in the published text in the light of the divergent earlier continuations of the 'Proto-Investigations'. The methodological question concerns parallelisms between Wittgenstein's philosophy of mathematics and his philosophy of psychology. We aim to assess the extent and nature of the illumination which these apparently disparate investigations might throw on each other.

2. *The early continuation of the 'Proto-Investigations' into philosophy of mathematics*

A discussion of parallelisms between the continuations of the 'Proto-Investigations' must be prefaced by a sketch of the salient features of Part

I of the *Remarks*. In comparison with standard works on philosophy of mathematics this text is extraordinary. Philosophers of mathematics would expect discussions of Russell's paradox, of how to construct real numbers from the rationals, of the acceptability of indirect proofs, or of the cogency of mathematical induction. Here we find none of this. Instead Wittgenstein investigated the concepts of proof and inference, compared calculations with experiments, juxtaposed logical with legal compulsion, and so on. His points are illustrated with very elementary examples, e.g. $25 \times 25 = 625$, or simple diagrammatic proofs of equations. Only the innumerate would have difficulty following these.

Apart from what the editors conjecture to be projected appendices on Cantor's theory of infinity, Gödel's incompleteness proof, Russell's logic and logicist definitions of natural numbers, Wittgenstein avoided the subject called 'the foundations of mathematics' (an amalgam of formal logic, number theory and real analysis). He incorporated no mathematical or metamathematical results into his work and he criticized attempts to extract philosophical theses from such proofs. This has evoked hostility among mathematicians and logicians, who have often misinterpreted this *methodological* disagreement as a manifestation of ignorance of sophisticated mathematics or even of philistinism. He abstained from frontal attacks on standard 'positions' in philosophy of mathematics, neither allying himself with logicists, Intuitionists or formalists nor lining up against them under some other banner (strict finitism or constructivism). But in the course of his investigations into mathematical concepts he made devastating criticisms almost *en passant* of each of the familiar triad. His reluctance to locate himself in some available pigeonhole has not diminished others' enthusiasm for completing this unfinished business on his behalf. Whatever positive conception he had must, it is sometimes thought, either be a synthesis of the three[3] or a purified version of one of them.[4]

Wittgenstein explored four interrelated topics in the text of the original continuation of the 'Proto-Investigations':

(i) *Inference*   Inferring or drawing a conclusion is not a mental process or act, but a transformation of expressions according to paradigms. It is not answerable to something external but is a movement within grammar. Rules of inference do not flow from the meanings of the logical constants, but rather constitute these meanings. To explain that fa follows from $(x)fx$ is to explain what the universal quantifier means, and to explain the nature of an inference is to teach someone the technique of inferring (drawing conclusions).

---

[3] The Vienna Circle surmised in their Manifesto that a synthesis of what is essential in each of the three views would be possible by using Wittgenstein's ideas.

[4] e.g. Intuitionism purged of psychologism.

(ii) *Proof and calculation*   Proofs in mathematics are commonly conflated with proofs (inferences) outside mathematics (and logic). But the
standard role of a mathematical proof or proposition is to supply a
paradigm for the transformation of empirical statements, i.e. to establish
a pattern of inference. The nature of mathematics is obscured by the fact
that we express mathematical 'results' in the form of declarative sentences,
but we might carry on mathematics without thinking that we were
dealing with propositions at all (RFM 93, 117). We construe mathematical proofs as demonstrations of propositions from other propositions,
but this too is inessential, since a proof may consist of a diagram or
geometrical construction to which the concepts of premises, conclusions
and inference are inapplicable. It is also misleading in suggesting that a
mathematical proposition is fully intelligible independently of its proof;
but a conclusion is best conceived as the end surface of a proof-body
(AWL 10). A proof establishes internal relations; it connects concepts and
thereby contributes to their identity. It creates essence by extending
grammar. Proofs and calculations are thus radically unlike experiments
(empirical verifications).

(iii) *Logical compulsion*   Logical inference seems inexorable. Anybody
who believes the premises of a valid argument seems to be logically
compelled to believe the conclusion. Misleading pictures surround the
'hardness of the logical "must"', e.g. that the conclusion is somehow
already contained in its premises, or that in grasping the premises the mind
foreshadows the thought expressed by the conclusion. These myths are
countered by clarifying the concept of inference. We are trained in the
techniques of inferring and compelled by our teachers and peers to
adhere to them. A specification of what conclusion to draw from given
premises is an intrinsic feature of the technique of inference. Hence we
are not forced by logic to draw a conclusion but are constrained in our
judgements about what is to be *called* 'a correct inference'. Wittgenstein's
account of inference does not derogate from the inexorability of logic but
merely eliminates misconceptions of it (cf. 'Grammar and necessity',
pp. 286f., 307ff.).

(iv) *The natural history of mankind*   The practices of inference, proof,
calculation and reasoning presuppose a ramifying network of regularities
in nature and human behaviour. We typically respond similarly to
patterns of training in arithmetical techniques. We normally agree in our
judgements when applying such techniques. Mathematicians rarely
quarrel over whether something is a proof. Certain patterns or re-
semblances are memorable for us, whereas we have 'blind spots' for
other possibilities or similarities. Such regularities are not parts of (do not
define) our concept of proof or inference. Rather, these regularities are
part of the framework within which we exercise these concepts. Without
these our language-games would lose their point. Hence, in clarification

of our concepts it is useful to note our established patterns of action and speech, our form of life, and also other contrasting ones, whether real or imaginary.

Even this cursory survey discloses affinities between the early 'mathematical' continuations of the 'Proto-Investigations' and the published text. Both give central positions to clarifying the concepts of a rule, of correctness according to a rule, and of following a rule. Wittgenstein argued that arithmetical equations and geometrical theorems should be viewed not as descriptions of numbers and shapes, but as rules for transforming empirical propositions. Arithmetic and geometry are akin to logic in that they all share this general function. Of course, the immediate rationale of the early continuations of the 'Proto-Investigations' is the elucidation of the concepts of mathematical proposition and proof for the purpose of removing prevalent philosophical confusions. This task is interwoven with the project of illuminating central normative concepts characteristic not only of mathematics but of language-use in general. Only the latter material has direct parallels in the published text.

At the cost of a thorough redrafting and rearrangement of the early text it seems that Wittgenstein could have separated out the remarks on rules, accord with a rule and following rules, and then treated these as a preface to his discussion of logical inference and mathematical proof. The result might have been something like the published text of §§189–242, followed by material on philosophy of mathematics rather than on the 'private language' and philosophy of psychology. Apparently something roughly like this idea occurred to him, probably in 1943 or 1944. Under the heading 'Plan' he outlined this programme:

Wie kann die Regel bestimmen, was ich zu tun habe?
Einer Regel folgen setzt Übereinstimmung voraus.
Es ist dem Phänomen der Sprache wesentlich, dass wir über gewisse Dinge nicht streiten.
Wie kann Übereinstimmung Bedingung der Sprache sein? . . . Fehlte die Übereinstimmung, d.h. könnten wir unsere Ausdrücke nicht zur Übereinst. bringen, so hörte damit das Phänomen der Verstandigung + der Sprache auf.
Worin besteht die Unerbittlichkeit der Mathematik?
Weg von dem was nicht Unerbittlich is zur Unerbittlichkeit. OBEN hat 4 Laute.
Ist ein math. Beweis ein Experiment? (MS 165, 30ff.)

(How can the rule determine what I have to do?
To follow a rule presupposes agreement.
It is essential to the phenomenon of language that we do not dispute about certain things.
How can agreement be a condition of language? . . . Were agreement lacking, i.e. were we to be unable to bring our expressions into agreement, then the phenomena of communication and language would disappear too.
In what does the inexorability of mathematics consist?

The way goes from what is not inexorable to inexorability. The word 'oben'
has four sounds.
Is a mathematical proof an experiment?)

Here the envisaged argument has the same general contour as §§189–242,
but it then diverges into a discussion of mathematics to remove the
objection that describing agreement in judgements as a presupposition of
language is inconsistent with the inexorability of mathematical propositions
and proofs. Apparently Wittgenstein contemplated deploying remarks
on inference, proof and logical compulsion to show in detail that the
need for agreement in judgement does not abolish logic though it seems
to do so, i.e. that acknowledging this framework condition for language
is not incompatible with recognizing the hardness of the logical 'must'
(in so far as this is intelligible; cf. 'Agreement in definitions, judgements
and forms of life', pp. 245ff., and 'Grammar and necessity', pp. 329ff.)
Consequently we might view the early continuation of the 'Proto-
Investigations' as an important complement to the final version. In
amplifying on the implications of agreement, it removes potential
misunderstandings.

3. *Hidden isomorphism*

It is a moot question how a uniform foundation, the 'Proto-Investigations',
can underlie each of two such divergent extensions. How is it possible
that a single chain of reasoning should lead smoothly into remarks on
mathematics and logic or alternatively into a discussion of psychological
concepts? One response, natural in the light of the foregoing observations,
would be that one must beware of exaggerating the divergence and of
overlooking the overlaps. As we just noted, in both texts Wittgenstein
discussed the internal relation of a rule to its applications, the autonomy
of grammar, and the role of agreement as a framework-condition for
following rules. Should one not view the final rule-following discussion
as part of the shared nucleus of the two extensions? Then the early
extension can be seen as exploring one main objection to the conceptual
role assigned to agreement, viz. that logic and mathematics (or more
generally, logical necessity) would be abolished. And the later extension
can be viewed as examining a second fundamental objection, viz. that a
language is conceivable (a 'private language') independently of even
the possibility of agreement. Accordingly the two divergent continuations complement each other, and each fits perfectly on to the 'Proto-
Investigations'.
    An alternative response, antithetical to the first would beware of
exaggerating the overlap. The pivot on which both continuations turn is

a set of remarks about following a rule; but is the pivot identical? There seems to be a shift of emphasis in the discussion of following a rule between Part I of the *Remarks on the Foundations of Mathematics* and the *Investigations*. Wittgenstein's focus of attention moved towards a sharper concentration upon the framework-conditions of rule-governed activities. *Investigations* §§185–242 stands at the culmination of this development incorporating and moving onwards from the scrutiny of the internal relations between a rule and its application that began in the 'Big Typescript' (if not before). One must not take for granted that there is no substantial evolution here, that the examination of rule-following in Part I of the *Remarks* has not been deepened and enriched in the *Investigations*. A *fortiori* one may not argue that the earlier extension of the 'Proto-Investigations' and *Investigations* §§243ff. are extensions of a homogeneous set of ideas dubbed 'Wittgentstein's rule-following considerations'.

Both responses are justified. We shall not attempt to adjudicate the question of what degree of continuity obtains and how extensive a change occurred. For our concerns the important point to stress is that the text of the 'Proto-Investigations' was written after much reflection on both philosophy of mathematics and philosophy of mind. It was informed by a unified conception of philosophy and philosophical methods that had been amplified and developed by application to both subjects. It was expressly designed to highlight sources of philosophical confusion rampant in both. Under the heading of 'Augustine's picture of language' the 'Proto-Investigations' drew together and surveyed a wide range of points that Wittgenstein had already made in earlier writings. The two divergent continuations fit on to this common foundation because it was crafted to support either, not as a result of personal idiosyncracy, but for deeper philosophical reasons. We shall justify this verdict by examining the two main ingredients of the Augustinian picture and by elucidating its role as an obstacle to philosophical understanding. This task involves pointing out parallels between Wittgenstein's philosophy of mathematics and his philosophy of psychology, neither of which will be thoroughly examined in this volume. So our observations will be schematic and provisional and must be treated as such.

(i) *Descriptions*   It is part of the Augustinian *Urbild* to take it for granted that the fundamental role of sentences, certainly of declarative sentences, is to describe something. Philosophers often *begin* their reflections from this presupposition. 'Eight is greater than five' is presumed to be a description, and the serious philosophical question is what it describes – a relation between abstract objects, marks on paper or mental constructs? Similarly, 'I have a toothache' is assumed to be a description and the philosopher's task is to determine whether it describes a private experience, a behaviour pattern or a brain state. This common presumption is a fundamental source of confusions about mathematics and the mind.

Mathematical propositions must be distinguished from descriptions. We should view them as instruments (AWL 157) and enquire into their roles, their use in practice (PR 134). We will then see that their characteristic use is as a rule for transforming expressions of empirical propositions (LFM 82, 246; AWL 154; PG 347), or, more generally, as a rule of representation for framing, *inter alia*, descriptions (see 'Grammar and necessity', pp. 269ff.). If one keeps the role, the use, of mathematical propositions in mind, then one will not mistake them for descriptions, just as 'you can't mistake a broom for part of the furnishing of a room as long as you use it to clean the furniture'. (PG 375) Similarly, geometrical theorems have the role of rules for framing descriptions of shapes and sizes of objects and of their spatial relations (LFM 44; PLP 47) and for making inferences about them. The contrast between descriptive propositions and mathematical propositions that play the part of rules of description is of the greatest importance (though that is not to say that it does not shade off in all directions (RFM 363)). Failure to draw this distinction is the source of rampant confusions in reflections upon mathematics, dragging in its wake further muddles about the concepts of truth, assertion, knowledge and verification (see 'Grammar and necessity', pp. 273ff.). Moreover, it breeds philosophical mythologies such as Platonism, which notes correctly that mathematical propositions are not descriptions of signs and jumps to the conclusion that they must be descriptions of something else (AWL 152), namely abstract entities. The formalist reaction to Platonism is equally awry, equally ensnared in the web of the idea that mathematical propositions describe something, if not abstract entities then signs (LFM 112). Finally, it obliterates the distinction between applying mathematical techniques *within* as opposed to *outside* mathematics. Such a statement as 'The real numbers cannot be put into a one–one correspondence with the natural numbers' sounds like a remarkable *discovery* about mathematical objects, but it is part of the construction of a mathematical calculus, not a discovery of mathematical facts but the creation of new norms of description.

In philosophy of psychology it is equally vital to distinguish expressions or avowals of inner state from descriptions. Avowals such as 'I have a toothache' and 'Now I understand' are instruments which have their uses (cf. PI §§416, 421). So too are descriptions (PI §290), such as 'He .has toothache' and 'Now he understands.' But these uses are characteristically different. Avowals are not typically employed to convey information (cf. PI §363), but to ask for help, solicit sympathy, signal an ability to do something. 'I have a toothache' sounds like 'I have a matchbox' but it is used in an utterly different way (LSD 44). A child is taught to use the sentence 'I have pain' to *replace* the moans which are the primitive, natural expressions of pain (PI §244); here the verbal expression of pain replaces crying and describes neither crying nor an 'inner state'. Similarly 'Now I know how to go on' is not a description, but corresponds to an instinctive sound, a glad start (PI §§180, 323). The contrast is of the greatest importance, even though it too shades off in all directions (PI p. 189). Failure to distinguish expressions or manifestations of inner states from descriptions of people as being in certain mental states is the source of widespread confusion in reflections upon the mind. It too drags in its wake misconceptions about self-knowledge and awareness, doubt and certainty, belief and verification. It breeds mythologies of the mental such as the Cartesian and empiricist conception of the mind as an 'inner world' accessible only to its owner by introspection which is conceived as 'inner sense'. And the behaviourist reaction to this picture of the mental is no less ensnared in the web of misconceptions. From these confusions grows the idea that the predicates I use to ascribe mental states to myself must be explained quite differently from the same predicates as applied to others. They seem to belong to a private language which is in principle intelligible only to me. The uncritical assumption that declarative sentences are uniformly descriptions plays as much havoc with our thought about the mind as it does with our reflections on mathematics.

(ii) *Names*   The second salient feature of the Augustinian picture is to treat every significant word as a name. This idea informs much reflection on philosophy of mathematics and of psychology alike. Mathematical expressions such as '0', '-2', '$\sqrt{-1}$', '$\aleph_0$', or even '$+$', 'x^4', 'e^x' are taken to be names of entities, and the question 'What do they mean?' is thought to boil down to 'What do they stand for?' Similarly, it is assumed that 'toothache', 'anger', 'understanding', 'intelligence', etc. are names and hence that they stand for something, and the debate centres on the question of what they stand for.

It is commonplace in reflections on mathematics to contrast the thesis that a symbol has content in virtue of standing for something with the claim that it is a meaningless mark and that the calculations in which it occurs are mere manipulations of empty symbols. Mathematicians for long held that nothing corresponds to the use of negative numbers, that these symbols do not stand for anything. Producing a rigorous explanation of what a symbol stands for, e.g. identifying a negative number with an equivalence-class of ordered pairs of positive integers, is taken to be a vindication of the claim that a symbol does have a meaning. (It is striking that such explanations play no role in conveying to a neophyte how these symbols might be used in the applications of mathematical calculations, e.g. in employing negative integers in banking or in mechanics.) Wittgenstein held that the preconception that all significant terms are names veils profound differences in use under a misleadingly uniform terminology. It further promotes the myth that differences in use mysteriously flow from differences in the natures of the objects allegedly 'named'.

We should, he argued, look on words as tools and clarify their uses in our language-games (PI §§10f.). We must not lose sight of the fact that number-words are instruments used in counting and measuring, and that the foundation of elementary arithmetic, viz. mastery of the series of natural numbers, lies in training in counting. Philosophers readily stray from such familiar points in seeking deeper foundations for arithmetic. Frege exemplified this error. He began his investigation of numbers from an examination of extra-mathematical count-statements such as 'Jupiter has four moons.' (LFM 166, 262ff.) But he then threw away his insight through his conviction that numerals are names of Platonic objects. He succumbed to the mesmerizing power of the philosophical question 'What are numbers?' and sought for a rigorous definition in response to it. Wittgenstein thought the question misleading (cf. PI §1: 'What is the meaning of the word "five"?' – 'No such thing was in question here, only how the word "five" is used') and the answers useless: 'What we are looking for is not a definition of the concept of number, but an exposition of the grammar of the word "number" and of the numerals.' (PG 321; cf. AWL 164) Assimilation of mathematical terms to names, especially the conception that they are names of ideal or abstract objects, is fundamental to confusions in reflections on mathematics. It is a prominent target of Wittgenstein's criticism (PG 52f.; PLP 46; LFM 33, 112, 144; RFM 137, 262f.) and is linked to a host of related muddles that he exposed.

In philosophy of mind there is a powerful temptation to construe psychological expressions as names of inner states or private experiences which the subject apprehends by introspection. Such names are given content, i.e. attached to what they name, by private ostensive definition. But we must, Wittgenstein argued, emancipate ourselves from the preconception that to understand a term is to know what it designates, and that to explain a term is to attach it to something as a name. Here too we should look upon such words as 'pain', 'thinking', 'anger' as tools and examine their functions in discourse. One cannot deduce how a word functions from categorizing it, e.g. as a sensation-word or an emotion-word, for such general categories are fluid and subsume con-cepts of different logical character. A careful scrutiny (PI §§51f., 66) of the actual use of various psychological concepts reveals surprisingly complex and variegated patterns of use. We use many of these terms in (first-person) avowals and in (second- and third-person) descriptions. Neither the explanations nor the use of such concepts have the formal simplicity and uniformity we seem to expect. Many are family-resemblance concepts (PG 74f.), some appear to be even more amorphous and heterogeneous, e.g. thinking (Z §§110ff.) or understanding (PI §532), and the use of many is related to complex behavioural criteria (cf. PI §§164, 182, 269, 580). In short, in every direction psychological terms burst through the conceptual bounds typical of paradigmatic names. 'That is to say: if we construe the grammar of the expression of sensation on the model of "object and designation", the object drops out of consideration as irrelevant.' (PI §293) The 'inner objects' which we introduce in order to make psychological concepts conform with the prototype of a name are grammatical fictions (PI §307).

(iii) *The influence of the Augustinian picture*   The twin ideas that every meaningful word is a name and that every sentence is a description Wittgenstein thought to be the central and typically unavowed inspiration of a widely ramifying *Weltanschauung* endemic in modern philosophy (see 'Augustine's picture of language: *das Wesen der Sprache*', Volume 1). It is, as it were, the magnetic pole of philosophical thought and hence something that must be identified by sensitive charting of the movements of philosophical arguments. *Investigations* §§1–88 examines the main aspects of the Augustinian picture at a level of comparative generality with examples of great diversity. Hence, to the extent that Wittgenstein's earlier reflections on the philosophy of mathematics and of psychology can be seen to be exploring the ramifications of deep misconceptions about words and names, sentences and descriptions, each of these two groups of investigations would complement the central theme of the 'Proto-Investigations'. For each would clarify how this *Urbild* shapes and distorts a major branch of philosophy. Provided that the Augustinian picture is indeed the focal point of the 'Proto-Investigations', the two continuations can be seen as parallel executions of a single strategy in respect of different domains of our language.

As an *Übersicht* of Wittgenstein's philosophy, this might seem to be purchased at too high a price. Are the ideas at the root of the Augustinian picture not manifestly ridiculous? Has any major philosopher affirmed that *all* words are names or *all* sentences descriptions? Is it not absurd to identify this as the target of Wittgenstein's criticisms? Such objections rest on misunderstanding. The components of the Augustinian picture are not official planks in anyone's philosophical manifesto. They are visible not so much in the theorizing of philosophers about their acivities as in the activities themselves. In philosophy of mathematics the picture is apparent in the orientation of the investigations, in philosophers' addressing themselves to the questions of what makes mathematical propositions *true*, how we attain *knowledge* of them, and *what* numbers are (what numerals *signify*). In philosophy of psychology, the Augustinian picture is manifested in philosophers' asking what *justifies* someone's saying 'I have a toothache', or speculating whether *introspection* is infallible and how one person can tell what another means by 'toothache'.

(One might add that in each case the power of the Augustinian picture is perspicuous in philosophers' outrage at Wittgenstein's calling mathematical propositions '*rules* of grammar' and his calling many first-person psychological statements '*expressions (Äusserungen)* of inner states'.) Commitment to this Augustinian picture is not something additional or external to philosophical reasoning, but a way of drawing attention to salient features of this reasoning. Wittgenstein's diagnosis might be challenged, but the grounds for doing so would *not* be that philosophers supposedly in the grip of this conception would indignantly repudiate the theses that all words are names or that all sentences are descriptions. Indeed, Wittgenstein anticipated resistance to his diagnosis of the deep sources of philosophical confusions. His therapy is intended to elicit the patient's acknowledgement of a motive in spite of his desire to disown it, i.e. to evoke a confession of error.

Eine der wichtigsten Aufgaben ist es, alle falschen Gedankengänge so charakteristisch auszudrücken, dass der Leser sagt, 'ja, ganau *so* habe ich es gemeint.' Die Physiognomie jedes Irrtums nachzuzeichnen. (BT 410)

(One of the most important tasks is to express every fallacious chain of reasoning in so life-like a way that the reader says 'Yes, *that* is exactly what I thought.' To capture the likeness of every error.)

Anybody who finds the Augustinian picture too crude to take seriously or who thinks its centrality in Wittgenstein's reflections to be absurd has not grasped the nature of deep philosophical confusion (or deep understanding!).

There is a further objection to our account. The themes of the Augustinian picture seem too superficial to be the source of so many deep confusions in philosophy. Would all these matters become clear if we kept reminding ourselves 'Words need not be names, nor sentences descriptions'? This response too is confused. The misconceptions of the Augustinian picture ramify into distorted ideas about symbols, explaining and understanding words, communication, representation, sense and nonsense, and so on. One cannot inoculate oneself against this host of interrelated confusions by taking a simple slogan and following it as one would a doctor's prescription. What is needed is a different point of view which can be fully achieved only by working through philosophical problems afresh, resisting the lures of the Augustinian picture throughout. One must turn oneself in a new direction and, once turned round, stay turned round (CV 53). This is not easy to achieve:

A philosopher says 'Look at things like this!' – but in the first place this doesn't ensure that people will look at things like that, and in the second place his admonition may come too late; it's possible, moreover, that such an admonition can achieve nothing in any case and that the impetus for such a change in the way things are perceived has to originate somewhere else entirely. (CV 61)

The strength of the Augustinian picture lies in its power to resist attempts to dislodge consequent misconceptions. It is as firmly an entrenched part of philosophers' *Weltanschauung* as the idea that the mathematician discovers laws about numbers or that poetry and music are essentially the expression of the emotions, experiences and inner states of their creators.

   If these objections are deflected, then it is obvious that no trivialization of Wittgenstein's work is implied by identifying the ramifications of the Augustinian picture as the trunk from which his critical investigations of mathematical and psychological concepts spring. Hence the apparent enigma of the divergent continuations of the 'Proto-Investigations' has a satisfying solution.

4. *A common methodology*

The foregoing discussion clarifies a crucial point of contact between Wittgenstein's philosophy of mathematics and his philosophy of psychology. They involve parallel diagnostic investigations into ramifying aspects of a single syndrome. But there are many further parallelisms and uses of remarks in one domain to illuminate the other. For example, Wittgenstein took behaviourism as an object of comparison for standard manoeuvres in philosophy of mathematics:

   Finitism and behaviourism are quite similar trends. Both say: but surely, all we have here is . . . Both deny the existence of something, both with a view to escaping from a confusion. (RFM 142)

Similarly, he argued,

   We might say that formalism in mathematics is behaviourism in mathematics. I could draw '2' and say 'That is the number 2.' This is exactly the same as pinching and saying 'This is pain.' – Mathematicians say 'Surely it is not just the numeral, it is something more.' (LSD 111)

So too one says that pain is not just behaviour, but something more (LSD 114f.). In both cases this response is misleading. It leads the mathematician to the idea that arithmetical equations describe relations among abstract objects and that they are true in virtue of corresponding to a mathematical reality. This generates a debate between 'formalism' and 'contentful mathematics' (as Frege put it) in which both sides make absurd assertions at variance with their day to day practice (PG 293). In the psychological case it leads to the idea that each person attaches the term 'toothache' to a private experience ascertainable only by himself, and hence to the solipsistic claim 'Only I have real toothache (or experiences).' This generates a debate in which the antitheses 'Only my experiences are real' and 'Everyone's experiences are real' are equally nonsensical (AWL 23). To escape from such absurdities one is tempted to deny that numbers are something more than sensations or that sensations are something more than behaviour. But this too is misleading. Numbers and sensations are not (different kinds of) shadowy objects. But neither are they just signs or just behaviour. The uses of 'numeral' and 'number', of 'behaviour' and 'sensation' are *different* (RFM 202). Formalism and behaviourism embody parallel insights into the uses of expressions, but both wrap up grammatical observations in a form that generates further confusion.

Wittgenstein's practice in philosophy of mathematics and philosophy of psychology indicates not only such parallels but a shared methodology. Notes taken of his lectures in 1929–36 show him frequently juxtaposing remarks about psychological and mathematical concepts. His own notebooks reveal similar frequent transitions from one domain to the other. The parallels exemplifying the shared method fall into two main types (though there are transitional cases). The first are explicit inter-polations of analogies to clarify or illustrate specific points, for example:

(i) 'The relation of expectation and its fulfilment is precisely that of calculation and result.' (LWL 62) Expectation anticipates its fulfilment just as a calculation anticipates its conclusion. In both cases the relation is internal.

(ii) One is inclined to assert that we can never really know what another person feels. This is parallel to the claim that we can never draw an exact circle. Both look like statements about empirical possibilities, but in fact they are misconceived statements of grammar (LSD 133f.).

(iii) Viewing visual impressions as 'inner pictures' is misleading, for this concept is modelled on that of an 'outer' picture. But the uses of 'visual impression' and 'picture' are no more alike than the uses of 'numeral' and 'number' (PI p. 196). The category differences in grammar are crucial.

(iv) One no more has the concept of colour in virtue of seeing coloured objects than one has the concept of a negative number in virtue of running up debts (Z §332). Concept-possession is not a matter of having had experiences, but of having mastered the use of expressions.

(v) Calculating in one's head is a kind of calculating. But the concept of calculating in one's head can only be mastered by someone who has the concept of (perceptible) calculating. The concept of calculating in one's head is confusing because it runs for a long stretch cheek by jowl with the concept of calculating aloud or on paper. These concepts are as closely related and also as different as the concepts of a cardinal number and a rational number (LW §§854, 857; PI p. 220).

(vi) The contrast between mathematical proof and empirical verification parallels the contrast between giving the agent's reason or motive for his action and specifying its cause. The connection between a reason and what it is a reason for, like that between calculation and result, is internal (AWL 4f.).

(vii) We use arithmetical equations as norms of description, e.g. as criteria for saying that something has vanished during a count. In science certain hypotheses have the same status as grammatical statements. Hertz used hypothetical 'invisible masses' to account for any deviation of observations from his laws. 'Unconscious mental events' play the same role in explanations of behaviour; they are introduced because we wish to say that there *must* be causes of human action. This is an arbitrary stipulation that makes determinism a property of the system of explanations of behaviour (AWL 15f.).

(viii) We confuse categorial differences in grammar with differences between kinds. We say that transfinite numbers are another kind of number than rationals, that unconscious thoughts are a different kind of thought from conscious ones. But the differences are not analogous to that between different kinds of chair, but to that between a chair and permission to sit in a chair. For the words 'thought' and 'number' are differently used when prefixed with these adjectives (AWL 32; BB 64).

The second type of methodological parallel is a matter of isomorphism in argumentative manoeuvre between self-contained arguments in philosophy of mathematics and philosophy of psychology. Consider this pair of cases. In logic we introduce pupils to the concept of a set by using lists to define class membership. We then suggest that there is an alternative to such an extensional conception of a set. We may define a set by a general condition, satisfaction of which by an object is a necessary and sufficient condition for the object to belong to the set. And we then point out that this intensional conception is preferable because it does not rule out speaking of sets whose members are too numerous to list, especially sets whose members are infinite in number like the set of the natural numbers. Logicians then proceed to point out the remarkable properties of infinite sets. It is easy to prove that two finite sets have the same number of elements if and only if they can be put in one-to-one correspondence and that a finite set cannot be put into one-to-one correspondence with any of its proper subsets. But an infinite set can! This is simple to show: the operation of doubling correlates the integers one-to-one with the even integers, but the even integers are a proper subset of the integers. With this paradoxical result the logician lures the pupil on into an exploration of the mysteries of sets, into the study of abstract set theory. And the expert prides himself in having surmounted the superstitions and prejudices that blinker the pupil and prevent him from seeing that only in the realm of finite sets does it hold that a proper part is never as great as the whole (cf. PG 465.). Wittgenstein argued that this entire chain of reasoning rests on a series of conceptual confusions. It is a fallacy to suppose that there is a single concept of a set which subsumes both sets defined by lists of their elements and sets defined by satisfaction of a predicate (WWK 102f.). In fact, these are different grammatical structures (PG 464f.); for, in the first case, any true statement of set membership (a ε A) will be a grammatical proposition, whereas in the second it will be equivalent to a proposition of the form $\phi(a)$ which will typically express an empirical statement (cf. AWL 150). There is, of course, no such thing as an infinite list (AWL 206). Hence, if the concept of a set is introduced extensionally, there is no such thing as an infinite set. The 'discovery' of infinite sets is an alteration in the concept of a set. It is misleading to speak of finite sets and infinite sets as two kinds of sets (WWK 192; PG 463f.). Similarly, the concept of one-to-one correspondence is subtly stretched and altered (cf. LFM 161ff.; AWL 168f.). We pass from the claim that two sets have the same cardinal if their members are correlated one-to-one (as cups and saucers are by laying them out so that each cup stands on a single saucer) to the claim that the sets have the same cardinal if their members *can* be correlated one-to-one (cf. AWL 148ff., 161ff.). We then think that we can prove that two infinite sets have the same cardinal; for although in writing out the table

0	1	2	3	4	5
0	2	4	6	8	10

one has arrived only at the sixth term of each series, one *can* correlate any specified even integer with an integer in the upper series, and vice versa (LFM 160). But in fact the concept of one-to-one correlation is now altered (LFM 161). There is no such thing as actually having listed against each integer the even integer which corresponds to it (PG 464), and equally no such thing as arriving at the end of the series of even integers to ascertain that none has been left out. The 'discovery' that an infinite set may be one-to-one correlated with a proper subset is a muddled report of a redefinition of one-to-one correspondence (LFM 161; AWL 209). The veil of mystery surrounding set theory is a sign that logicians do not understand what they are doing.

Wittgenstein gave a parallel diagnosis of the conceptual confusions enveloping talk of the unconscious in psychology. We have our everyday concept of a desire or motive. An agent often avows his motives if challenged to explain his actions, and his avowals have a crucial role in determining what his motives are. A psychologist may call attention to the fact that an agent may act as if he had a particular motive although he is unaware of it and would sincerely disavow it. The psychologist suggests that we speak here of an 'unconscious motive' (cf. RPP I §225), which he paraphrases by saying that the agent has a motive but does not know it. This seems like a genuine discovery opening new domains to psychological investigations and new possibilities for pinpointing the causes of behaviour (AWL 16). No longer is research limited to what is conscious; one can study all motives, feelings, thoughts, whether conscious or unconscious. The unconscious may turn out to obey remarkable laws and to have extraordinary manifestations in behaviour (as claimed in Freudian psychology). If anyone expresses scepticism or puzzlement as to how a desire or motive can be unconscious, the psychologist will say that it is a proven *fact* that there is such a thing, and 'he will say it like a man who is destroying a common prejudice.' (BB 23)

This drift of thought, Wittgenstein argued, likewise involves radical conceptual confusions. The phrase 'unconscious thought (motive etc.)' is misleading, for we suppose that unconscious and conscious thoughts are two kinds of thoughts. But this is *not* implied by the original explanation. By parity of reasoning someone might be said to have 'unconscious toothache' when he has a rotten tooth but feels nothing. In that case 'conscious toothache' must be understood to encompass *everything* ordinarily called 'toothache' (BB 57f.) and 'unconscious toothache' has a totally different use. It would be mistaken to object that there is no such thing as unconscious toothache, for the phrase 'unconscious toothache' has been given an intelligible explanation. Similarly, objectors to the unconscious do not appreciate that they are objecting not to empirical discoveries but to a new form of representation (cf. AWL 40). Psycho-analytic defenders of the unconscious are equally confused. They mis-construe unconscious desires as a kind of desire etc., and transfer parts of the grammar of 'desire' to 'unconscious desire'. Misled by their own novel convention of representation, they think they have, 'in a sense, discovered conscious thoughts which were unconscious' (BB 57). They think that an agent is cut off by a barrier from his own unconscious states, that consciousness is a screen against the unconscious. Such ideas, with the attendant aura of paradox and mystery, indicate that psycho-logists misunderstand their own discourse about the unconscious mind.

These two kinds of parallelisms between Wittgenstein's philosophy of mathematics and his philosophy of psychology are manifestations of the application of a single methodology and an overarching conception of the nature of philosophy, its problems and its resolution of its questions (cf. 'The nature of philosophy', Volume 1). We shall now briefly catalogue and classify the methodological parallels.

(i) *Pitting observation against prejudice* Philosophical prejudices stand in the way of apprehending how expressions are used, which alone can dissolve philosophical confusion. Our craving for generality, simplicity and formal definitions is a source of confusion in philosophy of mathematics and psychology alike, for we crave for a *Merkmal*-definition of 'number' or 'thought'. So we fail to recognize the existence and character of family-resemblance concepts. Our natural disposition to construct 'pictures' of whole domains of thought leads us into mythologies of symbolism. For the Platonist picture is profoundly appealing to many mathematicians; the conception of the mathematician as discoverer of the laws of non-empirical objects comes natural to us. The metaphors and idioms of our psychological discourse foster the picture of the mind as an inner realm in contrast to the external world, a realm only accessible by introspection.

(ii) *Focusing on use rather than on grammatical form*　We are readily impressed by forms of expression, and take common form to be indicative of a shared meaning. But it is *use*, not form, that shows shared meaning. We talk of the certainty of empirical propositions, of knowing or believing them, of verifying or falsifying them. We speak similarly of mathematical propositions. Hence, we think that the certainty of mathematical propositions is akin to, but much more secure than, empirical ones. And that we know mathematical truths in precisely the same sense in which we know empirical ones. And so on (see 'Grammar and necessity', pp. 287ff.). So too in philosophy of mind. The pronoun 'I' seems to refer to a person in just the way 'He' does. 'I have a toothache' is deceptively like 'I have a tooth.' But the shared forms mask radical differences in use.

(iii) *Exposing surreptitious changes in concepts*　This important philosophical technique has already been illustrated with the parallel examples of the contrasts between conscious and unconscious thoughts or motives, and finite and infinite sets. In such cases we mistake the introduction of a new concept for the scientific discovery of hitherto unknown *phenomena* subsumable under the old concept.

(iv) *Clarifying the completeness of language-games*　We are prone to view our language-games with all their complex articulations as essentially *completions* or culminations of the development of incomplete, gappy or essentially incorrect antecedent ones, or to view actual or imaginary language-games which lack such articulations as essentially incomplete. In arithmetic we think that the system of natural numbers contains gaps which are filled up by the negative integers (since we can frame within this system a problem which cannot be answered except by extending the natural numbers to include the signed integers). Similarly, in reflecting on perception, we are prone to think of colour-systems different from our own as incomplete, incorrect or gappy. Wittgenstein castigated such tendencies. There are no gaps in a grammar. A question makes sense within a grammatical system only if it has an intelligible answer *within that system*. Addition of new joints to a language-game may transform it altogether. Incorporating one language-game into another of greater multiplicity will transform *all* of the concepts of the more limited original one (like 'embedding' the number system '1, 2, 3, 4, 5, many' in our system of natural numbers).

(v) *Crossing language-games* It is a consequence of the previous point that errors ensue from failure to realize that the transposition of a concept from one language-game into another involves a shift in meaning. Both in philosophy of mind and in philosophy of mathematics Wittgenstein laid bare such confusions. Philosophers of mathematics are prone to overlook the fact that, for example, the concepts of addition or subtraction are redefined as one moves from the system of natural numbers to that of the signed integers; indeed, that the concept of number itself shifts as one moves from one system, e.g. the signed integers, to another, e.g. the rationals or reals. Similarly, we use the expression 'visual image' in connection with both seeing and imagining (imaging). So we assume, in philosophizing, a close similarity between these phenomena – that what it makes sense to say about seeing a tree (e.g. 'I didn't notice any birds' nests, but there may have been some') must also make sense about imagining a tree. In fact these language-games are radically different; the tie-ups are numerous, but there is no similarity (RPP II §§70f.), like one jigsaw puzzle on the reverse side of another.

(vi) *Transgressing the boundaries of language-games* Precisely because expressions have a meaning only within the language-game in which they are embedded, multiple confusions result from transgressing the boundaries of a language-game. For both in mathematics and in psychology we project one language-game not only into another but also into a grammatical void. It makes sense to ask whether there are four successive 7s in the first thousand places of the expansion of π. So we misguidedly think that it makes sense to ask whether there are four successive 7s in the expansion of π. Similarly, we use ostensive definition to explain the meaning of perceptual predicates and assume misguidedly that it makes sense to explain (to oneself) the meaning of psychological predicates by a 'mental' ostensive definition.

(vii) *Conceptual topology* Wittgenstein criticized the idea that our concepts mirror the essential nature of things. His most straightforward method is to imagine that certain general features of the world, including culture and history (CV 37), were different, and to consider what concepts would then be natural to us. He employed this method in philosophy of mathematics in imagining very different ways of measuring, weighing or buying and selling which would involve different grammars from our own. Even in the matter of counting, fundamental differences are conceivable, e.g. the number system '1, 2, 3, 4, 5, many' (which would be a natural enough system for what might be called 'visual numbers' that can be taken in at a glance). Such a number system is not an incomplete part of our own, but an autonomous system. The same method is conspicuous in his philosophy of mind. Our concept of a person seems justified by the nature of persons. But our use of proper names, of 'person' and 'same person' is 'based on the fact that many characteristics which we use as criteria for identity coincide in the vast majority of cases' (BB 61). But if things were very different, e.g. if we all looked alike and sets of character traits 'circulated' among these bodies, our present concept would be useless and various different concepts of a person might replace it (BB 62).

In these ways (and doubtless others could be mentioned too) one can see Wittgenstein's philosophy of mathematics and his philosophy of psychology as informed by a common conception of philosophy and a common array of methods.

5. *The flatness of philosophical grammar*

Philosophers fancy that they give explanations of the structure of our conceptual scheme and of the essential nature of the world, the mind and language. On Wittgenstein's view this is misconceived. Philosophy is purely descriptive. It clarifies the grammar of our language, the rules for the construction of significant utterances whose violation yields nonsense. Explanation would be possible only if it made sense to get behind these rules and supply a deeper foundation ('Grammar and necessity', p. 329ff.). But there is no behind, and rules are not answerable to reality in the currency of truth. Any deeper explanation would simply be another rule of grammar standing in the same relation to the use of expressions as the rules it allegedly explains. Therefore philosophy must be flat. This insight shapes the whole of Wittgenstein's philosophy.

The flatness of philosophy has two coordinate aspects. The first is that there are no theses or conclusions in philosophical grammar, i.e. nothing which could be called the terminus of a philosophical proof. For a grammatical proposition has no significant negation; it is not bipolar, rather its 'denial' is nonsense. Hence there is no such thing as demonstrating its 'truth' by ruling out the possibility that its negation is true by appeal to some further information. What Wittgenstein did is simply to 'draw the other person's attention to what he is really doing [to the rules according to which he is proceeding] and refrain from any assertions. Everything is then to go on within grammar.' (WWK 186) The result of philosophizing is not philosophical knowledge, but clarity (cf. 'The nature of philosophy', Volume 1).

This point must shape our conception of what Wittgenstein's arguments are meant to accomplish. We may be tempted to look at his discussion of avowals and ask where he *proved* that an avowal is not a description of the speaker's mental state, that it does not bear a truth-value, that it is not something he can be said to know or not to know. Similarly, we may enquire where he *proved* that an arithmetical equation is a rule for using number-words in empirical propositions, or that a consistency proof is irrelevant to the usefulness of arithmetic in building bridges. Such demands are pressed by his critics on the assumption that the admission that the required proofs are not to be found in his work derogates from his achievement, or perhaps altogether undermines it. This reasoning rests on misunderstanding. Wittgenstein's 'grammatical remarks' fall roughly into two categories. The first are evident truisms concerning our use of expressions and undisputed rules for their use, e.g. that it makes *sense* to say 'I know you have toothache', that 'to understand' has no continuous present tense, or that 'two' may be correctly explained by ostension. The second do not purport to be truisms and are often taken to express philosophical theses, e.g. that the sense of a sentence is its method of verification, that the proper answer to 'What are numbers?' is a description of the grammar of 'number' and of numerals, or that inner states stand in need of outward criteria. But to concede that these are not indisputable truisms is not to cast them in the role of explanations. They are rather intended to play the role of synoptic descriptions, i.e. of drawing together and interrelating a myriad of truisms in a single *Übersicht*. Achievement here is to be measured by the usefulness of these propositions in dissolving philosophical problems and promoting philosophical understanding exhibited in knowing one's way about among our concepts (cf. *'Übersicht'*, Volume 1). Whether any of these propositions does discharge this function may be disputed, but the dispute is not properly conducted by focusing on whether Wittgenstein has given rigorous enough proofs of his conclusions. For these propositions are totally misconstrued if treated as an axiomatic basis for the grammar of our language.

This point about the absence of theoretical explanations is likewise apparent in the second aspect of the flatness of Wittgenstein's 'grammatical' observations: there are no arguments *from* grammatical propositions in his work, i.e. no reasoning which takes the form 'Arithmetical equations are grammatical rules, so . . .' or 'First-person psychological utterances are manifestations, not descriptions of psychological states, so . . .' Instead such propositions appear uniformly as the coda of reasoning, the whole of which is presented independently of these observations. That is why he declared himself ready to give up any propositions that another wished to dispute or query; quite literally, nothing hangs on them. They promote insight and express surviews of complex networks of concepts, but they are *ex officio* disqualified from any part in 'explanatory deductions' in philosophy. This commonly overlooked feature of Wittgenstein's philosophy differentiates his use of his own synoptic observations from the use made of them by others, e.g. the Vienna Circle. He saw (and explained why there is) no inconsistency in calling mathematical propositions rules and speaking of them as being true. Members of the Circle saw themselves faced with a choice between alternative theoretical commitments. Similarly, he repudiated the idea that what the Vienna Circle called 'Wittgenstein's principle of verification' was part of a *theory* about language.

The 'flatness' of Wittgenstein's philosophy is difficult to keep in focus, and his readers often teeter on the brink of being unable to accept at his own valuation the insights he bequeathed us. Two observations might weaken our impulse to impute theories to him or to construe his grammatical observations as arranged under the headings of premises and conclusions of philosophical proofs. First, the primary role of many of his grammatical descriptions is not to disclose unity beneath apparent diversity, but rather to emphasize diversity in the face of apparent homogeneity. A striking example is his use (in the early 1930s) of the maxim 'The sense of a sentence is the method of its verification.' Some philosophers have seen this as highlighting a very abstract isomorphism between operationalist accounts of scientific concepts and constructivist accounts of mathematics, perhaps subsuming both under a completely general theory of meaning ('anti-realism'). Wittgenstein, however, employed the maxim for the opposite purpose. There is nothing more disastrous for philosophical understanding, he urged, than the assimilation of mathematical proof to the verification of a proposition on the model of the verification of an empirical statement by observation (PG 361). He emphasized the fundamental logical difference between the sense of a mathematical proposition and of an empirical one precisely by focusing upon the *differences* in the 'verifications' in these two cases (cf. PR 134). Secondly, his 'generalizations', or synoptic grammatical remarks, are intended to serve as reminders of a host of grammatical truisms. It is the arrangement of these, their juxtaposition with comparisons, analogies and disanalogies, that are powerful sources of insight and philosophical illumination. The grammatical 'generalizations' neither supersede nor theorize about these, but merely bring them into view to help the philosophically bewildered to find their way around.

This central feature of Wittgenstein's conception of philosophy informs his work in philosophy of mathematics and philosophy of psychology alike. For these are the two main branches that spring from his reflections on language, meaning and understanding in the 'Proto-Investigations'. It seems certain that close scrutiny of his writings on philosophy of mathematics can make decisive contributions to clarifying the *Philosophical Investigations*. Not only does this throw light on details of the text, it also promotes deeper understanding of his conception of grammar and of internal relations. Everything speaks for the proposition that this is an appropriate and fruitful strategy of interpretation.

Following a rule

(§§185–242)

INTRODUCTION

Sections 185–242 can be considered the seventh 'chapter' of the *Investigations*, complementary to §§143–84. There W. launched from an examination of mastering the technique of writing the series of natural numbers into a detailed discussion of the use of 'understand' in first-person avowals ('Now I understand how to go on'). Here he reverts to the topic of mastering related arithmetical techniques in order to clarify the concept of someone's understanding (and misunderstanding) the rule of an arithmetical progression. This investigation has two interwoven aspects. One is to elucidate the criteria for understanding a rule. The other is to eliminate philosophical misconceptions about the grammatical relation between a rule and a description of an act in accord with it; i.e. to clarify the concept of accord of an act with a rule. These two enterprises are carried out together in this seventh 'chapter'.[1]

These sections are the keystone of the arch in the architectonic of the *Investigations*. On the one hand, they hold in place the subsequent private language argument and pendant remarks on various psychological concepts. On the other hand, they are the culmination of the attempt to elucidate the concepts of meaning, use, understanding and explanation (and thereby to render perspicuous the shortcomings of philosophical reflections on meaning under the aegis of the Augustinian picture of language). Clarification of the concept of understanding a rule is the pivotal task in W.'s reflections. For explanations are held to be *rules* for the use of expressions; speaking a language involves *following* these rules, exhibiting mastery of them in practice, and *understanding* expressions is manifested both in giving correct explanation of what they mean and in applying them correctly. W.'s conception of meaning would disintegrate

---

[1] In Volume 1, p. 7, we characterized the topic of Chapter 6 as the subjective aspects of following a rule, and we contrasted this with the examination of the objective aspects of rule-following in §§185–242. Although this contrast points in the right direction, it does not indicate the two-sided nature of the discussion in Chapter 7, and it obscures the continuity of Chapter 7 with Chapter 6.

were it not that using a word correctly is a criterion for understanding it, and also a criterion for understanding an explanation of what it means. Only by apprehending the content of §§185–242 and the function of these remarks can one come to understand the *Investigations* aright.

Part A (§§185–97) opens by setting the stage: the pupil who previously mastered writing the series of natural numbers (§§143–6) is now taught to write arithmetical progressions in response to orders of the form '+ *n*', but when he first proceeds beyond 1000 he manifests his *misunderstanding* of the rule '+ 2' by writing '1000, 1004, 1008' (§185). §186 suggests that he has failed to *intuit* how to continue this progression, that he has not grasped what the teacher *meant* by the instruction '+ 2'. §§186–8 reject the idea that this provides a standard of what is in accord with the rule. §189 rebuts the implication that the rule therefore does not determine what is to be done; this rests on a misunderstanding of 'to determine the steps to be taken'. §190 makes the apparent concession that how the formula '+ 2' is meant determines what is to be done, but notes that this is expressed by an explanation of what it means, i.e. by another rule-formulation. From a new direction, §191 brings an objection against the previous line of reasoning: it seems as if we grasp the whole use of an expression in an instant, and this requires laying hold of something which (unlike a humdrum explanation of meaning) must somehow already contain the entire use of the expression in advance of our applying it. §§193–4 criticize the parallel ideas that the structure of a machine supra-causally determines its future movements and that it mysteriously contains the possibilities of its movements. §§195–6 ascribe the apparent mystery of instantaneous understanding to a misunderstanding of the grammar of the phrase 'to grasp the use of a word'. §197 rounds off the discussion by clarifying what it means to grasp the whole use of a word at an instant. This is compared with intending to play chess. In both cases there is a grammatical or conceptual relation with a set of rules – a relation transparent in teaching and in the activity of following these rules (i.e. of using the word in accord with its explanation and of playing games of chess).

(The following tree diagrams display the interconnections between W.'s numbered remarks. A broken horizontal line to a square bracket signifies a clear allusion or explicit reference to an earlier remark. Close clustering signifies tight thematic unity. These diagrams will be found useful only if consulted while studying W.'s text. The connections here delineated are clarified in the exegesis.)

Structure of Part A

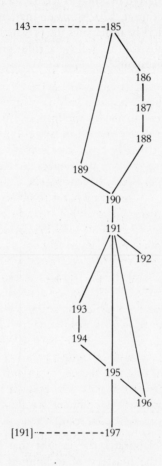

Part B (§§198–205) develops a fresh problem. In continuing the series + 2 by writing '1000, 1004, 1008', the pupil exhibited how he understood or interpreted the rule, and what he wrote is in accord with his interpretation. But if whatever one does can be brought into accord with this rule on some interpretation, how can the rule itself show one what is to be done at any step? §198 notes that the expressions of rules are connected with actions in training and that rules are conceptually related to normative regularities. §§199–200 elaborate the latter point. From the premise that any act can be brought into accord with any rule (§198), §201 first draws the (absurd) conclusion that there is neither accord nor conflict with a rule, and then infers that understanding (and misunderstanding) a rule is manifested in *acting* in accord with it (and contravening it), not only in interpreting it. §202 sums up matters in calling following a rule a *practice*; and it darkly anticipates the private language argument in declaring it to be impossible to follow a rule 'privately'. §§203–5 are various codas to the argument.

Structure of Part B

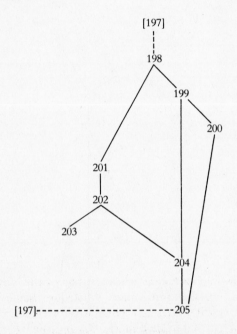

Part C (§§206–17) elaborates the insight that following a rule is a practice grounded in the mastery of techniques. §§206–8 explore the connections between the concepts of following a rule and of behavioural regularity. Regularities belong to the framework of acting in accord with rules (and speaking a language), but 'rule' cannot be usefully defined in terms of 'regular' or 'uniform'. §§209–12 criticize the idea that understanding a rule explained or formulated by examples must outstrip what is explained or explicit in the rule-formulation so that there is need for guesswork. Justifications of acts by reference to rules come to an end in forms of action accepted or acknowledged to be correct. §§213–14 add a coda critical of *intuition* as the arbiter between various possible interpretations of a rule formulated by examples. §§215–16 criticize the converse notion that the identity of a thing with itself provides an unequivocal standard for judging whether in acting *thus* one is doing the same thing as before (e.g. the same thing as in the examples used to explain or formulate the rule). §217 recapitulates the discussion in claiming that accepted patterns of action are the bedrock of justifications of what is done in following rules.

Structure of Part C

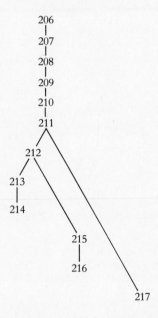

Part D (§§218–37) examines various aspects of the 'physiognomy' of following rules, i.e. the impressions which are made on us by the phenomena of following rules and which we express in certain figurative propositions and pictures. The remarks fall into three clusters. The first (§§218–21) investigates the notions that a rule is a visible section of rails reaching to infinity and that all the steps of following the rule are already taken in advance. The second (§§222–7) scrutinizes the picture that a rule *intimates* what is to be done, and it points out a tension with the idea that in following a rule one always does the same thing. The third cluster (§§228–37) opens with a criticism of the idea that knowing how to follow a rule depends on perceiving a *Gestalt*, i.e. on seeing it in a certain way (§§228–9). §230 connects this with the picture of a rule's intimating what is to be done. §§232–7 then round off the discussion by comparing and contrasting instances of following rules with cases of acting from inspiration. The features making up the 'physiognomy' of following rules are characteristic *accompaniments* of these activities, but not *criteria* for following rules.

Structure of Part D

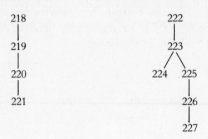

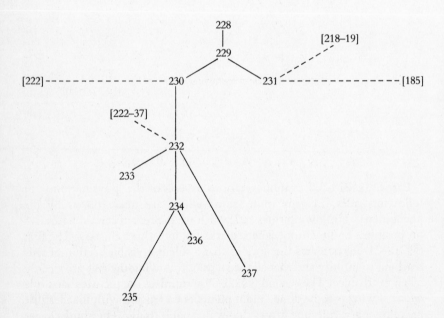

Part E (§§238–42) concludes the investigation of the concept of following a rule by drawing attention to the importance of the fact that there is a large measure of interpersonal agreement about the accord or conflict of acts with rules. It is as much a matter of course to draw the consequences of most rules as it is to call this colour 'blue' (§238). No reason is either required or available (§239). Absence of disagreement about what accords with a rule is part of the framework of speaking a language (§240). This agreement encompasses consensus about the truth of a large body of empirical judgements; the possibility of communication requires both agreement in definitions and agreement in judgements (§242). But this does not undermine the objectivity of truth and falsity (§241) or abolish logic (§242). It is agreement in form of life. This sets the stage for the private language argument.

Structure of Part E

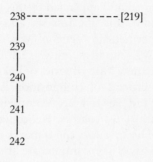

```
238 -------------- [219]
 |
239
 |
240
 |
241
 |
242
```

Correlations

PI	PPI	RFM Part I (§)	MS source
185	158		
186	159		
187	160		
188	161		
189(a)			
	162	1	117, 1–2
189(b), (c)			
190	163	2	117, 3
191		123	119, 35
192		124	119, 36
193		122	119, 28–31
194		125	119, 36–40
195		126	119, 41–2
196		127	119, 42–3
197		130	119, 44–6

The central third of the text of Part I, namely §§198–421, was composed in two distinct stages. First, W. produced a typescript (based on MS 129) of the so-called 'Intermediate Version' (*Mittelversion*). This was probably completed by January 1945, since the published preface was written then for this text. Professor G. H. von Wright has painstakingly reconstructed this text from fragments of the typescript and the manuscript underlying it. Secondly, W. made a compendium of remarks culled from most of his earlier manuscript books, the typescript called *Bemerkungen I* (TS 228). This was completed probably in the first six months of 1945. Some of this material was then inserted into the text of the 'Intermediate Version', more of it was rearranged and appended to this text (producing §§422–693 of the final version), and the rest set aside (mostly published in *Zettel*). Since the 'Intermediate Version' was a continuous chain of remarks, the effect of W.'s modification was to open some of the links of this chain and introduce new links or series of links between them.

Knowledge of this process of composition is important for understanding §§198–242, and so too are comparisons of the published remarks with their manuscript sources. Hence we have constructed two tables of correlation. The first lists the remarks drawn from the 'Intermediate Version' and gives their immediate source (MS 129) and the most important more remote source (MS 124). The second lists remarks drawn from *Bemerkungen I* and gives their immediate sources.

PI	PPI(I)	MS 129	MS124
198	198	25–6	205
199	199	26–7	206
200	200	27–8	
204	201	28–9	207–8
205	202	29	
206	203	29–30	
207	204	30–1	
208	205	31–2, 35–6, 88	209–10
209	206	35, 47–8	
210	207	33	210–11
211	208	33	211
212	209	34	211–12
213	210	34–5	212
217	211	33–4	
241	212	35	212–13

PI	TS 228 (§)	MS source
201	265	129, 119–20
202	266	129, 121
203	267	129, 121
215	677	119, 46–7
216	678	119, 47–9
218	337	129, 176
219	596, 597	128, 45
220	598	128, 46
221	599	128, 46
222	603	124, 152
223	339	129, 176–7
224	282	129, 130
225	613	124, 162
226	607	124, 153
227	608	124, 155
228	621	124, 184
229	338	129, 176
230	604	124, 152
231	622	124, 184
232	609, 619	124, 157
233	610	124, 157–8
234	616	124, 164
235	617	124, 164
236	612	124, 160–1
237	605, 606	124, 152–3
238	336	129, 175–6
239	38	116, 37
240	277	129, 127–8
242	279	129, 128–9

II

RULES AND GRAMMAR

1. *The concern with rules: the* Tractatus

Traditionally philosophy has been thought to study the most general and essential features of things, the nature of thought and the limits of possible knowledge. The metaphysician concerned himself with the essence of the world. The logician studied the nature of judgement and the laws of thought. The epistemologist studied the relations of ideas and their correspondence to reality. Philosophers did not conceive of their subject matter as the investigation of language, nor did they typically consider the study of the uses of words or sentences, *a fortiori* the rules for their use, as a crucial method to attain their goals. Such an investigation might at best be a propaedeutic to their proper business. Words, they held, signify things or ideas, and philosophy's proper business was to investigate and 'analyse' what is signified.

This conception has changed dramatically this century. The catalyst of change was the invention of function-theoretic logical calculi by Frege, Russell and Whitehead, which gave logicians an unprecedentedly powerful tool for the presentation of modes of inference. It was not unnatural to jump to the conclusion that this novel calculus had laid bare the hidden logical structure of any language fit for reasoning, arguing and inferring. The major reorientation resulted from the *Tractatus*, the goal of which was to elucidate the essence of any possible *language*, to clarify the nature of any form of representation. *All philosophy is a critique of language* (TLP 4.0031); the limits of thought are to be delineated by clarifying the limits of *language*. Logic is not an investigation into the nature of language-independent judgements, concepts and laws of thought, but an elucidation of the essential properties of *symbols* alone (TLP 6.113, 6.126). Metaphysics as traditionally formulated is nonsense, since it violates the bounds of sense. But what metaphysicians have tried to say is shown by the well-formed *sentences* of a language. Natural languages possess an essential underlying logical structure since logic is a condition of sense; there can be no such thing as an illogical language (or illogical *thought*).

This dramatic logico-linguistic reorientation of philosophy gave the concept of a *rule* of language a most important role in the *Tractatus*. Any possible language is governed by a complex system of rules of logical syntax. These rules determine the combinatorial possibilities of symbols, thus delimiting the bounds of sense. They are of two kinds. One kind of rule determines the modes of combination of atomic propositions into molecular propositions by means of logical connectives. The truth-tabular explanations of the logical connectives (which are not 'representatives', i.e. do not name functions or logical objects) belong to the rules of logical syntax. But logical necessity is not the product of syntactic conventions.[1] It mirrors the logical structure of the world (TLP 6.13), i.e. the possibilities of existence and non-existence of states of affairs.

The second kind of rule of logical syntax concerns names which are 'representatives'. These rules also are taken to reflect metaphysical necessities. The combinatorial possibilities of names mirror the combinatorial possibilities of the objects which are their meanings, and the proposition pictures the state of affairs which it represents. Since this relation is internal it is, according to the *Tractatus*, also ineffable. The correlation of a name with its meaning was conceived to be not *normative* but psychological. The projection of names on to objects is not a set of semantic rules, but a set of mental acts. However, in characterizing names of *complexes* as abbreviations. Wittgenstein allocated to syntax the equivalence of such a name with its analysis.

This conception of the rules which govern any possible language involves various striking peculiarities. First, many of the rules of logical syntax are hidden from view. They are not overt in the forms and structure of ordinary language, nor are they articulated in any practices of day to day explanations of meaning, teaching, correcting or criticizing. Secondly, these underlying rules generate consequences quite independently of human activities. We may recognize these when confronted with them, as we recognize the logical necessity of colour exclusion. Thirdly, the correct analysis of a significant proposition may be hidden and, in some sense, completely unknown to someone who understands it. Indeed, Wittgenstein himself was unable to give a complete analysis of *any* significant proposition in any language or to instance a single (logically proper) name. The 'ultimate analysis' of phenomena has yet to be achieved (RLF 171). Fourthly, in so far as a person has mastered a language, he must be presumed to have tacit or implicit knowledge of the rules of logical syntax (as it were, the essential grammar of any *possible* language). Of course, he will not be able to formulate them explicitly,[2] but he *must* follow these rules all the time, for they mark out boundary lines between sense and nonsense, boundary lines with which he is familiar. Understanding of natural languages is

---

[1] It is disputed whether the *Tractatus* gave a conventionalist account of necessary truth. Although its truth-table definitions were welcomed by logical positivists and used in the defence of consistent empiricism, that interpretation ignores many important remarks about logical constants and the nature of logic, e.g. the metaphor of logic as the scaffolding of the world, the idea that in it the *essential* nature of signs is manifest, the claim that logic is transcendental (TLP 6.124, 6.13).

[2] RLF 171 says that these rules cannot be *laid down* until we have reached the ultimate analysis of the relevant propositions. But this must surely mean: *be formulated*.

held to turn on enormously complicated tacit conventions which make it possible for speakers to express every sense 'without having any idea how each word has meaning or what its meaning is' (TLP 4.002).

Even more curiously, it seems that in a sense these crucial rules of logical syntax cannot be stated coherently at all.[3] For a coherent statement is a *picture of reality*, and an expression of a rule does not picture how things are in the world, but rather prescribes what is to be done. Moreover, since any rule of logical syntax cannot fail to hold, that it governs a particular language cannot be said.[4] For quite different reasons, an even more startling claim is made, namely that although inference is conceived to be manifested in logical syntax (i.e. rules for truth-operations), *rules* of inference which Frege and Russell invoked to *justify* inferences are superfluous, and disappear altogether (TLP 5.132). A further curious twist to the tale is given by the insistence that in a sense these rules of logical syntax cannot be violated! Logic takes care of itself, for a 'violation' of the rules of logical syntax yields *nonsense*, not a 'false sense'. And nonsense says nothing: 'Thought can never be of anything illogical, since, if it were, we should have to think illogically.' (TLP 3.03) Nonsense, one might say, is akin to a *natural* sanction attached to rules of syntax, as invalidity is akin to a natural sanction attached to laws stipulating the mode of exercise of legal powers. This has the consequence that nonsense need not (indeed, cannot (TLP 3.33ff.)) be banned by explicit prohibitions, as Frege and Russell had imagined in introducing explicit type-restrictions justified by reference to the meanings of signs. Purely syntactic prohibitions are also impossible, since the *logical* requirements on symbols cannot be expressed but only shown (NB 108).

This conception of rules of logical syntax which Wittgenstein had when he wrote the *Tractatus* and even 'Some Remarks on Logical Form' is a far cry from the conception of rules of grammar which dominates his later work. What was taken for granted earlier, what had seemed unproblematic, gradually assumed the spectacle of a philosophical quagmire in traversing which each and every step must be tested again, for any false move may sink one deep in the sludge of confusion. Many of the central theses of the *Tractatus* concerning logical syntax and its relation to reality now seemed muddles flagging treacherous terrain. There is no such thing as our following rules without our being able to explain or justify our actions by reference to them. There can be no hidden rules awaiting discovery, which we cannot yet formulate, but which we tacitly know and follow. Hence 'analysis' cannot wait for future discoveries. There is no such thing as meaning independently of

---

[3] This strange view is fully evident in Waismann's 'Theses' (WWK 240f.)

[4] This will be obvious if the rule incorporates formal concepts, e.g. the principle that the logical constants are not function names or that a proposition is not a name, but a symbolizing fact.

rules which determine how an expression is to be used. So names are given a meaning not by associating a form with an object in reality which is its meaning, but by a rule for its correct use. Such rules, however, are not rules correlating words with reality (that is a misconception of ostensive definition of 'indefinables'). Nothing counts as a rule independently of being used (or stipulated) as a rule, as a standard of correctness. The combinatorial rules for names do not mirror the logical forms of reality; rather the 'logical forms' of objects in the world are the shadows cast by grammar. 'The harmony between thought and reality is to be found in the grammar of the language.' (PG 162) For grammar is autonomous, a free-floating structure which is not answerable to reality.

Some of these issues will be examined in other essays in this volume; others have already been discussed in Volume 1; yet others must be deferred. The point of sketching some of the prominent claims about the rules of logical syntax is to make clear the origin, scope and nature of Wittgenstein's later concern with rules. It is rooted in an array of philosophical questions first broached in the *Tractatus*. What determines its scope is a range of problems in philosophical logic, philosophy of mind and metaphysics, e.g. the nature of meaning and explanation of meaning, of understanding, of necessary truth and valid inference, and of a form of representation and its limits. The concept of a rule, correctly apprehended, is a powerful elucidatory tool in the resolution of a multitude of philosophical questions. But if unclarity about rules persists, or if misconceptions abound, then this concept, far from clearing away the mists of mythology about symbolism, will multiply confusion, generating phantasmagoria of innate rules, hidden rules of depth-grammar, rules encoded in the brain, rules generating consequences which no human being can apprehend, and so on. This essay is intended to put some preliminary order into our reflections on the concept of a rule of language and to take the first steps necessary in order to come to grips with Wittgenstein's remarks on rules and rule-following.

2. *From logical syntax to philosophical grammar*

For present purposes it is fruitful to view Wittgenstein's later philosophy as an investigation of the conflicting pressures stored up in the conception of a language as a *system* of hidden *rules*. To a first approximation, what makes it plausible to describe languages as *rule*-governed, namely the motley of rules and principles used in language-teaching, visible in ordinary grammar books and dictionaries, manifest in daily explanations, clarifications and corrections of errors in language-use, does not manifest a system or constitute a calculus of rules. Conversely, what is typically offered in attempts to display a language as a systematic structure backed by a calculus of rules does not consist of anything having the *uses* characteristic of rules. Hence there is an intolerable tension.

When Wittgenstein returned to philosophy in 1929, he found fatal flaws in the logical and metaphysical theses of the *Tractatus*. In response to these he jettisoned the characteristic tenets of his logical atomism: the independence of the atomic proposition, the idea that all inference depended on truth-functional composition, the conception of sempiternal simple objects, the thesis of isomorphism crucial to the picture theory of the atomic proposition, the supposition that generality is reducible to logical sum or product. But, initially at least, far from *abandoning* the idea that any language is a calculus of rules, he remoulded and strengthened it. In the *Tractatus* he had thought that any possible language had the underlying structure of a logico-syntactical calculus connected to reality by logically proper names whose meanings were simple objects that constitute the substance of the world; he now argued that any possible language was an *autonomous* calculus of rules. For he now conceived of *meaning* as being bestowed on the primitive indefinables of a language partly by means of ostensive definitions which are in fact *rules*. And the samples employed in ostension are themselves elements of *the method of representation*. These rules are conjoined with other rules governing the uses of the indefinables, viz. category restrictions and rules laying down internal relations within a *Satzsystem* (e.g. colour exclusion). The meaning of an expression is not an object in reality but the *totality* of rules which determine its use within the calculus of language. The place of a word in grammar, its role in the calculus, is its meaning (PG 59, 63). In the *Tractatus* the rules of logical syntax governing the combinatorial possibilities of names were thought to mirror the nature of objects and the logical structure of the world. This Wittgenstein now stigmatized as a mythological conception of the rules for using expressions. In its place he substituted the idea that there is behind the use of language a definite body of autonomous rules.

This conception of meaning and language did not last long.[5] From 1931 onwards Wittgenstein moved gradually away from the idea that beneath meaningful discourse lies *a system of rules of a calculus* towards recognition of the fact that speaking a language is a many-faceted rule-governed *activity* or set of activities. He ceased talking of the calculus of language and instead began to talk of *comparing* a language with a calculus, a comparison which would reveal both similarities and differences. Subsequently he introduced the notion of a language-*game*, finding the analogies between speech and engaging in games, and

---

[5] Although certain aspects are permanent, e.g. the claim that grammar is autonomous, that there is (in the requisite sense) *no* connection between language and reality, that any difference in the rules for the use of an expression is a difference in meaning.

between the rules of games and the rules of languages, more fruitful than the analogy between speech and the operation of a calculus and that between rules of a language and the rules of a calculus. He thus displayed a movement away from focusing on *forms* of expressions and their patterns of relationships towards concentrating on *uses* – away from viewing discourse as patterned arrays of symbols towards seeing speech as part of the web of human life, interwoven with a multitude of acts, activities, reactions and responses.

The idea of a calculus *obstructs* our vision of the rules that govern languages. It obscures the motley of rules, the diversity of their forms and character, and the manners in which they are involved in linguistic activities. Wittgenstein had, in the *Tractatus*, seen that philosophical or conceptual investigation moves in the domain of rules. An important point of continuity was the insight that philosophy is not concerned with what is true or false, but rather with what makes sense and what traverses the bounds of sense. But his misconception of the normative character of language had led him there to erect a mythology of symbolism. Hence his later reflections on rules play a pivotal role in the whole of his mature philosophy.

Clarification of the concept of a rule and of following a rule were essential in order to shed light upon philosophical questions about meaning and understanding, sense and nonsense, necessity and possibility. These philosophical issues moulded the contours of his concern with rules. Hence numerous questions which have preoccupied philosophers in deontic logic, ethics, legal and social theory are passed by. He did not mention deontic modalities and their relations, criteria of existence and individuation of rules, distinctions between rules and principles, between duty-imposing and power-conferring rules, etc. This is not an incompleteness in his account. He aimed not to write a book on rules but to examine specific problems arising out of insights into the normative nature of a language, of logic and of reasoning. On the other hand, Wittgenstein concentrated on questions typically passed over in reflections on rules. Indeed the problems upon which he focused are not themselves readily understood, and have been extensively misinterpreted. What is it to act in accord with a rule? What is it for something to follow from a rule? How is it possible for a rule to have an open range of applications? What is it to understand a rule, and how does such understanding manifest itself? It is such questions that are the subject of Wittgenstein's reflections. Part of our task, in this and other essays, is to elucidate how these questions bear on the clarification of meaning, inference, necessity and mathematics.

The other main aspect of his investigations which needs clarification is what he called 'rules of grammar' – the heterogeneous rules for the use of symbols which he took to inform the activity of speaking a language.

These are the direct descendants of the 'rules of logical syntax' of the *Tractatus*. Like rules of logical syntax, rules of grammar determine the bounds of sense. They distinguish sense from nonsense, but not truth from falsity. Neither kind of rule furnishes empirical knowledge of the world. Points of contrast between logical syntax and 'rules of grammar' are, however, striking. The domain of grammar is wider than that of logical syntax. Its rules include *all* forms of explanations of meaning, not merely formal definitions but also ostensive definition, explanations by examples or paraphrase, gestures, etc. Mathematical propositions, which were conceived in the *Tractatus* to be pseudo-propositions, are now held to be rules of grammar. Metaphysical propositions which were held in the *Tractatus* to be literally ill formed are now argued to express, at least in certain cases, grammatical rules. On the other hand, Wittgenstein's conception of grammar also involves a radical transformation of what he had held to be the domain of logical syntax in the *Tractatus*. There he conceived his task to be the delineation of the essential nature of any possible language, whereas later he did not consider the rules of grammar to be universal. They are rules of particular languages at particular times, characteristic of particular forms of representation. Grammar consists of rules for the use of symbols (words, phrases, sentences, formulae) of natural languages (cf. PI §108), not of arcane and recherché entities such as 'logically proper names' and 'elementary propositions'. Although many languages which share a massive core of common concepts will have a large array of isomorphic rules, rules of grammar are in principle language-specific. Although philosophical problems are typically concerned with issues pertaining to concepts characteristically shared by most developed languages (substance, causation, personal identity, perception, logical necessity, etc.), different forms of representation, actual or *invented*, are of great philosophical interest. Different colour-geometries in different languages or different methods of counting and measuring shed light, by way of contrast, on our form of representation and serve to rid us of the illusion that ours is *correct* or *true to the facts*. Wittgenstein's 'rules of grammar' serve only to distinguish sense from nonsense. Unlike the depth rules of logical syntax, they do not reflect ineffable metaphysical truths. They do not give rise to any theses or doctrines. They settle what makes sense, experience settles what is the case. Hence also they are, in a deep sense, arbitrary (see 'Grammar and necessity', pp. 329ff.). Grammar is a free-floating array of rules for the use of language. It determines what is a correct use of language, but is not itself correct or incorrect. It is not answerable to the nature of reality, to the structure of the mind or to 'the laws of thought'. Grammar is autonomous.

Wittgenstein's conception of grammar has not been well understood and has met with a hostile reception. Clarifying it is an important exegetical task. Defending it is arguably a pressing philosophical need.

Preliminary steps in both directions will be taken in this essay. The task will be resumed in later essays.

3. *Rules and rule-formulations*

Obvious examples of rules are rules of games, legal rules, the traffic code or rules of etiquette. In selecting them, we show a preference for 'musts' and 'may nots' or for 'dos' and 'don'ts': 'Drive on the left', 'You must stop at the traffic lights if they are red', 'Don't eat with your fingers', 'Tax must be paid on . . . .' But in explaining a rule-governed activity we would also cite other kinds of rules expressed by other kinds of sentence, e.g. 'Spades trump clubs', 'The bishop moves only on diagonals', 'The winner is the one who has the highest score.' The range of sentence-types which may be used to state rules is very wide. Deontic sentences (i.e. declarative sentences containing a deontic auxiliary verb), imperatives, ordinary declarative sentences, sentences in what Bentham called 'the dominative tense' ('The prime minister shall form a cabinet within a week of being appointed') can all be used to specify rules. But it is noteworthy that such sentence-types can typically be used for altogether different purposes. One may, of course, adopt, for certain purposes, a canonical form for the presentation of a certain array of rules (a codification of rules). But its employment presupposes independent identification of the rules to be presented or a context in which it is laid down in advance that the *stipulation* of rules is to be expressed in these forms.

When confronted with the philosophical question 'What is a rule?', we typically respond by distinguishing a rule from its expression. A rule is not a rule-formulation, we rightly say (PLP 82). For the same rule may be written down three times on the same page; it may be stated on a notice board in three different languages. One may ask how many words there are in a rule-formulation, but not how many words there are in the rule. One may copy out the rule-formulation in smaller handwriting without the rule getting any smaller. Such considerations, correct as far as they go, nudge us gently towards Platonist vortices. If a rule is not a rule-formulation, and if we state rules by means of rule-formulations, then surely what a rule is must be *what is expressed by rule-formulations*! So just as sentences are distinct from the propositions which they express, and numerals are different from the numbers they denote (imperative sentences from orders, predicates from properties, etc.), so too rule-formulations differ from rules.

At this point the pressure to declare 'Rules are abstract entities' is very great. Nevertheless it should be resisted. While a thoroughgoing nominalism (rules are uniformly to be identified with rule-formulations) is patently misguided, Platonism is no less confused. That a rule, a proposition, a number is not identical with any spatio-temporal entity does not imply that it must therefore, *mirabile dictu*, be a non-spatio-temporal entity. Does it follow then that rules are *not* entities? And are we claiming that there *really* are not any rules, that rules do not 'exist'? Not at all; but the term 'entity' (not to mention 'exist') is the source of multiple confusions. The only serious questions are: what is it for there to be (or not to be) such-and-such a rule (of contract law in England or of international law, of cricket or football, of English grammar or etiquette), and what is it for an expression to be the formulation of a rule? And such questions boil down to the requirement for a careful examination of the ways in which we use the expressions 'rule', 'rule-formulation' and related terms. That in turn involves noting cases where they cannot be interchanged as well as those where they can. It is, in general, perfectly correct to say that a rule is what is expressed by a rule-formulation, as indeed it is correct to say that a number is what is signified by a numeral (PG 321). These are not ontological revelations, but grammatical trivialities. An investigation into what is expressed by a rule-formulation is an investigation into the grammar of the word 'rule' and the uses of rule-formulations.

Rule-formulations are not rules. We do not use the expressions 'rule-formulation', 'statement of a rule' in the same way we use 'rule'. But rules and rule-formulations cannot be simply segregated into separate 'ontological' categories, e.g. abstract entities and expressions. For the grammar of 'rule' and 'rule-formulation' runs, for a stretch, along parallel tracks. One may put the rules into the right logical order when transcribing them, underline the most important rules, leave some of the unimportant ones out, translate the rules into French, etc. (Similarly I write down my telephone number (not: numeral), draw a number in a lottery, etc.)

It is evident that neither 'rule' nor 'rule-formulation' wears the trousers. We noted that rule-formulations are not identifiable by their forms. We must rather examine how certain expressions are *used*, how they function in human affairs. Something expresses a rule only if it is used to express a rule, and it is that role which needs to be characterized. But equally, rules must be characterized by their role. An affinity in the grammar of 'rule' and 'rule-formulation' is manifest in the fact that an explanation of what a rule is and of what a rule-formulation is are overlapping and interdependent.

If called upon to explain what a rule is one might try different moves. Waismann (PLP 137ff.) takes us through various ones which he ultimately declares to be futile:

(1) *Rules are a means of learning how to engage in whatever activity they govern* We learn to play chess by learning its rules, how to read or write Latin by learning Latin grammar, and so on. Certainly rules typically

play a role in teaching and learning rule-governed activities. But, first, it is not logically necessary for someone to know how to engage in such an activity that he have learnt it, for innate knowledge is not logically impossible. But that would not render the rules obsolete, only pedagogically pointless. They would still have a role in justifying action, in criticizing mistakes (innate knowledge no more excludes occasional lapses than does acquired knowledge) and in evaluating correctness. Secondly, many rule-governed activities are learned by training, rather than by being taught rules (memorizing rule-formulations). Similarly, some activities can be learnt by observation rather than by being told what the rules are. Thirdly, some rules may play no role at all in teaching and learning. An example of one such type is that in chess a bishop cannot move off its own colour; an example of a quite different type is that one may not move pieces off the board.

(2) *Rules say what one ought to do* This too says something true, but not very much and nothing illuminating. First, orders, commands and advice tell us what we ought to do, but are not necessarily also rules. Secondly, not all rules tell or prescribe what ought to be done (e.g. the rule that the winner is the one who scores most points, or that doing such-and-such counts as scoring).

(3) *Rules describe prevailing practice* This is awry. One must not conflate statements of rules with descriptions of what most people do. 'This colour is called "red"' is typically used to formulate a rule, 'People generally call this colour "red"' is a description of behaviour. The former says what is *to be done*, the latter reports what is done. One might, of course, claim that rules describe what ought to be done, but only at the cost of stretching the term 'describe' and obscuring the nature of rules by forcing them into moulds appropriate for propositions and their internal relations to facts. Secondly, new rules can be introduced which are not yet part of prevailing practice. So rules cannot simply be descriptions of prevailing practice.

Many further such moves are available, and none is wholly pointless. Each comparison illuminates a facet of some kinds of rules. Reflecting on these similarities and contrasts, analogies and disanalogies, Wittgenstein was strongly inclined to repudiate any demand for a *Merkmal*-definition of 'rule'. The concept of a rule is a family-resemblance concept. There are no common features to all the things we call 'rules' *in virtue of which* we denominate them thus (PG 116f.). There may perhaps *be* common features, but if there are they play no role in determining the correctness or incorrectness of our use of 'rule' in contrast with, say, 'regularity', 'habit', 'custom', etc. and no role in explaining its use (AWL 155).[6] We

---

[6] It is important to note that claiming that a concept is a family-resemblance concept does not imply that items falling under it have no features in common (cf. Volume 1, 'Family resemblance', pp. 327, MU pp. 192f.).

are never, in our natural uses of language, called upon to distinguish rules from everything else there is. It is only in rather special contexts that we are required to draw a boundary between what is a rule and what is not, and then it is typically unproblematic, e.g. 'Is this a rule or a recommendation?', 'Are these the rules, or just a preliminary draft?', 'Is this a statement of a rule or just a description of what people do?' (PG 117)

This is not to say that we cannot specify salient features of (most) rules, compare and contrast rules with related things such as orders, statements and descriptions of behaviour. Rather the point is that we typically explain what a rule is by a variety of examples which show how the expression 'rule' is to be used (PG 118) and how 'an expression of a rule' likewise is employed (BB 98). And we may invoke general features of rules in particular cases to demarcate what is from what is not a rule, e.g. 'No, that is not a rule, it is insufficiently general.' (AWL 155) This clears up particular misunderstandings, but does not constitute an attempt to arrive at a *Merkmal*-definition of a rule.

With this proviso we can examine our humdrum concept of a rule more closely.[7] Light can be shed upon it by assembling reminders of the roles which rules fulfil in a rule-governed practice or activity. That an activity is rule-governed implies a certain *regularity* in behaviour (PI §§207f.). It is, as it were, a regularity from the point of view of the rule, for the concept of a rule and the concept of doing the same are internally, conceptually, related (PI §225) – a crucial feature which we shall examine later (cf. 'Following rules, mastery of techniques and practices', pp. 165ff.). If one follows a given rule, then one always does the same thing when the appropriate occasion arises. For rules are inherently general, laying down standards of correctness for a multiplicity of occasions.[8] Note, however, that this does not mean that a rule-formulation must always contain an expression of generality. An ostensive definition 'This ↗ is red' contains no such expression; nor does a rule of an arithmetical series given (correctly) by means of a segment of the series. The generality of a rule lies in its *use*, not (or not necessarily) in its form. We *guide* our actions by reference to rules: we teach and explain rule-governed activities by citing the rules that govern it. When in doubt about how to proceed

---

[7] Although it should be borne in mind that our ultimate purpose is to clarify Wittgenstein's conception of rules of *language*; hence much fine detail and many localized special cases which would be pertinent in a general treatise on normative theory or jurisprudence will be disregarded.

[8] Wittgenstein always stressed the requirement of generality in respect of occasion, 'that a rule is something applied in many cases' (AWL 155). Other kinds of generality may arise with respect to the subjects of a rule (e.g. of law) and the object (if any) referred to. What, in each case, generality amounts to is contentious (especially in legal and political theory) and arguably varies from context to context, case to case. But note his addendum: 'If I am a professor of logic and say a rule is something general or that for a rule generality is required, I am just making an ass of myself. For do you know any better how to use ['a rule'?] from this explanation? It is quite useless; it tells you nothing.' (AWL 155)

we consult the rules. Occasionally explicit reference to rules may be a natural phase in a rule-governed activity, as in employing conversion tables in measuring. But the forms of guidance by a rule are most varied; it is not at all necessary that for an activity to be guided by a rule the rule should enter into the activity or even cross the minds of those engaged in it (chess players do not think about the rules of chess as they play; they know them too well (WWK 153f.; PLP 129ff.)). But neither is it enough that the behaviour of someone following a rule merely conforms with the rule (a chess computer follows no rules). Nor is it sufficient that he once learned the rule – for that is past history (PG 86) and the issue here is his present possession of an ability, not its genesis. Nor would it suffice that the rule might be encoded in his brain (whatever that might mean); for being caused to act by the encoding of a rule is precisely *not* to follow a rule (PLP 119ff.).[9] That a person's action is normative, that he is following a rule, that he is guided by a rule (or better, guides himself by reference to a rule) is manifest in the manner in which he uses rules, invokes rule-formulations, refers to rules in *explaining* what he did, *justifying* what he did in the face of criticism, *evaluating* what he did and *correcting* what he did, *criticizing* his mistakes, and so forth. It is to these familiar but often overlooked features of rules and rule-governed practices that we now turn.

(1) *The instructional aspect*   We typically teach a rule-governed activity by citing rules, i.e. by using sentences as formulations of rules: '*This* is a pawn; it moves *thus*'; 'If the ball knocks the bails off, the batsman is out'; 'Stop at the traffic lights if they are red.' But it is not essential to teaching or mastering every rule-governed activity that all of its rules be formulated in the course of instruction.

(2) *The definitory aspect*   Rules define actions, e.g. castling in chess, making a valid will or contract, and obeying an order. Hence they generate forms of description and determine the applicability and in-applicability of corresponding (normative) characterizations of be-haviour (e.g. 'He castled'). Just as the rules of chess define what is called 'playing chess' (and also what is called 'trying to play chess', 'wishing (intending, refusing) to play chess'), so too rules of inference define what is to be called 'a valid argument'. In laying down such rules we typically mould concepts. In making connections between rules (in stipulating that compliance with a given rule is an operative fact relative to another rule) we are engaged in concept-formation, introducing new criteria for the applicability of concepts.

(3) *The explanatory aspect*   Since the rules are necessary to render

---

[9] Current jargon of 'neural representations' of rules is manifest nonsense since only symbols with a use can function as a representation (formulation) of a rule, and nerve cells are not symbols. Being knocked sideways by a board on which is written 'Turn left!' is not to *follow* the rule to turn left, but only to be caused unwittingly to conform to it.

intelligible descriptions of acts within a rule-governed practice, they also
underlie a standard form of the explanation of the particular actions of
those engaged in the activity. They provide part or the whole of answers
to questions of the form 'Why did he do that?': e.g. 'He is walking off
because he is out', 'He stopped because the lights were red', 'He
exchanged queens because of the threat of perpetual check.' Such
explanations are not causal, but teleological. An action is thus explained
by giving the agent's *reason* why he acted as he did, and the rule which
the agent follows provides part or the whole of his reason (cf. Exg.
§211). Note that it is a presupposition of any such explanation that the
agent is *following* the relevant rule; accidental conformity of his behaviour
with an unknown rule cannot provide his reason for what he did. Only
reference to a rule that he is following is what is called a (teleological)
explanation of his actions. Note too that the mastery of rule-governed
techniques provides foundations for predictions. An explanation of an
agent's action by reference to his reasons for doing something does not
assert that there are regularities in behaviour (even in the agent's
behaviour), and hence it cannot be falsified by any statistical evidence;
rather, such an explanation presupposes that there are general regularities
in the behaviour of persons who follow the rules which define the rule-
governed activity. When people have this as their reason or that as their
goal, they generally act *thus*. Hence we may predict that he will castle
now since he is a good chess player, or that he will calculate the product
of 25 × 27 to be 675 since he is a competent mathematician (cf. RFM 193).
Without the possibility of predictions of actions within rule-governed
activities, there would be no such thing as teleological explanations of
actions by citing rules as reasons.

(4) *The justificative aspect* A rule is cited in justifying (and criticizing)
an action. When challenged, I may justify what I have done by reference
to a mandatory rule (e.g. 'I had to sacrifice my queen because a king
cannot be left *en prise*') or by the claim that an operative condition of such
a rule is satisfied (e.g. 'I stopped at the intersection because the lights
were red'); or I may claim that I am entitled by a permissive rule to have
done what I did (e.g. 'I have the right to grow prickly pears in my rock
garden').

(5) *The evaluative aspect* Rules constitute standards of correctness
against which to 'measure' conduct as right or wrong. The dimensions of
normative evaluation vary according to the nature of the activity (e.g.
legal or illegal, grammatical or ungrammatical, sense or nonsense, valid
or invalid) and to the specific definitory aspect of the rule. Wittgenstein
stressed the metaphor of measurement. Rules are what measure, not
what is measured. Hence an expression cannot, on one and the same
occasion, be used to express a rule and also as an application of that rule.
Hence if a sentence expresses an ostensive definition, it cannot also (on

that very occasion) be an application of the defined expression, and so cannot be giving an *example* (cf. 'Ostensive definition and its ramifications', Volume 1, pp. 178ff., MU pp. 91ff.). Note that expressions have been transferred in both directions across this metaphorical bridge. 'Rule' (or in French *règle*) as in metre-rule is derived from *regula* (rule or norm).

These five aspects of rules are manifest in what we shall label 'normative activities', viz. teaching, explaining, justifying and criticizing, evaluating and defining rule-governed activities. We use this term of art to refer to the activities which constitute the background or framework of the possibility of following a rule. Hence we shall *not* call playing chess a normative activity (even though it is following a set of rules), for we shall reserve that term for the background activities, actual and potential, which make rule-following actions (logically) possible.

Our rehearsal of some salient logical features of the role of rules in our rule-governed practices[10] are meant to bring out what might be called the *dynamic* or *functional* aspect of rules. Rules are *instruments* (BT 241). Something is a rule only dynamically, only in so far as it is *used* in a certain way, viz. in normative activities, only in so far as it is thus involved in rule-governed practices. But, of course, such comments are at best misleading, at worst nonsense. A lever, Wittgenstein emphasized, is a lever only in use; disconnected it is just a rod. A word, he stressed, has a meaning only in the context of a sentence – a dictum which should be understood as saying that something is a symbol only in so far as it actually fulfils a role in a system of symbols. But rules, unlike levers or marks on paper, and like propositions or numbers, are not in general to be equated with physical objects that can be used in various ways, or not used at all, but just left idle. We can say that it is no longer a rule that one ought to do so and so, but there is no answer to the question what it is that is no longer a rule! Yet the inchoate thought that a rule is a rule only in use moves in the right direction. There are, in a sense, no *idle* rules,[11] i.e. rules which have (or worse, *could* have) no role in guiding action, in justification or explanation, in teaching and correcting, evaluating and criticizing. Hence also there can be no 'hidden rules' buried in the

[10] We have omitted numerous other features that may be of philosophical interest in other contexts. One might classify rules according to their normative function (viz. to prohibit, prescribe, permit, empower, constitute or identify) or according to their social functions (e.g. to discourage deviant behaviour, encourage desired conduct, create normative relationships at will, and facilitate settlement of disputes). Such features are not our concern, which is both more general, viz. to explore the logical nature of normative conduct, and more specific, viz. to illuminate the nature of rules of language.

[11] Of course, one must make room for legal rules that are not enforced for long periods, but could be. This is a peculiarity of complex normative systems with sophisticated authority structures. One must also make room for rules of games that are not played for centuries but are then rediscovered by antiquarians who find the original rule-formulations. Did the rules 'exist' all the time? The question is misleading, but the facts are clear.

unconscious mind or encoded in the brain, for what is thus hidden has no place in any normative activities.

We might elaborate the idea of the dynamic or functional character of rules in terms of the use of symbols as rule-formulations. For an expression or symbol to formulate a rule it must (tautologically) be *used* to formulate a rule. But it is so used only if it is given a role in normative activities. This fact is important, for whether a deontic or imperative sentence (for example) formulates a rule depends on what role it fulfils in discourse. Such items as blueprints can function as descriptions or as rules.[12] For the architectural historian or engineering student the blueprint describes the building or machine. It is *used as* a description; and if the building or machine are other than as is drawn in the blueprint, then the blueprint is false. But for the builder or engineer, the blueprint is used as an instruction or rule dictating how he should construct the building or machine. And if what he makes deviates from the blueprint, then he has erred, built incorrectly and must try again. Similar considerations apply to charts, diagrams, or maps of a route (one to *be* followed, or one that *was* followed).

Whether a form of words formulates a rule depends on its use. Once this is realized, scruples about the propriety or correctness of certain formulations of rules may disappear. The source of these scruples is the commonplace observation that we sometimes formulate a rule by means of an authoritative example or a series of precedents. I may instruct children in what is to be done by saying 'When we attend mass, watch me and follow my example' or 'In French "is" is pronounced like *this* . . ., "on" like *this* . . . .' And judges in England appeal primarily to previous decisions to settle whether a particular course of conduct manifests negligence. Though familiar and typically unproblematic in practice, such rule-formulations are apt to arouse qualms in somebody reflecting on the nature of rules and of guidance by rules. These formulations seem defective, mere expedients to be used for lack of a proper expression of the rule (or for fear that this expression would not be understood by the rule-subjects). The *real* rule, it seems, is merely hinted at by examples or precedents, and it can and should be formulated in full generality.

These misunderstandings and confusions crowd around explanations of meaning by speakers of natural languages (on the assumption that explanations of meaning are correctly conceived as rules). We often explain the meaning of an expression by a series of examples. And in reflecting on the nature of meaning, we are strongly tempted to suppose

---

[12] One might doubt whether a blueprint *is* a description or a rule, instead suggesting that it can only be part of a description or a rule or perhaps akin to a description or a rule. But in clarifying its use, such refinements have no place.

that these gesture in the direction of a full understanding of the expression which for some reason we are unable to put into words. For it seems that the items cited in such an explanation are items that themselves fall under the general concept being explained. So it in turn must be determined by some genuine general rule in virtue of which these items are subsumed under it. So the examples are really a *means* for making one see what is in common. Once one sees that, the examples are redundant, since one can see the common features (the *Merkmale*) in a single instance. Or so it seems! But this, as we have seen (Volume 1, 'Family resemblance') is to succumb to a mythology of symbolism. A form of words or a sign expresses a rule if it is used in normative activities in characteristic ways. There is no higher standpoint from which we can legitimately deny that it is a proper rule-formulation. It is not the form of words, but the use we make of them in practice, that makes them an expression of a rule (just as being a sample is not an intrinsic feature of an object but a feature of our use of it). In particular, an expression is an explanation of meaning (whatever its form may be) if it is used as an explanation of meaning. Hence 'examples are decent signs, not rubbish or hocus-pocus.' (PG 273) Note that in using a series of examples to give a rule for the use of an expression one is *not* giving examples of the application of the rule; one is stating the rule. The supposition that such a rule-formulation is provisional, defective or a mere second-best is misguided. A rule and its expression are in order if they fulfil their function. (For further analysis of the formulation of rules by examples, see 'Accord with a rule', pp. 94ff.).

A rather different galaxy of errors clusters around our practices of *codifying rules*. In so doing we normally choose a canonical form for the expression of the rules. Note that even here it is not their form that *makes* the sentences into rule-formulations; their form *signals* that they are being so *used*. The practice of codifying is prone to distort our philosophical vision, for it encourages a mythology of rule-*discovery*. It fosters speculation about the real *form* of a rule, what is *really* a complete rule and what is only *part* of a rule. So one may think that the systematizing activities of the codifier mirror objective structures in the 'normative sphere'. A few remarks may make this clear, and serve as a warning.

Because economy of expression, ready surveyability, and memorability are among the purposes of codifications, codes of rules impose system upon the phenomena they represent. Indeed, that is their purpose (see Bentham's methodological discussions of principles of codification). When grammarians began the task of tabulating rules of Latin grammar for foreigners who wished to learn the language, they imposed order upon linguistic usage by complex systems of classification of declensions, conjugations, moods, etc. The rules they then formulated were not rules anyone had hitherto *used* or enunciated (no Roman mother had ever corrected her child's mistakes by pointing out that *avis* belongs to the third declension and *therefore* has a genitive plural ending in -*ium*). But these 'rules' subsumed many particular rules that were put to use in teaching children and correcting deviant speech of native speakers (compare spelling rules in English). And the grammarians' tabulations *became* the rules foreigners (and even native speakers) employed in learning and teaching Latin. It is easy to see how one might think that the traditional descriptive grammarian *discovered* the 'real rules' of a language (as opposed to giving a systematized synopsis of them). One might even think that speakers knew these 'discovered' rules only imperfectly and incompletely, even though they spoke the language impeccably according to these rules! How much more tempting it is, when one is confronted with the activities of the modern theoretical grammarian, to think that we are being presented with discoveries of the real, hitherto unknown (or, perhaps, 'tacitly known') rules.

A related, reinforcing misconception concerns the notion of completeness. In order to avoid tedious repetition, to enable easy learning and to facilitate surveyability, codifiers must make decisions as to what is to count, for their purposes, as a single rule and what as merely part of a rule. The results may be highly useful. But conceptual confusion creeps in if one thinks that these economical formulations actually reflect, not a purpose-relative decision, but an objective fact about the unity of a rule and about its parts. For then one will be prone to conceive of the results of codifications as capable of constituting *discoveries*, statements of rules which were hitherto hidden from view and only imperfectly understood.

A complementary error is to think that there is an absolute standard of completeness for codification of the rules governing an activity (cf. AWL 21: 'There is no such thing as a completed grammar'). For one readily conceives of the codifier or grammarian as aiming to tabulate the *totality* of rules. But we should pause to wonder what that means, what we are going to *call* 'the totality of rules' (Z §440). This conception, applied to rules of language in particular, leads to confusion. For it is operating with the wrong picture of the practice of using language. And this in turn leads to a misconception of explanation of meaning and of shared understanding. If we reflect upon our normative practices of teaching, explaining the meanings of words, correcting mistakes, we shall see that the notion of a context-free, purpose-independent conception of the totality of rules for the use of an expression is out of place. An explanation of the meaning of a word functions as a rule for its correct use in standard contexts. Someone understands the explanation if he goes on to use the word correctly, if he applies it in accord with the explanation (i.e. if he applies it in the way that we call 'correct'). Of course, he may misapply it; in which case we shall give a further explanation, a further rule for the use of the word. Does this show that the initial explanation was incorrect or incomplete? One is tempted to say so, for we are prone to conflate different cases. If Cephalus explains that 'justice' means repaying one's debts, that explanation is correct, but can well be said to be incomplete. For 'justice' is also standardly used to talk of laws, punishment, respecting the rights of others, etc., and these uses of 'just' are not applications of Cephalus's explanation. By contrast, an explanation of what 'red' means by reference to a standard sample is not incomplete for failing explicitly to exclude green, or even for failing to draw a sharp boundary line between red and orange. But if a learner misapplies 'red', calling a reddish-orange object 'red', we will correct him. It is tempting to respond to this simple fact as the interlocutor in PI §87:

'But then how does an explanation help me to understand, if after all it is not the final one? In that case the explanation is never completed; so I still don't understand what he means, and never shall.'

But this rests on a misconception, viz. that an explanation is complete only if it gives *all* the rules for the use of a word, and so serves to exclude all possible misunderstandings and misapplications. That, however, is absurd; it rests upon a chimerical ideal of explanation and of a totality of rules (cf. Volume 1, 'Explanation').

As though an explanation as it were hung in the air unless supported by another one. Whereas an explanation may indeed rest on another one that has been given, but none stands in need of another – unless we require it to prevent a misunderstanding. One might say: an explanation serves to remove or to avert a misunderstanding – one, that is, that would occur but for the explanation; not every one that I can imagine.

    . . .

    The signpost is in order – if, under normal circumstances, it fulfils its purpose. (PI §87)

    Hankering after such a totality of rules for the use of an expression ramifies into mythologies of 'analysis' on the one hand (as pursued by philosophers) and mysteries of 'depth-grammar' on the other. Speakers agree in the use of a word, share a common concept, if they accept as correct the same explanations and if they use the word in the same way (in what is called 'a correct use') in accord with those explanations. This does not mean that shared understanding rests upon agreement over a yet-to-be-discovered or 'tacitly known' totality of rules for the use of a word. Rather lack of shared understanding manifests itself in differences of use and disagreement over some particular rule or explanation. If someone misuses a word and justifies his use by citing a rule (giving an explanation) which another person does *not* recognize as correct, then the former expresses a different concept by that word.

    These questions and the general issues behind them may look pedantic and academic. But appearances mislead, for on these issues many aspects of the modern 'sciences' of theoretical linguistics and cognitive psychology turn. It is not our purpose to pursue these matters further here, merely to issue warnings. The moral to be born in mind is that codifications are purpose-relative. What counts as a whole rule and what as part of a rule depends upon our purposes and the context in which such a question is raised. Similarly what, if anything, counts as a complete list of rules is settled by criteria which we must, in relation to our purposes, lay down.

4. *Philosophy and grammar*

Philosophy, Wittgenstein claimed, is a grammatical[13] investigation (PI §90) in which philosophical problems are resolved and misunderstandings eliminated by describing our use of words, clarifying the grammar of expressions and tabulating rules (WWK 184). Remarks concerning conceptual relations are 'grammatical notes' (PI §232) or 'grammatical remarks' (PI §574); logical questions are said to be actually or properly 'grammatical' (Z §590). These claims, of course, need justifying. They are not an optional extra, but pivotal for Wittgenstein's general conception of philosophy. Their justification lies in the corpus of his later writings (and our account of their justification in the essays of these volumes). Our present task, however, is primarily one of clarification.

The claim that philosophical elucidations are grammatical remarks must not be understood to mean that the subject matter of philosophy is grammar and its product a list of grammatical rules. The subject matter of philosophy is philosophical questions, which are best characterized by a range of examples and their features (see Volume 1, 'The nature of philosophy'). These questions typically concern what is necessary or impossible, what is possible even though not actual (hence what is conceivable or imaginable). They often have the form of questions about the nature or essence of this or that, or about the essential relationships between kinds of things. Hence many philosophical questions have the appearance of questions in physics or natural science. This is misleading. When the philosopher asks such questions as 'What is colour?', 'What is perception?', 'What is dreaming?', he is not concerned with theories about light waves, nerve receptors, or rapid eye movements. He is concerned with the *concepts* of colour, perception or dreaming, and to

---

[13] In speaking of ordinary grammar, he meant the traditional subject-matter of grammarians (descriptive grammar and historical linguistics), not the twentieth-century 'science' of theoretical linguistics. It is, however, noteworthy that explanations of meaning are ordinarily conceived of as belonging not to grammar but to lexicography. To that extent Wittgenstein *is* stretching the use of 'grammar'. Presumably he would have argued that in both cases we are concerned with rules for the use of words.

investigate these concepts (which are *presupposed* by the scientists' empirical investigations) is to investigate the use of these and cognate expressions in a language. If someone (whether philosopher or scientist) claims that colours are sensations in the mind or in the brain, the philosopher must point out that this person is misusing the words 'sensation' and 'colour'. Sensations in the brain, he should remind his interlocutor, are called 'headaches', and colours are not headaches; one can have (i.e. it makes sense to speak of) sensations in the knee or in the back, but not in the mind. It is, he must stress, extended things that are coloured. But *this* is not a factual claim about the world (an *opinion* which the scientist might intelligibly gainsay). It is a grammatical observation, viz. that the grammar of colour licenses predicating 'is coloured' (primarily) of things of which one may also predicate 'is extended'. And minds and sensations are not extended, i.e. it makes no *sense* to say 'This pain is 5 cm long' or 'This itch is 2 cm shorter than that.' Such utterances are not *false* (for then they *could* be true) but senseless. So too it makes no sense to say 'My mind is $2\,\text{ft}^2$ larger today than it was yesterday.' These are grammatical observations, not theoretical ones. Physicists could not show these claims to be false, for they are not factual claims at all. Does not grammar involve theories, does it not embody a naïve theory of colour, matter, space, etc.? No, it determines *sense*, it does not pronounce upon the facts.[14] Determination of the *meaning* of 'colour', 'matter', 'space', the rules for the use of these words, is not a theory about anything. It is *antecedent to all theories*, and presupposed by them. (If they do not 'presuppose' the grammatical rules for the use of these words, then they are not talking about colour, matter, space at all, but about something else.)

The wayward interlocutor may insist that he is using 'colour' and 'sensation' in a special, new sense, a sense more useful perhaps for scientific purposes. This may be so; as long as he does not claim that his new sense is *correct*, truer to the facts, we may accept what he says. But now we should elicit from him the new rules according to which he is proceeding, pointing out where they differ from our rules. We should now stress why the concepts *differ*, and how it is that what seemed a startling discovery (that colours are in the mind or are really dispositions to cause sensations) is either no more than a recommendation to adopt a new form of representation (for which he has yet to make a case) or a confusion of different rules for the use of homonyms. 'Thus I simply draw the person's attention to what he is really doing and refrain from

---

[14] It is, of course, open to the 'scientific realist', if he is so foolish, to deny that any extended objects are coloured. He may insist that they are colourless, i.e. like a window pane! But though what he says is patently false, it does not deny what grammar affirms, since all that grammar affirms here is that is makes *sense* to predicate colour primarily of extended objects.

any assertions. Everything is then to go on within grammar.' (WWK 186) If, however, our interlocutor contends that his new use is the *correct* one, we must explain to him that there is no such thing as a *correct* rule of grammar. (It can only be correct or incorrect, true or false, that *this is* a rule of our grammar.) For there is no such thing as justifying grammar by reference to reality. Grammar (logic) is antecedent to truth. Philosophical questions concern the bounds of sense, and these are determined by the rules for the use of words, by what it makes sense to say in a language. *This* is the source of philosophy's concern with grammatical rules. For by their clarification and arrangement philosophical questions can be resolved and typical philosophical confusions and paradoxes dissolved.

It might now appear as if Wittgenstein were claiming that there are two sorts of grammar, the traditional linguists' variety and a new type, viz. a philosophical grammar. Traditional descriptive grammar concerns itself with parts of speech (such as nouns, verbs, adjectives, adverbs), examines forms of pluralizing nouns, regularities and irregularities in the conjugation of verbs, and so on. This seems to have nothing to do with philosophy. And then there is the new and obscure kind of grammar that philosophy should allegedly concern itself with. As Moore put it, grammar is the sort of thing one teaches small children at school, e.g. 'You don't say "Three men *was* in the field" but "Three men *were* in the field"'; that is grammar. And what has that to do with philosophy? To which Wittgenstein replied that this example indeed has nothing to do with philosophy, since here all is perspicuous. But what about 'God the Father, God the Son and God the Holy Ghost *were* in the field or *was* in the field?'[15]

This in turn may suggest that philosophical grammar is more complete and inclusive than traditional descriptive grammar. For while philosophy *may* have to concern itself with such trivialities as verb pluralizations and their matching, it *also* concerns itself with many other things which lie outside the scope of ordinary grammar. The question of the scope of grammar (or 'grammatical rules') will be examined below. But the thrust of this question is misplaced.

There are not two kinds of grammar (although it is true that grammarians do not concern themselves with, for example, ostensive definitions, category distinctions such as sensation/perception, paraphrastic rules such as Russell's theory of descriptions), but two kinds of interest in the rules of a language, determined by very different purposes (AWL 31). Philosophy is concerned with rules of grammar, rules for the use of expressions, only in so far as they shed light upon particular philosophical problems (hence the range of its concern cannot be

---

[15] We owe this charming anecdote to the late Charles Stevenson, who was present at the exchange.

determined in advance). Where the grammarian's concern is with a particular natural language (or languages) and its forms and structure, the philosopher is typically concerned with forms shared by many languages (although language-specific enquiries are not precluded, e.g. attention to variant colour-geometries or variant symbolism in mathematical proof). But this general concern is *not* because philosophy aims at a universal grammar. It does not aim at producing a grammar at all, but at resolving philosophical questions. Where the grammarian classifies parts of speech into nouns, adjectives, etc., the philosopher will typically concern himself with different classifications, e.g. sensation-words, words for feelings, emotions, moods, attitudes, etc. The philosopher can dissolve conceptual puzzles and resolve confusions about perception and our knowledge of the world, for example, by clarifying, arranging and contrasting the different rules for the use of sensation- and perception-words. He will point out that it makes sense to say 'I see better, more distinctly than you', but not 'I feel pain better, more distinctly, than you'; it makes sense to say 'I think I can see a house in the distance, but I'm not sure; let's go closer', but not 'I think I feel a pain in my knee, but I'm not sure', and so on. Even where the grammarian's classification is of philosophical interest, e.g. the classification of nouns into concrete or abstract, the nature of the philosopher's interest differs from that of the grammarian. For what concerns him here is the fact that while we may claim that concrete nouns are names of (concrete) substances, we may not claim that abstract nouns are names of (abstract) substances. And this itself is the tip of a large philosophical iceberg that needs dissolving, but which is of no concern to the grammarian. Grammar, as Wittgenstein understood the term, is the account book of language (PG 87). Its rules determine the limits of sense, and by carefully scrutinizing them the philosopher may determine at what point he has drawn an overdraft on Reason, violated the rules for the use of an expression and so, in subtle and not readily identifiable ways, traversed the bounds of sense.

5. *The scope of grammar*

Wittgenstein, like the traditional grammarian, talks of the grammar of words (BB 24; PI p. 18n., §§187, 257), of expressions (BB 20, 109; PI §660), of phrases (BB 70), of sentences or propositions (BB 51, 53; PI §353). He also speaks, in the material mode, of the grammar of states (PI §572) and processes (PG §41), and he calls 'I can't have your pain' or 'Every rod has a length' grammatical statements (BB 49; PI §251). A superficial reaction is to insist that states and processes cannot have grammars because they are not words, and that 'I cannot have your pain' is not a grammatical statement because it is not about words at all but about ownership of pain.

This is too hasty. To insist pedantically that we should always speak of, for example, the grammar of the *word* 'state' would be to insist that rules for the use of expressions are only correctly given by mentioning rather than using the word thus explained. But that is patently false (cf. 'Grammar and necessity', pp. 281f.).

This initial reaction is, however, symptomatic of non-trivial anxiety about Wittgenstein's procedure. For it seems that he deviated substantially from ordinary usage in calling things 'rules' which no one would dream of so doing. Equally, he seems to have extended the concepts of grammar, grammatical rule, and grammatical statement far beyond their ordinary scope. We shall first examine the issue of his use of 'grammar', then his use of 'rule', in particular 'rule of grammar'.

Even in introducing talk of grammar in his lectures in 1930 (M 276), he made some controversial claims. The colour octahedron is not really part of psychology, but belongs to grammar (PR 51f.; WWK 42). Euclidean geometry is not a theory about space but is part of grammar (WWK 38, 62). And he developed even more radical ideas: mathematical equations are really grammatical rules (PR 130); certain metaphysical statements too are grammar, in the guise of super-physics; and so on. Moore suggested that the expression 'rule of grammar' is here used in a special sense, but Wittgenstein insisted that it is not (M 276f.; LWL 98). Elsewhere he admitted that he included items in grammar which one would not find in ordinary grammar books, e.g. ostensive definitions, Russell's theory of descriptions. (He might have added: explanations of meaning in general, since ordinary grammars do not include the vocabulary.) Yet this is an unimportant difference (AWL 31). He conceded that he had to justify calling his comments on the expression 'Time flows' grammatical (e.g. contrasting different explanations of 'to flow'). But he evidently thought this could be done.

Three central points stand out. First, philosophical grammar is *concerned with rules for the use of words*, just as ordinary grammar is. In this respect it is unlike those rules of logical syntax which were conceived to be concerned with 'super-expressions' (elementary sentences and logically proper names) that await discovery, or unknown 'thought-constituents' which psychology must bring to light. Secondly, the important difference between the grammarian's interest in the use of words and the philosopher's lies in their purposes. True enough, grammarians (as opposed to lexicographers) concern themselves relatively little with meaning, focusing on syntax, whereas the philosopher is concerned largely with meaning. But Wittgenstein clearly thought *(infra)* that there was no essential dividing line in the patterns of use of words between so-called 'syntax' and 'semantics'. It is our *interests* that make us draw these distinctions, and from some points of view they are highly artificial. Thirdly, Wittgenstein was inclined to characterize grammar very generally as all the conditions, the method, necessary for comparing the proposition with reality (PG 88). It incorporates any rules for using expressions correctly. Since explanations of meanings of words are standards for their correct use, *all* explanations of word meaning fall into grammar. Grammarians are prone to distinguish grammatical nonsense 'The was it blues no' from gibberish 'Ab sur ah' and from 'sensible nonsense' e.g. 'Green ideas sleep furiously', the latter being a 'well-formed' sentence of English. Wittgenstein disagreed: nonsense is nonsense; the only difference lies in the jingle, the *Satzklang* (AWL 64). And philosophy's major concern with grammar lies in detecting well-concealed forms of nonsense. It is this camouflaged nonsense which pervades philosophy, and which it is the philosopher's task to bring to light.

Wittgenstein incorporated into the category of rules of grammar a whole host of items which hardly anyone hitherto had ever conceived of as *rules*, let alone as rules of *grammar*. Was he claiming that grammarians, mathematicians, and philosophers were *wrong* to deny that ostensive explanations and colour-charts, statements of arithmetic or geometry, certain propositions of metaphysics are rules; that they had made a *mistake*? Or was he stretching the meaning of 'rule' and 'rule of grammar'? Waismann was certainly inclined to say that the term 'rule' was being stretched here (PLP 66f., 136f.), that a new terminology was being *recommended*, and that it was justified because of pervasive analogies and similarities between those items on Wittgenstein's list and things which we would unhesitatingly call 'rules'. At the end of the day, he suggested, it does not matter whether we *call* mathematical equations or some metaphysical statements 'rules'. What matters is that we note the similarities in function, the analogous relations to truth and falsity, sense and nonsense, verification and falsification which these propositions have to paradigmatic rules. This is the more conciliatory position to adopt. There is, however, little sign that Wittgenstein looked upon his remarks here as mere recommendations to *compare* axioms, equations, various metaphysical propositions, etc. to rules of grammar. It was his contention that they *were* rules, and that if one did examine their role and function one would see this. He was not trying to persuade one to alter one's usage, but rather to bring one to recognize that one uses axioms, equations, some metaphysical propositions, ostensive explanations, explanations by paraphrase, etc. *as rules*, taking as his premise that what is used as a rule *is* a rule. In particular, we must not assert that mathematical or certain metaphysical propositions do *not* have the uses of rules just because we do not *call* them 'rules' (and so too for concrete samples, charts, blueprints, signposts, etc.). According to either view, the primary philosophical task in elucidating Wittgenstein's thoughts here is to make clear the similarities between the uses of such items and rules uncontroversially so called.

First steps may be taken after reflecting on the following sample, in which Waismann deliberately expresses himself in the formal mode (PLP 135f.):

(i) The verb 'to see' is an irregular verb.

(ii) In Latin, the preposition *cum* takes the ablative.

(iii) The verb 'to master' may only be used transitively.

(iv) A proper name cannot be the predicate of a sentence.

(v) The adjective 'identical' cannot form a comparative or superlative.

(vi) The word 'north-east' should not be used in the contexts 'north-east of the North Pole' or 'north-east of the South Pole'.

(viii) The words 'it is true that . . .' should not be used with an adverb of time.

As we move towards the bottom of Waismann's list we arrive at items which would not normally be taken to be grammatical rules. Grammarians typically contend that 'north-east of the South Pole' is *grammatically* correct though logically awry. Such a distinction is defensible on pragmatic grounds (classificatory convenience, pedagogical efficiency, division of labour) but then it is not one of principle, and may be differently drawn when different purposes are in view. Alternatively the distinction might be based on dogmatic adherence to the idea that there are absolute and determinate distinctions between syntax, semantics and pragmatics. This idea can be challenged. Certainly Wittgenstein attacked a main presupposition of the sharp demarcation of semantics from pragmatics. He held that whether a sentence has a meaning is often a circumstance-dependent question (BB 9ff.). Hence it is misguided to think that the utterance of a sentence in an inappropriate context is always meaningful, that one understands what is then said but not its point or purpose. (So too, if I see you with a saw in hand, sawing away wildly in thin air, I do *not* understand what you are doing). He held that the boundary between sense and nonsense is typically context-dependent (AWL 20f.). Hence the idea that 'semantic rules' determine once and for all what makes sense is absurd. The repudiation of the *Tractatus* version of the Augustinian picture of meaning in favour of the conception of language as an autonomous calculus meant that he was no longer willing to segregate purely syntactical rules for the use of signs (e.g. truth-table definitions of the logical constants[16]) from considerations about meanings. Both involve rules of language; neither connects language with reality or mirrors any metaphysical truths about the world. There is no sound basis for an absolute distinction among the motley of rules for the use of an expression between a syntactic subset and a semantic one. If it is

---

[16] Only in the 1930s did these kinds of definitions come to be called 'semantic' (cf. Carnap and Tarski). That betokened not discernment of earlier error, but shift in conceptual boundaries, i.e. a conceptual change.

claimed that semantic rules assign meanings to sentences by specifying their truth-conditions, and assign meanings to sub-sentential expressions by specifying their contributions to the truth-conditions of sentences in which they may occur, it is obvious that this is not Wittgenstein's conception.

Ordinary grammar lays down that 'north-east of' must be followed by a noun or pronoun in the accusative case. It does not lay down what *sort* of noun one must use (e.g. a place-designation). Two reasons explain this. First, such category distinctions are *not* peculiar to particular languages. Since ordinary grammar books are written for people who already speak a language, these restrictions can be presumed as known. Secondly, grammatical classifications do not go beyond the rather simple categories of (syntactical) parts of speech (and there are reasons for this too). But it would be wholly arbitrary to accept that it is a rule of grammar that 'north-east of' must be followed by a noun or pronoun in the accusative, yet to deny that it is a rule of grammar that these must themselves be designators of a place, an object or person at a place, or of an event occurring at a place. And if greater precision is necessary in demarcating sense from nonsense, we would surely wish to add that 'North Pole' and 'South Pole', though they satisfy the previous requirement, are nevertheless excluded. This provides a transparent rationale for viewing (vi) in Waismann's sample as a rule of grammar (PLP 136).

It is noteworthy that the potentially misleading 'metaphysical' correlate of this grammatical rule is 'One cannot travel north-east of the North Pole (or, South Pole).' This is misleading in as much as it sounds like an empirical proposition such as 'One cannot travel by sea around North America (because there is no north-west passage).' But it is just the rule of grammar expressed by (vi) dressed up in the *form* of a scientific proposition (BB 55ff.). It is characteristic of many metaphysical propositions that they conceal grammatical rules (see 'Grammar and necessity', pp. 269ff.).

Initial surprise at finding Wittgenstein referring to ostensive definitions or tables of correlations as rules may diminish on reflection. Certainly ostensive definitions do not have the form usually associated with rules. Indeed, they have the superficial form of a description. 'This ↗ is red' seems akin to 'This chair is red', a simple empirical statement. But this appearance vanishes if the ostensive definition is paraphrased by saying 'This colour ↗ is red', since it is not a contingent fact that this colour ↗ (viz. red) is red. This explanation functions as a norm of correct use, in as much as anything which is this colour ↗ (pointing at the sample) is correctly said to be red. It may be viewed as a substitution rule: instead of saying 'A is red' one may say 'A is this colour ↗ [pointing at the sample].' It does not 'connect language to reality', but connects a word with a sample, a gesture and the utterance 'This is'. The sample is best considered an instrument of grammar, not something *described*, but part of the method of representation, a symbol. Hence an ostensive definition is illuminatingly conceived as a linguistic rule with a central role in teaching, learning and explaining the words of a language (cf. Volume 1, 'Ostensive definition and its ramifications').

It seems similarly eccentric to call tables of correlation such as colour-charts, conversion tables or the key at the foot of a map 'rules'. Again, it is true that they do not have the forms typical of rule-formulations. But what *is* important is that we *use* them in the same ways as we use rules. The key of interpretation at the foot of a map is employed as a rule for reading the map. 'There is marshland north of Barchester' we may say, pointing to a symbol on the map. 'No', we may be corrected, 'those clustered dots mean sand-dunes. Look at the table.' The table (or key of interpretation) can be considered as a group of rules for interpreting the symbols on the map, functioning as a guide and as a standard of correctness. It is cited as a justification if challenged, and deviation from it is criticized. Note also that tables or charts can be used as alternatives to other rule-formulations. Thus a colour-chart may be employed as an equivalent of a series of ostensive definitions of colour-names. And logic books often give a rule for the use of a logical connective by correlating the symbol with a truth-table. In all these cases there are correlations of symbols with symbols. We are prone to see a truth-tabular explanation as reflecting some kind of 'logical reality', the essence and nature of logical constants. But this is a fallacy; the truth-table for disjunction is just another symbol instead of ' ∨ ', no closer to any 'logical reality' than 'or'. For whether something is a symbol depends upon its *use*, and these objects (drawings on a key of interpretation, truth-tables, samples) are used as symbols.

Having followed Wittgenstein thus far, we will no longer find it excessively strained to say that a ruler with centimetres calibrated on one side and inches on the other is itself a rule. For it is in effect, and is used as, a table of correlation of inches and centimetres, a conversion table (LFM 118). By consulting it we may learn that instead of '2 in' we may say or write '5.08 cm'. So the ruler functions here as a system of substitution rules. We convert imperial measurements to metric ones *on the ruler* (RFM 40f.). Of course, we may still plague ourselves with qualms. If the ruler is a rule, does it follow that we can hold a *rule* in our hand, break it in two, etc.? Or if a colour-chart is a rule of grammar, can a rule (or part of grammar) go up in smoke? Well, we may say such things, although this is very misleading (rather should we say that we *use* the ruler as a rule of conversion and that we might well cease to do so). Equally, we may say that one can pick up something with an infinite magnitude! – namely a ruler, which has an infinite radius of curvature (LFM 142). Here philosophical puzzles dissolve into jokes.

The similarities and analogies in use between items which we would all unhesitatingly denominate 'rules' or 'expressions of rules' and such things as explanations of word-meanings, ostensive definitions, charts, tables, rulers are intended to persuade us to shrug off our initial scruples. But our credulity may well be stretched when Wittgenstein takes us still further. Notoriously he claimed that mathematical propositions are rules of grammar. This idea seems revisionary (but cf. Hilbert and Schlick). We have firm preconceptions that in these cases we are dealing with deep truths, not arbitrary rules. Truths of mathematics strike us as the bedrock of certainty, objects of reason not creatures of the will, the subject matter of *a priori* sciences not stipulations that could be otherwise. We deal with these objections below (cf. 'Grammar and necessity').

6. *Some morals for the moderns*

Wittgenstein's reflections on rules reveal deep difficulties and confusions in the ideas informing much contemporary theorizing in linguistics and philosophy of language, cognitive psychology and philosophy of mathematics. These subjects are committed to the intelligibility of hidden rules which are tacitly or even innately known, even though *no one* knows them explicitly. Rules are conceived of as explanatory hypotheses, or as laws of correlation which correlate entities independently of us. Theorists speculate about rules being encoded in the brain, and conceive of people following rules of which they have never heard and which they could not understand. Of course, such theorists are aware of difficulties, and hope for enlightenment from future research.

Four problem areas illustrate their unease that perhaps not all is in order in their theory construction:

(i) *Consistency* A putative system of rules may be vitiated by a hidden contradiction, conflict or inconsistency among the rules. Since the only role of such *postulated* rules is theoretical and explanatory rather than normative, contradictions may lurk unbeknown to anyone. It seems to be the task of the theorist to 'ensure' that his system of rules is consistent. Equally, a putative rule may fail to be a rule (e.g. the axiom of choice might introduce inconsistency into set theory, like the naïve comprehension axiom).

(ii) *Uniqueness* In so far as rules are conceived as hypotheses to fit data (whether the 'behaviour' of numbers or of people), the scientist seems (theoretically) crippled by the under-determination of an hypothesis by the data. Alternative hypotheses may fit equally well, and it is unclear how to choose between them. It is, of course, wholly unclear what these hypothetical rules *are*, since no one *uses* them overtly. As they play no role in normative activities, do they have a *causal* role in the generation of behaviour?

(iii) *Source*   Since, in these subjects, rules are postulated by the working scientist (linguist, cognitive psychologist, mathematician), there is a mystery about their source. What validates them? Are these rules merely part of our *description* of how languages (or numbers) work? Or are they part of the workings (the 'machinery') of language, the software of the biological computer? Are they innate or acquired? What would it be to have knowledge of a *rule*, which though innate is only tacit?

(iv) *Expressibility*   If it does make sense to *postulate* rules as explanatory mechanisms, then surely these rules must be 'realized' in some form. If, as linguists argue, a child's ability to learn a language presupposes its tacitly knowing a complex array of rules and principles, how are such rules 'represented' in the child's mind? Is it that every natural language presupposes a 'language of thought'? Or are the rules of 'universal grammar' written in letters of DNA? Can there be rules which have never been expressed? Does mathematics not offer us an indefinite range of such rules in the form of functions, conceived as laws of correlation?

These clusters of questions are no more than conceptual muddles dressed up as theoretical problems. Thus arrayed they distract attention from philosophical analysis of the *concept* of a rule, an investigation which plots the bounds of sense in these matters and hence delimits what can intelligibly be said about rules. Some indication of this is given by the following principles (dogmatically stated) which follow from Wittgenstein's argued case:

(i) *Any rule can be expressed*   There is no such thing as a rule which cannot be expressed, or a rule every expression of which transcends the understanding of the persons who are following it. For what is inexpressible cannot be consulted for guidance, cited in justification or criticism, used as a standard of evaluation of action, etc. There is no such thing as a rule-governed practice the rules of which cannot be tabulated, and no such thing as rules of a practice which *nobody* is in a position to formulate. Of course, expressions of some rules may require non-verbal instruments, e.g. samples, actions, or concrete symbols; and in the case of complex social practices and institutions (e.g. legal systems) individuals following the rules may grasp only a fragment or aspect of the rules, and have recourse to experts when more is necessary. But even there it would be unintelligible to suppose that there existed rules unknown to *all* the experts, or that the experts were normative scientists in the business of discovering rules.

(ii) *It must be possible to follow (or violate) a rule*   Rules which cannot in principle be followed or violated, i.e. with respect to which nothing *counts* as complying or transgressing, are merely pseudo-rules, like scales upon which nothing can be weighed or metre-rules against which nothing can be measured. Putatively innate rules or rules realized in neural mechanisms cannot be followed (for there is no way to determine what would *count* as following, as the rules are hidden from us; and causal determination cannot, in principle, establish internal relations). Nor can they be violated, since any apparent violation would disprove the existence (or correct characterization of the content) of that rule itself. For this 'rule' is conceived as an explanatory hypothesis.

(iii) *Rules are creatures of the will* Rules may exist independently of stipulation or legislation. And some rules have the appearance of superhuman sempiternality (rules of inference, laws of thought). But rules are human creations, made not found. They are not true or false, and they are not answerable to reality; in this sense they are *arbitrary*. So it must always make *sense* to modify or annul a rule in practice.[17] But can postulated rules conceived as innate be abrogated or altered by human agreement?

(iv) *Rules are standards of correctness and guides to action* For an activity to be rule-governed at all is for rules to have a role in justifying or criticizing performances, in teaching or explaining. They function as standards against which to evaluate performances as correct or incorrect, and by reference to which actions are correctly characterized by one normative description or another. But the conception of a rule that informs current speculation offends against this basic principle.

(v) *Rules must be more or less transparent to participants in a rule-governed practice* One can no more follow completely opaque, unknown rules than one can see completely invisible objects. In the particular case of the grammar of language, Wittgenstein remarked:

The wrong conception which I want to object to in this connection is the following, that we can hit upon something that we today cannot yet see, that we can *discover* something wholly new. That is a mistake. The truth of the matter is that we have already got everything, and we have got it actually *present*; we need not wait for anything. We make our moves in the realm of the grammar of our ordinary language, and this grammar is already there. (WWK 183)

But the rules concocted by theorists of meaning or theoretical linguists are completely opaque to competent practitioners. They are allegedly *discovered* by observation and research, confirmed by experiment (independently of the speaker's recognition or acknowledgement of the 'rule').

---

[17] Although not without *consequences*. For if a given rule *defines* a certain act or procedure then a change in the rule will imply that following the (new) rule will no longer *count* as falling under the concept defined by reference to the (old) rule. The rule of *modus ponens* partly defines what we call inference. Nothing *stops us* following the rule of affirming the consequent; but we do not call *that* inferring (correctly). Note that following such a rule would not bring us into conflict with any *truths*; we would just be engaged in a very different activity, a different language-game – which might have its uses.

These contrasts should give us pause. What contemporary philosophers and theoretical linguists are now prone to subsume under the label 'rule' differs from paradigmatic rules on almost all important points. (Compare these 'theoretical rules' with rules of games, or of etiquette, the rules of the road or the rules of the local cooperative society.) Even family-resemblance concepts are resistant to the maxim that *anything* goes! Not only is the concept of a rule misused, but also no problems are solved, dissolved or clarified. On the contrary, mystification and confusion are generated in the guise of newly discovered scientific profundity.

Wittgenstein's examination of the concept of a rule is, by contrast, subservient to the overall purpose of removing perennial philosophical perplexity. Bafflement about the grounds of logical necessity or the source of knowledge of necessary truth, about the apparently essential connection between language and reality, or the semipiternality of the laws of thought, is *removed*. Problems are laid to rest, perplexity is resolved and the aura of false mystery is eliminated.

SECTION 185

1 Having rounded off a long sequence of remarks clarifying the grammar of 'understands', including its use in avowals of understanding, W. reverts to the example of §143. The point of so doing is to resume discussion of the relation between meaning, which is given by an explanation of meaning (i.e. a rule), and the use of an expression. We typically understand an expression immediately ('at a stroke') when we hear or say it, but how can what we thus grasp at a stroke agree or fail to agree with the myriad acts of using that expression (PI §139)? This question is but a special case of the question: how can a rule determine what accords with it? We are inclined to conceive of understanding as 'laying hold of' a rule ('by means of our logical faculties' as Frege might put it) from which all the particular applications flow. Understanding is then conceived as a *state* which is the *source* of the correct use (PI §146), and the rule one 'lays hold of' is thought of as something which forces a particular application upon one (cf. PI §140). A model for this misconception is the derivation of a series from its algebraic formula (PI §146) as one is naturally inclined to think of it. These questions led to the long analysis of understanding. It is not a state, but akin to an ability, to mastery of a technique. 'Now I understand' is not a description of an inner event or process, but a signal of understanding (PI §180). This being now established, W. picks up the threads: what is it to understand a rule? The arithmetical example is being used to shed light upon the nature of understanding the meaning of an expression.

To raise the issues he wishes to examine, W. needs to enrich the example of §143. Judging by the usual criteria, the pupil has mastered the series of natural numbers. We now teach him to follow orders of the form '+ n', where this formula constitutes a rule for a series of natural numbers. We do tests with him up to 1000. He now proceeds beyond 1000, and writes the *wrong* sequence. We correct him. If he responds by insisting that he *has* carried on after 1000 exactly as he was supposed to, that he *was* doing the *same* after 1000 as he had been doing before, it will, of course, not help to repeat the original examples and explanations. For his performances hitherto are irreproachable. The futility of any such repetition is driven home by the suggestion that it might come natural to the pupil to understand '+ 2' as we understand 'Add 2 up to 1000, 4 up to 2000, etc.'

(d) adds the observation that this abnormal reaction has similarities with the failure of the natural human reaction to pointing exhibited in looking in the *opposite* direction to the one pointed at. It is part of human nature to react to pointing by looking in the direction pointed at (whereas a cat will look at the hand (PG 94)), and equally natural to learn to carry on the pattern in response to the usual kinds of training and teaching. Furthermore, on the basis of the primitive reaction to pointing we construct more complex language-games of directing a person to go over that ↗ way, or of pointing out to him that there is a rabbit in the field there ↗, or of pointing at a colour or shape of an object. So too, on the basis of standard reactions to certain kinds of training, we can teach the use of such expressions as 'carrying on in the same way' (e.g. in learning to copy a pattern in carpet making or tapestry weaving no less than in learning to expand arithmetical series), 'correct', and 'incorrect'.

Note that the identification of what is correct (and incorrect) is presupposed. We know that writing '1004' after '1000' is not in accord with the rule '+ 2' (because we have mastered addition), and the identification of his performance as incorrect is our ground for judging that the pupil does not understand the order correctly. He manifestly contravenes the rule '+ 2'. If this were not acknowledged, W. would not have succeeded in raising a puzzle about the concept of understanding!

Note too that the remark about what comes natural to the pupil is an aside which also takes for granted an *independent* criterion of what is correct. It is quite absurd to suppose that W. here proposes, as an explanation of what 'to continue correctly' *means*, 'to continue as most people would find it natural to continue'. (cf. 'Agreement in definitions, judgements, and forms of life', pp. 237f., 243ff.).

1.1   (i) 'Wir sagen: "Du solltest doch *zwei* addieren"': 'we say: "You should have added *two*."' The translation should preserve a distinction between this remark and the later suggestion (§186) that what is correct is what the teacher *meant* the pupil to do.

(ii) 'Ich dachte, so *soll* ich's machen': 'I thought that was how I *had to* do it.'

(iii) ' "But I went on in the same way" ': from his perspective, he did go on in the same way (just as a child, asked how many xs there are in '$3x + 2x + x$', might intelligibly respond 'three'). Of course, the learner did *not* go on the same way since up to 1000 he followed the rule 'Add 2' and beyond 1000 he contravened it. And following the rule is not doing the same as breaking it! But the notion of sameness or identity provides the learner with no independent handle to grasp what to do at the 500th step. What counts as 'doing the same' depends on the instruction 'Add 2', and it is this that he has misunderstood. The issue is discussed in PI §§223ff.

2   Br.B. 141, but not EPB 214, introduces the expression 'interpret' into an early draft of §185. 'We might, in such a case, say that this person

naturally understands (interprets) the rule [+ 1] (and examples) we have given as we should understand the rule (and examples) . . .: "Add 1 up to 100, ..."' This highlights a connection between §185 and §§198ff. which is less explicit in the text of PI.

LFM 22ff. presents the material distributed in §§185–97 in the setting of a discussion of a philosophical puzzle about what is meant by saying that one understands a phrase or symbol. This puzzle is claimed to arise because there seem to be two different sorts of criteria for understanding. One criterion seems to be having a diagram or set of rules in mind; the other the actual use made of the symbol. The first (the 'momentary act of understanding') is compared with having an algebraic formula in mind; the second with writing down the terms of the series determined by this formula. For this reason the discussion of continuing a series in accord with an algebraic formula is taken to bear on the different criteria for understanding a symbol and on the apparent possibility of conflict between them. In that lecture the overall purpose of the material of §§185–97 is made explicit.

LFM 27f. moves off in a different direction. We teach someone to square numbers, and test him up to 1,000,000. Should we then say – 'We can never really know whether he has understood the rule "n^2", since he may produce a different answer from the one we would produce if asked to square numbers larger than 1,000,000'? Does this show that one can never know whether another person understands the meaning of an expression? W.'s riposte is to turn the tables on this solipsistic drift. How do *I* know that I understand a symbol? I know about myself neither more nor less than I know about him, namely that I have and can cite certain rules, that I have worked out examples, that I explain the rule by reference to such examples in these and these ways. Does it then follow that I do not know what I mean by the square of a number? It is ironic that this rhetorical question has called forth the answer 'Yes' from some contemporary writers. But this bizarre form of scepticism rests on a misconception of what it is to know what I mean (cf. Exg. §187).

RFM 80 (cf. Vol. XIV, 30) notes that if, when my attention is drawn to my misapplication of a rule of inference, I respond 'Oh, that's how I should have applied it', then I'm playing the game. 'But if I simply reply: "Different? – But this surely isn't different!" – what will you do? That is: somebody may reply like a rational person and yet not be playing our game.' Note that playing the game thus, inferring thus, is conceived as constitutive of rationality: this is what we call 'rational argument'.

2.1   (i) 'an order of the form "+ n"': Br.B. 141 discusses the same issue in terms of following *rules* of the form '+ n'. Commands and rules alike provide standards for the evaluation of action as correct or incorrect, and guide people in what they do (cf. PI §206).

(ii) '"But I went on in the same way"': Br.B. introduces the issue after a detailed examination of the idea that concepts are applied only on the grounds of possession of common properties. This culminates in a discussion of 'the same'. In certain contexts, with certain legitimate applications of 'pointing in the same direction' in mind, one would correctly say that these two arrows → ← 'point the same way' (Br.B. 140); in other contexts, with other legitimate applications in mind, one would say that these → → 'point the same way'. Similarly, when we hear the diatonic scale, we say that after every seven notes the same note recurs (only an octave higher). But someone might say that he heard the same note alternately after every four or three notes (calling the tonic, the dominant, and the octave the same note). Does he *hear* something different from those of us who have learnt to apply 'the same note' to the octave only?

LFM 26 considers the idea that the identity of an object with itself constitutes an unequivocal paradigm for explaining 'going on in the same way'; see Exg. §215.

Section 186

1   The apparent implication is that our understanding of the rule '+ 2' goes far beyond our ability to explain it, and W.'s interlocutor draws this conclusion. He is impressed by the futility of trying to correct the pupil by saying 'Didn't I tell you always to add 2?', or 'Can't you see that you haven't gone on in the same way?', or by repeating the previous examples and explanations. So he concludes that what has been explained to the pupil falls short of what is to be understood. Consequently, something must fill the gap between the explanation of '+ 2' and our understanding of this formula in virtue of which going on '1002, 1004, . . .' is correct. The interlocutor makes a familiar move: a *new insight* or *intuition* is needed at *every step* to carry one from the rule to each of its applications. It is intuition that tells one that writing '1002' after '1000' is doing the same to '1000' as one did to '998' in writing down '1000' after it. Otherwise how could one know what to do at each step? (After all, one might say, 1000 is not the same as 998; so even if one writes '1000' after '998', how should we know without a fresh insight what the result of adding 2 to some *different* number, viz. 1000, will be?)

W. parries this proposal quickly here (but cf. LFM 30). Intuition presupposes an independent determination of correctness; it is not one's intuition that *makes* doing thus-and-so correct, rather one intuits that the correct thing to do *is* thus-and-so. But what determines what the correct thing to do *is* (i.e. what it is that insight or intuition might reveal)? Like *guessing what is right*, intuiting presupposes precisely that which is here perplexing.

The interlocutor accepts this and tries a fresh move. If intuition will not provide a standard of correctness to bridge the (apparent) gulf between the explanation of the rule (and the previous correct performances) and its application at this point, then surely what the learner needs to do is guess what the teacher *meant*. The *correct* step is the one that *accords* with the order *as it was meant* by the teacher. This proposal is not *incorrect* (cf. §187). But it only gives the appearance of resolving the difficulty in so far as it is incorrectly understood. When the teacher gave the order, did his meaning 'Add 2' consist in his meaning the pupil to write '1002' after '1000', and also in his meaning him to write '1868' after '1866', and so on? In short, does giving the order 'Add 2' and meaning it in such-and-such a way consist in performing an infinite number of acts of meaning correlating every even number with the next even number in the series? This is doubly absurd. First, to mean something by what one says is not to perform a special mental act accompanying the utterance. Hence also to understand the rule the teacher gave to the pupil, the pupil does not have to guess what mental act (or process) accompanied the teacher's utterance (as if that interior act of meaning will bridge the apparent gap between the rule 'Add 2' and the acts that accord with it). Secondly, and consequently, to have meant the pupil to write '1002' after '1000' (as well as '1868' after '1866') does not consist in having performed in a flash an infinite number of separate acts of meaning (any more than the infinite divisibility of the distance of one pace implies that, in taking a pace, one performs an infinite number of acts).

The interlocutor accepts that this is absurd. But he persists in his recourse to the mind in order to build the bridge between the rule and its applications, a bridge which seems necessary in view of the fact that explanations seem to fall short of articulating what the teacher understands (and the pupil does not). An infinite number of acts of meaning is ridiculous, but why does the resolution of the difficulty not lie in the performance of a *single act of meaning* which will *contain* all the acts that accord with the rule in advance of their performance? So he suggests that in giving the order 'Add 2' the teacher meant that the pupil should write the next but one number after *every* number that he wrote. From this all the particular steps follow, and this provides a standard of correctness against which to measure the pupil's performances.

This is futile. If the order 'Add 2' is not understood it is no use saying that what the pupil lacks is apprehension of the fact that the teacher means him to write the next but one number after every number he writes. For that is just a paraphrase of the fact that he does not understand that he is meant to follow the rule '+ 2'. If the pupil is, after all the explanations and examples he has been given, at a loss what to do in applying the rule '+ 2' after '1000', he will be equally at a loss in applying the rule 'Write the next but one number after every number you write' after '1000'. For the latter is merely a reformulation of the former, and if what is in question is what follows from, what is called 'being in accord with', the rule '+ 2' at the 500th step, that is the very same question as 'What follows at the 500th step from the rule "Write the next but one number after every number you write"?' So it is no use saying that what the teacher meant when he uttered 'Add 2' was this latter formulation, and from *it* everything follows. Hence the intrusion of a mythical 'act of meaning' to mediate between rule and its application is futile. For to specify what he meant is simply to paraphrase the rule he gave. So this merely returns us to the point of departure after a useless detour.

W. concludes with the aside that it would almost be more correct to say that a new decision, not an intuition, is needed at each stage. It looked (to the interlocutor) as if a separate intuition was necessary at each step to carry one from the rule to what accords with it at that particular step. But, as we have seen, it makes sense to talk of intuiting what is correct only if there is an independent determination of correctness. Yet that is just what is in question – how does the rule determine what accords with it? Now it seems that we need a separate rule at every step in the application of the general rule '+ 2' to determine that *this* is what accords with the rule at *this* step. But that is tantamount to *deciding* what is to be called 'accord' at each step. Of course, the pupil does *not* make a new decision at each stage. He is taught (if teachable) to do as we all do, in learning arithmetic as in learning the moves in chess.

1.1   (i) 'intuition': intuition and insight alike suggest discovering that things are, independently of intuition, thus-and-so. But in calculi or techniques there are two alternatives. Either one can learn by drill, repetition, exercises and tests to operate the calculus, to employ the technique *as it is to be* operated or employed (i.e. as those who have *mastered* it *do*, in general, operate or employ it). Or one can invent new extensions of the calculi or techniques, introduce new rules, establish new internal relations by stipulating that *this* is to count as applying *this* rule to *this* case. But there is no *gap* between learning (and exemplifying that one has learnt correctly) and inventing (or stipulating) in which to locate any discovery. Internal relations can be learnt, or established, but not discovered (LFM 86).

(ii) 'Und auch mit der *Meinung*, die du damals dem Satz gegeben hast . . .': since English uses 'meaning' for both 'Bedeutung' and 'Meinung', better – 'and also with how you meant that sentence – whatever that may have consisted in'.

2   Br. B. 141ff. (EPB 213f.) connects this passage with a host of cases in which we labour under the illusion that an intermediate step links two

apparently independent things. A man *must* understand an order before he can obey it, *must* know where his pain is before he can point at it, *must* know a tune before he can sing it. So too here, between the statement of a rule or issuing of an order ('Add 2') and its individual applications, there must be some link that makes writing '1000, 1002, 1004' correct. This link may, we think, be forged by apprehension of the instructor's meaning the trainee to go on thus, or by an insight or intuition into the essential nature of the rule (conceived as 'containing', in a shadowy form, everything that follows from it), or by an interpretation. The idea that the possibility of understanding a sentence, an order or rule requires an intermediary between the words and the response is a recurrent theme. (See 'Accord with a rule', pp. 86ff.)

2.1   (i) 'a new insight – intuition – is needed': Vol. XIV, 4 introduces this gambit differently. 'How do I know to continue the series thus?' resembles 'How do I know that this colour is red?' In both cases I do not doubt for a moment that . . ., but the absence of doubt does not mean that I have grounds or reasons that compel me to continue the series thus, or to say that this is red. 'But how can I know this', the interlocutor responds, 'if reasons do not compel me? There is only one other possibility: I know it by intuition!' Do I always have to presuppose a mental reservoir, W. responds ironically, from which what I say and write flow?

(ii) 'To carry it out correctly': cf. RFM 234f. If, instead of saying that one needs an intuition at every step, one said that one must *guess right* at every step, this would make evident the uselessness of invoking intuition. For while the phenomenon of guessing is psychological, the phenomenon of guessing *right* is normative. Then it is perspicuous that something other than the guessing (or intuition) itself must determine what is to be called 'right'.

(iii) 'an infinite number of such propositions': there is an interesting parallelism with the question of how a proposition *can* 'contain' its entailments going back, in W.'s work, to pre-*Tractatus* days. To say that if *p* entails *q* then the sense of '*q*' is contained in the sense of '*p*' is merely to disguise this very question in the form of an answer to it. The matter is raised, but not resolved, in PG 247f. A general proposition may entail a logical sum of a hundred terms, of which we do not severally think when we utter the general proposition. And yet, what follows from a thought must be involved in thinking it:

For there is nothing in a thought that we aren't aware of while we are thinking it. It isn't a machine which might be explored with unexpected results, a machine which might achieve something that couldn't be read off from it. That is, the way it works is *logical*, it's quite different from the way a machine works. *Qua* thought, it contains nothing more than was put into it. As a machine functioning causally, it might be believed capable of anything; but in logic we get out of it only what we meant by it.

After a lengthy discussion, W. concludes that the idea that in thinking of a proposition one must also think of all its logical relations rests on a misconceived psychologism. Only what is contained in the signs and rules concerns us.

(iv) 'and with the *mean*-ing you then put into the sentence': Br.B. 142f. elaborates this. The mental act of meaning or intending is conceived to inform the rule and to give it power to contain its own applications in advance of its being applied.

AWL 132 observes that when we respond to the learner's error by saying 'I *did* not mean you to do that', the past tense fosters the illusion that something *occurred*, whereas nothing at all need have occurred other than my issuing my instruction (cf. Exg. §187). This illusion is a special case of another, namely that the chain of reasons has no end. For in response to the question, why must the learner write '110' after '100' in the series + 10, we think that we must find a further reason, and interpose the teacher's *meaning* as such a reason.

(v) 'not that an intuition was needed . . . but . . . a new decision': this verdict concludes W.'s own successive adherence to and subsequent repudiation of each of these moves. PR 170f. suggests that a new insight is necessary at each step in a proof. Since each number is different from every other, every application of a general rule containing a variable requires a fresh recognition that the rule applies in this individual case. 'No act of foresight can absolve me from this act of insight. Since the form to which the rule is applied is in fact different at every step.' To this W. later added a marginal note: 'Act of *decision*, not *insight*.' However, a residue of the idea that insight is necessary still appears in PG 347. By 1933–4, however, he had definitely shifted ground. AWL 133f. criticizes mathematical intuitionists. They were right to see that a general rule does not compel one at each step, but wrong to think that an insight is necessary, as if the absense of a *reason* betokened the presence of revelation. 'If any mental process is involved, it is one of decision, not of intuition. We do as a matter of fact all make the same decision, but we need not suppose we all have the same "fundamental intuition".'

In Br.B. 143 this too is repudiated. Talk of an act of decision is less confusing than talk of intuition, but it too is misleading. For no act of decision, or of deliberation (EPB 216), need occur. We may just write down or say what the next number in a series is. What is misleading is not merely that we do not have to make decisions, but the underlying suggestion that something must *make* us follow the rule in *this* manner. But *'we need have no reason to follow the rule as we do.'* W. clarified the two points involved here in different places. The relation between the terminus of reasons and a decision is adumbrated in LSD 125. Of course, if I instruct someone to continue the series '1, 1 + 1, . . .' there is a right continuation and wrong ones. If the instruction was 'Add 1' then it is wrong to go on (1 + 1) + (1 + 1), but right to go on 1 + 1 + 1. That is *not* at issue; the question is whether I could give a reason why it is right. I have a reason for writing '1 + 1 + 1', namely that I was given the rule '+ 1'. But do I have a reason for holding that '1 + 1 + 1' is the third step in continuing the series '+ 1'? 'I might just say "That is what I meant", or just "Well you've got to do that." – "It is right" is a *decision* which I make. I can't give reasons *ad infinitum*.' Nevertheless, it is misleading to talk of a *decision*. W. elaborated this point in LFM 30f., 237: intuitionism boils down to saying that one makes a new rule at each step in a calculation or in each application of a rule; for since one can only intuit what can, by other means, be determined as being there independently of intuition, the so-called 'intuition' is in effect a new rule. Or, less misleadingly, a decision! But that too is wrong: 'You don't make a decision: you simply do a certain thing. It is a question of a certain practice.' (LFM 237) Intuitionists speak of a *Grund-Intuition* by which the series of natural numbers is given us. One can be said to know that such-and-such by intuition if one knows without calculation what others know on the grounds of calculation. But none of us knows on the basis of calculation that 1 + 1 = 2, or that 3 follows 2 and 4 follows 3 in the series of natural numbers. 'The real point is that whether he knows it or not is simply a question of whether he does it as we taught him; it's not a question of intuition at all . . . it is more like an act of decision than of intuition. (But to say "It's a decision" won't help so much as "We all do it the same way.")' (LFM 30f.)

Section 187

1 The interlocutor feels that W. is pushing him off an important truth. Surely he *already knew* when he gave the order that the pupil should write '1002' after '1000'. So writing '1002' is correct because it accords with the teacher's already knowing at the time that the pupil ought to write just that. Of course, W. concedes, you knew it. As indeed you meant it. But just as having meant it did not consist in performing one of a multitude of acts of meaning, so having known it did not consist in *thinking of* this step from 1000 to 1002 (let alone in thinking of an infinite number of such steps).

Having ruled this out, W. offers a diagnosis. The interlocutor's saying 'I already knew at the time . . .' amounts to saying that if one had been asked what number is to succeed 1000, one would have said '1002'. And so doubtless one would. But this is an *assumption or hypothesis*, analogous to 'If he had fallen into the water, I should have jumped in after him.' This observation is evidently meant as a decisive criticism, since it is followed by the query 'Now what was wrong with your idea?', which is answered in §188 (cf. BB 142; EPB 215; AWL 131; LFM 28). What *is* this crucial countermove? The interlocutor is trying to answer the question of what determines what is the right step to take at any stage in following the order '+ 2'. He invokes two related notions: that he *meant* the pupil to do thus-and-so, and that he *knew* that the pupil should write thus-and-so. In both cases the past tense of the verb suggests an occurrence simultaneous with the order, i.e. the performance of an act of meaning, or a process of thinking of such-and-such. It is, the interlocutor implies, the accord of the pupil's reply with what the teacher *already* meant or knew that rendered it correct. This thought is both confused and misleading. It is confused because 'I meant . . .' and 'I knew . . .' do not refer to any past events or processes. Of course I *knew* that the pupil should write '1002' after '1000', since I *know* (and *have known* for years) what the series of even integers is, what 'the series of even integers' means. This innocuous expression is misleading in this context precisely because the temporal qualification 'I *already* knew *at the time*' distorts one's apprehension of the fact that this knowledge is *mastery of a technique* (not an event or process). The anomalousness of 'I already knew . . .' is evident in the riposte 'When did you know that he should say "1002" after "1000" in expending the series of even integers?'

Although one might paraphrase 'I knew at the time . . .' by 'If I had been asked, I would have said . . .', this paraphrase, by replacing the categorical 'I knew at the time' by a conditional, undermines the inter-locutor's case. For I *was not asked*, and I *did not say*. So there was no past event accord with which made answering '1002' correct. And a merely potential yardstick (what I *would* have said if . . .), one might say, is no yardstick at all. But, of course, I did mean him to write '1002'. Indeed, if I had not meant him to write '1002' after '1000', I could not have meant him to expand the series of even integers, since in that series '1002' succeeds '1000'. And if I did not know that '1002' comes after '1000', I would have not understood what this series is.

1.1   (i) 'Denn du meinst ja nicht': better translated 'For you don't mean that . . ..'
         (ii) 'Dein "Ich habe damals schon gewusst . . ." heisst etwa': better translated 'Your "I already knew at the time . . ." means, say, ...'

2   §187 is merely the tip of an iceberg, the nether regions of which are visible in earlier works. The key recurrent themes which are associated with this argument are four: (a) that meaning, understanding, knowing are not states of mind; (b) that 'I meant (knew)' does not refer to a past event; (c) that one's having meant such-and-such can be explained by a

conditional of the form 'If I had been asked . . ., I should have said . . .',
but nevertheless one's confidence that one meant it does not rest on
privileged access to one's dispositions; (d) whether someone meant such-
and-such typically turns on whether he has mastered a technique of using
an expression correctly, in accord with its meaning. These themes are
evident in the following:

(i) WWK 167f. argues that understanding is not a state (like a
toothache) from which exemplifications of understanding flow. If I use
the name 'Napoleon' in sentences, and am asked 'Did you mean the
victor of Austerlitz?', I should say that I did. But my having meant the
victor of Austerlitz is not a continuous state of mind, and the use of the
past tense 'I meant . . .' refers not to an act of meaning but to the past
utterance of the sentence about Napoleon. It may be misleading to talk of
understanding an expression at a certain time, if this suggests that what is
essentially akin to a capacity is an instantaneous event, or a state
obtaining at a particular time. PG 103 embroiders: when I said 'Napoleon'
I meant the victor of Austerlitz, but *in the kind of way* that I also knew that
$6 \times 6 = 36$.

So in using words one typically means by them whatever it is that they
mean. For to know the meaning of a word is to have mastered the
technique of its use. It involves being able to use it correctly, to respond
appropriately to its use and to explain it correctly. So if one has
employed a word 'W', and if the correct explanation of 'W' is 'G', then,
of course, other things being equal, in using 'W' one meant G, because
that is what 'W' means.

(ii) AWL 90ff. discusses the mental cramp generated in reflecting on
the relation between a rule and its application. A rule, we are inclined to
think, should contain its own application, otherwise an unbridgeable gap
seems to open between the two. And it will seem inexplicable how
understanding a word, knowing the rule for its use, is related to using the
word correctly, applying it in accord with the rule. Our confusion results
from conflating two related but distinct statements, viz. the statement of
a rule and an experiential proposition. W. illustrates this by a parallel
example. We might conceive of love as just a matter of having certain
feelings. In a given case, we say that A loves B. Later B's life is
endangered, but A does nothing to help B. We might now be inclined to
say 'A cannot really have loved B.' This looks like a piece of empirical
reasoning, but it is not. Rather, it reflects the fact that we are not going to
call this 'love' if A did not save B when he could have. That most people
who have such-and-such feelings usually behave thus is an empirical
proposition. That if A did not save B when B was endangered, then he
cannot have loved him, is the expression of a grammatical rule concerning
what is to be called 'love'. A second confusion W. warns against is the
supposition that in conditionals of the form 'If A loves B, then A will

behave thus', love is conceived as a state from which the behaviour follows, as if from a mechanism which generates the behaviour.

The latter kind of confusion is also exemplified by misunderstandings of understanding. For we are inclined to misconceive understanding as a state of mind from which behaviour manifesting understanding flows. W. does not elaborate fully the analogy. Arguably one might do so. The conditional 'If I had been asked what number comes after 1000 in the series + 2, I would have said "1002"' is a counterfactual hypothesis. But the compound conditional 'If I understood the expression "the series of even integers", then if I had been asked . . ., I would have said . . .' is a grammatical statement. Parallel to the grammatical statement about love, this is an expression or reflection of a rule for the use of 'understands the expression "the series of even integers"'. For, other things being equal, if he had said that '1004' follows '1000' in the series of even integers, we should *deny* that he understood the expression. We are, however, inclined to conflate the hypothesis and the grammatical statement. In particular, we are prone to view understanding as a state of mind from which behaviour follows as if *generated* by that inner state, so that this mechanism is, as it were, the foundation of the counterfactual. Here, as elsewhere in philosophy, we are prone to view logical, conceptual, connections as super-mechanical ones (partly, no doubt, because of the verbs 'must' and 'makes').

The argument is resumed at AWL 131: we are inclined to explain why the pupil had made a mistake by saying that the teacher meant the pupil to go on *thus*. But this is misleading, for no acts or processes of meaning accompany the instruction. The confusion disappears when one realizes that 'I did not mean you to go on thus' is not a report of a mental act the teacher performed at the time. The teacher might justify himself by saying 'I would have said . . . if I had been asked . . .'. But this is irrelevant, since it is either a hypothesis or a rule. If it is a rule, it is irrelevant since it was not given. So *that* cannot be what makes going on thus correct. If it is a hypothesis, it is irrelevant, since the teacher was *not* asked.

(iii) Br.B. 142 (cf. EPB 215) elaborates: in response to 'Surely I knew . . .', W. replies that this presumably means either that I performed an infinite number of acts (e.g. saying to myself 'I want him to write . . . after . . .') or that 'knowing' signifies a disposition. But the first alternative is absurd, and the second problematic. For only experience can teach us what it is a disposition *for*. And (EPB 215) if I say 'If I had been asked . . . I should have said . . .', *that* is a hypothesis (like 'If N had fallen into the water, I should have pulled him out'). Yet surely my confidence that I knew that he should write . . . does not rest on observation of my dispositions (but on the arithmetical techniques which I have mastered). W. repeats his point about the misleading character of

'I meant', and emphasizes that 'I meant . . .' no more implies 'I thought of . . .' here than my meaning by 'Napoleon' the victor of Austerlitz involved my thinking, when I said 'Napoleon was crowned in 1804', that Napoleon won the battle of Austerlitz. Although, of course, if you had asked me whether by 'Napoleon' I meant the victor of Austerlitz, I would have agreed, i.e. *I know who Napoleon was.*

(iv) Vol. XIV, 7f. has the interlocutor ask: 'But now, without any sophistry, didn't you mean, when you gave the order "+ 2", that he should, when he came to that point, write *that* number?' First, W. replies, I did not think of that number when I gave the order. Secondly, if I had thought of it, I would have explained that transition *as the one I meant!*

(v) LFM 28 has a different nuance: to the argument that having meant something does not mean having thought of it, one might respond 'I am sure I meant him to write . . . when he came to this step.' This is, W. implies, muddled. For it is like 'I am sure that I should have jumped into the water if Arabella had fallen in.' The suggestion seems to be that in this context 'I am sure I meant . . .' is anomalous. For one's insistence that one meant the pupil to write '1002' is not comparable to one's certainty about one's behavioural dispositions. The latter rests on self-knowledge, the former on knowledge of arithmetic. If I instruct a pupil to expand the series of even integers, of course I meant him to write '1002' after '1000'. But to say that I am sure that I mean him to do this implies that it is conceivable that I might be *unsure*; but then, by the same token, I would not fully understand the instruction I gave him.

2.1   (i) 'you should not let yourself be misled by the grammar of the words "know" and "mean"': the analysis of a person's meaning something by his words is a recurrent theme in PI. Here is a list of some of W.'s straightforward points: (1) 'I mean . . .' or 'I meant . . .' is not like 'when I said . . . I thought of . . .'. (PI §§692–3, p. 217) (2) To mean something by what one says is not an act (PI §678), or an activity (PI §693). (3) It is fallacious to think that meaning such-and-such by one's words is what gives the words their life, endows them with sense. *Inter alia*, meaning is not a process accompanying one's utterance (PI §675), for no process could have the consequences of meaning (PI p. 218). (4) We adopt a false picture whereby what we want to say or what we mean is present somewhere in one's mind before one says it (PI §334). But in so far as I meant such-and-such before I spoke, this is not because I performed any antecedent mental act; it is made possible by my mastery of the language (cf. PI §337). (5) 'I mean' is not like 'I imagined.' I cannot, by saying 'a, b, c, d', mean that the weather is fine. But that is *not* because I do not *associate* 'a' with 'the', 'b' with 'weather', etc. (PI §508). (6) 'I meant', like 'I intended', refers to a particular time, but not to an experience at that time (PI pp. 216f.). (7) 'I meant', like 'I intended', has no experience-content, for whatever accompanies my then meaning *that*, or my intending then to do such-and-such, is not *what* I mean or intend, let alone my meaning or intending (PI p. 217).

In MS 165, 52f., which succeeds a draft of PI §693 (which clearly belongs to this discussion), W. remarks that once it becomes clear that different psychological verbs such as to mean, think, fear, be startled, expect, etc. have categorially distinct applications, the investigation of a special case will no longer present such fearful difficulties.

A brief parallel investigation of 'I knew at the time' occurs in LW §§843ff.: if asked whether I already knew at the time that . . . or whether it was only later, I should, of course, insist that I knew it at the time. But knowing is not an experience. Indeed, if I were to say that when I said 'Expand the series + 2' I knew that he should write '1002' after '1000', this may well be a way of saying precisely that I did *not* rush through the series in my mind, *since I already knew it*. Were I to say, 'When I told him to add 2, I did not know that "1002" comes after "1000"', this would imply that I only found it out later, which in turn would imply that I myself did not fully understand what I said.

(ii) 'If I had been asked': cf. LW §716; after all, I was *not* asked, but I *did* know at the time. But the consequent of the conditional is not an event that would have flowed forth from the state of knowledge in the event of being asked. For knowledge is not a state of mind.

SECTION 188

1   This is part of the answer to the question posed at the end of §187, viz. what was wrong with the idea that the right step at any stage in expanding the series is determined by its according with the order *as it was meant*. Rather than analysing the notion of meaning something, a task begun in §§186f. and resumed later, W. here brings to light the mythology which underlies the idea.

Because we cannot see how the words of the order 'Add 2' can of their own accord, as it were, determine '1002' as the correct thing to write down at the 500th step, we seek to interpose a link between the words (the order, the rule) and the steps that constitute compliance. What better agent than the mind to make the connection, 'think the method of projection', from the rule to its applications! The way it is done is by *meaning* the order. But if meaning it is to do the necessary work, then the mind must fly ahead of the order, executing it *in petto* before giving it, so that the pupil's acts will have something with which they may uniquely and unambiguously accord. And so it seems as if the act of meaning can anticipate reality.

In PPI §161 and in TS 239 W. added the parenthesis 'we shall come across this delusion again frequently' (deleted in PPI(I)). So, indeed, in PI this phenomenon of a sentence or utterance casting a shadow before it crops up again and again. An order seems to anticipate its own execution, by ordering just that which is later carried out (PI §§458ff.). A wish or an expectation determines now what will later fulfil it (PI §§437, 465). An intention too anticipates the future, since I now intend precisely that which I later do when I do what I intended. Like a crystal ball, my intention seems to contain a picture of what I shall subsequently do. And even a false proposition seems to cast a shadow on reality, for it determines, as it were, how it is that the world is *not*. All these puzzles are facets of a problem which preoccupied W. from the very start of his philosophical career, the problem of the 'harmony between language and reality'. (See 'Accord with a rule', pp. 85ff.)

.1   (i) 'in some *unique* way': so that *just these* steps and no others would fit the rule; hence the misconception of the mental act of meaning as 'the final interpretation':

What one wishes to say is 'Every sign is capable of interpretation; but the *meaning* mustn't be capable of interpretation. It is the last interpretation.' (BB 34)

(ii) '"The steps are *really* already taken, even before I take them in writing or orally or in thought"': the steps are 'really already taken' because I mean just *these* steps and no others. But if I take them by meaning them, and if my meaning takes place in my mind, then is not my meaning them something I do 'in thought'? No. For §187 has already established that meaning is not thinking of what one means. So my meaning these steps must outrun even my thinking.

The scrutiny of this phrase is resumed at §219.

.1   (i) 'your mind as it were flew ahead': cf. Br.B. 142, 'Your idea really is that somehow in the mysterious act of *meaning* the rule you made the transitions without really making them. You crossed all the bridges before you were there.'

(ii) 'took all the steps before you physically arrived': EPB 215 invokes a different picture. 'According to the *sense* of the order, one ought to write . . .'; here one thinks of the sense as a shadow which hurries ahead, and which, in a shadowy way, performs all the transitions in advance. But W. mocks the picture: if the transitions have been executed in a shadowy way, what shadow will now mediate between the shadow-transitions and the real ones? If the words of the order cannot anticipate the transition from one number to the next, then no mental act accompanying the words can do so either (cf. Br.B. 143). These pictures are the product of not understanding the logic of a language.

(iii) ' "The steps are *really* already taken, even before I take them in writing or orally or in thought" ': that the conception crystallized in this statement also belongs to the picture of the *rule* (or formula of the rule) determining the steps that follow from it is shown by RFM 45. Russell presents *modus ponens*, a fundamental rule of inference in *Principia*, as being *right* or *correct*. What is implied by a true premise is true.

In his fundamental law Russell seems to be saying of a proposition: 'It already follows – all I still have to do is to infer it.' Thus Frege somewhere says that the straight line which connects any two points is really already there before we draw it;[1] and it is the same when we say that the transitions, say in the series + 2, have really already been made before we make them orally or in writing – as it were tracing them. (RFM 45)

---

[1] Frege, GA i, 88; cf. FA 24: 'The truths of arithmetic would then be related to those of logic in much the same way as the theorems of geometry to the axioms. *Each one would contain concentrated within it a whole series of deductions for future use*, and the use of it would be that we need no longer make the deductions one by one, but can express simultaneously the result of the whole series.' (our italics) See also FA 93; cf. WWK 165.

III

ACCORD WITH A RULE

1. *Initial compass bearings*

After the detailed examination of understanding, of the 'experience' of being guided by a rule, and of avowals of understanding, Wittgenstein turns aside to allocate 58 remarks to a discussion of what it is for someone to follow a rule. He focused on the seemingly trivial example of someone's writing a sequence of numbers according to the rule 'Add 2'. But are there really any deep problems buried here? A superficial reading may well leave one bemused as to the motivation underlying the discussion, puzzled about its targets, and bewildered about the thrust of the argument. It is no coincidence that for two decades after publication this part of the *Investigations* was largely neglected. A slightly less superficial reading may give one the impression that Wittgenstein was elaborating a form of scepticism about following rules, which he then tried to resolve. This suggestion, for a multitude of reasons,[1] is definitely wrong. The first requisite in approaching this part of the book is to clarify what are the problems he saw, and what role these remarks play in the overall strategy of the book.

Although the subject of this essay concerns the concept of accord with a rule, it should be borne in mind that the remarks on this topic in *Investigations* §§185ff. are subordinate to the theme of following a rule, which is in turn part of Wittgenstein's extensive examination of the nature of understanding. Having completed the investigation into the special use of 'understand' in avowals of ability (§§151–84), Wittgenstein reverted to the problem previously broached (§§145–50) of what it means to say of the pupil in §143 that he has understood a certain part of our system of arithmetic. The original example concerned the technique of writing the series of natural numbers. This is now enriched to include writing out progressions in response to orders of the form '+ *n*'. This deliberately introduces explicit formulations of *general* rules into the system that is to be understood.

The discussion begins with the homely example of teaching a pupil to extend the series of even integers. The pupil errs when he goes beyond 1000, and we may wonder how to explain to him that he has not applied the rule '+ 2' correctly, that he has not proceeded in the same way as

---

[1] Having discussed it exhaustively in G. P. Baker and P. M. S. Hacker, *Scepticism, Rules and Language* (Blackwell, Oxford, 1984) we shall not dwell on it here.

before. There is no room for doubt whether the pupil is right or wrong; we know that he is wrong. The correct steps are determined by the formula '+ 2' (PI §189); it would be absurd to deny this, since such a formula is what is called 'a formula which determines a series'. But reflection may cause us to lose our grip on these platitudes. For *how do we know* that 1002 follows 1000 in the series + 2? What *justifies* our verdict that 1002 is the next term in this series, that the pupil's answer '1004' is incorrect? What *reasons* do we have? These questions seem embarrassing. Standard manoeuvres for trying to answer them are also suggested to be futile. Intuition affords no *grounds* at all, and the appeal to what we meant the pupil to do would provide a general standard of correctness only if the mind could traverse the entire series of even integers in a flash (PI §§187–8). Similar perplexity arises from pondering on the idea that the *formula* determines what is the next term in the series. How can an *expression* settle what is correct and incorrect? Is this not a mythology of symbolism? We might instead claim that it is *the rule* itself, i.e. what is expressed by the formula, which determines the terms of the series. But is this not a Platonist mythology? Does it not depend on the weird conception that a rule is a mechanism which inexorably generates consequences independently of human intervention? We might suggest that the reason for writing '1002' turns on our giving an *interpretation* of the rule. But then we must face the fact that every formulation of a rule can be variously interpreted, each interpretation yielding different verdicts about what is correct or incorrect (PI §198). Now we seem driven to deny that it makes sense to say 'the *formula* + 2 determines what follows 1000 in the series 2, 4, 6, ...' Our whole pattern of speaking about following rules, the network of our concepts, seems to be thrown into confusion by philosophical scruples.

What was Wittgenstein's purpose in these remarks? It is tempting to interpret the *Investigations* as advocating scepticism or conceptual nihilism about what is in accord with a rule. This should be resisted. Wittgenstein did not urge us to abandon the convictions that we *know* what acts accord with a rule and that a formula (expression of a rule) does *determine* what steps are to be taken. For it makes *sense to say* that someone knows what accords with a rule, and it can typically be readily verified; and so too it makes sense to say of certain formulae that they determine given results. These are not theses that may intelligibly be disputed; rather they are delineations of part of the grammar of the concepts of a rule and of following a rule. Denials of these propositions would be not false but nonsensical. Hence these propositions do not need evidential support. Still less do they require any reconstruction of our concept of following a rule. Wittgenstein did indeed remark 'following a rule is a practice' (PI §202), that thinking that one is following a rule is distinct from following it (§202), and that following a rule is not something which only one man could do only once in his lifetime (§199). But it is definitely wrong to interpret these comments as suggesting that what determines whether an act accords with a rule is something other than the rule itself.

Wittgenstein did not set out to construct a case for some particular opinion (e.g. common sense (LFM 103)) about the phenomena associated with following rules. Rather he intended to clarify the *concept* of following a rule. If we find ourselves in the position of feeling compelled to deny propositions which delineate parts of the grammar of our concepts, we have fallen into confusions. The only appropriate remedy is to expose them. This is what is done in *Investigations* §§185–242. Wittgenstein examined a wide range of pictures and metaphors which we are inclined to employ in reflecting on following rules, and he pinpointed both the illuminating and the misleading aspects of these turns of phrase. Some of these expressions capture insights in a distorted way (e.g. 'all the steps are *already taken* (§§188, 219) or 'the line *intimates* to me the way I am to go' (§§222, 230)); these are all too easily misunderstood. Others, though apparently anodyne, are also easily misconstrued (e.g. 'the way the formula is *meant* determines what steps are to be taken' (§190), 'the steps are *determined* by the algebraic formula' (§189), or 'we grasp the use of a word in a flash' (§§191f., 195ff.)). Far from challenging grammatical truisms, Wittgenstein reined in an interlocutor tempted to deny them. The inclination to assert that no formula determines what steps to take is brought up short against the grammar of the expression 'the steps are determined by the formula' (§189), and the idea that any act can be brought into accord with any rule is diagnosed as resting on a misunderstanding (§201).

A full understanding of these remarks presupposes a grasp of their role in the overall strategy of the book, in particular to relate this discussion to the topic of meaning and understanding which dominates the preceding remarks. Wittgenstein connected the concept of meaning both with the *use* of an expression and with an *explanation* of its meaning. Are these two *independent* clarifications of the same concept? It may superficially seem so. This impression is strengthened when the nexus between meaning and understanding is pressed. For the meaning of an expression is, tautologically, what someone understands when he understands or grasps the meaning of the expression. His understanding is manifest in how he explains the expression, and also in how he uses it. But, surely, he may explain it correctly and then go on to misapply it. Conversely, someone may use an expression correctly, yet explain it wrongly. So, it seems, by one standard he understands it, by another he does not. The concept of understanding seems riven by internal incoherence. This apparent dilemma must be resolved by making it clear how explanation and use are related and how the criteria of understanding mesh. It is an illusion to suppose that the ability to explain a word and the ability to use

it correctly are independent of each other, and it is important to realize
that understanding or misunderstanding of a correct explanation is
manifested in correct or incorrect use of the expression explained (cf. PI
§§28f.). Grasping such relations between the concepts of explanation and
use should forestall our concluding that the concept of meaning is shown
to fall apart by Wittgenstein's clarification.

But there is another antithetical danger of a fundamental misconception.
Dimly aware that the concepts of explanation and use do interlock, we
may oversimplify the relations between them and thereby be tempted to
embrace certain illusions of reason. Wittgenstein identified the idea of the
instantaneous understanding of an expression as pregnant with potentialities
for confusion. It does of course make sense to speak of a person's
understanding a word at a stroke; he may fully grasp the meaning when
he is given an explanation of what it means. On the other hand, to grasp
the meaning is to understand how it is used. But its use seems to be
extended in time, so how can what someone understands at an instant be
its use (PI §138)? Similarly, his understanding (or lack of it) will be
manifested in the correct (or incorrect) use that he later makes of the
word; so how can what happens at an instant (his immediate grasping of
its meaning) anticipate or encapsulate his future acts? In reflecting on
these matters, we are inclined to conclude that the future use of the word
is in some queer sense already present (PI §195) or else that we cannot
really grasp the whole use of a word at an instant (PI §§191, 197). Or
perhaps we infer that understanding a word is a very mysterious process
(PI §§196f.); the mind effects the miraculous feat of traversing the
boundless applications of the word in a moment (cf. PI §188). Or we
might conclude that the explanation somehow contains all the uses of the
word, so that its applications flow forth from the explanation inexorably
like the products of some magical machine (cf. PI §§193ff.). Bizarre as
these conclusions are, misconstruals of the concepts of understanding
and meaning lead to them.

Wittgenstein's strategy for removing such puzzlement about the
concepts of meaning and understanding was to investigate what it is to
follow a rule. He noted that explanations of meaning are standards
employed in determining whether words are used correctly or incorrectly; they function in our practice as *rules* for the use of expressions.
Moreover, speakers who understand a word or know what it means
must have the abilities to say or explain what it means (cf. 'Explanation',
Volume 1), to justify their own uses of it, to correct mistakes, etc.; in
short, they manifest the capacities characteristic of *following* the rules
(explanations) for using the word. Consequently, someone's uses of an
explained expression constitute the following of a rule (namely the
explanation). Therefore the relation of the explanation of a word to its
use is a special case of the relation of a rule to its applications.

Wittgenstein sought to clarify the former by investigating the latter, and to shed light thereby upon the nature of understanding.

The puzzles about the relation of explanations of meaning to the uses of words are all replicated in puzzles about the relation of rules to acts which accord with them (i.e. the relation of rules to their applications). On the one hand, reflection inclines us to declare that understanding a rule is one thing, while following it is something quite different. On the other hand, we think that misapplications of a rule evidence defective or deviant understanding of the rule applied, and we may well add that the rule as it is to be understood determines what is correct and incorrect. Consequently, we become entangled in the very same problems previously rehearsed. What is lacking is understanding of what it means to say that a rule determines what accords with it. To grasp the relations between meaning, use, explanation and understanding, we need an *Übersicht* of how the concepts of a rule and of an application of a rule interlock and a clarification of the concepts of following a rule and acting in accord with a rule. Our approach to these questions will be indirect. For a correct apprehension of the movement of Wittgenstein's thought is possible only against a background of questions that preoccupied him ever since the *Tractatus* – questions which he referred to as 'the problem of the harmony between language and reality'.

2. *Accord and the harmony between language and reality*

The accord of an act with a rule is one of a range of concepts that preoccupied Wittgenstein in the early 1930s. Others are the satisfaction of a desire or wish, the fulfilment of an expectation, the compliance with an order, and the verification of a description. All exemplify what he called 'the harmony between language and reality'. In every case what is at issue is the mesh, fit or correspondence between something in the world (that which satisfies a desire or wish, fulfils an expectation, complies with an order, makes true a proposition) and something expressed in words. He thought this matter to be a focal point of philosophical confusions, and during this period he wrote about it extensively. In his view he resolved these problems and did not return to them. In particular, the *Investigations* does not examine *in detail* the concept of the accord of an act with a rule. The remarks on the general topic of the harmony between language and reality (§§431ff., 440, 442ff., 460f.) are garnered from early manuscripts. The moral is not that one should ignore these matters, but rather that they are taken for granted as part of the background to the discussion of following a rule in the *Investigations* and, in particular, to the conception of accord with a rule that is there put to work.

Misconceptions about the 'harmony between language and reality' are part of the *raison d'être* of the picture theory of meaning. We can understand a proposition (a sentence in use) without knowing whether it is true or false – indeed, independently of whether it is true or whether it is false. But if what makes it true (if it is true) is a fact, what we understand cannot be a fact, since that would exclude the possibility of understanding a false proposition. On the other hand, when we understand a proposition, we know what must be the case *if* it is true. We can read off from the proposition what fact will make it true if it obtains. This may well seem mysterious. How can a proposition thus anticipate reality? Surely, the *Tractatus* argued, by virtue of containing a logical picture. The core of this conception was elaborated by the picture theory of the atomic proposition and the doctrine of isomorphism between language and reality. An elementary proposition consists of logically proper names whose meanings are sempiternal simple objects. The proposition itself is a fact which in virtue of its structure pictures a *possible* concatenation of objects, a (possible) state of affairs. An elementary proposition is therefore a model of reality, a logical picture of a state of affairs which would make the proposition true if this state of affairs were actualized. Hence the proposition, as it were, determines reality completely save for a 'Yes' or 'No'. The possibility depicted by it is so close to actuality that all that is missing from it *is* reality (cf. PG 136). Only thus can one explain how it is possible to think what is *not* the case, and make clear how we can read off from the proposition what must be the case *if* it is true.

The relation between a true proposition and the fact that verifies it is *internal*[2] (TLP 4.014). The proposition would not be the proposition that it is if it did not depict the state of affairs that it does. Hence it is inconceivable that the possibility depicted by a proposition be actualized and yet the proposition *not* be true. This picture theory of the proposition is a version of the correspondence theory of truth, but with the peculiar twist that the relation of correspondence, being internal, indeed metaphysical, is ineffable. The mechanism of this correspondence or harmony between language and reality is the possible situations which propositions depict. The possibility of propositions depends on their being essentially connected with situations because they are composed of signs which represent objects (TLP 4.03ff.). Possible situations (states of affairs) are, as it were, shadows that mediate between propositions and facts.

---

[2] A property is internal if it is unthinkable that its object should not possess it, and a relation between two objects is internal if it is unthinkable that *these* two objects should not stand in *this* relation (TLP 4.123). In Wittgenstein's writings the expression 'internal relation' does not indicate any adherence to Bradley's metaphysical doctrines which Russell and Moore had vigorously assailed. (See below, pp. 104f.)

It is arguable that at the time of writing the *Tractatus* Wittgenstein would have extended this account to explain other forms of 'correspondence' or 'harmony' between language and reality (cf. NB 96, 129; TLP 5.541ff.). For one might use the same metaphysical apparatus to explain how a command, wish or desire can anticipate what will satisfy it. For surely one can read off from a command what will fulfil it, whether or not it is executed; one can say what it is one wants in advance of getting it, and even if one does not get it. But how can one's present state of desiring anticipate what will satisfy it? Surely only by containing a logical picture of what will fulfil it. The relation of an order to the act which executes it, of a desire to what fulfils it, of a wish to the event which makes it come true, is patently internal. And that seems to be explained by reference to the idea that a command, desire or wish contains a picture of what will satisfy it.

This idea was not explicitly developed in the *Tractatus*. But when, in the 1930s, Wittgenstein came to reject the picture theory of meaning, the conception of a metaphysical harmony between language and reality was brought under critical scrutiny. In the course of resolving this issue and of dispelling the metaphysical miasma, Wittgenstein initially extended the scope of the *apparent* harmony between language and reality to include the relation between command and its execution, desire and its satisfaction, wish and its fulfilment. For in all these cases something that is expressed in language seems to anticipate reality, to contain a picture[3] of an event in the world. His favourite example of this wider 'harmony' was the fulfilment of expectation. My expectation that a gun will go off seems to anticipate its fulfilment, i.e. the gun's going off. But, of course, it cannot contain the event itself, since it has not yet occurred and may never occur (cf. PR 67). It now seems mysterious how I can ever expect something; for is what I expect something *other* than the event which, once it occurs, fulfils my expectation? Can I expect a particular explosion if this event does not yet even exist? And how can I know that *this* explosion *is* the fulfilment of my expectation? Did it sound just as loud in my expectation (PG 134; PI §442)? It seems that my expectation must foreshadow its fulfilment in virtue of containing a model or picture of a possibility (as the elementary proposition seemingly must picture a possible situation in order that it should fit the fact that makes it true – if it is a fact). For what I expect must be the same whether or not my expectation is fulfilled. The realization of this possibility is the fulfilment of my expectation. One finds a particular comparison irresistible:

---

[3] This was no longer unpacked in terms of the metaphysics of logical atomism. For the picture theory of meaning with its logical atomism was part of a logico-metaphysical solution to the *problem* of the *pictoriality* of the proposition. Obviously the problem can and should be stated independently of this misguided solution.

A man makes his appearance – an event makes its appearance. As if an event even now stood in readiness before the door of reality and were then to make its appearance in reality – like coming into a room. (PG 137)

Here again a possibility plays the role of a shadowy intermediary to link the two terms of an internal relation: the relation of a fulfilled expectation to the event fulfilling it.

These logico-metaphysical illusions are precisely what Wittgenstein shattered here. The apparent harmony between language and reality is not the product of isomorphism between proposition and fact; nor is the 'mechanism' of the apparent harmony a matter of shadowy intermediaries, possible situations or possible events. The apparent harmony is the echo of a grammatical orchestration. What seems to be a metaphysical correspondence is actually an intra-grammatical articulation.

It seems as if the expectation and the fact satisfying the expectation fitted together somehow. Now one would like to describe an expectation and a fact which fit together, so as to see what this agreement consists in. Here one thinks at once of the fitting of a solid into a corresponding hollow. But when one wants to describe these two one sees that, to the extent that they fit, a *single* description holds for both. (On the other hand compare the meaning of: 'These trousers don't go with this jacket'!) (PG 134)

What I expected was expressed by the sentence 'The gun will go off'; and what now fulfils my expectation is the event described by the sentence 'The gun has gone off.' Here it is evident that '*expectation* uses the same symbol as the thought of its fulfilment'; *hence* it is inconceivable that there be any language in which 'expecting that *p*' was described without using '*p*' (PR 69; cf. PG 139). 'If you see the expression of the expectation, you see what is expected.' (PG 132; PI §452) What appeared to be a metaphysical fitting together of entities of different types is the shadow cast by an intra-grammatical connection. The metaphysical harmony between language and reality is a reflection of a transparent connection between the uses of symbols, e.g. 'the expectation that *p*' = df. 'the expectation that is fulfilled by the event *p*' (cf. PG 161f.). In the light of such familiar rules of grammar it is evident that no shadowy intermediaries are necessary to connect an expectation and its fulfilment, since they are connected *in language* (PI §445).

Precisely the same therapy applies to the apparent metaphysical fit between proposition and fact which the elaborate picture theory of the proposition attempted to explain. 'The proposition that *p* corresponds to the facts' is not a description of a relation between entities belonging to different 'realms', Language and the World; nor is it a violation of the bounds of sense, attempting to say what can only be shown. It does not call for ontological theses about proposition and facts. Rather it is merely an idiomatic variant of 'It is true that *p*.' Facts and true propositions are connected in various ways by familiar rules of grammar. 'It is a fact that *p*' is typically interchangeable with 'It is true that *p*' or 'The proposition that *p* is true.' Similarly 'the proposition that *p*' = 'the proposition which the fact that *p* makes true' (PG 161), and 'the fact that *p*' = 'the fact that makes true the proposition that *p*'. Facts and propositions make contact in language (cf. PG 140; PI §445). The internal relation between a true proposition and the fact that verifies it owes nothing to the good offices of a possible situation or state of affairs. There is here no metaphysical *fitting* of entities from different realms; rather, true propositions and facts belong to each other (cf. PI §136 and Exg.). They make contact *in language*.

Wittgenstein invoked parallel points to demolish related misconceptions. One such target (merely alluded to) is Frege's idea of the 'sense of a sentence' (cf. BB 32, 36) or 'thought' conceived of as a Platonic object. On Frege's view it is only in virtue of having or expressing a sense (an entity distinct from the sentence) that a sentence may name the True or the False, and may be used to state something true. To understand a sentence, according to Frege, is to 'grasp' its sense, and to do that is to know the condition under which the function which is the meaning of the constituent function-name has the value 'the True' for the object which is the meaning of the constituent argument-expression (GA i, §32). Frege's rationale for introducing such shadowy entities as 'senses of sentences' differed from the *Tractatus* rationale for states of affairs. Nevertheless, the grammatical articulations that render superfluous the metaphysical apparatus of states of affairs equally make redundant Frege's metaphysical apparatus of senses and the True and the False. Certainly, if the proposition that this apple is red is true, then this apple must have the property red, must fall under the concept red. But these are (contorted) grammatical propositions; and they require no metaphysical harmony between expressions, senses, functions, arguments and an object called 'the True'. Nor do we need to conjure Platonic entities such as 'senses of sentences' to mediate between a sentence that is understood and such a mythical object. For a person understands a sentence '*p*' if he understands that what it says is that *p*, and if he understands *that* he also understands that it is in fact true if it is the case that *p*. These grammatical articulations require no ontological harmonies in a function-theoretic key.

Another target is Russell's account of the satisfaction of desire in *Analysis of Mind*. Russell argued that I cannot foresee with certainty what will constitute the satisfaction of my desires; indeed I cannot tell what I desire until I see what brings about the quiescence of my craving or a feeling of satisfaction. Here Wittgenstein's objection is not merely that the feeling of satisfaction is a misguided mechanism invoked to explain an internal relation by mediating between the relata, but that Russell wrongly denied that the relation of a desire to its satisfaction is *internal* (PR 63ff.; cf. PI §441) and then introduced the feeling of satisfaction into his analysis in order to bolster this misconception. But 'the desire to eat an apple' means the same as 'the desire which is satisfied by eating an apple'. If the occurrence of an independently identifiable feeling of satisfaction determines whether a desire which I express is satisfied, then there will be *no* grammatical connection between the expression of the desire and the description of its satisfaction, and that is unintelligible. Moreover if quiescence of the desire identifies what is desired, then if I say 'I want an apple' and am given a punch in the stomach that gives quiescence to my desire, then what I really wanted was the punch – which is absurd!

Philosophical puzzles about such internal relations have straightforward analogues in conundrums about rules and acts in accord with them. The rule of castling in chess seems to anticipate the acts that accord with it, i.e. particular acts of castling correctly. But the rule cannot *contain* the acts that accord with it. They lie in the future, and may never be performed. So how can the rule determine in advance what will accord with it? And how can I be sure that *this* move is what the rule licenses? How do the rule and an act in accord with it fit together or agree with one another? This range of puzzles overlaps with the perplexities that emerge in *Investigations* §§185ff. and link them naturally with the 'harmony between language and reality'.

Tempting strategies for explaining the fit between rule and what accords with it parallel previous manoeuvres. One (aping the *Tractatus*) would be that a rule contains a picture of what accords with it (for one *can* read off from the rule what act will accord with it). A rule must be or contain a picture of a possible act, a possibility which is depicted whether or not the rule is followed. If an act fits this picture, then it accords with the rule, it realizes the possibility depicted. A second strategy (aping Frege) would be that the rule has a 'sense' which fixes whether a particular act is in accord with it or not. Platonic machinery determines accord independently of human intervention. A third strategy (aping Russell) would be to deny that the rule does determine what is in accord with it; the measure of accord is external to the rule, lying perhaps in the fact that most people in the community of rule-followers feel satisfied that everyone would be inclined to act *thus*. On the first two views, a shadowy intermediary is introduced as an explanatory mechanism underpinning an internal relation, whereas on the third it is invoked while denying that there is such a relation. Similar (but *not* identical) moves are essayed in *Investigations* §§184ff. Wittgenstein's interlocutor is tempted to interpose mediating entities between the formulation of a rule and the acts that accord with it. The rule, he suggests, makes contact with what accords with it only via the teacher's *meaning* just those acts (PI §186). Alternatively he conceives of the rule-formulation as expressing a rule, conceived as a mysterious Platonic object which, as it were, *contains* its applications in advance (cf. PI §§191ff. and Exg.). And he is sorely tempted by the idea that it is an *interpretation* that builds the bridge between the expression of the rule and one's actions, so that understanding the rule consists in laying hold of the correct interpretation.

Unlike his interlocutor, Wittgenstein does not try to explain how a rule can determine what accords with it (or how we can know what accords with it) by reference to mediating entities. Just as the apparent harmony between language and reality was dissolved by clarifying grammatical articulations, so too the relation between a rule and what is in accord with it is rendered unmysterious and perspicuous by grammatical remarks. If the rule reads 'No castling through check' then *'my not castling through check'* describes an act in accord with this rule, and *'my castling through check'* an act that contravenes it. More generally, it is a grammatical truth that an F's ϕing in circumstances C is an act in accord with the rule that F's should ϕ in C; and equally 'The rule that F's should ϕ in C' = 'The rule that is followed by an F's ϕing in C'. Like the relation between a true proposition and the fact that verifies it, the relation between a rule and an act in accord with it is internal (WWK 157; cf. MS 123, 74). This rule would not be the rule that it is, nor would this act be the act that it is, if this act were not in accord with this rule. Because the relation is internal, no intermediary can be interposed between its two terms to effect a connection. Nothing can be inserted between a rule and its application as mortar is inserted between two bricks (WWK 154ff.). It is a grammatical platitude that a rule determines what acts are in accord with it, just as a desire determines what satisfies it and a description determines what must be the case for it to be true. Hence it is nonsense to suggest that the rule + 2 for the series of even integers leaves undetermined what it is correct to write after '1000' (PI §§189, 198). Likewise, to understand a rule is to know what acts are in accord with it,[4] just as to understand a description is to know what would be the case if it were true or what facts would make it true. The rule and its 'extension' are not two things that can be grasped independently of one another (LFM 85, 108), but are internally related. The rule 'Add 2' would not be the rule it is if writing '1002' after '1000' were *not* in accord with it. It is *in language* that a rule and the act in accord with it (or a rule and its 'extension') make contact. This point (which we shall clarify further) is fundamental to understanding the discussion of following rules in the *Investigations*.

---

[4] Though, of course, in certain cases that may involve reasoning or calculating.

3. *Rules of inference and logical machinery*

This simple account of the accord of an act with a rule has the merit of perspicuity, and it also eliminates metaphysical mysteries. But like the clarification of the correspondence of propositions and facts, it may leave anxiety that something deep has been trivialized. Worse, it appears open to serious objections. Two such objections were examined by Wittgenstein, and his responses to them further illuminate his conception.

The first turns on the role of principles of logic or rules of inference in the determination of the accord of an act with a rule. For it seems that such principles insinuate themselves between the terms of this internal relation; and that would undermine Wittgenstein's account altogether. The problem can be formulated by using his arithmetical example. The rule for the series of even integers is that one write the next but one number after each number that one has written. 1002 is the next but one number after 1000, so writing '1002' after '1000' is in accord with the rule. 1004 is not the next but one number after 1000, so writing '1004' after '1000' is not in accord with it. Each of these verdicts rests on an *inference*. So the description of the act of writing '1002' after '1000' seems to make contact with the rule 'Write the next but one number after every number previously written' only *indirectly*, via the logical principle of universal instantiation 'From $(x)fx$ infer fa.' In the absence of this principle of inference, how could there be any question of accord or conflict between a *particular* act and the *general* rule? So are not the laws of logic the ultimate grounds of accord and conflict of acts with rules?

In fact, this is a special case of a general problem. On the one hand, it seems evident that all *logical* relations among propositions are *internal* (cf. TLP 5.131, 5.2); the propositions $(x)fx$ and fa would not be the propositions that they are if the first did not entail the second. On the other hand, logical relations seem to be described by the propositions of logic (e.g. $(x)fx \supset fa$) and enshrined in rules of inference (e.g. from $(x)fx$ infer fa); and this suggests that all logical relations among propositions are cemented by the truths of logic or laws of thought. But how can the laws of logic be essential to relate propositions that are already intrinsically, internally, related?

The appearance of conflict arises out of misconceptions about the role and status of rules of inference. We shall examine these issues in detail in 'Grammar and necessity' (pp. 307ff.); here a schematic treatment suffices. One should start from the question of what an inference is, and of what it is to make one. Inferring is a human activity; in one sense of 'inference', an inference is an act or performance (a far cry from an ordered *n*-tuple of sets of truth-conditions!). The simplest case of making an inference is making one assertion after another, given that the final assertion is (and is intended to be) a transformation of the previous ones according to certain paradigms. An inference is an act of transforming symbols,[5] and hence a rule of inference is a norm governing symbolic transformations. We say of a person that he has inferred such-and-such if the *expression* of what he has inferred is (or is intended to be) a transformation of other propositions (e.g. the expressions of what he believes) according to such a paradigm. A rule of inference must have the roles characteristic of rules, viz. the functions of teaching people to make inferences, of justifying and criticizing their reasoning, and of describing and giving normative explanations of what they have done. The rule of universal instantiation or double-negation elimination is a paradigm for transforming expressions, and it is put to use in making a particular sequence of assertions. (It is misleading to describe a rule of inference as a *means* for making a transition from one assertion to another.)

This clarification of rules of inference interlocks with Wittgenstein's account of the meanings of words. Whether particular symbolic transformations are licensed is clearly an aspect of the *uses* of symbols. Hence in so far as it turns on particular constituents or features of complex symbols, it is a matter of the *meanings* of these expressions. For example, it is uniformly legitimate to infer *fa* from $(x)fx$; therefore the rule of universal instantiation embodies part of the *meaning* of the universal quantifier. Similarly $\sim \sim p \vdash p$ represents part of the *meaning* of negation. (This is a crucial, and by no means trivial, claim. Its consequences are explored in detail in 'Grammar and necessity', pp. 312ff.) For if we did not make or acknowledge inferences of the form $\sim \sim p \vdash p$, then '$\sim$' would not mean what it does. This is a platitude; it is indeed part of the established use of '$\sim$' (and 'It is not the case that . . .') that $\sim \sim p \vdash p$ is a paradigm of (correct) inference. If someone argued '$\sim \sim p$, so $\sim p$' (or condemned the inference '$\sim \sim p$, so p') we would say that he did not understand the meaning of '$\sim$', did not understand how it is used. This rule of inference perspicuously constitutes part of the meaning of '$\sim$'.

To acknowledge that rules of inference are in part *constitutive* of the meanings of logical constants makes it clear that an inference rule cannot appear in the guise of a *deus ex machina*, making connections *in logic* between internally related propositions. In logic you cannot 'connect two things by means of a third one'; they must already stand in a connection with one another (WWK 155). Rules of inference are indeed essential parts of the grammar of language, essential in the explanations of the meanings of logical operators. But the rule of universal instantiation is not something pasted on to an independently understood proposition containing the universal quantifier (or 'All'). This pattern of inference

---

[5] More generously, we speak of an inference where such a transformation is licensed.

cannot be *discovered* to hold between the propositions $(x)fx$ and fa. In short, a rule of inference does not engineer a fit between independently given propositions, as it were cementing together two bricks. Rather, it makes perspicuous the fact that a pair of propositions belong to one another, that they *are* internally related.

So too in the case of a rule (such as the rule for writing down the sequence of even integers) and the acts that accord with it. Already in 1931 Wittgenstein observed that 'There is no rule that interposes itself between the expression "x/x^2" and its application to numbers, like the mortar between bricks; I have already to read a certain kind of application into the expression.' (WWK 155) Similarly, to understand the rule 'Add 2' *is* to know that the number to write after '1000' is '1002'. Therefore appeal to universal instantiation in determining that a particular act is in accord with a general rule confirms rather than confutes the claim that they are internally related. A rule and an act that accords with it make contact in language, in the way in which the rule is explained, in the manner in which the act is described, and in the criteria for understanding the rule. Writing '1002' at the 500th step in following the rule 'Add 2' is what we *call* 'acting in accord with' this rule.

4. *Formulations and explanations of rules by examples*

The second objection is the reverse of the first in as much as it starts by taking the relation between a general formulation of a rule (e.g. 'Write the next but one number after *every* number') and what accords with it to be wholly perspicuous. Obviously writing '1002' after '1000' is correct. But many formulations of rules are not thus explicitly general. They may take the form of a geometrical pattern which is to be repeated (PI §208) or a segment of an arithmetical progression (e.g. '2, 4, 6, 8, . . .') which is to be extended (PI §§213f.). Here in *formulating* the rule one seems *already to be applying it*:[6] in the simplest case the rule-formulation itself will be incorporated in the product of following the rule, as when a child continues a pattern or fills in the blanks in the sequence '0, 2, 4, 6, . . ., . . ., . . .'. In all these cases it is natural to say that the rule is formulated by giving a sample or series of examples of its applications. While it is transparent that the rule given by '0, 2, 4, 6, 8, 10, . . .' makes contact in language with the first six terms of the series, it may well seem opaque how it makes contact with (and hence determines as correct) the segment '998, 1000, 1002, 1004' of this series.

[6] This idea has a deeply distorting effect on the way one views ostensive definitions. For we are constantly tempted to think that 'This ⟋ is red' is an *application* of 'red' rather than a rule for its use (and indeed, sometimes it is, but then it is not an ostensive definition). See 'Ostensive definition and its ramifications', Volume 1, pp. 180ff., MU pp. 93ff.

This worry is easily transformed into a full-blown objection. A leading idea of modern mathematics (and much philosophy of science) is that any function is underdetermined by a proper subset of pairings of values with arguments. This idea seems immediately applicable to the rule-formulation for writing the series of even integers when it is given in the form '0, 2, 4, 6, 8, 10, . . .'. With sufficient ingenuity, some function can be specified which yields as its values *any* continuation of '0, 2, 4, 6, 8, 10' for the series of arguments 6, 7, 8, ... This seems to imply that writing any sequence of numbers is in accord with the rule formulated by '0, 2, 4, 6, 8, 10, . . .'. From a logical point of view, it appears, the formulations of a rule by examples leaves wide open what acts are in accord with the rule. On some interpretation of the rule *any* continuation is correct (cf. PI §§198, 201). This seems manifestly to refute the idea that such a rule and an act in accord with it make contact in language.

These doubts are infectious. Rules which are *not* formulated by examples are often *explained* by examples, and the argument from underdetermination can then be turned against these rules too in virtue of their explanations. The rule '+ 2' in *Investigations* §185 is to be understood as a general formula equivalent to 'Write the next but one number after every term of the series' (PI §186). But this formula is explained by giving the pupil examples of how to follow it and making him do exercises until he displays mastery of the technique of writing arithmetical progressions. Hence there seems no essential difference between following the rule formulated by examples and following the rule + 2 outside the range of examples and exercises that occur in explaining it. On some interpretation of the rule *as explained, any* continuation of the series outside the range of instruction will accord with it. Unless our understanding of a rule is ineffable (perhaps requiring recourse to intuition or intimation), the rules *must* apparently leave partly undetermined what acts accord with them. And if fundamental rules in terms of which all others are explained (e.g. elementary arithmetical operations) are themselves typically explained by examples (cf. MS 124, 17f.) then there is a perfectly general objection in principle to claiming that a rule and its 'extension' make immediate contact in language. On the contrary, accord would be mediated by interpretations.

The issue has a more general bearing on the argument of the *Investigations*. Family-resemblance concepts are explained by examples. Such explanations are not merely provisional and tolerated *faute de mieux*, but function as rules for the use of the explained words. Explanations of 'proposition', 'number', 'language', 'game', etc. are, in this respect, comparable to the rule-formulation '0, 2, 4, 6, 8, 10, . . .'. Furthermore, it is a general principle of Wittgenstein's argument that an explanation of meaning is itself a *symbol* which can (in certain circumstances) be substituted for what is explained. Hence if the formulation '+2' were explained by the phrase 'the series 0, 2, 4, 6, 8, 10, . . .', then the former can be worth no more than the latter.

The objection is clearly absurd. We do formulate rules by examples; we are taught to respond in definite ways to the demand to continue the series 0, 2, 4, 6, . . . or 1, 3, 7, 13, 21, 31, . . . and we discriminate between what is correct and what incorrect in such cases. We have no qualms about speaking of *the* series 0, 2, 4, 8, 10, . . . or *the* operation of multiplication; and we do not acknowledge that replacing the dots by *any* numbers whatever is in accord with this rule because there is some function which generates such a sequence. And our explanations of general formulations of rules by reference to examples fulfil their function perfectly well. How the absurdity is to be defused, however, is less obvious.

Several misguided responses are alluring. One might have recourse to the mind as the determinant of accord with a rule. In giving a rule (whether by a general formulation *or* by examples) one means the pupil to act thus-and-so (to write '1002' after '1000'). Accord with a rule is a matter of fitting what one meant (PI §§186ff.). This either involves a mythology of acts of meaning, or else presupposes what it is supposed to explain, since what one meant the pupil to do is precisely what the expression of the rule means (cf. Exg. §§186ff.).

As an alternative one might suggest that in giving the rule one has a certain *interpretation* in mind, so that an act is in accord with a rule if it fits the intended interpretation. This is defective. First, it drives a wedge between what is said and what is meant. Is the correct interpretation of 'Add 2' *different* from what is said in uttering 'Add 2'? Secondly, it is only of any use if one can make sense of ineffable intentions, for if the intended interpretation could be expressed, then the mind would drop out of the account and accord would boil down to a grammatical relation between the act and the *preferred* formulation of the rule. Finally, if one has qualms about the relation of the act to the rule, one must have equal qualms about the relation of the act to an interpretation of the rule.

One might suppose that *logical* underdetermination of the accord of acts with a rule is compensated for by *empirical determination*. This might be characterized as psychological. Though the rule-formulation '0, 2, 4, 6, 8, 10, . . .' (and '+2', if it is thus explained) logically leaves open what counts as the correct continuation, no continuation other than '12, 14, 16, 18' (etc.) ever crosses our minds. This, and only this, is what 'comes natural' to us. Alternatively the determination might be thought to be social rather than psychological; not human nature, but social pressure and community habit singles out a unique 'correct' continuation out of a myriad of logically possible ones. This pair of manoeuvres is likewise incoherent, representing an internal relation as an external one, and trying to cement the relata with socio-psychological glue (see 'Agreement in definitions, judgements and form of life', pp. 237ff.).

Wittgenstein's own response locates the fundamental misunderstanding at the point from which the whole chain of reasoning takes off. A symbol that is used to formulate a rule is understood only if it is taken to *be* a rule-formulation, indeed only if it is understood to formulate *a particular rule*. When we give someone a pattern to copy or ask him to construct a series in accord with the rule '0, 2, 4, 6, 8, . . .', we do not judge him to have understood the instruction merely because he looks at it, or merely if he understands the numerals '0', '2', '4', '6', '8' *irrespective of what he does*. His understanding (or lack of it) is manifest in his actions, in what he copies out or writes down, in how he employs the rule-formulation as a standard of correctness. It is a criterion for a decorator's understanding a sample as a rule for painting a frieze with a certain pattern that he carry out the decoration *thus*. 'Dieses Muster, *so* aufgefasst, ist nur *so* fortzusetzen' ('This sample, understood *in this way*, must be continued *in this way*') (MS 165, 85). It is a criterion for *mis*understanding the rule '0, 2, 4, 6, 8, . . .' that someone write '12, 20, 45' as the next three terms. If he understands the rule, he *must* write '10, 12, 14' as the next terms. There is no mysterious necessitation here (he might say that he has better things to do!). The 'must' marks the determination of a concept. To write anything other than '10, 12, 14' here is not what is called following the rule '0, 2, 4, 6, 8, . . .' (cf. MS 124, 17f.), and hence too is a criterion for not understanding it (PI §201). The same holds with respect to giving a general formulation of a rule that is (if necessary) further explained by examples.

The apparent logical gulf between a rule and its 'extension' arises from the mistaken assumption that understanding a rule is at least partly independent of how it is projected on to actions. But however it is formulated or explained, a rule is understood only if it is correctly projected. To be ignorant or mistaken about what acts are in accord with it is to be ignorant or mistaken about what the rule is. To understand a rule *is* to know what acts accord with it and what violate it (just as to understand a proposition is to know what is the case if it is true). This connection of concepts is completely distorted in comparing the understanding of a rule formulated by examples with the concoction of a hypothesis to fit a set of observational data in science. The data may be apprehended and the descriptions of the data be understood independently of accepting or even understanding the hypothesis. This is an essential feature of inductive reasoning, and it has no analogue in the case of the relation between a rule (whether given by examples or not) and the acts that accord with it.

5. *Interpretations, fitting and grammar*

We have clarified Wittgenstein's account of the accord of an act with a rule by reference to his dissolution of the puzzles about the 'harmony between language and reality'. We shall now further exploit this exegetical strategy to illuminate Wittgenstein's observations about *interpretations* in *Investigations* §§198, 201 and his remarks about 'belonging' (internal relations) and 'fitting'.

We noted (p. 82) that when puzzled about how a rule can determine what must be done to act in accord with it, one is tempted to invoke an interpretation to mediate between the rule and its extension. The interpretation, thus conceived, will infallibly determine what to do. Just before the original draft of *Investigations* §198, Wittgenstein sketched this idea:

> Ich will aber eine 'Auffassung' statuieren (etwas wie die alter 'Proposition'), die die Reihe so bestimmt, wie eine unfehlbare Maschine, durch die ein Band läuft.
> So also, dass nur diese Fortsetzung zu dieser Auffassung passt. (MS 165, 86f.)

> (I wish, however, to construct an 'interpretation' (something similar to the old-fashioned 'proposition') that determines the series just as an infallible machine does through which a strip runs.
> In such a way then that only this continuation fits this interpretation.)

An interpretation appears to be the only possible bridge between a rule and the acts that accord with it, e.g. between the rule + 2 and what is to be done after writing '1000'.

This suggestion runs into immediate difficulties. For it is now supposed that the act of accord will fit the interpretation. But this 'fitting' was precisely what was to be explained by the interposition of an interpretation. Not only is it not thus explained, but further, 'Whatever I do can, on some interpretation, be brought into accord with the rule.' (PI §198) But if 'anything goes', there *is* no following of a rule at all! This move was anticipated earlier in the *Investigations* in the discussion of grasping the meaning of a word at a stroke. We might think that what we understand when we hear a familiar word cannot be the whole use of the word; so what comes to mind must be something like a picture, which will *fit* the use. And this is precisely analogous to an interpretation.

Well, suppose that a picture does come before your mind when you hear the word 'cube', say the drawing of a cube. In what sense can this picture fit or fail to fit a use of the word 'cube'? – Perhaps you say: 'It's quite simple; – if that picture occurs to me and I point to a triangular prism for instance, and say it is a cube, then this use of the word doesn't fit the picture. – But doesn't it fit? I have purposely so chosen the example that it is quite easy to imagine a *method of projection* according to which the picture does fit after all. (PI §139)

Applied directly to the idea that an interpretation mediates between a rule and what accords with it, this argument constitutes a *reductio ad absurdum* of that idea, which is explicit in §201;[7] for then

no course of action could be determined by a rule, because every course of action can be made out to accord with a rule. The answer was: if everything can be made out to accord with the rule, then it can also be made out to conflict with it. And so there would be neither accord nor conflict here. (PI §201)

Hence, of course, 'any interpretation still hangs in the air along with what it interprets, and cannot give it any support. Interpretations by themselves do not determine meaning.' (PI §198)

The analogy which Wittgenstein explicitly drew in MS 165, 86 (above, p. 98) between an interpretation which will infallibly determine what 'fits' and what he called 'the old-fashioned "proposition"' is revealing. Moore, for example, argued that 'proposition' is

a name for what is before your mind, when you not only hear or read but *understand* a sentence.[8] It is, in short, the meaning of a sentence – what is expressed or conveyed by a sentence: and is, therefore, utterly different from the sentence itself – from the mere words.[9]

Wittgenstein criticized this conception that a proposition is a shadow which uniquely fits the fact that verifies what is stated (BB 35ff.). This in turn connects up *indirectly*[10] with his criticisms of the picture theory of meaning which, as we have seen, gave a metaphysical explanation of the 'harmony between language and reality', the 'fit' between sentences-in-use and facts. Following this indirect route will lead us back to the discussion in the *Investigations* from a new and revealing angle.

One source of the conception of a proposition as a shadowy intermediary between a sentence and a fact (which will ensure that the sentence pictures precisely *this* fact) is that in some cases of reading or hearing a sentence an image which more or less corresponds to it comes to mind. This image, which is, as it were, a picture of what the sentence says, is of a kind which we understand immediately. It stands in need of no interpretation, the intention of the picture *cannot be questioned* (BB 36). Moreover, it is a 'picture' by similarity – or so it seems to us. It is tempting, when we reflect upon the fit between a sentence we understand and what it describes, to think that the sentence and fact (if it is a

---

[7] But already embedded in one line in the original draft of §198 in MS 165, 88.

[8] We do not know whether Wittgenstein had Moore in mind. But note the *precise* parallel with PI §139.

[9] G. E. Moore, *Some Main Problems of Philosophy* (Allen and Unwin, London, 1953), p. 259.

[10] Indirectly, because Wittgenstein never succumbed to the temptation to reify propositions.

fact) are cemented by such a proposition, which is a kind of shadow of the fact and fits it perfectly.

The *Blue Book* blocks this drift of thought by drawing attention to the fact that not all pictures, portrayals or representations are representative in virtue of similarity. There are different methods of representation, different ways of projecting things into pictures, and conversely different methods of reading pictures. 'If we keep in mind the possibility of a picture, which, though correct, has no similarity with its object, the interpolation of a shadow between the sentence and reality loses all point.' (BB 37) For while a picture, which is not a picture by similarity, needs a method of projection to be a picture of what it is, it needs no intermediate entity to connect it to what it depicts. For the method of projection is not such an intermediate entity. It is rather the rule-governed *use* of a symbolism. So the sentence *itself* can be viewed as a picture which stands in need of no shadowy entity to stand between it and what it depicts. To understand it involves mastery of the *technique of projection*, not a grasp of a mediating entity, a 'proposition' thus conceived. What holds of sentences applies similarly to rules and their formulation. No interpretation is *necessary* to bind a rule to its extension; indeed, none is possible until the rule has a certain use, i.e. until it is employed as a standard of correctness. For only then is there anything to interpret! (A signpost is not just a piece of wood pointing in a certain direction.) Following a rule is a practice (PI §201), a matter of *using* rule-formulations in normative activities (see 'Rules and grammar', pp. 41ff.) as standards of, and guides to, action.

The picture theory of meaning did not reify propositions (if anything, it invoked states of affairs as shadows to mediate between sentences and the facts they fit). But it is noteworthy, and relevant to our concerns, that Wittgenstein later remarked that in the *Tractatus* he had confused the method of projection with the lines of projection.[11] What he meant was this: in the *Tractatus* the propositional picture was conceived to be connected to the objects in reality by means of correlations or lines of projection ('the feelers of the picture's elements, with which the picture touches reality' (TLP 2.1515)). These correlations of the picture's elements with objects Wittgenstein called 'the pictorial relationship'. It was this, he thought, that ensured the connection between picture and reality: the picture, by means of these projection lines, reaches right out to reality (TLP 2.1511). Conceiving thus of the elementary proposition, he explicitly included the pictorial relationship (the lines of projection on to objects) in the picture (TLP 2.1513). This, together with the metaphysics

---

[11] He said this in a discussion with R. Rhees; see P. Winch, 'Introduction: The Unity of Wittgenstein's Philosophy', in *Studies in the Philosophy of Wittgenstein*, ed. P. Winch (Routledge and Kegan Paul, London, 1969), p. 12.

of logical atomism and the doctrine of analysis into simple names, appeared to explain the fit, the metaphysical harmony, between language and reality. It was of this idea that he remarked 'The lines of projection might be called "the connection between the picture and what it depicts"; but so too might the technique of projection.' (Z §219) If we compare the method or technique of projection to lines of projection,

This comparison conceals the fact that the picture *plus* the projection lines leave open various methods of application; it makes it look as if what is depicted, even if it does not exist in fact, is determined by the picture and the projection lines in an ethereal manner; every bit as determined, that is to say, as if it did exist. (It is 'determined give or take a yes or no'.) In that case what we may call 'picture' is the blueprint [of an object to be made] plus the method of its application. And we now imagine the method as something which is attached to the blueprint whether or not it is used. (One can 'describe' an application even if it doesn't exist.) (PG 213)

What connects the picture with what it pictures is the way in which it is used in practice, how it gets compared with reality, or, in the case of the blueprint, how the artefact gets matched against the blueprint (the manner in which the blueprint is used as a standard for the correct production of the object). But when we are puzzled about the fit or harmony between proposition and fact, expectation and fulfilment, rule and what accords with it, we are tempted to assimilate the method of projection *into* the picture, as if the method of projection were lines of projection 'reaching right out' to reality and ensuring the fit. And we take it that the proposition, expectation or rule must include such 'projection lines' in some form or other, otherwise they would not fit the fact, event, or act which they do fit. But this is wrong; for here one imagines

that the difference between proposition and reality is ironed out by the lines of projection belonging to the picture, the thought, and that no further room is left for a method of application, but only for agreement and disagreement. (PG 214)[12]

Yet the picture *together with the lines of projection* can be variously applied. And this is precisely the point made in *Investigations* §141:

Suppose, however, that not merely the picture of the cube, but also the method of projection comes before our mind? – How am I to imagine this? – Perhaps I see before me a scheme showing the method of projection: say a picture of two cubes

---

[12] This conception is intimately related to the idea that ostensive definitions infallibly link language with reality. The system of ostensive definitions seems to supply the lines of projection once and for all for all propositions. It is this philosophical confusion that is the target of the notorious (and widely misinterpreted) remark that an ostensive definition can be variously interpreted (and misunderstood) in every case (PI §28).

connected by lines of projection – But does this really get me any farther? Can't I now imagine different applications of this scheme too? (PI §141, cf. Exg.)

In the case of a rule and what accords with it, the analogue of the projection lines is an interpretation. For the interpretation is meant, like the projection lines, to carry us infallibly from the formulation of the rule to what accords with it. But an interpretation gets us no closer to an application than we were before. It is merely an alternative formulation of the rule, another expression in the symbolism which paraphrases the initial one. It too must be *used*, and different ways of using it are imaginable. It does not *fit* the 'extension' of the rule any *better* (more ineluctably) than the initial rule-formulation.

Of course, one can describe a method of application (and, in a sense, an interpretation is such a description). But this description is again a symbol – which can be variously applied:

You may say: I count the projection lines as part of the picture – but not the method of projection.

You may of course also say: I count a *description* of a method of projection as part of the picture. (PG 214)

If one wishes to conceive of the method of projection as a bridge between symbol and what it symbolizes, between proposition and fact or rule and what accords with it, at any rate, 'it is a bridge which isn't built until the application is made.' (PG 213) For a description of a bridge is not a bridge! So 'any interpretation still hangs in the air along with what it interprets.' (PI §198)

The connection between a rule and the acts which accord with it is effected (cf. PI §197) in the practice of using the rule in training, teaching and instructing, in the regular employment of the rule as a standard of correctness (PI §198), in the practice of following it (PI §202), and in the explanations and justifications of actions by reference to it. Our understanding of a rule is not an interpretation of it: nor in understanding a rule do we typically lay hold of an interpretation. Rather, our understanding is exhibited in what we *call* 'following the rule' and 'contravening the rule' in actual cases (PI §201). The rule and what accords with it, like the proposition and what makes it true, or an expectation and what fulfils it, are internally related. But this requires no metaphysical explanations or interposition of mediating entities. They make contact in grammar, sometimes directly or transparently (e.g. in the case of the proposition (sentence in use) that p and the fact that p, where the same expression is visibly used in both cases) and sometimes indirectly, as in the case of the rule '0, 2, 4, 6, 8, . . .' and writing '. . . 1000, 1002, 1004'. That is what we *call* 'adding 2 to 1000', what we call 'applying the rule "0, 2, 4, 6, 8, . . ."' (i.e. the rule for the series of even integers) at the 500th step'. If

'1002' were *not* the right thing to write at this point, this series would not *be* what we call 'the series of even integers'.

Because these relations are internal, it is wrong to talk of two things *fitting* here, and misleading to talk of a harmony between language and reality. Rather, one might say that they *belong* to each other (PI §136). In the remainder of the above quoted remark (p. 98), *à propos* the idea that only *this* continuation of '+ 2' fits this interpretation, Wittgenstein observed:

In der Wirklichkeit aber sind es nicht zwei Dinge die hier zusammenpassen. Man könnte aber sagen: Du bist durch Deine Erziehung so konditioniert/ /eingestellt/ /, dass Du immer ohne Bedenken etwas bestimmtes als das Passende erklärt. Etwas was mit dem übereinstimmt was Andere für das Passende erklären. (MS 165, 87)

(But in fact there aren't here two things that fit together. But one could say: You are so conditioned//prepared//through your upbringing that without reflecting you always declare some particular thing as what fits, something which agrees with what others declare to be what fits.)

The relata of internal relations, *appropriately specified*, belong to each other in the sense that the very identity of each is bound up with the other. Hence one cannot grasp one without grasping the other; and the 'cannot' here is *grammatical*, i.e. *there is no such thing*. One cannot understand the rule + 2 and *deny* that '1002, 1004, . . .' is part of this series; for to deny that would show (be a criterion) that one does *not* understand the rule. The rule determines this (and nothing else) to be what follows '1000' (PI §189). But one could also say that people are so educated to use the formula '+ 2' that they all write down the same sequence of numbers. (And in *that* sense the letter 'L' *fits* on to the series of letters of the alphabet up to 'K', and 'true' and 'false' can be said to *fit* propositions (PI §137).) For given our education in arithmetic, for us the order 'Add 2' completely determines every step from one number in the series to the next; that is how we use the sign '+ 2' (PI §189).

6. *Further misunderstandings*

Care is necessary in handling Wittgenstein's own metaphors. If it is wrong to say that rule and what accords with it fit each other, is there then a gap or gulf between them, one that is bridged only in practice, in the application of the rule? He certainly raised questions built upon this metaphor. How can one make the transition from a rule to its application (MS 180(a), 75; MS 129, 117 and 182)? How can one jump the gap between the two (MS 180(a), 68)? Do rules by themselves not hang in the void, aloof from their applications (PI §198; MS 180(a), 75), leaving us in the lurch when it comes to *doing* something (MS 180(a), 68f.)? This line of thought leads in the direction of a kind of logical existentialism. Rules cannot bridge the gulf separating them from their applications, so pure acts of will are required. One is tempted to say that a new *decision* is necessary at each application of a rule (PI §186).

Striking as these pictures are, they are, of course, *not* what Wittgenstein was trying to defend, but expressions of certain misunderstandings that he was trying to resolve. There is no bridge between a rule and what accords with it, for there is no gulf to bridge. There is, on the one hand, the expression (formulation) of a rule, and on the other a description of what is called acting in accord with this rule. These are grammatically related. No bridging apparatus, whether fabricated by metaphysics or supplied by social services, is either necessary or possible in order to connect what cannot intelligibly be sundered. It is similarly misconceived to think that it makes sense to ask 'How can I make the transition from grasping a rule to acting in accord with it?' For to grasp a rule is to understand it, and understanding a rule is not an act but an ability manifested in following the rule. There is no question of making a transition from doing one thing to doing another, but rather of performing acts that manifest (and are criteria for) an ability. It would be patently ridiculous to worry about the question 'How can I make the leap from being able to add numbers to actually adding 58 and 67?' It is no less absurd to address the question how one can make a transition from an understood rule to its applications (cf. MS 180(a), 68f.). For if this is not a version of the previous question, it must be about the transformation of a rule into descriptions of acts which are in accord with it. But this is a straightforward matter of grammar, not a mystery calling for blind decisions or courageous leaps into the void.

Potential misunderstanding no doubt lies in the claim that a rule and what accords with it, like an expectation and what fulfils it, are internally related. We have found it illuminating to employ this expression in this context in order to bring out the similarities between the puzzles about rules and acts which accord with them and the questions Wittgenstein associated with the apparent 'harmony between language and reality'. But one must beware of mystification here (a danger which explains why he was chary, in his later writings, of using the expression 'internal relation' and preferred to talk of 'grammatical' relations, connections or propositions). That A and B are internally related implies that it is inconceivable that they should not be thus related. And we may add that it is of the *essence* of A and B to be thus related. At this point our anti-metaphysical hackles may rise. But no metaphysical mysteries are involved here. Like everything apparently metaphysical, internal relations are to be found in the grammar of the language (cf. Z §55). An internal relation between two objects is not a relation between them as an external relation is. It is not as if there are between A and B various relations, some internal, some external and we must investigate which of them are which (LFM 78f.). That would be absurd, for one could not identify A and B *as* A and B, i.e. as subsumable under those concepts, unless one understood that they are thus related (compare the application of Leibniz's Law in the different cases). One might therefore say that an internal relation is a relation between two *concepts* (LFM 73). Consequently a sentence asserting an internal relation between two things (e.g. 'writing "1002" after "1000" is in accord with the rule "+ 2" at the 500th step') never expresses an empirical proposition and is not a description of two objects. It is rather the expression of a grammatical rule (e.g. that instead of 'He acted in accord with the rule "+ 2" at the 500th step' one may say 'He wrote "1002" after "1000"') and could be said to be constructing concepts (cf. LFM 73). An internal relation *is* a shadow of grammar, and can as well be called a grammatical relation. The statement of an internal relation is a grammatical statement, a norm of description.

A different kind of misunderstanding stems from failure to bring into proper focus Wittgenstein's explanation of the grammatical relation between a rule and what accords with it. For looked at wrongly it may seem that he is propounding a deeply distasteful form of irrationalism. How do I know how to apply a rule, how to continue a pattern, how to extend a series in accord with a rule? 'If that means "Have I reasons?" the answer is: my reasons will soon give out. And then I shall act, without reasons.' (PI §§211, 217 and Exg.)

It should now be evident that Wittgenstein's remarks about the terminus of justification are not intimations of a bizarre form of logical existentialism. What he wrote was that my reasons will soon give out, not that I have none. But when I have given my reasons, I need not and typically do not have reasons for holding the reasons I have given to be reasons. For I will quickly reach bedrock, exhaust all justifications, and say 'This is simply what I do' or 'This is what is called doing thus-and-so.' But this does not mean that I have no justification for what I do. On the contrary, I cite the rule I am supposed to be following as a justification. It is the pattern for my actions. Nor is any justification *missing*, for it makes no sense to *justify* a grammatical nexus.

Hence too the remark 'I follow the rule blindly' signifies not the blindness of the sleep walker but the certitude of one who knows his way. I know *exactly* what to do. I do not choose, after deliberation, for I have no doubts at all. The rule 'always tells us the same, and we do what it tells us' (PI §223), 'we look to the rule for instruction and *do something*, without appealing to anything else for guidance' (PI §228), 'it is my last court of appeal for the way I am to go' (PI §230), 'I draw its consequences as a matter of course.' (PI §238) These remarks do not signify yawning chasms of irrationality beneath our rule-governed activities. On the contrary, they point towards the firm grounds of grammar and of our practices of using language. To be sure, these have no support, but they no more need support than the globe itself.

SECTION 189

1   Paragraph (a) (which in PPI occurs as the last paragraph of §188) links this remark with the previous discussion. It seemed unclear how the order '+ 2' (the algebraic formula) could fix what counts as compliance at the 500th step (§185). But the attempt to provide a standard of correctness by appeal to something more, e.g. what the teacher *meant* by the expression he uttered, proved a fruitless detour (§§186–8). The steps in the expansion of the series are *not* 'really' already taken in shadowy form by an act of meaning (§188). Consequently the determination of correctness (or incorrectness) seems to have evaporated; which seems absurd. Hence the interlocutor responds in bewilderment 'Are the steps then *not* determined by the formula?' (for surely, not *anything* goes!). W.'s reply is that this question rests on a misunderstanding of the sentence 'the steps are determined by the formula.' For it presupposes that the formula determines the steps *somehow*, that it *makes* these right, those wrong by some logical mechanism.

    The sentence 'the steps are determined by the formula' may be used to state facts about normative behaviour. People may be trained so to use an algebraic formula that they uniformly work out the same value for each number as argument, just as at a more elementary level pupils are drilled to produce invariant answers to simple addition problems. Such people *will all know what they are to do in response* to orders framed in terms of simple algebraic formulae such as '$y = x^2$'. For them the steps to be taken are completely determined by the formula – 'by the formula' because no further instructions are needed. (Just as what a driver is to do is determined by traffic signals, signposts, etc.) By contrast, children who have not yet mastered these techniques will not know what they are to do. For them, we might say, the steps to be taken are not determined by the formula. Whether, for a given person or group, a formula does or does not determine the steps to be taken, is an empirical question. It does so if there is a *normal* pattern of response to it (cf. §141).

    However, the sentence may also be used to state a grammatical truth. Against the background of a general practice of algebraic calculation we can differentiate two kinds of formulae, exemplified by '$y = x^2$', and '$y \neq x^2$'. The former, but not the latter, may be said to determine the number y for a given value of x. That a given formula does (or does not) determine a value for each argument is a statement about the type of formula; not an empirical truth about behaviour, but a truth of grammar.

The question whether a given formula determines a unique value for every argument makes sense only in rather special circumstances, e.g. when it is an open question whether some formula (perhaps only obliquely characterized as 'the formula written down there') is of the one kind or of the other. But to ask whether a *paradigm* of a formula which determines a unique value for any argument (e.g. $y = x^2$) is of the one kind or the other only makes sense in testing whether a pupil understands this use of the verb 'to determine' or in demanding that he prove that x has only one square for any real number. Outside such contexts it has as little sense as 'Am I here now?' or 'Is this ↗ [pointing at a ripe tomato in good light] red?'

The interlocutor's question 'Are the steps not determined by the formula?' was not an inquiry into the uniformity of people's behavioural responses to the order to expand the series from the formula. But the question 'Does the formula "$a_0 = 0$; $a_{n+1} = a_n + 2$" determine the steps to be taken?' is not an open one. As a question about the *type of formula*, it is *trivially* true that this formula determines a unique number for every step. But the interlocutor did not mean this either. His mistake was to think that there is some sense of 'determine the steps' in which, if a formula (rule) determines the steps, it is the formula which *makes* these steps correct, as if the *formula* takes the steps in advance of us (cf. §188 and RFM 45f.). But this is confused. Nothing *makes* it correct; it *is* correct, in accord with the rule. This is what we *call* 'the correct application of the formula (rule) . . .'; the series of even integers is partly *defined* by this sequence (cf. RFM 37). A misconception of 'determination' fosters philosophical illusions (exemplified by Russell and Frege).

1.1   'by the algebraic formula': the rule-formulations '+ 1', '+ 2', etc., are here called algebraic formulae. (cf. Vol. XIV, 7: 'Etwa "+ 2" oder ein anderer algebraischer Ausdruck' ('say "+ 2" or another algebraic formula').) Although they do not contain letters, in this context these symbols are not used to name positive integers (as they are in the question 'what is the sum of + 2, − 4, + 1 and 0?'). The philosophical issue here discussed would be unaffected if '+ 2' were replaced by the recursion formula '$a_0 = 0$, $a_{n+1} = a_n + 2$'.

2   (i) The failure of the psychologistic explanation of what 'determines' how to continue the series '+ 2' after 1000 leads to a Platonist variant. This form of determination *seems* to be even more rigid than a causal or physical one.

How queer: It looks as if a physical (mechanical) form of guidance could misfire and let in something unforeseen, but not a rule! As if a rule were, so to speak, the only reliable form of guidance, But what does guidance not allowing a movement, and a rule's not allowing it, consist in? – How does one know the one and how the other? (Z §296)

To which the correct answer is that guidance not allowing a movement consists in causal necessitation, as the rails guide the train in *this* direction, not allowing it to go *that* way. But a rule's not allowing a movement *necessitates nothing but the applicability or non-applicability of a description* (RFM 328f.).

MS 124, 201 links the normative and mechanical pictures of necessitation, presciently describing the philosophical illusions which would only reach full flower in the computer age.

'Die Regel bestimmt, was ich auf jeder Stufe zu schreiben habe.' Das kann man so auffassen wie: 'Die Konstruktion des Mechanismus bestimmt die Bewegung dieses Teils für jede Lage der Kurbel.' Der Mensch ist also//hier//die Maschine, die mit Hilfe der Regel, des Befehls, der die Regel enthielt, der Abrichtung im Befolgen von Befehlen (etc.) gezwungen wurde, auf dieser Stufe *dies* zu schreiben (*so* zu handeln).

('The rule determines what I have to write at every step.' One can conceive of this as follows: 'The construction of the mechanism determines the movement of this part for every position of the crank.' So//here//the person is the machine which with the help of the rule, the order which contained the rule, the training in following orders, etc., is forced at *this* step to write *this* (to behave in *this* way).)

In this picture following a rule is assimilated to being causally determined to produce just *this* answer (to write '1002'). But the rule is not the cause of our producing this answer, it is the ground. And no cause could determine this answer as the *right* or *correct* answer. So we think of the rule as determining what occurs at the *n*th step in its application, quite independently of anyone being ordered to follow it. And *then* we think of this rule, thus determining its consequences, as existing in our mind. And in this way, it can, it seems, determine what we do when ordered to apply it. But we forget, W. concludes (MS 124, 202), that this rule-in-my-mind must itself be called forth in signs, and that this pattern has to be projected (in the mind). But if my mind can follow this sign, why can't my hand?

(ii) RFM 45 explores the idea that the rule determines its consequences, so that all *we* have to do is infer what is already there, independently of us (cf. Exg. §188, 2.1(iii)). But examine first cases where one really can say that one determines the transitions someone is to make in expanding a series, e.g. where we write down in another notation the very segment he has to write down and he has only to translate it, or where we write it down faintly and he has only to trace it, or where we dictate what he has to write down. Here, especially in the latter two cases, we would say that what the pupil has to write down is already there, in advance of his writing. A sure way of determining what steps someone is to make, is to make them first.

But when we teach pupils a technique of rule-application, we determine the transitions in a quite different sense. Here we succeed, i.e. have taught the technique to the pupils, when they go on to steps that we have never demonstrated for them, and yet we can predict with certainty that they *will take* the steps that they *are to take*. Here, we might say, they are 'determined' by training and exercises. And we might naturally, but wholly misleadingly, say 'the steps are already taken and he is just writing them down'. But this 'already taken' means no more than that in this calculus, these steps *count as the correct steps* to take in performing this operation. One might say, towards the end of a game of chess, 'There is no need to go on. It is checkmate in four. The steps are already taken.'

(iii) RFM 81 (cf. LFM 28f.) when discussing logical compulsion employs the distinction between two kinds of order, one that determines uniquely what counts as compliance, one that does not.

(iv) Vol. XIV, 160f. follows up a similar discussion of 'determination' with the interlocutor's querying, 'But do you want to say that the expression "+ 2" leaves you in doubt over what you should write after 234?' No, W. responds, I will answer, without reflecting, '236'. But just because of that it is superfluous to suppose that anything was determined in advance. That I have no doubt about how to answer does not mean that the question was already answered beforehand.

2.1   'The steps are determined by the formula': it is exceedingly important to realize that this is not wrong. It is only wrong under the aegis of a misunderstanding of determination.

> When you get the picture of 'being determined' out of your mind, then you get rid of the puzzle. – But still one can say the algebraic expression determines his actions – and perfectly correctly. But now you have got rid of the cramp. (LSD 24)

SECTION 190

1   This dovetails the discussions of how a formula is meant and of the formula's determining the steps to be taken. One can indeed say that what is meant by the formula determines which steps are to be taken. But correctly understood, this will not serve the purpose which the wayward interlocutor had in mind. For what the teacher *meant* by the formula, e.g. that he meant that the pupil should write '1002, 1004, . . .', is not the content of his past (or present) acts of meaning, but of the techniques of arithmetic which he has mastered. What he meant by the formula (and hence also what he meant the pupil to write) is what is, in general, meant by the formula, what the formula means. The criteria for what is meant are impersonal, viz. the established use of the formula and

the standing procedures for teaching its use. What is meant by '+ 2' is what is explained in standard explanations of its meaning, viz. in giving examples of its application and getting the pupil to do exercises (as in §185).

Bearing this in mind, as well as the analysis of 'determines', (b) provides a context in which it has a point to say 'What is meant by the formula determines which steps are to be taken.' Faced with someone using a sign unknown to us, we might conjecture what he means by it. If by '$x!2$' he means x^2, then what he means is a formula which determines each step to be taken; in particular it determines, for example, the value 9 for the argument 3. That is the nature of the formula. If he means $2x$, then again what he meant by the formula determines which (different) steps are to be taken (whereas if he means $\pm 2x$, it does not). How then does he manage to mean the one formula rather than another? Not *any* how! In particular, not by any special acts of meaning. One does not mean x^2 (as opposed to $2x$) by performing anything. But, of course, what one means is manifest in how one uses the formula, and is given by one's explanation of meaning, viz. to the question 'What do you mean by "$x!2$"?', one replies 'I mean x^2.'

(c) dryly concludes the discussion: *this* is how one's meaning such-and-such can determine the steps in advance. But of course this is not what the interlocutor was hankering for. He had thought to locate an explanation in the mind by way of acts of meaning which predetermine the correct steps, or, failing that, to locate explanatory machinery in mathematics by way of a formula (or perhaps the 'sense' of the formula) *making* such-and-such steps the ones that really *follow* (and that is *why* our inferences are correct (RFM 44f.)).

1.1   (i) 'wie die Formel gemeint wird': perhaps better translated: 'What is meant by the formula'. Note the impersonal form. The established manner of using the formula is the criterion for how it is, in general, meant. The meaning of an expression is its use; hence how it is used is the criterion for how people who have mastered its use mean it. An explicit connection between what someone means by a sentence and how he explains it (in particular what he would take as verifying the proposition expressed) is drawn in PI §353 (cf. PI §540).

(ii) 'wie wir sie ständig gebrauchen': how we standardly use it, the established way in which we use it.

(iii) 'Wie macht man es, mit . . .': 'How does one do this *meaning* the one thing or the other by . . .' or 'How does one manage to mean the one thing or the other by . . . .' The irony is lost in the existing translation.

1   Here once again the interlocutor manifests his unease that something crucial has been omitted from W.'s account. §190 argued that *explaining* what a formula means is specifying what is *meant* by it, and that the steps of applying the formula are in this way determined in advance. But of course the explanation itself may be misunderstood and misapplied, however full it is. Consequently, W. seems to allow no scope for the possibility of instantaneous understanding. For if there is to be any such thing as grasping the whole use of a word at a stroke, then it seems that there must be something to seize hold of other than an explanation which is only *fallibly* connected with the established pattern of correct use; there must be something that effects a harder, more rigid form of determination. Unless an explanation is merely a pointer at something else, the phenomenon of understanding in an instant becomes apparently baffling. For how can the whole pattern of use of a word be packed into an explanation such as 'This $\nearrow$ is red', 'By "$x!2$" I mean x^2'? And how could one grasp in an instant something like the whole use of an expression (the applications of a rule)? 'It is as if', the interlocutor claims; for he thinks that we do not really grasp the whole use in an instant (how can the use, 'which is extended in time' (§138), be grasped in an instant?). So what we grasp, when we understand a word, must be something that 'contains' the whole use in some special way, something from which the applications of the expression will unfold automatically, inexorably. But then equally the suggestion that how an expression is *meant* is fully explained by an explanation of its meaning must be wrong. Rather such an explanation must be an indirect means of enabling one to grasp something from which its use will unwind.

Just as the interlocutor's conception of a formula's *determining* the steps to be taken involved a mythology of symbolism and a misapprehension of this use of 'determines', so too his conception of *grasping the use of a word at a stroke* involves a parallel mythologizing and misapprehension. His scruples, manifest in his prefix 'It is as if', are misplaced (cf. Exg. §§195, 197). We do indeed typically grasp the whole use of a word at a stroke when given an explanation. In what sense? In the sense that given the explanation, one can typically go on to use the expression correctly, in what is called 'accord' with the explanation. But this mundane 'grasping at a stroke' will not satisfy the interlocutor. He hankers for something that *generates* or *necessitates* or *determines* just those applications of an expression that constitute its whole use, but which cannot be contained in any mere explanation.

But, W. responds, he has no model for this super understanding-at-a-stroke, no genuine object of comparison to give his philosophical simile

('It is as if') genuine content. All his simile really expresses is a certain kind of philosophical craving. He craves for a special kind of grasp of an expression which will bridge the apparent gulf between an explanation of the meaning (the rule for its use) and its applications, a kind of understanding of a symbol in which we grasp, as it were, the spirit of the symbol which hovers over all its applications. This is the confusion in which he is enmeshed. For there is no such thing. His craving is not for the moon but for moonshine. The life of a sign lies in its use; our immediate understanding of a sign does not consist of our 'laying hold, by means of our logical faculties' of its sense, which is a sort of logical machine, but of our mastery of the technique of its application.

The illusion that we can grasp the whole use of an expression in a 'much more direct sense' than the mundane one stems from the crossing of different pictures (cf. Exg. §191, 2.1). An example of such 'crossing of pictures' was in effect given in §189, where the interlocutor's misconception of 'determining the steps to be taken' derives from crossing the empirical sense of 'determines' with the grammatical sense. Here, too, we project our inexorable commitment to using an explanation of the meaning of a sign as a standard of correct use on to the explanation. Then it seems to us that the rule for the correct use must inexorably determine the use, contain the use, in advance of our using the sign. And when we see that our ordinary explanations fail to meet this metaphysical ideal, we are inclined to view them as ersatz explanations which point towards the real explanation, the genuine rule which determines the use of the expression. And it must be this which explains our feeling that when we understand it is 'as if we could grasp the whole use of the word in an instant'. (A further elaboration of the 'crossing of different pictures' is given in §§193–4.)

1.1   'mit einem Schlag': 'in a flash' smacks too much of 'a flash of understanding', i.e. a sudden insight, whereas what is at issue is not insight but *instant* understanding. So better 'in an instant' or 'at a stroke'.

2   (i) Vol. XV, 35 contains an early version. The context is a discussion of 'the hardness of the logical *must*' now to be found in RFM 84. This is followed (as in RFM) by PI §193. Then W. examines the remark 'Don't think the machine has, in some mysterious way, got its movements within it.' One appears to be telling someone who does so think that he is labouring under an *illusion*. But this is not so, even though the form of words suggests it. It is, rather, a nonsense. Through a comparison (between a machine and a machine-as-symbol) one is led to say that the further applications of a symbol are inexorably determined – inexorably, that is, relative to any empirical determination. But this is a confusion not an illusion, since one knows of no such thing as this super-inexorability; one 'has no model for it'. One is merely inclined to use this

expression. This remark is followed by PI §191. W. then compares this confusion with the absurdity of 'The metre-rule is unalterable, no matter how the lengths of things change.'

(ii) LFM 198 makes a similar point about the idea of logical machinery. W. wants to say that there is no such thing. And this seems absurd, since one is inclined to say that one must know what it is whose existence one is denying. So too with the idea of the super-rigidity of logic. What must be done is to show that these misleading expressions, which we are inclined to invoke, are meaningless, that the phrase 'logical machinery' does not signify a kind of machinery that happens to be logical, that 'super-rigidity' is not a species of rigidity.

2.1   'the crossing of different pictures': LFM 196ff. compares the idea of logical machinery invoked in explanations of logical necessity with the 'ideal machinery' invoked in kinematics. The idea of logical machinery is of something that underlies the symbols we use and which explains why *this* determines *this*, why *this* follows from *this*, why from *this* you must infer *this* (if you wish to attain truth). The 'senses of expressions', for example, are paradigmatic logical machines in philosophers' imaginary workshops. It is, we think, because of the *sense* of '$(x)fx$' that 'fa' follows. But there is no such thing as 'logical machinery'.

When we invoke the picture of logical machinery in explaining logical necessity, we produce an idea of the parts of the logical machine (e.g. senses, functions, operations) which are, as it were, made of infinitely hard material. For logical necessity, we think, is much *more* necessary than other kinds of necessity. So only logical machinery made of infinitely rigid material could explain the absolute inexorability of its consequences.

This confusion W. explains in two ways. First, by analogy with the use of the machine-as-symbol in kinematics (see Exg. §§193f.). Secondly, by analogy with the law. Suppose, in a certain society, murder is punished by death. In due course, some judges condemn every murderer, others do not; so one then speaks of inexorable and lenient judges. One may also speak of inexorable laws, meaning laws which allow no discretion (analogous to formulae that 'determine a unique solution') and lenient laws, meaning laws with loopholes or allowing judicial discretion (analogous to formulae of the form $y \neq x$, or $y = \sqrt{x}$). But then we may 'cross different pictures'. We take the notion of 'inexorability' as applied to the judge (viz. he is quite merciless, since he condemns every accused) and apply it to the law. Now when we say that the law is inexorable, we no longer mean: it is of the non-discretionary type, or it is of the kind that allows no loopholes. Rather we mean: it is even more inexorable than the judge. And now we may claim that even though the judge may be lenient, the law is always inexorable. (Thus, we may pride ourselves, we live under the rule of the Laws, not of men!) Hence we dream of a super-inexorability of the Law.[1]

So what two pictures do we cross here? We are inexorable (like Judge Jeffries) in our use of the rule 'Add 2'. We *never* accept as according with it a sequence such as '622, 624, 625, . . .'. We teach our children that when told to expand the series '+ 2' they must *always* go on thus . . . (although not if the house is burning down!). We use the rule as a yardstick against which to measure progressions. And we *call* '2, 4, 6, 8, . . .' the terms of this series. Then, especially when doing philosophy, we project our inexorability in applying the rule thus on to *the rule itself* (cf. RFM 82). The rule, we think, inexorably produces just these numbers and no others at each stage. So, when we grasp a rule, we grasp at a stroke something (the logical machinery) which has within it the power to produce just this.

Section 192

1 A coda to §191. The 'superlative fact' is the interlocutor's alleged grasping the whole use of the word at a stroke in the 'special sense' in which *what* he thus grasps contains the whole (so that in grasping the formula, its meaning, its sense, one grasps immediately the infinite series that flows from it). But we really have no idea, no 'model', of what this extraordinary object might be. It is our misconceptions about meaning and understanding, necessity and derivability, which seduce us, by the crossing of different pictures, into transforming the mundane expression 'grasping the use at a stroke' into a super-expression, a philosophical superlative. The theme is resumed in §197.

This illusory superlative grasping is, of course, realized in the Platonist *Bedeutungskörper* (meaning-body)[2] conception (cf. 'Grammar and necessity', pp. 316f.). Hence it has as its corollary the mythology of special privileged philosophical explanations of meaning which do contain, in some sense, the whole use of the terms they explain. Thus, for example, the definition of the concept of a natural number as '0, ξ, $\xi + 1$' (TLP 6.03) may seem to crystallize the general form of a number, and hence to 'contain' the whole series of natural numbers in advance of our thought. So too the truth-tabular explanations of the logical connectives seem to unfold the true essence of negation, conjunction, etc. Here, we may think,

---

[1] Apropos the duelling corps among German students, Mark Twain observed, 'The public authorities, all over Germany, allow the . . . corps to keep swords but *do not allow them to use them. This law is rigid; it is only the execution of it that is lax'*: *A Tramp Abroad* (Century Publishing Co., London, 1982), p. 23.

[2] Cf. Exg. §138.

after immense intellectual effort, which may have continued over centuries, . . .
humanity at last succeeds in achieving knowledge of a concept in its pure form, in
stripping off the irrelevant accretions which veil it from the eyes of the mind.[3]

Such definitions finally bring to light what it is that we grasp when we
truly understand these expressions, for they contain within themselves
all the truths of the propositional calculus (all one needs to do is turn the
crank, i.e. mechanically write down the appropriate Ts and Fs). This is
misleading and incorporates a fallacy that needs to be exposed.

2.1   'a super-expression . . . philosophical superlative': this terminology is
clarified elsewhere. Vol. XV, 34 speaks of the imaginary *super*-inexorability
(Über-Unerbittlichkeit) with which the further application of a symbol is
determined. For it is determined 'superlatively' relative to any empirical
determination. LFM 199 associates the idea of the super-rigidity or
super-inexorability of logic with the (Platonist) conception of logical
machinery. Of course, there is no such thing as this 'super-rigidity'. It
does not lie on the same scale, only higher up, as the rigidity of wood or
steel. Rather, it comes from the interference of two pictures, viz. the
rigidity of materials, and the employment of machines as symbols in
kinematics (cf. Exg. §§193f.). This is parallel to crossing 'The law
punishes killing with death', 'The judge inexorably (mercilessly, without
fail) punishes killing with death' to yield the misbegotten 'The law
inexorably punishes killing with death.' The latter 'inexorably' is a
'philosophical superlative'. RFM 84 suggests that 'the hardness of the
logical *must*' is another such superlative (cf. LA 15f.).

    It is noteworthy that the explicit and transparent internal reference in
Vol. XV, 34 (viz. that 'Über-Unerbittlich' is an *Über-Ausdruck*, hence a
philosophical superlative) is masked in RFM 86 and lost in PI.

3   (i) Frege provides an example of invoking such a superlative 'grasping
the whole use at a stroke' without having a 'model' for this. The sense of
an expression is conceived as an abstract entity with a variety of super-
physical properties (it determines reference; combines with other senses,
which may be complete or incomplete; bears truth-values; etc.). This
entity we grasp when we understand an expression. But what is this
grasping? It is

a mental process! Yes, indeed, but it is a process which takes place on the very
confines of the mental and which for that reason cannot be completely
understood from a purely psychological standpoint. For in grasping something
comes into view whose nature is no longer mental in the proper sense, namely
the thought; and this process is perhaps the most mysterious of all. But just
because it is mental in character we do not need to concern ourselves with it in

---

[3] Frege, FA p. vii.

logic. It is enough for us that we can grasp thoughts and recognize them to be true (PW 145).

(ii) An example of the use of a philosophical superlative in connection with 'the hardness of the logical *must*' is Łukasiewicz. The logical calculus seems like

a mighty construction, of indescribable complexity and unmeasurable rigidity. This construction has the effect on me of a concrete tangible object, fashioned from the hardest of materials, a hundred times stronger than concrete and steel. (cf. Exg. §97 for a fuller quotation.)

SECTION 193

1   This illustrates 'the crossing of different pictures' mentioned in §191. The illusion that a machine predetermines its movements in advance, that it 'has it in it' to move just thus, is parallel to the thought that the general formula of a rule contains in advance the steps to be taken, and to the idea that 'I meant him to go on *thus*' signifies that the steps to be taken have already been taken in some sense in the mind of the teacher (cf. Vol. XIV, 183). Hence also, it illuminates the confusions involved in the supposition that what we 'grasp in a flash' is something from which the use unfolds.

This machine analogy is particularly apt here. First, we are prone to view a rule as being akin to a mechanism (cf. LFM 282) which correlates with each relevant situation (an item of input) the correct response (a particular output). Simple mathematical functions, conceived as rules for correlating numbers, fit this picture; e.g. x^2 can be seen as a 'machine' which generates a number as its value for each number as its argument. Secondly, we are prone to misconceive dispositions and abilities as hidden mechanisms which generate actions on appropriate occasions. Here a postulated mechanism is thought to explain overt performances (a 'black-box' explanation) as the hidden mechanism of a watch explains the visible movements of its hands. Thus we think of understanding a word as an unknown mechanism that generates a person's correct uses of the word.

The purpose of §193 is to examine the illusion that the action of a machine is somehow contained in it in advance. It might seem absurd to say that a part of a mechanism *must* (not just *will*) move thus-and-so if another part moves thus. For surely such a conditional expresses a mere hypothesis! But it is not absurd, for we use bits of machines (and drawings of machines) to symbolize laws of kinematics. A pair of cogwheels, for example, is commonly used to demonstrate the principle that one *must* revolve clockwise if the other turns anti-clockwise. In such cases, a simple mechanism is used to demonstrate a law of kinematics, and this law has the status of a theorem of geometry, not of a generalization in a manual of practical mechanics.

In so using a machine to symbolize an action, we speak as if it were impossible for the parts to move in other ways, and we ignore the possibility that they may bend, break or jam. Of course, the fact that the parts of the machine we use as a symbol *may* break or bend (are not super-rigid) does *not* show that it is improper to use it for this purpose, any more than the fact that the drawing of a triangle consists of lines with a width (and which are not 'perfectly straight') shows the drawing to be improper as part of a demonstration. Equally, just as it would be a mistake to suppose that the 'imperfect triangle' on the blackboard represents an *ideal* triangle which cannot be fully realized and of which the theorems of geometry hold, so too it would be confused to suppose that the machine-as-symbol represents an ideal machine which is described by the laws of kinematics. It would be no less misguided to suppose that in using a machine to symbolize movements we *assume* that its parts will not bend or break, and hence that the principles of kinematics hold only relative to the truth of this hypothesis (RFM 83f.).

These misconceptions (analogous to those familiar from school-masters' explanations of geometry) stem from misunderstanding the role and nature of symbolism and the use of 'concrete' symbols. Two features of the use of machines or drawings of machines as symbols make clear the confusion. First, we use machines (or pictures of them) to describe movements, and we *derive* from such symbols the subsequent movements (e.g. where the piston will be when the driveshaft has reached a certain position (LFM 195) or what figure a part of a machine will trace out (RFM 434)). Contemplating the possibility that machine-parts might bend or break is no part of this technique. Even if actual machinery were used and broke while we carried out a derivation, nothing essential would be lost, since the machinery as it had been before breaking could be used to derive a series of *pictures* of movements. Secondly, in using a machine (or picture) to symbolize a mode of action there is nothing that represents the expansion, contraction, bending, breaking or seizing up of the parts. The symbolism does not provide for these possibilities (as is evident in engineering designs). To see a pair of interlocking cogwheels as a demonstration of the principle that one *must* rotate clockwise if the other revolves anti-clockwise is inconsistent with viewing these wheels as ones whose teeth may shear off when they start to turn. If, however, they do so shear off, this deviant behaviour of the mechanism has no *symbolic* role (just as partial smudging of a machine-drawing by exposure to rain has no symbolic significance).

This is the background to W.'s discussion of the illusion expressed by 'The machine's action seems to be in it from the start.' We would find it absurd to say this in a context in which we were predicting a machine's action (e.g. when purchasing a second-hand car). But it is much more alluring when we use a machine as a symbol of a mode of action in a kinematic demonstration. It seems the only adequate expression of our wonder at the insight that the movement of one part means that another part *must* move in a certain way. Something stronger than a causal connection between a present state and future actions seems to be indicated. We seem driven to conclude that the movements of the machine-as-symbol must be (in a mysterious sense) *already present*. And although this is, of course, muddled, it is true that the movement of the machine-as-symbol *is* predetermined in a quite different, non-causal, sense from the predetermination of the movement of an actual machine. For it is predetermined as a *form of description*.

Our confusion stems from two mistakes. First, we confuse two senses of 'determine' or 'predetermine' – a causal sense in which future actions are determined, and a grammatical sense in which the applicability of a description is determined. Secondly, we confuse two uses of a machine, viz. to produce something (an action or movement) and to symbolize something (a pattern of action). We cross the picture used to describe the functioning or malfunctioning of a particular machine with the picture used to formulate a kinematic principle. Hence we are tempted to speak of the machine-in-use in idioms reserved for the machine-as-symbol.

.1   (i) 'the machine as symbolizing its action': mechanisms thus used are concrete symbols, parallel to samples in ostensive definitions. (The misconception that the machine-as-symbol must consist of super-rigid components parallels the misconception that the 'indefinables' in a language must stand for indestructable simple objects (cf. Volume 1, pp. 201ff.; MU pp. 114ff.).) The manipulation of a mechanism which is being used to symbolize a movement might be mistaken for an experiment, but it has the role of a proof (RFM 259, 434).

     (ii) 'a machine . . . is the first of a series of pictures': W. also describes the machine-as-symbol as an expression, or as part of a language (Vol. V, 269; below, Exg. §193, 2.1).

2   RFM 84 (Vol. XV, 28–31) incorporates this remark into a discussion of logical necessity. The hardness of the logical 'must' is compared with the 'must' of kinematics. Elsewhere (BB 3f., 39f., 117f.; AWL 80ff.) the misconception of the machine as containing its future actions is used to illuminate misunderstandings of dispositions and abilities (in particular understanding) as mental mechanisms.

.1   (i) 'The machine as symbolizing its actions': two corollaries of using a mechanism as a symbol are easily overlooked. First, it must be stipulated or explained how these symbols are to be used; the *grammar* of this

symbol-system must be laid down, Secondly, as a symbol, a mechanism
is an expression, or *part of a language*, and so too are its operations; a
system of signs in which machines symbolize actions will be partly
concrete (like a language incorporating samples and gestures). These
points are both emphasized in early remarks:

In einer Maschine gibt es, was man einen vorstellbaren Anschlag nennt; nach
ihm richtet sich die Länge der Bewegung eines Maschinenteiles.

Das ist immer wieder, als ob zwar nicht in der Maschine selbst die Allgemeinheit
liegen könnte, aber in der *Auffassung* der Maschine.

Und wieder nicht in der Auffassung durch einen Menschen (einer Tätigkeit
eines Menschen), sondern in einem Zeichensystem. Als ob die *Auffassung*
niedergelegt sein könnte in der Grammatik eines Zeichensystems. (Vol. V, 225f.)

(In a mechanism there is what might be called a visual pathway, with which
the length of the movement of a machine-component conforms.

It seems again and again as if the generality could not lie in the mechanism
itself, but rather in the way the mechanism is conceived.

And again, not in the way it is conceived by a person (a person's activity), but
in a system of signs. As if the way of conceiving it could be embodied (only) in
the grammar of a system of signs.)

Wir können wohl eine Maschine zur Illustration der Koordination zweier
Vorgänge, der Abbildung des einen in dem andern verwenden, aber nur die
Maschine *wie sie funktionieren soll*, also die Maschine in ganz bestimmter Weise als
Ausdruck aufgefasst, also als Teil der Sprache. (Vol. V, 269)

(We can indeed make use of a mechanism to illustrate the coordination
between two processes, the mapping of one on to the other, but only the
mechanism *as it should function*, hence the mechanism conceived in an altogether
specific way as an expression, i.e. as a part of language.)

If this pair of points is borne in mind, we will find perspicuous how the
movements of the machine-as-symbol are determined in advance. It is
the rules of grammar which govern the symbolic uses of these concrete
mechanisms that are expressed in such sentences as 'If this part moves
thus-and-so, that part *must* move in such-and-such a way.' The inter-
connection of the movements of a machine-as-symbol are forged in
grammar. This is a connection of a different kind from the connection
between my turning the key in the ignition of my car and the engine's
starting. That makes clear why one movement *predetermines* another in
different senses in these two cases.

(ii) 'the way it moves must be contained in the machine-as-symbol far
more determinately *(viel bestimmter)* than in the actual machine': this is
the conception also expressed by the sentence 'The *must* of kinematics is
much harder than the causal *must* compelling one machine part to move
like *this* when another moves like *this*.' (RFM 84) Both locutions are

radically confused, for they make comparisons of what are altogether incomparable. Against the second, W. argues 'The connection which is not supposed to be a causal, experiential one, but much stricter and harder, . . . is always a connection in grammar.' (RFM 88) Against the first, he objects that it conflates being determined by a matter of fact *(die Bestimmtheit einer Erfahrungstatsache)* with being determined by a stipulation *(die Bestimmtheit einer Abmachung)* (Vol. XV, 33). The movements in the two cases are predetermined *(vorausbestimmt)* in different senses of the word 'predetermined'.

(iii) 'determined in advance' *('vorausbestimmt')*: it is an illusion that time enters into statements of laws in kinematics. In using a machine to symbolize interactions in a gear-train, we often use the future tense to state principles of movement: we say, for example, 'This part *will* turn clockwise if this one turns anti-clockwise.' Hence, we appear to predict the *future* behaviour of the mechanism, to determine how it will move *in advance* of observing its behaviour. But time does not really enter in (AWL 87). The allusion to the future is 'mere clothing' (RFM 318). Kinematics makes no predictions; one of its principles, demonstrated by a mechanism, makes no *assumptions* about what will happen to the mechanism (cf. LFM 195). The principle read off from a mechanism (or its picture) does not say what the actual mechanism will do (RFM 250), though, in as much as it stipulates a form of description, it assists us in making predictions (in a way different from the report of the results of experiments (RFM 241f.)). The mechanism, or a diagram of a mechanism, may have the role of a proof; in this case it convinces one that a particular part of the machine will move in such-and-such a pattern when the mechanism is set in motion, but we must separate the proof from the prediction (RFM 235). What is proved has an aura of certainty which a prediction never wears (cf. RFM 316ff.); it has the status of a stipulation, a rule for describing motions of machines. The statement *proved* by employing a mechanism or a diagram of a mechanism is a statement of geometry, not of physics (AWL 84), and the mechanism itself has the status of a geometrical proof (RFM 259f.). Kinematics is the geometry of motion, and hence it has no more connection with time than plane or solid geometry. W. stressed that no utterance can simultaneously be described as a prediction and as a rule of grammar. Geometry and arithmetic (and kinematics) make no predictions (AWL 177, 189), while predictions cannot state what *must* happen. Conflating the two carries in its wake a conflation of proofs with experiments. These fundamental confusions are particularly captivating in kinematics because of the practice of using the future tense.

1   §193 explored the thought that the action of a machine is in it from the
start, that its movement is, in some special sense, predetermined. §194
examines an analogous idea, viz. that the *possible* movements of a
machine are contained in it in some mysterious (non-empirical) way.
This idea, too, occurs to one typically when philosophizing. It is induced
by the way in which we talk about machines and their capacities, in
particular by our use of 'has' and 'can' in the *present tense* when we
attribute potentialities to machines. We say that a machine *has* such-and-
such possibilities of movement, and this form of representation makes it
appear as if possibilities exist alongside reality in a shadowy kind of way
(BB 117; PG 283), as if they were shadowy occurrent states. This
conception is further sustained by the realization that while the possibility
of a movement is obviously distinct from the movement itself, it must
also be distinct from the physical conditions for the movement (e.g. that
there is play between socket and pin). For the empirical conditions of the
movement could be otherwise. But the possibility of this movement
could not be anything other than the possibility it is. It must be even
more intimately connected to the actual movement than a picture could
be (as a shadow is related to what it is a shadow of). For the possibility of
this movement (unlike a picture of it) must be the possibility of just *this*
movement, not of any other, however slightly different.

These reflections produce intellectual vertigo. Possibilities seem to
take on magical properties, to be like shadows of movements that have
not yet been made. Yet we no more know of such shadows than we have
a model for 'grasping the whole use of a word in an instant' in a special
and direct sense (§191).

(b) restores our sense of balance by focusing on the everyday use of the
phrase 'possibility of movement' in discourse about machines. W.
displays how our philosophical misconceptions emerge from misconstruals of ordinary turns of phrase. While explaining principles of
mechanics one may exhibit the possibility of a movement by using a
drawing of the movement. And a wayward philosopher (whose remarks
are in single quotation marks in §194) may be inclined to say: 'So
possibility is something which is like reality.' Here again we have a
'crossing of different pictures', for the drawing of a movement whereby I
show the possibility of movement is indeed 'like reality' (since it is a
drawing of it), but the possibility of moving thus, which I show by *using
the drawing*, is not 'like reality'. (It is not unlike it either – for these
combinations of words are senseless.) Similarly, one may finish assembling
a machine and say 'It is not moving yet, but it already has the possibility
of moving.' This too encourages the thought that possibility 'is some-

thing very near reality', for all the machine has to do, one might think, in order to transform its possibility of moving into actual moving is to move! Here the 'already has' misleads us. How near to reality is this possibility which the machine already has? Well, it might be five minutes away, or five hours – depending on when one starts the motor!

How does the philosopher get the idea that a possibility is even more closely related to reality than a picture, that it is like a shadow of reality? W. develops further the argument of (a). We may doubt whether loosening a particular cogwheel will make this clockwise movement possible (this is a question of the physical conditions for moving). But we never query whether this possible clockwise movement is the possibility of a clockwise movement or of some other (e.g. anti-clockwise) movement. Hence the philosopher may conclude, 'so the possibility of the movement stands in a unique relation to the movement itself, closer than that of a picture to its subject.' For it makes sense to doubt whether this picture is a picture of this or that, but one cannot doubt whether *this* possibility is the possibility of this or that movement (it is, he might add, of the *nature* of this possibility to be just this possibility and no other). While experience will show whether loosening this nut will give the pin the possibility of a certain movement, it would be senseless to suppose that experience might show that this possibility is the possibility of precisely this movement. But the philosopher altogether misconstrues these grammatical trivialities. 'So it is not an empirical fact that this possibility is the possibility of precisely this movement', he concludes triumphantly, thinking that it is a metaphysical fact. A grammatical nexus is misinterpreted and taken to signify metaphysical marvels.

(c) formulates a general diagnosis of this kind of philosophical mystery-mongering. In doing philosophy we do indeed attend to our mode of expression about possibility; that is just what the wayward philosopher in (b) has been doing. But we grotesquely misconstrue them, like the Lilliputians who thought that when Gulliver looked at his watch to see whether it was time for lunch he was consulting an oracle who told him what to do at every hour of the day.

1   'Wir achten auf unsere eigene Ausdrucksweise': 'We pay attention to our own mode of expression.'

2   (i) RFM 87 (Vol. XV, 41) adds a further remark: 'Imagine someone not understanding our present tense: "he has had it." – He says: " 'he has' – that's present, so the proposition says that in some sense the past is present." ' This is analogous to: 'It already *has* the possibility of movement – that's present, so the future possibilities of movement are in some sense present.' This is linked with a remark omitted from §195 (cf. Exg. §195, 1.1(iii)).

(ii) This misguided inference from present-tense forms of auxiliary

verbs is often pinpointed by W. as a primary source of the idea that
possibilities mysteriously foreshadow actualities. 'He is capable of . . .',
'He is able to . . .', 'He can . . .' look like descriptions of existing states
of affairs (BB 117), and seduce us into thinking that the future behaviour
which manifests a possibility or ability is already contained in the
present. Against this W. urged (Vol. XV, 32f.):

Lass Dich . . . durch [die] Ausdrücke unserer Sprache [nicht irren], wie: 'ich
kenne' (Gegenwart) oder 'verstehe' die Wirkungsweise der Maschine, und nicht
dazu verleiten, zu denken, es müsse da ein unerhörter Fall der Gegenwärtigkeit
des nicht Gegenwärtigen vorliegen, da jetzt schon in unveränderlicher Weise
bestimmt sei, was geschehen wird.

(Don't let yourself be misled by the expressions of our language such as 'I *know*'
(present tense) or 'I understand' the action of the machine, and don't be seduced
into thinking that here there must be a fabulous case of the presence of what is not
present, because here what will happen is already determined in an *unalterable*
way.)

The combination of the present tense with the future tense in framing
kinematic principles is what we find bewildering. It appears as if the
sentence 'I *know* that this wheel *will* revolve thus if this piston moves in
this way' relates a future event to a present state of mind. But the future
tense here is no more used to frame a prediction than the present tense is
used to describe a state of mind.

   (iii) W. repeatedly inveighed against the conception of possibility as a
shadow of reality: 'It is one of the most deep-rooted mistakes of
philosophy.' (PG 283) It originates in grammatical analogies (PG 137)
and a too primitive conception of our language (PLP 342).
   W. criticized this conception in four different domains. In *logic* it leads
to the idea that what a sentence expresses is a possible state of affairs (or a
proposition, or the sense of a sentence), which mediates between a
sentence and the fact that makes it true. And this idea carries in its wake a
whole mythology of symbolism. In *philosophy of mathematics* construing
possibilities as shadowy actualities leads to a multitude of confusions on
two of which W. focused: (i) that the axioms and theorems of geometry
describe ideal geometrical objects in a Euclidean heaven rather than
stipulate possibilities (i.e. what it makes sense to say) (LFM 144f.; PG
52ff.; PLP 44ff.; cf. 'Grammar and necessity', pp. 283ff.); (ii) that
elementary arithmetic has foundations in set theory, since it seems that
natural numbers can be defined in terms of equinumerosity of sets, and
equinumerosity seems to be established by the mere *possibility* of a one-
one correlation (PG 355; AWL 157; LFM 158ff.). In *philosophy of mind* it
leads to the idea that expecting, wishing, believing, wanting, etc.
essentially involve transactions of the mind with shadowy go-betweens
(cf. PR 63ff.; BB 40; PG 135ff.). For we are inclined to think of these as

mental states or processes whose objects (or contents) are a curious entity which is, in a mysterious way, a shadow of the fact that will, e.g. make our belief true, satisfy our expectation, fulfil our wish (cf. 'Accord with a rule', pp. 87ff.). Finally, in reflections on *powers and abilities*, potentiality is misconceived as a shadowy form of actuality (cf. PG 159; BB 54ff., 111ff.; LFM 57, 87, 91, 144ff.).

In all these cases we project grammatical articulations on to reality in the form of mysterious and remarkable metaphysical theses.

SECTION 195

1   This connects §§193–4 with the unfinished business of §191. The interlocutor's claim there that it is as if we could grasp the whole use of a word at a stroke is parallel to the thought that it is as if the future movements of a machine were in it from the start, not merely empirically (causally) determined, but 'in a mysterious sense – already *present*' (§193).

The interlocutor falls into a parallel crossing of pictures in claiming that his grasping the whole use of a word does not determine his future use *causally*, but rather that the whole use seems 'in a *queer* way' already present. Why does it so seem? When we reflect on such utterances as 'Now I understand this word' or 'He grasps the entire use of . . .' we are inclined to construe them as descriptions of occurrent mental acts, processes or states on analogy with other sentences containing present-tense verbs (cf. BB 117). But this 'state' of immediate understanding is distinct from one's future acts of using the expression understood. So it appears that unless the future use *is* 'in some sense' present, then the relationship between present understanding and subsequent use can only be external and causal, needing the support of evidence drawn from experience. But this, we feel, cannot be so. We do say such things as 'But I knew, when I gave the order, that he ought to write "1002" after "1000".' But philosophers behave like savages and misinterpret this familiar expression (§187).

Philosophers are pulled in opposite directions when they reflect on the nature of understanding. On the one hand, one is inclined to think, when I hear or utter an expression, I typically understand it. I *now* grasp the use of the word. On the other hand, somebody who repeatedly misuses a word cannot correctly be said to understand it. So my current act of grasping the use, or my current state of understanding cannot ensure subsequent performance. For current acts or states can at best only causally determine future acts. But now it seems that only the future can tell whether one really understands. Yet that seems absurd. For given that I do now understand an expression, my future use of it is *not* a mere causal consequence of my present understanding.

So the interlocutor's opening exclamation is a dim apprehension of the truth. Of course, if it is established that one now understands an expression, it does not *follow* that one will use it correctly tomorrow, next week, next year. For one may forget what it means; or deliberately misuse it; or make an inadvertent mistake. Yet it is not an inductively established fact, which could be otherwise, that someone who understands an expression does typically use it, and continues to use it, correctly. Just as it is not a matter of induction that someone who *can* swim, typically *does* swim when he tries. For understanding is neither a state of mind from which future applications flow nor a special mental act of laying hold of a peculiar object (e.g. a Fregean sense) which determines future applications in advance. It is rather akin to an ability. And an ability is not a reservoir from which its exercises flow. Nor is it the *cause* of those acts that constitute its exercise. Rather are they *manifestations* of the ability. Furthermore, abilities are not related to time as are states. If I *now* have the ability to φ, that does not mean that I have the ability to φ-only-*now*.

Apprehending these features only 'through a glass darkly', the philosopher seeks for an account of understanding in which what one understands will determine subsequent use non-causally, inexorably, so that when one understands one will in some sense be logically compelled (e.g. by the rule for the use of the expression understood) to go on correctly. The rule, as it were, must trace out the lines along which it is to be followed through the whole of space (§219), and to understand it, is, so to speak, to place oneself on the lines. In this 'queer' way, the future use is already (in some sense) present!

W.'s riposte runs parallel to §191. Just as it is not *as if* we can grasp the use of a word in an instant, but we really, unmysteriously can, so too the present qualifications 'in a queer way', 'in some sense' are symptomatic of persistent confusion. They intimate a special, yet to be discovered, sense in which the use of a word may be present. But this is just as bogus as the idea that the future movements of a machine are (in a special sense) already present in its actual structure.

If one drops these qualifications, there is a legitimate, unmysterious, use of the phrase 'the use itself is present' (cf. §191). Philosophical confusion is generated by transposing expressions from their homely context into one in which they do not fit, and is countered by reminders of their everyday uses (cf. §116). 'Now I understand' is not typically used to describe a mental act (§180). Phrases such as 'He now grasps the entire use of the verb "to book"' or 'He has not fully grasped the use of "möglich"' are at home in pedagogic discussions of language-lessons. If we do not bear these humdrum facts in mind, we risk embracing absurdities parallel to the supposition that a tailor can sew without cloth.

This therapy lays bare the mythology of the mental. We do indeed say

'I knew that he ought to write "1002" after "1000"' (§187), but this does not indicate any magical powers of the mind to fly ahead and make all the transitions of an infinite series (§188) or to latch hold of a Platonic mechanism which will by itself make all of these transitions for us.

1　(i) '(beim Erfassen)': since this refers back to §191, it would be better translated: '(in grasping the whole use of the word)'. There is no implication that the notion of a Fregean sense is involved here, and the difficulties of the thesis that the sense of a word determines its use should not be suggested.

(ii) '*kausal* und erfahrungsmässig': §169 affirms that causation is established only by experiment or experience (though not necessarily by the observation of regular concomitance).

(iii) 'But of course it is, "in *some* sense"!': an earlier version (RFM 87) adds the clarifying parenthesis: '(And don't we also say: "the events of the years that are past are present to me"?)'. The point is to make clear that we can and do quite properly say 'The whole use of the word is present in my mind.' This is an acceptable way to express the thought also expressed by 'I now fully understand this word' or 'I know how to apply this word in *any* standard situation' or 'The method of applying this word is something that I have in mind.' (cf. §141) To add the phrase 'in *some* sense' or 'in a *queer* way' is to manifest scruples that are out of order, as if what was said were nonsensical. If an elderly person exclaims 'The battle of the Somme is present to me' or 'I can still see the dogfights over Kent in the Battle of Britain', it would be wrong to retort 'What nonsense – the past is never present and nobody (not even Alice!) has good enough eyesight to see events that took place many years ago.' If we are troubled by these familiar locutions, this is a sure sign that we have ripped them out of the contexts in which they have unproblematic uses and found analogies between them and other expressions with no use at all (e.g. 'I am now seated on the armchair which I burnt to ashes yesterday in a bonfire').

SECTION 196

1　We misconstrue the use of the word 'grasp' in the phrase 'to grasp the whole use at a stroke' (§191), and hence we take it, in the utterance 'I grasped the whole use of . . . at a stroke', as the expression (or outward manifestation) of a queer inner process. For it seems as if understanding a word must consist of laying hold of something which 'contains' the use of a word in advance (e.g. a *Bedeutungskörper*).

In a parallel way philosophers are seduced into taking time to be a queer medium or the mind to be a mysterious substance (cf. AWL 13ff.;

BB 26f., 47ff.). Here too we misunderstand the use of the word 'time' in such phrases as 'Time passed quickly', 'Time stood still', or of the word 'mind' in locutions such as 'I know what I have in mind', 'He has a mind of his own.'

1.1   (i) 'die unverstandene Verwendung . . . als Ausdruck . . . gedeutet': more literally, 'The not understood use of the word is interpreted as the expression of a queer process.' Vol. XV, 42 has 'Die seltsame Verwendung . . .', and W. deleted 'seltsame', replacing it by 'unverstandene', presumably because in the preceding remark (here §195) he has just stressed that the sentence is *not* queer at all when viewed in its proper context.

(ii) 'a queer process': cf. §308; to conceive of grasping the use of a word, of understanding, as a *mental process* is a disastrous error (cf. 'Understanding and ability', Volume 1, pp. 597ff.; MU pp. 323ff.).

2   RFM 88 (and Vol. XV, 42f.) adds the remarks: 'The difficulty arises in all these cases through mixing up "is" and "is called".' We fail to examine *what is called* 'grasping the use in an instant' or 'understanding at a stroke'. So we imagine that grasping in an instant is a quite different, altogether mysterious, language-game from the one it is. We imagine that to understand in an instant must be laying hold of something in the mind from which the subsequent applications of the word will flow like water from a reservoir (PLP 359).

In precisely parallel a way we dismiss ordinary explanations of meaning as not being *real* explanations, but only hints at explanations or provisional explanations awaiting the advent of a Socrates or Frege who will give definitive ones. We think so because an explanation such as 'That ↗ is red' (pointing at a sample) does not 'contain' the application of the word 'red'. It can be misinterpreted; it may be misapplied. Here too, we fail to advert to what we *call* 'an explanation' and concoct a mythology of what explanation is under the spell of philosophical confusion.

RFM and Vol. XV then interpolate two remarks before §197. First:

The connection which is not supposed to be a causal, experiential one, but much stricter and harder, so rigid even, that the one thing somehow already *is* the other, is always a connection in grammar.

This links §194 ('the possibility of this movement must be the possibility of just this movement') with §197 ('what kind of super-strong connection . . .'). The illusion of a super-connection is always a misunderstood convention, part of our form of representation. Second:

How do I know that this picture is my image of the *sun*? I call it an image of the sun. I *use* it as a picture of the *sun*.

This illustrates the distinction between 'is' and 'is called'. This is my image of the sun not because of resemblance, or some other discoverable empirical relationship, but because of convention and use in accord with that convention (cf. PI §§354f.).

SECTION 197

1   W. here deepens his diagnosis, drawing together the threads of §191, §194 and §195. Grasping the use of a word at a stroke is perfectly ordinary. It only seems queer if we think that the present 'act of understanding' must contain all future applications of the word (as we think that the machine contains its possible movements (§194)). We are driven to that conclusion by the apparent tension between the correct contention that we typically understand words completely here and now, in advance of future applications, and the equally correct claim that the meaning of a word lies in its use. And how can something like use be 'present in an instant'? This tension manifests itself in our uneasy hedging that the future use is 'in some sense' and 'in a queer way' present (§195). 'But *this* isn't how it is!' – we say, 'Yet *this* is how it has to be!' (§112)

The pressure is relieved by an analogy between understanding at a stroke and intending to play chess. The analogy also paves the way for the ensuing discussion of rule-following. The points of analogy W. stresses are three. (i) There is no doubt, when I wanted or intended to play chess, that it was *chess* and not some other game that I wanted or intended to play. Similarly, there is no doubt that I often understand a word in an instant. (ii) Chess is the game it is in virtue of *all* its rules. And a word would have a different meaning if *any* of the rules for its use were different. (iii) When I truthfully say 'I want to play chess' I do not quickly run through all the rules before I speak. And when I understand a word in an instant, I do not survey the whole use of the word in a flash.

These three observations about the intention to play chess might lead to the thought, parallel to the puzzle about understanding, that the rules of chess are in some *mysterious way* present in the mental act of intending to play chess. For if there were no super-strong connection between the act of intending and what is intended, how could there be any confidence about what one intends in advance of doing it?

W.'s strategy is to exploit this parallelism in misunderstanding the concepts of intending to play chess and of grasping the whole use of a word at a stroke. Apparently he supposes the illusion to be more transparent in the first case than in the second, and hence he offers only the briefest hints about the misconceptions in the first case to suggest correctives to the misconceptions in the second. Four points stand out:

(a) Although chess is what it is in virtue of all its rules, it would be absurd to suggest that I do not know what game I wanted to play until I have played it and have seen which rules I was following. (No more do I have to drink a glass of water in order to discover whether it was a glass of water and not a hot bath that I wanted.)

(b) Equally absurd is the other side of this dud coin, viz. that my 'act of intending' contains, in some queer way, all the rules of chess, and that that is why I rightfully, unhesitatingly say that I am going to play *chess*.

(c) My confidence that it is chess I wanted to play does not rest on an inductive correlation between a mental event and subsequent chess playings. It is not as if I have learnt from experience that whenever this curious feeling comes over me (the 'feeling of wanting' (or 'intending')) I will shortly afterwards play chess.

(d) Hence it does *not* follow that there is some doubt that I now want to play chess (since I lack grounds!). Indeed, if my grounds were inductive, it would (absurdly) be an empirical hypothesis that I intend to play chess. So instead of saying 'I'm going to play chess', I should say 'I have the queer feeling I always get before I play chess, so I think I am going to play. Let's see!'

These have obvious counterparts for the clarification of grasping the use of a word at a stroke:

(a) It would be absurd to suggest that I do not know what I understand by a word until I have applied it.

(b) My 'act of grasping the use at a stroke', my understanding, does *not*, in some queer way, contain the whole use of the word (and my understanding of the order 'Add 2' does not 'contain' the acts of writing out the terms of the infinite series of even integers).

(c) My understanding a word at a stroke does not determine the future use causally (a point conceded, of course, by the interlocutor (§195), who draws the wrong conclusion from it). We do not establish inductive correlations between immediate understandings and subsequent correct uses.

(d) My saying that I have understood, grasped the use of a word, is not to be qualified in the form 'I have the experience of grasping what you said, so I think I can use this word. Let's see!' (Although, of course, one *sometimes* thinks one understands, only to find that one does not (PI p. 53 n.).)

So much for the nonsense. But where now is the connection, which must be 'stronger' than a mere causal one (and hence must be grammatical (RFM 88)), between my intending and what I intend? (And, by implication, between my grasping the use of a word and using it?) I express my intention by 'Let's play chess', and *what* I intend is: to play chess, i.e. the game played by *these* rules. It would not be chess that I intend to play if it were not just *this* game with *these* rules. So where is the connection between 'Let's play chess' (my expression of intention) and the rules of the game? In the list of rules, the teaching of the game, in the day to day activity *(Praxis)* of playing.

LFM 25 enlarges on this point. The expression 'I intend to play chess' is used by people about to sit down at a chessboard. Or it is said when not sitting down; but then someone typically goes to get a board and pieces. (No one says 'I now intend to play chess' and then undresses.) Chess is taught by citing its rules, which are exemplified in the teaching. It is played according to these rules, which are explicitly appealed to in disputes. The complex context connects the words by which the intention is expressed with the rules of the game. 'An intention is embedded in its situation, in human customs and institutions. If the technique of the game of chess did not exist, I could not intend to play a game of chess . . ..' (PI §337)

Similarly the connection between grasping the use of a word at a stroke and the use lies in the rules for the correct use of the word. And the connection between understanding and the rules for the use of the word is forged by explaining the word (giving the rules) both in teaching and in appeals when mistakes are corrected or meanings clarified.

All this might be conceded, yet bafflement remain, for the question 'How do I know that I intend to play chess?' (or 'How do I know that I have grasped the use?') has not apparently been answered. But this is incorrect. The question was answered, or rather rejected, in §§153–5 (cf. Exg.). Understanding is not a mental process, and the avowal 'Now I understand' is not a report of such a process, nor is it justified by any inner accompaniment (cf. §180). Likewise intending is neither an act nor a process, and 'I intend to play chess' is not a description of an inner event (§§645ff.).

1.1   (i) 'was ich spielen wollte': 'which game I wanted to play'.

(ii) 'was zu tun ich beabsichtigte': 'what I intended to do'.

(iii) 'in der täglichen Praxis des Spielens': it is important to realize that 'Praxis' here signifies the *activity* of playing (cf. Exg. §202).

2   (i) PG 49ff. explores these issues in detail.

(ii) Vol. XIV, 8f. argues that 'When I gave you the order, I meant you to write "264, 266"' is like 'When we sat down at the chessboard, I meant that we should play chess and that he who first took his opponent's king should win.' For here too one would not have *thought* of this rule of chess. Yet, *of course one meant that.* But if one no more thought of this rule than, perhaps, of its opposite, with what right can one say that one meant it? This surely has to do with the fact that it is a custom to play the game thus, that this is what is called chess.

(iii) The theme of sudden understanding is resumed at PI §§321ff., and of one's certainty that one can do something (e.g. continue an arithmetical series) at §§324f. This certainty does not rest on induction. It has no grounds. Yet we are groundlessly certain, and right to be so. And daily, in thousands of ways, we are borne out: we are certain that we can do something, and we go on to do it.

SECTION 198

1   How can a rule guide one in a particular application, e.g. the transition from 1000 to 1002 in expanding the series '+ 2'? Any rule can be misunderstood, misinterpreted. And whatever I do can, on some interpretation, be brought into accord with the cited rule. And if that is so, how *can* a rule show me what I have to do?

Two preliminary points are noteworthy about W.'s strategy. First, the question raised here was already mooted in §146 (cf. also §§139f.). There it was argued that understanding seems (wrongly) to be the *state* from which applications of a rule flow, as water from a reservoir. One's (confused) model for this is the derivation of a series from its formula (the formula conceived as 'containing' its applications). But, W. objected, 'we can think of more than *one* application of an algebraic formula; and every type of application can in turn be formulated algebraically.' This parallels the opening move of §198,[4] i.e. however one continues the series in response to the order '+ 2', some formula (an interpretation) can be found which will present the sequel as being in accord with the rule '+ 2'.

Secondly, it is important to bear in mind the position of this question within the grand-strategy W. is pursuing (cf. 'Accord with a rule', pp. 83ff.). His task is to show that explanations of meaning are internally related to the correct use of an expression in order to make clear that explanation and use are two facets of a single concept of meaning.

Against this background we can clarify the interlocutor's reasoning in §198(a). It is always possible to give an interpretation of a formulation of a rule, e.g. '+ 2', or '$a_0 = 0$; $a_{n+1} = a_n + 2$', or a signpost pointing thus: '→'. Thus the order 'Expand the series + 2' (§185) is given an interpretation by the explanation (§186): 'The pupil should write the next but one number after every number that he wrote.' This is merely the substitution of one expression of the rule for another (§201). But rules are misunderstood. The pupil in §185 wrote '1000, 1004, 1008, . . .', and that is wrong. We might say that he understood our order 'Expand the series + 2' as *we* should understand the order 'Add 2 up to 1000, 4 up to 2000, 6 up to 3000, and so on'. And then we would also say that he *misinterpreted* the order (rule). But what he wrote is in accord with the rule as he interpreted it. Hence, it seems, *whatever* he writes can be brought into accord with the order *on some interpretation*. And if 'anything goes', then the rule does *not* show me what I have to do. So there really is no such thing as following a rule (MS 165, 88).

---

[4] Cf. also §§139–40: the picture that comes to mind on hearing the word 'cube' is akin to an interpretation. This too can be variously applied, according to different methods of projection.

W.'s initial response to the interlocutor's predicament is to condemn the self-evidently absurd conclusion that anything goes and hence to deny the explicit premise of his reasoning. We ought *not* to say 'Whatever I do is, on some interpretation, in accord with the rule'. (In §201(b), he identifies and negates an implicit assumption of the interlocutor's reasoning.) Rather, we should say that any interpretation still hangs in the air along with what it interprets. This response does not seem perspicuous. The nature of the misconception embodied in the interlocutor's seemingly plausible premise is not pinpointed; presumably it turns on a muddle about the concept of interpretation, but this topic is not raised until §201(b)–(c). Equally unclear is how to explicate the metaphor of an interpretation's hanging in the air together with what it interprets, although this is the centrepiece of W.'s response.

The interlocutor is apparently troubled by the philosophical problem of how one makes the transition from a symbol (rule-formulation) to doing something, and W. addresses the misconception that an interpretation must bridge the gap between the rule and one's action. The metaphor encapsulates the thought that interpretations accomplish nothing towards resolving this puzzle. For one's interpretation of a rule is a *mental* symbolization of the rule. It can have no powers that an ordinary rule-formulation cannot have, and hence, in this context, it can be replaced by a formulation of the rule in external symbols (words, pictures, diagrams, etc.). (This move is one of W.'s standard manoeuvres against the introduction of allegedly explanatory mental entities in attempts to resolve philosophical problems (cf. BB 4).) But now it is *obvious* that an interpretation is powerless to bridge the gap between a rule and one's action. It is just another formulation of the rule, and hence it is no 'closer' to one's action than the original rule-formulation was (cf. MS 165, 33). If the latter hangs in the air, then so does the former. (Of course, this is an *ad hominem* argument, because the interlocutor's puzzle is illusory.) Like other mental acts of understanding which are alleged to breathe life into dead signs, interpretations of rules do not determine meanings. Rather the meanings of rules, like those of all symbols, lie in their *use*.

§198(b) opens with the interlocutor's suggesting what seems to him to be the obvious conclusion from the previous argument. If interpretations accomplish nothing by themselves but leave rules still hanging in the air, then must it not follow that a rule-formulation gives no guidance whatever about what is to be done? And then, of course, there would be no such thing as following rules at all. So the interlocutor asks in bafflement whether he is meant to understand that anything can be brought into accord with the given rule.

This idea is self-evidently absurd. It implies that the expression of the rule has *nothing* to do with my actions. The rule-formulation would then have no role whatever, either in guiding my actions (providing me with a reason, e.g., for turning left – in the case of the signpost) or in evaluating what I do as correct or incorrect. But, W. counters, there *is* a connection between the expression of a rule and what we do. Indeed, there is no such thing as a *rule-formulation* independently of the use of expressions in such normative activities (i.e. to *be* a rule-formulation *is* to be used in such-and-such ways). We are, for example, *trained* to react to the expression of a rule in such-and-such a way. We are taught that when such-and-such is said, or such a sign encountered, *this* is what is to be done. We learn to follow rules as we learn to swim – in practice. In the simplest kind of case, we learn to follow a signpost by being taught to go in the direction pointed. (Note the connection with §197.)

(c) raises an objection. This apparently 'genetic' answer seems to give only a causal explanation of why, in response to a signpost or sign, we act thus-and-so. We *react* thus because we were so trained. This does not explain what *following* the signpost 'consists in'. (So too, in the antecedent discussion of reading, one sought to discover what being guided by the letters 'consisted in'.) But this is wrong! Something is a signpost only in so far as it has the use characteristic of signposts, i.e. in so far as there is a customary procedure of using such objects to guide journeys and to correct wayward wanderings. A person can *follow a signpost* only in so far as he has mastered this technique. In acquiring such a skill one is not 'trained to react' like Pavlov's dogs, but rather one is further taught that going *thus* is correct, going otherwise incorrect. One learns that a signpost is a *reason* for acting (not a cause which elicits a conditioned response). *Using* a signpost (citing a rule) is a crucial element in our concept of the relevant normative action. One refers to it in justifying one's having gone this way, or in correcting another who has gone that way. One guides oneself by it when one consults it, taking it as a reason for acting *thus*. In these activities the connection between the concept of the expression of a rule (rule-formulation) and the concept of acting in accord with the rule is transparent.

1.1   (i) 'was immer ich tue, ist doch durch irgend eine Deutung mit der Regel zu vereinbaren': this would be better translated: 'Whatever I do can, by some interpretation, be brought into accord with the rule.' That everything *can* be interpreted as being in accord with the rule does not mean that everything *is* in accord with it (cf. RFM 414).

In fact, there are three readings of this sentence which differ in respect of what is interpreted and what things are brought into accord. First, one might claim that whatever I do (my actions) can be variously interpreted, and that on some interpretation my action is in accord with the rule, which is not itself interpreted (cf. RFM 341: 'da doch, was immer ich tue, als ein Folgen gedeutet werden kann'). Secondly, one might hold that any rule can be variously interpreted, and that whatever I do is in accord with some interpretation of the rule though not necessarily with the rule itself (cf. RFM 341: 'da ich doch jede Handlung mit jeder Deutung in Einklang bringen kann'). Thirdly, an interpretation of a rule might be thought to be an instrument which can be used to bring about accord between whatever I may do and the rule which is thus interpreted. It is not clear that the interlocutor intends to draw any such subtle distinctions or that W.'s response turns on differentiating among these contentions.

The interlocutor's premise seems to be exaggerated as well as unclear. It is not true that *whatever* I do can, by some interpretation, be brought into accord with the rule + 2 at the 500th step. This pre-supposes that there is no restriction whatever on what may correctly be called 'an interpretation' or 'a misinterpretation'. But would *whatever* one says when asked to explain the rule + 2 count as an *explanation* (mistaken, of course) of this rule? Likewise, would *whatever* one does manifest a *misunderstanding* (misinterpretation) of the rule + 2? These ideas seem very dubious.

One might further object that the interlocutor conflates interpretations and misinterpretations of rules. Any rule may be misinterpreted in indefinitely many different ways, but there are severe restrictions on what qualifies as giving an interpretation (or reformulation) of it. *If it is understood*, the rule + 2 cannot be interpreted by the explanation 'add 2 up to 1000, 4 up to 2000, etc.', though it can be given the interpretation 'Write the next but one number after every number previously written.' Since one's writing *this* sequence '1000, 1002, 1004, 1006' is a *criterion* for one's following *this* rule (RFM 317ff.), one could not be said both to understand the rule and to give an interpretation of it according to which writing '1000, 1004, 1008' counts as following it. In other words, the symbol '+ 2' leaves open what counts as an interpretation only if it is *not* understood. W. noted this point: 'If I see the thought symbol "from outside", I become conscious that it *could* be interpreted thus or thus.' (PG 147)

(ii) 'What has the expression of a rule – say a signpost – got to do with my actions?': here as in some other places W.'s use of the term 'rule' seems idiosyncratic (see 'Rules and grammar', pp. 57ff.).

(iii) 'Well, perhaps this one': misleading translation of 'etwa diese', since this *is* one kind of connection. So better 'Well, this one, for example.' Other kinds of connection obtain too, e.g. I explain why I turned right by reference to the signpost, I look at the signpost before I turn, I tell those who are with me to follow it thus.

(iv) 'only in so far as there exists a regular use': cf. PI §454, 'The arrow points only in the application that a living being makes of it.'

2   (i) RFM 341f. raises a parallel problem about obeying the simple imperative 'Slab!' (in language-game §2).

(ii) MS 165, 38ff. (MS 179, 1f.) links §198(a) immediately to a remark related to §201(b), viz.:

Wie kann ich einer Regel folgen? Wie kann sie mir zeigen wie sie mich zu führen hat? – Wenn ich sie so oder so auffasse, wie kann ich diese Auffassung festhalten, wie kann ich sicher sein, dass sie mir nicht unversehens entschlüpft ist?

(How can I follow a rule? How can it show me how it is to guide me? – If I understand it in this or that way, how can I hold tight to this way of understanding it, how can I be sure that it hasn't slipped unawares?)

The *next* remark is an early version of §217. When justifications (interpretations, rules for applying rules, etc.) run out, *there lies action*, which we call 'in accord with this rule'.

(iii) MS 165, 33 illuminates the apparent predicament. Understanding a rule is itself like understanding a sign; and how can a sign show me what I have to do? Whatever I add to a sign by way of interpretation, it is still by a sign that I guide myself. So an interpretation does not, in principle, help. Interpretations and explanations are in the end at the service of practice (activity). ('Die Deutungen und Erklärungen dienen am Schluss nur der Praxis.')

MS 165, 78ff. explores further. A rule is not an extension, the set of acts that accord with it, but rather to follow a rule is to construct an extension according to a 'general' expression (a formulation of a rule). To ask what 'according to' means here is akin to asking how the execution of an order is related to the order, how the act is connected to the words. And the answer, in both cases is: through a general practice. Giving and following orders, complying with rules, are possible (these *expressions* make sense) only in the context of established practices, regular patterns of action and response in certain typical settings. 'Nicht die *Deutung* schlägt die Brücke zwischen dem Zeichen und dem Bezeichneten//gemeinten//. Nur die Praxis tut das.' ('It is not the interpretation which builds the bridge between the sign and what is signified//meant//. Only the practice does that.')

MS 165, 86f. holds up the temptation for scrutiny. One is inclined to say that a sample of a series, say, seen in such-and-such a way, must be continued thus. He is, W. writes, yearning for an interpretation (*Auffassung*) by which the series is determined as by an infallible machine from which it emerges; so that only this continuation fits this rule, thus grasped. But in reality there are not two things here that fit together (presumably they 'belong' but do not 'fit', cf. PI §136ff.). However, one may indeed say that one is so educated that one will always, without thinking further, explain a certain thing as fitting. And as L fits K in the series of letters of the alphabet, or 'It is true that' fits a declarative sentence, that will also accord with what others explain as fitting.

This passage is followed immediately by a version of PI §198(a) in which the interlocutor's observation is followed by:

> Aber das hiesse doch, es gäbe nicht/ /kein/ /'einer Regel folgen'. Was immer ich tue ist ja durch irgend eine Deutung mit ihr zu vereinbaren.
>
> Nein. So sollte ich nicht reden. Sondern so: Jede Deutung . . ..
>
> (But that would mean that there is no such thing as 'following a rule'. Whatever I do can be brought into accord with it through some interpretation or other.
>
> No. I should not put it that way. But rather: any interpretation . . ..)

This makes it evident that §198(a) is a *reductio* of the supposition that a rule shows me what to do only by means of an interpretation. It also makes it fully evident that §201(a) restates the thought implicit in §198(a).

2.1   (i) 'What has the expression of a rule . . . got to do with my actions': if the interlocutor were to argue that a pupil understands a rule only because he adds something to it, namely an interpretation, the question of what made him give just *this* interpretation would arise. If the answer is: the rule itself, then the rule was already unambiguously understood, since it demanded just this interpretation. But if the interpretation were attached arbitrarily, then what he understood was not the rule but only what he made of it (cf. PG 47). In the first case the interpretation is redundant, in the second case the action has nothing to do with the expression of the rule.

(ii) 'say a signpost': MS 124, 205 adds 'no matter how many interpretations I add to it'.

(iii) 'I have been trained to react . . .': cf. MS 165, 84f.:

> Man richtet ein Kind ab, dass es einem Regel folgt: aber sagt man ihm auch: 'Wenn Du der Regel folgst, so *musst* Du dahin kommen/ /Du das schreiben/ /?'
>
> 'Wenn Du etwas andres schreibst so hast Du die Regel nicht verstanden oder missverstanden.' Ist das ein Erfahrungssatz?
>
> Du lehrst einem Mensch eine Regel, Du richtest ihn ab, auf einen bestimmten Befehl so und so zu handeln.
>
> Das 'muss' sagt, was anerkannt wird.
>
> (One trains a child so that he should follow a rule: but does one also say: 'If you are following the rule, you *must* get there/ /write this/ /?'
>
> 'If you write anything else, then you have not understood or misunderstood the rule.' Is that an empirical statement?
>
> You teach someone a rule, you train him to behave thus and so at a certain order.
>
> The 'must' says what will be acknowledged.)

It is most important to realize that W.'s recurrent talk of training is not a manifestation of a kind of stimulus/response conception of accord with a rule. The training in question is a training in a normative activity. The pupil learns what to do, and also what is to be done, what is called 'right', 'in accord with this rule', 'correct' (cf. Z §300). But the very possibility of his training rests upon generally shared human reactions:

> The origin and the primitive form of the language game is a reaction; only from this can more complicated forms develop.
> Language – I want to say – is a refinement, 'in the beginning was the deed.' (CV 31)

(iv) 'and so I now react to it': but only 'in so far as there exists a regular use'. RFM 414 elaborates this. The teacher interprets the rule for the pupil by the explanations and training he gives him –

And the pupil has got hold of the rule[5] thus interpreted, if he reacts to it thus-and-so.

But *this* is important, namely that this reaction, which is our guarantee of understanding, presupposes as a surrounding particular circumstances, particular forms of life and speech. (As there is no such thing as a facial expression without a face.)

(This is an important movement of thought.)

This movement of thought connects PI §198 with §§199–200.

Section 199

1   This is continuous with §198. One can be said to 'follow a signpost' only in the context of a regular use of signposts. More generally, one can talk of following rules only in the context of temporally extended normative practices. This is not because it is logically necessary that a normative practice have a history (although as a matter of fact our normative practices do have histories). It does not preclude the logical possibility of being born with a fully fledged ability to speak English (PG 188; BB 12; cf. 'Explanation', Volume 1, pp. 70f.; MU pp. 30f.). Following rules, making reports, giving and understanding orders, and playing games (such as chess) are essentially connected with regularities, viewed normatively (although not necessarily *past* regularities). They are customs, established patterns of (correct and incorrect) behaviour. To judge an act to be a case of following a rule is to see it as an instance of a normative regularity (or against a context of related normative regularities). Hence it is not possible that in the history of the world only one

---

[5] 'Und der Schüler hat die Regel (*so gedeutet*) inne, wenn er so und so auf sie reagiert.' The RFM translation 'he possesses the rule inwardly' is misleading; cf. PI §146 'Hat er das System inne', i.e. 'has he got hold of' it.

man should follow a rule only once. Note that W. is not concerned here with socio-psychological facts about learning and acquisition of skills, or with the conditions under which it might be said that a rule was invented (cf. PI §204). His concern is with the *concept* of following a rule (RFM 322), and the impossibility he notes is a logical or grammatical one (MS 124, 206).

Is the impossibility analogous to the obvious impossibility of only one man's buying or selling something, marrying or making a promise? Or is it analogous to the impossibility that only one man, on only one occasion, buys something from another, marries a woman, or promises something to someone? The latter. For while it is possible for each of us to get married just once and never again, it is only possible because the institution of marriage exists. (That it needs two people is true, but uninteresting here.) But cannot one person establish, institute, a solitary practice? The issue is not raised here (but see 'Following rules, mastery of techniques and practices', pp. 169ff.).

The role of this section in the development of the argument is to replace false pictures of the relation of explanation to use, of rule to application, by a correct conception of a normative practice. It is not the timeless senses of expressions which atemporally determine a consequence, fix the reference, determine whether an object falls under a concept or not. If this picture made sense, it would also, *prima facie*, make sense for one man on just one occasion 'by means of his logical faculties, to lay hold of'[6] the sense of an expression and apply it. For if the sense of an expression is something from which the applications flow, and if understanding is 'grasping' a sense, then one might grasp it completely and apply the expression just once (or even, not at all!). But it is not such Platonic machinery which determines what follows from a rule, nor is it what makes possible what we call 'following a rule'. This Fregean picture is only implicitly assailed. The explicit purpose is to make clear the fact that the criteria for following a rule, hence too the criteria for understanding in general, presuppose a complex context of normative regularities.

We are inclined to think of making a report, giving an order, etc. as acts of an individual that depend only on his *intentions*; hence, it seems, any such act might occur in glorious isolation from the whole web of human behaviour. But understanding and using language involve the mastery of many interrelated techniques. One can no more understand a single sentence of a language and no other[7] than one can follow just one rule just once in a lifetime. One cannot make a move in chess without being able to play chess. One cannot understand a sentence without also

---

[6] Cf. Frege, PW 181.

[7] Although an English speaker may, of course, know what just one sentence in Chinese means.

understanding (perhaps only poorly) the language to which it belongs. To understand a language is to have mastered a technique (PI §150) of using (and responding to the use of) signs. Mastery of a technique is manifest in its exercise on a multiplicity of *occasions*. (Note that W.'s emphasis here is not on the need for *joint* activity, but on recurrent activity. The concept of following a rule is here linked with the concept of regularity, not with the concept of a community of rule-followers.) It is not only that it is thus that we determine whether one has understood signs and how one has understood them. Rather is it that only in this case is there any *sense* to talk of understanding.

2   (i) MSS 124, 206 and 129, 26f. preserve the link with the previous remark by retaining the reference to a signpost: the first cites a signpost as an example of a rule, the second argues that it is not possible that only once in human history was a signpost followed.

(ii) RFM 334, having observed that a game, a language, a rule is an institution, raises the question of how often a rule must have been applied before it makes sense to talk of a rule. There is no hard and fast answer, any more than there is to the question of how many times a pupil must have added, multiplied, etc. before he can be said to have mastered these techniques.

(iii) RFM 193 emphasizes that consensus among calculators is an essential feature of the phenomenon of our calculating. But does that not mean that a solitary human being could not calculate? His answer is careful: 'Well, *one* human being could at any rate not calculate just *once* in his life.' The question is raised again at RFM 349, where W. responds with the query; 'Is this like "Can one man alone engage in commerce?"' He does not answer his query. Clearly the answer is negative. (Cf. 'Following rules, mastery of techniques and practices', pp. 169ff. and Exg. §204.)

(iv) RFM 346 observes that one cannot say that just once in the history of mankind someone followed a signpost, although one could say that once someone walked parallel to a board. 'The words "language", "proposition", "order", "rule", "calculation", "experiment", "following a rule" relate to a technique, a custom.' This point is picked up in MS 124, 187f.: if I were on Mars, and observed a creature who looked at something like a signpost, and then walked parallel to it, I would *not* be justified in judging him to be *following* it (even if I knew all about his occurrent feelings). But surely, W.'s interlocutor responds, he must know whether he is following it! But not by introspection, W. replies. (How do I know that I am doing so? Well, how do I explain what I am doing? How do I react when I notice that I have turned the wrong way?)

RFM 351f. imagines someone making a gesture, as if to say 'Go!' and the other person goes away with a frightened expression. Even if this happened only once, could it not be called 'order and obedience'? But in other cultures quite different gestures correspond to 'Go away!', and our gesture may there be a token of friendship. The interpretation of a gesture depends on what precedes and follows it, and gestures no less than words are, in the activities of ordering and obeying, interwoven in a network of relationships. This remark makes evident the connection between §199 and §200.

.1   'To understand a sentence means to understand a language': this idea surfaced in the early 1930s as part of a criticism of the conception that understanding is a mental accompaniment of hearing or speaking a sentence, that the mind breathes life into signs. Instead, W. suggested, understanding a sentence depends on seeing it as an element of a calculus of signs of which one has mastery. Without the system, one might say, the series of signs constituting a sentence would be dead (cf. PG 172; BB 5). The philosopher must attend to the system of language (PG 171), not mental acts of meaning and understanding (BT 1ff.). For his purposes, it is useful to call a proposition 'a position in the game of language' (PG 172). 'The role of a sentence in the calculus is its sense.' (PG 130; cf. BB 42) It is only in a language that something is a sentence; to understand a sentence is to understand a language (PG 131; BB 5). For a sentence is a sign in a system of signs, one combinatorial possibility among many others, and in contrast to many others (cf. PG 63). Hence understanding a sentence is conceived as an aspect of mastery of the calculus to which it belongs. (Equally, one might say, something is understood as a picture only within a picture-language (cf. PG 171).)

    In later writings W. retained and developed this idea, but he divorced it from the conception of a language as a calculus. That came to seem a one-sided and distorting way of viewing language. What gives life to a sign is its *use*, its role as an element in human *activity*. The sense of a sentence is its *employment* (PI §421) or its role in the *language-game*; a proposition is a move in the language-game (cf. PI §22). This thought is gradually deepened:

> What, in a complicated surrounding, we call 'following a rule' we should certainly not call that if it stood in isolation.
> Language, I should like to say, relates to a *way* of living.
> In order to describe the phenomenon of language, one must describe a practice, not something that happens once, *no matter of what kind*. (RFM 335)

It makes sense to talk of understanding, of mastery of the 'techniques' of using language and responding to its use, only in the context of a form of life in which these techniques are used. They are part of our complex natural history (PI §25). 'Words have meaning only in the stream of life.' (LW §913)

SECTION 200

1   Here W. offers two linked clarifications of the concept of playing a
game of chess (hence of following the rules of chess). First, imagine a
tribe lacking the very idea of a game. We can envisage two tribesmen
sitting at a chess-board, going through all the moves of a chess game,
even feeling, for example, a sudden anxiety or flicker of triumph
appropriate to the 'move' being made. If we were to see them, knowing
nothing of their form of life, we should say they were playing chess. And
we should obviously be wrong. For though their behaviour *looks* like the
playing of a game of chess, it is not. To play chess is to engage in an activity
governed by rules. Only in certain circumstances, in a complicated
surrounding against the background of a way of living, do these actions
constitute playing chess.

Conversely something that did not *look* remotely like a game, let alone
a game of chess, might, in certain circumstances, be one. Imagine a
mapping of chess moves on to yells and stampings of feet. One can then
imagine two people yelling and stamping in such a way that if their
behaviour is translated into chess moves a coherent game results. Are
they playing chess? Again, knowing nothing of their form of life, we
would not say so. We would not even be inclined to say that they were
playing a game. Perhaps they were dancing or performing a ritual. Yet,
in certain circumstances, these antics would count as playing chess (just
as writing down moves in chess notation is, in appropriate circumstances,
playing a game of chess). What would give us the right to say that this
(apparent) dance was a chess game? The larger context, against which
these actions can be seen as 'customs, uses, institutions', in which the
concept of a game, and of following the rules of chess can get a grip
(cf. PI §§152–5).

The point of §200 is not to establish some form of scepticism about
whether an individual is following a rule. (As if one could never tell from
his behaviour, but must make ever more extensive investigations into his
social surroundings.) Rather, W.'s aim is to reinforce the clarification of
§199. For if whether two people are playing chess depended *solely* on
what they did and what they thought while doing it, then it would be
inconceivable that an initial judgement that they are (or are not) playing
chess could be upset by investigating what kind of regularities stand in
the background of these doings. And therefore it would also be possible
for just two people on a single occasion to play a game, or, *pari passu*,
for just one person once to follow a signpost, make a report, issue an
order, etc.

2   (i) BT 153 clarifies a connection between §200 and §197. Chess is
certainly characterized in terms of its rules. And a person playing a game
of chess, who makes a move, is doing something different from someone
who cannot play, but moves a chess-piece in the same manner. But this
phrase 'doing something different' is misleading; it inclines us to think
that the difference consists in an accompanying brain-process (cf. §§153–4),
whereas it does not even consist in the player's thinking of the rules as he
moves, any more than intending to play chess involves thinking of the
rules of the game.

Just as it is possible to *intend* to play chess only in the context of the day
to day practice of playing, teaching, discussing the game (PI §197), so
too it is possible for particular acts of moving pieces to be moves in a
game of chess only in the context of established customary techniques of
playing.

(ii) PG 294 gives a homely example of imagining a complete set of
chess moves being carried out in a context in which we would deny that
what was going on was a game of chess, viz. if the two participants are
collaborating in solving a chess problem. Also, one might add, if they
were collaborating on going over the moves of a famous chess tournament.
Here, of course, these activities are parasitic on the practice of playing
chess.

(iii) MS 124, 206 also places a variant of §200 after an early draft of
§199. W. sketches the picture of two people, just once, sitting at a chess-
board, going through the moves of chess, with whatever mental
accompaniments one wishes. But this would not make their activity into
a game of chess, for it could just as well be the mad activities of two
lunatics. So, W. concludes

Was wir Spiel nennen ist eine menschliche Gepflogenheit mit einem bestimmten
Platz unter andern menschlichen Gepflogenheiten. Und ebenso ist das auch die
Sprache in allen ihren Formen.

(What we call a game is one human custom with a particular place among other
human customs. And so too is language in all its forms.)

This is immediately followed by PI §204.

(iv) RFM 336 imagines a God creating in a wilderness, for just two
minutes, a replica of a part of England, with people in it engaged in all
typical activities. If one such two-minute man were doing just what an
English mathematician were doing when calculating, does it follow that
he too is calculating? Could we not imagine a wholly different past and
future for these two minutes which would incline us to call this activity
something quite different?

1   §201(a) repeats the theme of §198(a). The 'paradox' restates the
argument, viz. a rule cannot determine an action as correct, show me
what to do, stipulate what is to be in accord with it. Why not? Because
every course of action can be made out to accord with the rule by means
of some interpretation. In §198 the interlocutor was driven into the
nonsensical conclusion that whatever he does is (on these premises) in
accord with the rule; which is tantamount to saying that there is no rule
and no following of rules. §201 reaches the same conclusion; the paradox
evolves into a self-evident absurdity. For if every course of action can be
made out, on some arbitrary interpretation or another, to accord with
the rule, then by the same token it can be made out to conflict with the
rule. But then the very notions of *accord* and *conflict* are deprived of any
meaning. And therewith also the concept of a rule itself.[8]

   (b) offers a diagnosis that enlarges upon §198. The absurdity into
which we have been driven stemmed from the idea that it is an
interpretation and only an interpretation which determines what is the
correct application of a rule. That this involves a misunderstanding is
evident from reflection on the development of the argument since §185.
How the teacher *meant* the pupil to continue seemed to be what
determined '1002, 1004, . . .' as the correct way to continue – *until we
notice that the expression of how he meant it could itself be variously interpreted.*
What our absurd predicament shows is that not all *understanding* of rules
can consist in assigning interpretations. How I understand a rule is
shown not only by the interpretation (explanation) I give of it if asked,
but also by what I *do* in following it. How I understand it is manifest in
that action which, in each case, I *call* 'following the rule' and 'going
against it'. Of course, I may understand it right or wrong. If A, in
response to the order 'Continue the series 2, 2, 2, 2' goes on '2, 2, 2,
2, . . .' that shows how he understands it. If B goes on '3, 3, 3, 3, 4,
4, . . .' that shows that he understands it differently. (And nothing has so
far been said about who understood it right!)

   Going on '1002, 1004, 1006, . . .' is *what we call* 'Expanding the series
+ 2'; anything else we call 'going against' that rule. The *grammatical*
relation between the rule and what accords with it is manifest in our
normative activities, the way we teach others what a rule-formulation
means and what is called 'acting in accord with it', the way in which we
correct ourselves and others when the rule is flouted, the way in which
the expression of the rule is cited as a canon of correct action. We talk

---

[8] This removes any possibility of formulating a *sceptical* problem about what counts as
accord and conflict with the rule.

correctly (cf. §189) of the rule as determining what steps to take. But we are inclined to misconstrue this idiom as if the rule in some mysterious way already contained all its applications independently of us. The truth is that *we* fix these steps as what we *count* as being in accord with this rule. And this is manifest in the motley of our normative (or, more particularly, mathematical) activities, in teaching, explaining, criticizing, justifying, etc. Hence the pupil's getting just these results (1002, 1004, 1006, . . .) is what it is to be following the rule correctly at this point. Moreover, since how he understands the rule is manifest in his actions, the correctness of his understanding turns on the correctness of his acts according to the standard set by the rule. He understands the rule *(ceteris paribus)* if he writes down just this sequence, since that is what we fix as 'following this rule'. It has just been argued that our understanding of a rule is exhibited in what we *do*. But if we are still inclined to think that one cannot act in accord with a rule without interpreting it somehow or other, we may insist that acting in accord with a rule *is* an interpretation of it. For when we see the pupil writing '1000, 1004, 1008, . . .' we do say 'He has interpreted it to mean . . .' But this is misleading in this context. For 'He has interpreted . . .' here just *means* 'He has understood it to mean . . .'; it does not mean 'He has given the rule an interpretation, namely ". . .", on which he has now acted', for then his action might manifest a misinterpretation (i.e. a misunderstanding) of *his interpretation*. But we want his 'interpretation' to be something that he can't further misinterpret (cf. LSD 22). (It was supposed that it would carry him unerringly to the action.) Moreover, in saying 'He has interpreted the rule to mean . . .', we want to draw attention to the fact that he has misinterpreted *the rule* (i.e. misunderstood it), not something *other than* the rule, viz. a (mis)interpretation of the rule such as 'Add 2 up to 1000, 4 up to 2000, ...' So, in this context we ought to restrict the term 'interpretation' to the substitution of one expression of a rule for another, and say of the pupil simply 'He has misunderstood the rule.' We take his behaviour as exhibiting how he understands the rule, and our statement of how he understands it may well be said to be an interpretation (or rather, a misinterpretation) of the rule.

1   (i) 'dass es eine Auffassung einer Regel gibt': 'Auffassung' has a standard use similar to 'Deutung', but here these two terms stand in contrast to one another. The point at issue here is that *how one understands* the rule is manifest not just in the interpretations one gives, but also and essentially in what one does. To capture this it is advisable to break with the German syntax and translate 'what this shows is that how one understands a rule need not be an *interpretation*, but may be exhibited . . .'.

   (ii) 'sei ein Deuten. "Deuten" aber sollte man . . .': 'is an interpreting. But we ought to restrict "to interpret" to . . ..' This is not a general

thesis about the correct use of 'Deuten' or 'interpret', and W. uses the
term in other standard ways (e.g. RPP I §20; LW §179). He evidently
means to prevent a confusion from arising in this context. It is important
to distinguish two different ways in which how one understands a rule is
exhibited, viz. in explaining what the rule is and in following the rule (in
the acts called 'following the rule'). But saying that every act according
to a rule *is* an interpretation obscures this distinction.

2   (i) §201 does not occur in any of the earlier typescripts of PI (PPI(I)
moves from PI §200 to PI §§204–13). It was worked in from B i §265. Its
ultimate source seems to be MS 180(a), 72f. The context is the discussion
now located at PI §§377–81 (this too did not occur in PPI(I).) This begins
from an examination of aspect-seeing (MS 180(a), 52ff.). Do I *interpret*
the figure Ⅎ now as an F, now as a reversed F? Do I see everything
always *as* something? Do I need words for such 'visual interpretation', or
are words only necessary to communicate what I see (cf. Z §208)? The
concept of 'interpreting' needs to be clarified. How did we ever come to
this concept of 'visual interpretation'? Only by means of different verbal
reactions, e.g. to puzzle pictures. It seems though that I can recognize my
visual impressions (of F or Ⅎ), identify them, and *then* express this
recognition in words.
    Then follow early drafts of PI §§377–81. W. undermines the idea that a
recognitional process mediates between having an image and saying
what image one has, or between seeing a colour and saying what colour
it is. For we are inclined to think that one must recognize what colour
one is imagining before one names it. This pushes one in the direction of
relying on a private, inner, ostensive definition (MS 180(a), 65). but this is
incoherent; justification must be public (PI §378). I use *no criterion* in
saying that I have a red visual impression (PI §377). Private tables of
samples are comparable with idle doodling when thinking; they have no
normative role. So how *does* one know that this colour is red (PI §381)?
One might answer: I have learnt English. (Comparable with: how do
you know that 'H' comes after 'G'? – I have learnt the alphabet.)
    But how can any teaching help me when I have to make the transition
from experience to words? Isn't it right to say: I see the colour and
recognize it as red? No, W. insists, this is a misuse of 'recognize'. For is
one to say that I see that it is red, but don't know what it is called (until I
recognize it)? Then what use is this wordless 'seeing that it is red'? Do I
rather see that it is *this* colour, and, of course, I know what this colour is
called? But which colour is *this* colour? Or do I see *what* colour it is,
namely *this* colour? Which colour?
    At this point we have the first draft of PI §201:

    Ich erkenne also es ist *so*. Und nun muss ich zu Worten, oder Handlungen//
Handlungen: Worten z.B.//übergehen.

Ich war (früher) in der Schwierigkeit dass eine Regel keine Handlungsweise bestimmen könnte da eine jede mit der Regel in Übereinstimmung zu bringen sei. Die Antwort war: Ist jede mit der Regel in Übereinstimmung zu bringen, dann auch zum Widerspruch. Daher verlören hier 'Widerspruch' und 'Überein-stimmung' ihren Sinn völlig.//Daher gäbe es hier überhaupt weder Überein-stimmung noch Widerspruch.//

Das Missverständnis zeigt sich darin dass wir überhaupt in diesem Gedankengang Deutung hinter Deutung setzen wodurch wir zeigen dass es für uns eine natürliche Auffassung einer Regel gibt die *nicht* eine *Deutung*//das Hinzufügen einer *Deutung* //ist, sondern sich vor Fall zu Fall darin äussert was wir der Regel folgen und was wir ihr entgegen handeln nennen.

(Thus I recognize that *this* is how it is. And now I must turn to using words or acting//acting: using words, for example.//

I was (earlier) in the difficulty that a rule could not determine any way of acting since every way of acting could be brought into accord with it. The answer was: if everything can be brought into accord with the rule, then also into conflict with it. Hence 'conflict' and 'accord' here would lose their sense entirely.//Hence there would here be neither accord nor conflict at all.//

The misunderstanding is manifest in the fact that we, in the course of this argument, set interpretation after interpretation, whereby we show that how we naturally understand a rule is *not* by an *interpretation*//the attaching of an *interpretation*//but is exhibited in what, from case to case, we call following the rule and what we call going against it.)

Here W. invokes the argument of PI §198, which occurred on p. 1 of MS 180(a). That this *was* what he meant by §198(a) is evident from MS 165, 87 (above, p. 137). For the current predicament runs parallel to the earlier one. There it was argued that interpretations alone do not determine meaning, and that the possibility of bringing anything into accord with a rule by some interpretation or other does not indicate that rules do not show one what to do. Here there is a parallel confusion. The interposition of a succession of 'visual interpretations' in order to explain how I know that this is red (or that this is the same image) is similarly futile.[9] Each fresh 'visual interpretation' generates the same problem again. And what this shows is that there is a natural way of under-standing a rule (in *this* case, a *public* ostensive definition) that involves no interpretations but action, the exhibition of an ability, the mastery of the technique of using a word, of the application of the rule. How we under-stand the rule, what we understand by it is exhibited in the custom (§198) of going by it, in the normative regularity of following it – of doing what we *call* 'following' it.

---

[9] W. added later in MS 180(a), 73 the incomplete remark: 'als beruhige uns eine jede wenigstens für einen Augenblick bis wir an eine weit . . .' (as if each contented us at least for a moment, until we thought of yet anoth . . .).

The following conclusions may be drawn: (i) In its original locus, §201 applied §198 (after elaboration) to the question of aspect-seeing and the bogus intervening process of recognition in judgements about mental images and impressions, and to the immediate application of colour-predicates. (ii) It did not propound any new paradox, but merely cross-referred to a difficulty introduced and dissolved in the argument of §198. (iii) Transposing §201 from the discussion of §§377–81 involves a reorientation of purpose, and minor modifications of reference, but no change in significance. Its role is now simply to amplify §198. The reference to the succession of interpretations (i.e. 'visual interpretations' and futile attempts to *express* one's experience *antecedent* to 'recognition') shifts to the discussion of PI §§186–90. (iv) In MS 180(a) it explicitly presupposed the conclusions of the private language argument.

MS 129, 116ff. confirms this interpretation. There an early version of PI §377 precedes an independent discussion of colour recognition.

Ich sehe, dass es rot ist – aber was hilft mir das, wenn ich nicht weiss, was ich zu sagen habe oder sonst meine Erkenntnis zum Ausdruck bringen soll? Denn einmal muss ich nun den Übergang zum Ausdruck machen. Und bei diesem Übergang lassen mich nun alle Regeln in Stich. Denn sie hängen nun alle wirklich in der Luft. Alle guten Lehren hilfen mir nichts, denn am Ende muss ich einen Sprung machen: Ich muss *sagen* 'dass ist rot', oder in einer Weise *handeln*, die auf's selbe hinaus kommt.

(I see that it is red – but how does this help me if I do not know what I have to say or how, in some other way, to give expression to my knowledge? For sooner or later I must make the transition to expression. And at this transition all rules leave me in the lurch. For now they all really hang in the air.[10] All good advice is no help to me, for in the end I must make a leap. I must *say* 'That is red' or act in some way, which amounts to doing the same thing.)

The following material includes PI §§380(a)–(b), 378–9. Then comes a redrafted version of PI §201 beginning 'Ich befand mich in der Schwierigkeit, dass es schien, die' (I found myself in the difficulty that it seemed[11] that). W. crossed this out and replaced it by 'Unser Paradox war dies' (This was our paradox). Then came a new remark:

(Dass wir eine Regel 'aufgefasst haben' zeigt sich, unter anderem, an der Sicherheit, ich meine, dem Fehlen des Zweifelns und Tastens, bei ihrer Anwendung.)

(That we 'have understood' a rule is shown, among other things, in our certainty, I mean the absence of doubt and fumbling in its application.)

---

[10] In MS 180(a), 68f. W. explains that 'advice (or teaching) leaves me in the lurch. I must now make a jump' means here 'a "seeing-that-this-is-red" does not help if I still have to find the words that fit this situation.'
[11] In MS 129 the draft of §198 occurs on p. 25.

This precedes PI §§202f. and then a brief discussion of aspect-seeing.

This confirms the conclusions drawn from MS 180(a), particularly since remarks from MS 180(a) were transcribed into MS 129. The concluding remark makes clear that the primary concern in these sections is not to emphasize that following a rule is a *social* practice, but that it is an *activity*, a normative regularity of conduct which exhibits one's understanding of a rule, one's mastery of a technique of applying rules, which is a practical *skill* shown in *action*.

(ii) PG 47 explores the idea that understanding always involves interpreting. We think that an interpretation must fill the gap between an order and its execution, so that one understands only because one *adds* an interpretation to the order. But then why add just *this* interpretation? If it is the order itself that demanded it, then it was unambiguous and needed no interpretation. If not, then interpretation is arbitrary, and what is understood is not the order but what one makes of it.

An interpretation is given in signs. So the idea that every sentence needs an interpretation amounts to the suggestion that no sentence can be understood without a rider. But this is absurd, for then the rider would need an interpretation. We do sometimes interpret signs. But when asked 'What time is it?', we do not. We react, and our understanding is manifest in what we do. Cf. PG 147: that a symbol *could* be further interpreted does not show that I interpret it further. I use a railway timetable without being concerned with the fact that it can be differently interpreted.

(iii) BB 34 adds that to say that every interpretation can be further interpreted is merely to say that what for us is the last interpretation need not be.

(iv) RFM 79ff. applies the very same argument as §§198, 201 to logical inference. Am I not *compelled* to go in such and such a way in a chain of inferences? No – I can do as I please, W. replies. But if one wants to remain *in accord* with the rules of inference, one *must* go on thus! Not at all, W. responds; it depends what one calls 'accord'. And so on. However many rules one suggests in 'defence' of our patterns of reasoning, someone can add a rule justifying a different pattern (which *he* calls 'the same'). This seems absurd: does it mean that one can continue such and such a series as one likes, and so infer *any*how? (Here the argument runs precisely parallel to PI §201.) Not at all, W. replies, for then we should not call what he does 'continuing the series' and 'inferring'. For we *define* the series '+ 2', for example, in terms of the sequence '. . . 998, 1000, 1002, 1004'. Getting this result is a *criterion* for applying the operation '+ 2' (RFM 317ff.). The rule and its application are internally related, for we define the concept 'following this rule' by reference to *this* result.

(i) 'paradox': a paradox is a paradox only in a defective surrounding. If this is remedied the appearance of paradox will vanish (RFM 410). For every paradox is disguised nonsense, and hence may never be accepted and bypassed by other arguments. It must be dissolved by clarifying concepts. Here the defects of the surrounding are various. (1) A confused conception of determination, in which we project on to the rule our determination to use it as a standard of correctness. (2) A misconception of understanding: since how I understand a given rule is something I typically explain by giving an interpretation, we are inclined to think that to understand it *is* to interpret it. (3) A false picture of the internal relation between rules and their applications, according to which something must mediate between the two. (4) A confusion between the correct thought that further interpretations are possible and the false thought that they are necessary.

But note that in view of MS 180(a), 72 (see above, p. 148) it might well be held that 'paradox' in PI §201 means no more than difficulty.

(ii) 'Hence there is an inclination to say: every action according to a rule is an interpretation': a temptation to which W. succumbed; cf. LWL 24:

> How do we know that someone had understood a plan or order? He can only show his understanding by translating it into other symbols. He may understand without obeying. But if he obeys he is again translating – i.e. by coordinating his action with the symbols. So understanding is really translating, whether into other symbols or into action.

Section 202

1   This smoothly continues the argument of §201(b). If how one understands a rule is *exhibited* in what we call 'following the rule', then of course following the rule is an activity, something one does *in practice*. Otherwise how we understand a rule would *not* be exhibited in action. Interpreting a rule is not following a rule, and while any rule can be given an interpretation, it is not possible that every rule-following should require an interpretation in advance of acting. (This impossibility is conceptual or grammatical.) Hence 'following the rule' designates a practice, a normative regularity.

This repeats the point made in §§198–9: to follow a rule is not just to act in such and such a way; it is, in general, to exemplify a regularity of conduct, a mastery of a technique. It is characteristic of what W. calls 'a technique', e.g. a technique of calculating, that there are criteria of correctness in applying it. If you multiply 25 and 27, you must get 675; otherwise you have not multiplied these numbers. If you follow this rule, we say, you *must* get *this*; i.e. getting this result is fixed as what is called 'following this rule'. Such internal relations are not discovered, but stipulated and then taught and learnt. Hence the connection between rule and acting in accordance with it is visible in training, teaching, inculcating (PI §198).

It is important to remark that the notion of a practice here invoked is that of a normative regularity, not of a social practice. It may well be the case that the only kinds of symbol-using practices likely to interest philosophy are common, shared practices, but that is a further matter. W.'s emphasis throughout is not upon the multiplicity of people necessarily involved in rule-following (as if the concept of following a rule required a team of rule-followers in order to be justifiably applied, as does cricket-playing). The contrast that concerns him is not between an aria and a chorus, but between a score and singing an aria. Following a rule is an activity that manifests mastery of a technique, not a one-off affair, but something generally exhibited on a multiplicity of occasions (see below, Exg. §202, 1.1 and 2), and this is what W. means by 'Praxis'.

'To think one is following a rule is not to follow one' prefigures PI §258. The rule is the yardstick against which the act is measured. But a yardstick which expands or contracts according to what one *thinks* is the length of the measured object is no yardstick at all. Merely believing that what I do accords with a rule must not suffice for accord with it. This is clear enough in the two kinds of distinguishable cases: (a) If the rule requires me to φ, and I ψ in the false belief that I am φing, then my belief that I am following the rule is clearly false. (b) If the rule requires me to φ, and I believe that that rule requires me to ψ, and I ψ in the belief that I am following that rule, then again my belief is false. I am not following the rule I take myself to be following. Accord with a rule is something *objective*. Whether one complies with a rule in acting is not determined by whether one believes one is complying. It is fixed by what is called 'following this rule', by what *counts* as complying in the normative regularity of action.

Hence also it is not possible to follow a rule 'privately', as the private linguist purports to do in judging that he is in pain by comparing what he 'has' with a recollected 'private mental ostensive definition' (a putative rule for his use of 'pain'). W. here anticipates the private language argument (see below, Exg. §202, 2).

1   (i) 'Praxis': used in the sense in which we speak of doing something in practice (and not just in theory), with the rider that it is action exemplifying a technique, hence a normative regularity. Earlier in PI 'Praxis' occurs at §51: 'in the technique of using language' *(Praxis der Sprache)* and in §197: 'in the day to day practice of playing' *(in der täglichen Praxis des Spielens)*. In both cases the emphasis is on activity that instantiates an established technique. RFM 333 clarifies: 'In order to describe

the phenomenon of language, one must describe a practice, not something that happens once, *no matter of what kind.*'[12]

(ii) 'to obey a rule "privately"': why the scare-quotes? Because 'privately' does not mean 'not in public' (since it makes sense to say that we follow rules in privacy); cf. similar use of scare-quotes in §§256, 653. 'Privately' (in scare-quotes) precludes the *possibility* of 'publicly'!

2   (i) MS 180(a), 76 is the ultimate source. (For its context see above, Exg. §201, 2.) Following the occurrence there of §201, which argued that how one naturally understands a rule must be exhibited in action, W. continues his examination of 'visual interpretation', of the suggestion that a process of recognition mediates between seeing and saying. One is tempted to think that on seeing a colour I first recognize it, and then apply a colour-name to what I see. Against this W. makes two convergent moves. First, one could say that the rules for the use of a colour-name would leave one in the lurch here, because there is no transition from seeing that it is *this* to seeing that it is red; i.e. no rule can guide the application of a word to a private and incommunicable *this*. (This was already argued in the private language argument; and as W. has observed eight pages earlier, if I need a justification for using a word, it must also be one for someone else (cf. PI §380); similarly (MS 180(a), 70) if the words fit the situation, then it must be possible for everyone to judge whether they fit.) Secondly, one could say that the rules leave one in the lurch here because there is no technique, no institution of going by the rule. This move builds on the preceding draft of §201 as well as on §§198–9 (MS 180(a), 1f.). Following a rule *here* would not exhibit one's understanding in action. The putative transition from the postulated 'what is seen' to the words would be a 'private' one (cf. PI §381(c)). If one cannot make the transition from looking to the word 'red' without the mediation of recognition, then one would not be able to make it by means of a rule anyway.

Niemand kann mir helfen; kann mir sagen wie ich den Übergang zu machen habe.
Darum beziehen sich die Worte 'einer Regel folgen' auf eine Praxis die nicht durch den Schein einer Praxis ersetzt werden kann.

(No one can help me; can tell me how I am to make this transition.
Therefore the words 'to follow a rule' refer to a practice which cannot be replaced by the appearance of a practice.)

---

[12] Cf. RFM 432 where *an employment of a concept* is called a 'Praxis'. MS 165, 33 (in a passage anticipating PI §198) insists that explanations and interpretations are useless in telling me what I must do except in so far as they are subordinate to the practice of employing the sign.

This is followed by a draft of the last two sentences of PI §242.

The putative following of a private ostensive definition yields only the semblance of a 'technique' of application. But for there to be a genuine following of a rule (and a genuine rule to follow) there must be a *Praxis*, a normative regularity of conduct. Note in particular: (i) the argument here presupposes the private language argument in respect of the claim that there can be no such thing as a 'private' sample; (ii) the notion of a *Praxis* here is not concerned with multiplicity of interacting agents, but with publicity of behaviour (with 'obtaining and stating results of measurement').

(ii) MS 129, 121 contains the full draft of §202. (The context was given above (p. 148).) Note that MS 129 prior to this already contains 48 out of the 74 sections of the private language argument (PI §§243–317); in particular, it contains PI §258 (MS 129, 43f.) with the remark, apropos private ostensive definition, that 'one would like to say: whatever is going to seem right to me is right. And that only means that here we cannot talk about "right".' Consequently the redrafting of MS 180(a), 76, in which the words 'which cannot be replaced by the appearance of a practice' were replaced by 'And to *think* one is obeying the rule is not to obey the rule', most probably echoes that earlier remark. The final sentence certainly refers *back* to the private language argument. Transposing this remark to its locus at §202 has transformed a perspicuous back reference into an opaque anticipation.

(iii) MS 163, 133f. reflects upon the idea of my impressions providing grounds for my use of words or pictures. This only makes sense if there are rules justifying the application of words. Of course, W. concedes, one can imagine a subjective picture of the following of a rule. But does one who thinks he is following a rule follow a rule? What is the criterion for someone's following a rule? Is 'I am following the rule . . .' a subjective expression *(Äusserung)* [of following a rule] like 'I have a pain'? This remark is followed (p. 136) by the ancestor of PI §259: the balance upon which impressions are weighed is not the impression of a balance.

IV

FOLLOWING RULES, MASTERY OF TECHNIQUES AND PRACTICES

1. *Following a rule*

Fundamental to Wittgenstein's conception of philosophy is the comparison of speaking a language with playing a game in accord with definite rules. He initially likened a language with a calculus and speech with carrying out calculations. Incurring less risk of confusion, he later compared speaking with playing chess, words with chess pieces, explanations of words with the rules of chess, and the meanings of words with the powers of chess pieces. This picture is built into his employment of the term 'language-game'. Making use of expressions is engaging in some language-game whose structure is given by a set of rules (especially by explanations of meaning). The task of philosophy is to clarify the rules for the use of expressions, especially to remove philosophical misunderstandings by rendering these rules surveyable.

Not only do rules define calculi or games, but also they constitute individuals' *reasons* for doing things and they *inform* actions within those rule-governed practices. The rules here are immanent, not transcendent. They are *put to use* both in calculating and in moving chess pieces, and hence they are *transparent* to agents engaged in these activities. It is precisely these aspects of making calculations and playing games that give point to Wittgenstein's analogy. Explanations of meaning inform speech; they are put to use in giving descriptions, asking questions, giving orders, etc., and they are transparent to language-users. Consequently it is vital to have a correct conception of how rules enter into making calculations and playing games.

It is first necessary to elucidate how rules of grammar make contact with the motley of speech activities. If somebody's understanding of an expression is embodied in a particular explanation of what it means, he must *acknowledge* this rule for using it; he must willingly *cleave* to it. Otherwise the rule cannot be his *reason* for using the expression as he does. There is no such thing as compelling somebody against his will to accept an explanation of what he means by a word. The cure of a conceptual confusion, like Freudian psychotherapy, depends on securing the patient's agreement about what he meant, in this case what rules or standards of correct use he conceives himself to be following. Explanations of meaning are irrelevant in philosophy as long as they are considered to be *causes* of an individual's using words as he does. We are not interested in the mere history of verbal reactions (PG 81, 90) or in causal mechanisms underlying speech production (PLP 124). We may disregard any such 'action at a distance' of explanations of meaning (PG 81; BB 17), focusing instead on how rules of grammar are manifest in the activities of speaking a language. For this purpose, it is obviously not enough to apply the concept of somebody's acting in a way that happens to accord with a rule. An infant, a monkey or a robot might move pieces on a chess-board, and we could intelligibly say of any such move that it was in accord with a rule of chess. But it would be nonsensical to describe such acts as being informed by the rules or to say that these rules were there put to use in providing reasons for actions. The concept of *following* a rule is applicable only to beings who understand rules, apprehend actions as according or conflicting with rules and intentionally act in accord with rules. Clarifying this claim will expose the nonsense in supposing a parrot, a gramophone, a word processor or a computer to speak English. It will also reveal the confusion in the idea that a formal calculus, theory or analysis could discover *hidden* nonsense or contradictions in our linguistic practices, or hitherto unsuspected explanations of our expressions.

We speak of *following* a rule, *conforming*, acting *in accord*, or *complying* with it, and of *obeying* it. These phrases are variously employed for different purposes, sometimes interchangeably, sometimes to draw contrasts (it is odd to speak of 'obeying' a permissive rule). Our concern here is with the issues of whether an agent knows that there is a rule, understands it, and intentionally moulds his actions to it. Hence we shall differentiate 'acting in accord with a rule' and 'conforming with it' from 'following a rule', reserving the latter for cases in which the agent puts a rule into practice, in which he could, and in certain circumstances would, cite it as a reason for actions. Our present topic, then, is the difference between following a rule and (merely) acting in accord with it.

Much of the background to Wittgenstein's remarks on this topic has already been filled in. Two fundamental points must be borne in mind. (i) The concept of a rule interlocks with the concepts of guiding oneself, justifying and criticizing actions, teaching techniques, and giving teleological explanations of behaviour. These conceptual connections are summed up in the observation that the concept of a rule is a dynamic or functional concept (see 'Rules and grammar', pp. 47f.). (ii) The relation of accord between an act and a rule is an internal relation. The rule itself, not some third entity, determines what accords and conflicts with it. Hence to understand the rule is to know what accords with it (see 'Accord with a rule', pp. 102f.). It is a corollary of these two points that the concept of acting in accord with a rule should not be thought to be logically prior to the concept of following a rule; for, in the absence of the normative activities and guidance distinctive of following rules, there would be no such thing as rules at all (and hence no possibility of accord or conflict with rules).

Wittgenstein took two principles for granted from the outset. The first is that the statement that someone has followed a rule entails that he has acted in conformity with it. In this respect 'to follow a rule' resembled 'to know (that)' and 'to calculate'. These expressions are 'success-verbs'. The action of following a rule has an objective aspect. There is no such thing as X's following the rule R in ϕing unless X's ϕing constitutes his acting in accord with R, just as there is no such thing as X's knowing that p if in fact it is false that p. This has important corollaries. (a) It is always possible to distinguish someone's trying to follow a rule from his actually following it; the first issue turns primarily on his intentions but the second depends primarily on what he actually does. (b) Somebody's sincerely believing that he is following a rule never logically guarantees that he is following the rule; whether he really follows the rule requires that his action conforms with it, and this is not settled by his believing himself to have followed it. In short, a rule must determine what counts as acting in accord with it, and it is a truth of grammar that a person on a particular occasion is following a given rule only if he acts in accord with this rule.

The second principle in Wittgenstein's reflections was that X's ϕing counts as his following the rule R only if R is his *reason* or part of his reason for ϕing. Part of his justification for ϕing must involve reference to the fact that ϕing accords with R. It is not enough to support the statement that X is following R in ϕing to observe that X has previously received instruction including formulations of R or that prior exposure to R plays a role in the causal explanation of his ϕing. Rather, it seems, he must understand what the rule requires (permits, etc.), and intend to act in conformity with it. We are tempted to conclude that there is no such thing as his following a rule of which he is completely ignorant, or which he does not (or cannot) understand, or which he intends to violate. With appropriate qualifications to accommodate second-hand knowledge and understanding within complex systems of rules (e.g. a layman's follow-ing a tax code), these ideas indicate important aspects of the connections between the concept of following a rule and the concept of a reason for an action.

In several early attempts to clarify following rules, Wittgenstein was lured into error. He avoided the mistake of arguing that an agent follows a rule only if he has it in mind at the time of acting or in the course of prior deliberation. On the contrary, the mind is irrelevant since the agent may follow a rule in making use of a written rule or a concrete rule-formulation (signpost or traffic light). Here the occult appearance of mental processes is avoided by replacing such processes by acts of looking at real objects (cf. BB 4). On the other hand, this leaves a difficulty in trying to clarify the difference between reasons and causes for actions. Here Wittgenstein tried to tie following a rule to an agent's deliberations without falling into myths about mental processes. As a model he took a calculation in which a rule-formulation *visibly* plays a part. A chess novice may work out how to make each move by consulting a table showing the powers of the different pieces (BB 13f.; PG 86; PLP 129); he might be said to calculate what do from the rule (cf. WWK 168ff.). Likewise, in working out the continuation of the series 1, 4, 9, 16, . . ., someone might write down the schema

$$x \quad 1 \quad 2 \quad 3 \quad 4 \quad 5 \ldots$$
$$x^2 \quad 1 \quad 4 \quad 9 \quad 16 \quad 25 \ldots$$

and use the formula x^2 to calculate the further terms (cf. PG 99ff.). In both cases rules are transparent parts of rule-governed activities, unlike causes, which are not contained in their effects (PG 80). Here, Wittgenstein argued, are paradigms of activities with reference to which someone's having learned a rule is not merely the *cause*; rather, the rule (previously learned) is 'involved in' his activity as a *reason*. And Wittgenstein evidently thought that *comparing* actions with these paradigms would illuminate the distinction between acting in accord with a rule and following a rule (PG 86).

At this stage he attached importance to elaborating and clarifying this concept of a rule's being involved in an action:

Take an example. Someone teaches me to square cardinal numbers; he writes down the row

$$1, \quad 2, \quad 3, \quad 4$$

and asks me to square them . . .. Suppose, underneath the first row of numbers, I then write:

$$1, \quad 4, \quad 9, \quad 16$$

What I wrote is in accord with the general rule of squaring; but it obviously is also in accordance with any number of other rules . . .. Supposing, on the other hand, in order to get my results I had written down what you may call 'the rule of squaring', say algebraically. In this case this rule was involved in a sense in which no other rule was.

We shall say that the rule is involved in the understanding, obeying, etc. if, as I should like to express it, the symbol of the rule forms part of the calculation . . ..

Teaching as the hypothetical history of our subsequent actions . . . drops out of our considerations. The rule which has been taught and is subsequently applied interests us only so far as it is involved in the application. A rule, so far as it interests us, does not act at a distance. (BB 13f.)

This general conception of involvement is applied to clarify how explanations of meaning bear on the use of expressions from the viewpoint of philosophy. An ostensive definition of 'yellow' is of interest only in so far as it is put to use, e.g. when someone calls a flower yellow (BB 11ff.), only if it is put to work every time the word is used (PG 80f.). A philosopher is concerned with explanations of meaning only to the extent that they are *reasons*, not *causes*, of the applications of expressions; as it were, he is interested in the 'geometry' not the 'physics' of language (PLP 124ff.; cf. PG 273). Languages are to be viewed not as mechanisms but as calculi. This is meant to highlight the idea that explanations of meaning are of philosophical interest only if they are involved in the use of words, just as explicitly cited rules of derivation are involved in a formal proof (e.g. in *Principia Mathematica*). Speaking a language is thus compared with operating a calculus of rules (BT 143; PG 63; BB 42). An explanation of 'yellow', e.g., 'as a part of the calculus cannot act at a distance. It acts only by being applied.' (PG 81) It provides a chart; so if I now work without the chart as if it had never existed, then the explanation becomes 'mere history' (PG 86).

Wittgenstein's comparing languages with calculi articulated the conceptual connection between explanations of meaning and the uses of expressions. The striking metaphor that rules cannot act at a distance was tied to this comparison. Both the analogy and the metaphor disappeared from his later reflections, but neither was completely inept. They capture important aspects of the contrast between reasons and causes, thereby illuminating the idea that explanations of meaning are rules of grammar. But this whole strategy of clarification came to seem misleading. The concept of following a rule is tied too closely and narrowly to the agent's overt behaviour. It is the *potentialities* of an agent for using a rule in *normative activities* that is crucial for his following this rule, not the actual occurrence of a rule-formulation in his visible activities. This point applies as directly to the concept of carrying out derivations within a fully formalized calculus as to other examples of following rules. Citing rules to justify each step of a formal derivation achieves nothing if the calculator has not mastered how to use them. And most instances of carrying out computations or calculations do not involve any consultation or formulation of the rules of a calculus, just as competent chess players seldom advert to any rules of chess in playing games. This Wittgenstein had noted much earlier but tried to push aside (e.g. WWK 153; PG 61, 85f.; PLP 129ff.). Later he came to appreciate that operating a calculus, far from being an object of comparison to illuminate the concept of following a rule, is itself an *instance of what needs to be clarified*. The comparison remained important, but now for the purpose of stressing differences rather than close similarities.

What seems to have lured Wittgenstein into the mistaken strategy of tying the concept of following a rule to acts which 'involve' rules is the natural thought that following a rule is doing something *more* than merely acting in accord with it. The question to be answered seems to be 'What more?' Apart from a misguided detour into a mythology of psychological processes, this question seems to leave no acceptable answer. The point then to appreciate is that the fault lies in the question itself. The illusion that there is something more arises from the platitude that it is possible to act in accord with a rule without following it. We are tempted to conclude that the difference must be intrinsic to the act, whereas in fact it turns on the *circumstances* that surround the act.[1] 'What, in a complicated surroundings, we call "following a rule" we should certainly not call that if it stood in isolation.' (RFM 335) It would make no sense to describe two persons as playing chess (or following the rules of chess) if they belonged to a culture unacquainted with games (PI §200). And it would undermine the claim that someone in our culture was following the rules of chess if he waited on whispered instructions from another or if he had been drilled to perform a single invariant sequence of moves. It is only against a certain complex background that acting in accord with a rule counts as following the rule. So if we were still to say that there is something *more* to following the rule than merely acting in accord with it, then this would be the circumstances of someone's actions that entitle us to say that he has followed the rule (cf. PI §§154f.).

What Wittgenstein needed to clarify are the criteria for someone's following a rule. This question turns primarily on the criteria for understanding a rule and for intending to conform with it. Such understanding and intentions involve the possession of *abilities*. To understand a rule is to be able to determine what acts are in accord with it (e.g. to be able to answer the question whether a suitably described act accords or conflicts with it). And to intend to follow the rule presupposes the ability to employ this rule in normative activities. Human *abilities* are the key to a correct analysis of the concept of following a rule, not actual calculations in the medium of the mind let alone electrical operations in the brain or in a computer. Whether someone has followed a particular rule depends on what he would have done if he had been challenged or called upon to make his behaviour intelligible. His having followed the rule presupposes the truth of certain hypotheticals (cf. PI §187),[2] and the support for these encompasses earlier and later behaviour. There is no such thing as someone's following a rule who lacks all of the abilities bound up with understanding or intending to conform with this rule. Consequently, it is nonsense to say that a planet, an ant, a dog or a calculating machine *follows* a rule (though of course the behaviour of any one of these things may, in a sense, *conform* with a rule). *Pari passu*,

---

[1] This point is perfectly consistent with the truism that someone who follows a rule must *intend* his act to conform with the rule. For the criteria for his having meant this also belong to the general framework of his rule-conforming act (cf. PI §190 and Exg.).

[2] Cf. H. L. A. Hart, *The Concept of Law* (Clarendon Press, Oxford, 1961), pp. 136ff.

teleological explanations involving rules are literally nonsensical when applied to the behaviour of any such thing. For example, no rule can provide the computer's reason for performing as it does; that a rule is a reason *for X* and that it *can* be X's reason presupposes the possibility of X's following this rule, and this is totally lacking in these instances.

The concept of someone's following a rule, not the concept of acting in accord with a rule, is the primary focus of *Investigations* §§185–242. This affects the interpretation of the text at the strategic level. It makes clear the role of these sections in exploring the relation of explanations of words to meaning and understanding as well as elucidating the nature of philosophy as an investigation of rules of grammar. At the tactical level it is vital to the articulation and integration of Wittgenstein's remarks. Many of them have no obvious place in a discussion of merely acting in accord with a rule, e.g. comments about intention (§205), absence of choice (§§219ff.), and intimation (§§222, 230ff.), but all of them fit together into a clarification of the concept of following a rule. The same point is vital to the correct interpretation of individual remarks. It is following a rule (e.g. going by a signpost) which is said to presuppose a regular use or custom (§198), not to be possible for a single person to do only once in his life (§199), and to rest on mastery of a technique (§199). And most important of all, it is following a rule which Wittgenstein called a practice (§202). This is all perspicuous if we bear in mind the contrast between following a rule and merely acting in accord with it. A person can be said to follow a given rule only if his behaviour is sufficiently complex and regular to make it intelligible to describe his actions as manifesting understanding of the rule and the intention to act in conformity with it. This in turn makes sense only against a background of his mastery of a distinctive range of techniques, skills or customary practices, since otherwise he cannot exhibit any of the abilities essential to the possibility of his following the rule. Consequently it seems natural to characterize following a rule, *unlike* acting in conformity with it, as a practice, use or institution.

The philosophical task of clarifying the concept of following a rule cannot be accomplished by formulating a simple definition. That is easy enough (cf. AWL 153f.; RFM 321). We could, for example, explain that somebody follows a rule if he intentionally acts in conformity with it. But this would not help to dissolve any of the philosophical puzzles or confusions that surround the phrase 'to follow a rule', and it would shed no light on how rules function as reasons for actions and how they are put to use in practice. Something much more discursive and less easily circumscribed is required. We need to survey a complex network of interlocking concepts, to appreciate how following a rule is related to reasons for actions, to justification and criticism, to deliberation, and to descriptions and explanations of human behaviour. Above all, we must acknowledge how *fundamental* the concept of following a rule is to nearly all of our reflections. Only this will provide a sure defence against the temptations to try to ground following rules in something more basic (the biological nature of *Homo sapiens*, stimulus/response conditioning, the phenomenon of established habits and customs, etc.).

2. *Practices and techniques*

Wittgenstein emphasized the conceptual connection between following a rule and both techniques and practices. The possibility of following a rule presupposes the existence of an established use or custom (PI §198). Following a given rule requires mastery of a technique (§199), hence following a rule is a practice (§202), custom, use or institution (§199). These are not causal hypotheses about rule-following or empirical observations, but grammatical remarks clarifying the concept of following a rule (§199).

A technique is not the same as a practice, although the concept of a technique is internally related both to the concept of a rule and to the concept of a practice. For there to be a rule by reference to which certain acts are judged to be correct or incorrect, in accord with the rule or contrary to the rule, there must be a technique of applying the rule. If something is to count as the expression or formulation of a rule, it must be used (or be understood as being appropriate to be used) as a standard of correctness against which to measure actions. Consequently there must be a technique of so using it, as it were a method of projection of the rule on to conduct. To understand a rule is to be master of the technique of its application, i.e. to possess a certain array of abilities. To understand a language is to be master of a technique (PI §199), indeed of a wide range of complex, interlocking techniques. Counting, calculating, making geometrical constructions, measuring, inferring, correlating members of sets are all techniques (LFM 31, 42, 61f., 79ff., 153, 202, 206f., 285). To engage in these activities is to exemplify mastery of these techniques, to display the ability to use and follow the various rules that define them.

Mastery of a technique is manifest *in practice*, in doing certain things. But, of course, a single act in accord with a rule is not (save in complex settings) an exhibition of mastery of a technique. Nor, save against a complicated setting which presupposes possession of a wide array of rule-following skills, is it a matter of following a rule. For, as we have argued, to follow a rule presupposes possession of a variety of abilities. Someone does, indeed, manifest his mastery of a technique of following a rule in a particular act of applying it, but only against a complex background of behaviour exhibiting his abilities and comprising *a practice*, a custom or regularity of applying it (or other rules).

The concepts of a technique of using and applying rules and of a practice in which mastery of such techniques is manifested have many interrelated facets. We shall single out four:

(i) *Regularity*   We can speak of a technique and its exemplification in practice only where an established pattern of behaviour is discernible. Something must be identifiable as a standard procedure, and hence occasional deviations must be identifiable as exceptions to a pattern (cf. LFM 25). This grammatical observation has two aspects. First, tasks within a practice of employing a technique of following a rule recur, as do accompanying normative activities. Many are routine. A competent practitioner must address the same task in the same way and do what is required. Secondly, acquiring the mastery of many techniques typically involves drill, training and exercises (PI §208). A person must learn how to do certain things, and mastery of a technique is judged by the exhibition of the necessary abilities in successful performances. Regular behaviour of the right kind is the criterion for the acquisition and persistence of mastery of a technique. (But someone's mastery of a technique *need not* be related to regularity in the behaviour of *others*; that is relevant only to establishing mastery of a *shared* technique.) Note that the concept of a normative regularity, of 'doing the same thing' in a practice is not independent of particular techniques (see §3 below, 'Doing the right thing and doing the same thing'). What is crucial about a regularity exemplifying a technique of applying a rule is that the agent not only acts in a regular fashion (a bee or bird does *that*), but also that he sees a certain pattern *as* a regularity and that he intends his actions to conform to this pattern. The behaviour of a bee is a natural expression of a regularity, or uniformity, but following a rule is manifest in a regularity which presupposes *recognition of a uniformity* (RFM 348). It might be that whenever someone looked at the sign ❀ a numeral occurs to him, which he then writes down; and when he looks at the sign and the numeral, another numeral occurs to him, which he again writes down. So whenever people look at ❀ they naturally produce the series 123123123 . . . .. But the sign ❀ is not the expression of a rule, and the behaviour is not an instance of following a rule but only a natural expression of a uniformity (RFM 347f.).

It is a corollary that the concept of a technique is connected with the possibility of making predictions (cf. RFM 192), and, moreover, these predictions are not *causal* ones. Mastery of a technique licenses predictions about behaviour (at least relative to motivation). Were predictions not warranted, there would be no discernible regularities in putting a technique into practice, and hence there would be no technique at all: 'We should not call something "calculating" if we could not make such a prophecy with certainty. This really means: calculating is a technique. And what we have said pertains to the essence of a technique.' (RFM 193) However, this feature does not determine what the contours of the technique are, i.e. what is correct and incorrect (cf. Exg. §186); indeed, the prediction will in each case be that the person competent in the technique will do what is correct, and so presupposes an independent differentiation of correct and incorrect procedures. Indeed, in making the prediction we rely on the technique (cf. LFM 96).

(ii) *Action versus theory*   A technique is exhibited in a pattern of *behaviour* or *activity* (RFM 331), a practice. Our rule-following techniques are part of our form of life. We are inclined to think of counting, calculating, inferring or constructing proofs as primarily cerebral activities. The essential business seems to be carried on in the medium of the mind (or the circuits of computers), and any overt actions seem mere symptoms of something deeper and more ethereal. This is profoundly misleading. These are all rule-following *techniques*, and it is of their *essence* to be employed in practice, in daily transaction with people and with objects in the world. We count money and pay our debts, we calculate loads and build bridges, we infer conclusions and act on them.

(iii) *Criteria of correctness*   Essential to any technique is the stipulation of what procedures and what results are correct. Laying down such criteria of correctness is necessary to delineate the scope and content of any technique. Indeed, criteria of correctness are intrinsic parts of techniques. If somebody in counting out marbles says '1, 2, 4, 5, 6' and hands out one at each step in this series, we would say that he miscounted; and if he regularly proceeded in this way, we would judge that he did not know how to count. These verdicts are not based on a discovery (or intuition) that 3 comes between 2 and 4 in the series of natural numbers. Rather, uttering the sequence '1, 2, 3, 4, 5, 6' is something that we fix (LFM 83) or lay down as a rule for correct counting (cf. LFM 107), without which there would be no such thing as counting (or miscounting!). Before criteria of correctness are fixed within a technique, there are no right or wrong results (LFM 95) and hence there is no such thing as a technique to be mastered. And once such criteria are laid down, there is no room for *experimenting* to find which results are correct. It is a corollary of this general point that a change in criteria of correctness produces a different technique. In the case of explanations of meanings, it is part of the technique of application that using a given word *thus* is correct, e.g. that calling an object 'red' is correct if it is *that* ⟋ colour [pointing at a sample], that 'Shut the door!' is obeyed by shutting the door, and so on.

It might be objected that in very rudimentary cases, e.g. in teaching a child to continue simple patterns, the child may master a technique of repeating the pattern without any conception of a rule. This rests on three misunderstandings. First, we may talk here of a technique only because of the normative activities with which *we* surround the activity. Mere natural repetition, as when a thrush repeats the same phrase in its song, or a chimpanzee idly scratches the same figure, does not amount to exhibiting a technique (RFM 344f.). Secondly, one must not conflate a conditioned response inculcated by drill with exercise of a technique. Not until the pupil manifests in his behaviour his taking certain continuations to be correct, and others incorrect, can we say that he has set about following a pattern (as opposed to reacting to a stimulus). Finally, one must not so inflate the concept of a rule that a simple pattern which the child is taught to follow is not thought of as a rule (and hence that the child has mastered a technique without grasping a rule). Provided such patterns figure in normative activities, they are (used as) formulations of rules ('Rules and grammar, pp. 48f.).

(iv) *Objectivity*   Since mastery of a technique is exhibited in acts which satisfy the criteria of correctness internal to the technique (doing what is called 'applying the rule'; PI §201), this manifestly guarantees the possibility of distinguishing between a person's thinking that he is following a rule and his actually doing so. It is, however, tempting to construct an explanation for this objectivity by reference to the idea that techniques are inherently *social*. On such an interpretation, 'correct' (relative to a given technique) would be defined or explained by reference to what most qualified members of a practice do from case to case. This *seems* to be supported by Wittgenstein's using 'custom' and 'institution' as rough equivalents of 'technique' and 'practice' (PI §199; RFM 322, 334, 346) and his emphasis on the importance of agreement (PI §§241f.).

This account is radically mistaken (see §4 below, 'Shipwrecked on the shores of grammar'). Here we merely wish to note three points. First, any definition of 'correct' in terms of consensus or statistical regularity treats correctness as externally related to the technique of applying a given rule, whereas stipulating criteria of correctness is an essential part of explaining any rule whatever. It also conflates a natural expression of a regularity with the recognition of a regularity and the employment of the pattern of the regularity as a norm (above, p. 162). Secondly, it violates Wittgenstein's most fundamental principal of the autonomy of grammar, since it tries to uncover *foundations* (justifications) for grammatical propositions in human agreement (see 'Agreement in definitions, judgements and forms of life', pp. 243ff.). Thirdly, it wrongly takes Wittgenstein's conception of a practice to be necessarily a *social* practice (as if 'social practice' were a pleonasm). But it is not part of the general concept of a practice (or of Wittgenstein's concept) that it *must* be shared, but only that it must be *sharable*. It must be possible to teach a technique of applying a rule to others, and for others, by grasping the criteria of correctness, to determine whether a given act is a correct application of the rule. It must be *intelligible* that others can qualify as masters of any genuine technique. Hence if I engaged in a sort of arithmetical calculation in which I awaited inspiration and hearkened to an inner voice to arrive at a result, then I would not be exhibiting a *technique* at all (cf. PI §§232f. and Exg.).

The purpose of these observations about Wittgenstein's use of the terms 'technique' and 'practice' is to articulate what he meant (and what he did *not* mean) by his grammatical remarks about the concept of following a rule. In observing that 'rule' and 'following a rule' relate to a technique or custom (RFM 346) or that 'following a rule' is a practice (PI §202), he located these concepts in a wider and widely ramifying grammatical context of the concepts of regularity, doing the same, agreement, justification and explanation. The network formed by the articulations of these (and further) concepts is central to the clarification of such concepts as counting, measuring and inferring, and hence he indicated the appropriateness of employing some general remarks about these various special techniques to clarify the concept of following a rule. Conversely, the conceptual connection between techniques and rules makes clear how central the clarification of following rules is to a wide range of issues in philosophical logic and the philosophy of mathematics.

3. *Doing the right thing and doing the same thing*

The endeavour to reduce such normative concepts as accord with a rule, and a technique of applying a rule to regularities or human dispositions, is in principle misguided. But even if Wittgenstein's arguments against such reductionism carry the day, we may still be tempted by philosophical scruples. The argument is straightforward. The same action cannot be treated now as correct, now as incorrect (in the same circumstances) within a single coherent practice. If what was done previously was correct, then surely doing the same thing again must be correct. And whether the same act is performed twice can be settled by inspection. Conversely, if what someone does is unprecedented in a given rule-governed practice, then it must apparently fall outside the scope of the technique exhibited in the practice. Hence, the question of its correctness must be either nonsensical or open. And this thought leads immediately to the idea that *new cases* relative to a practice cannot be predetermined by the relevant rule.

Wittgenstein held that such ideas rest on confusion about the concept of identity or doing the same thing (PI §§208, 215f., 225ff.; LFM 26f., 58f., 176, 180), confusions which obscure the autonomy of grammatical rules and practices. It is a truism that, relative to a given rule, doing the same thing as before must be correct if what was previously done was correct. But this does not make the practice (the application of these rules) responsible to something external. Metaphorically, it is the practice itself which is the arbiter of what is doing the same thing. In teaching someone a technique of applying a rule, we teach him a new use of 'the same'. We may give him a pattern to follow, saying 'Watch me and do the same thing' or 'Study this pattern and go on the same way.' (cf. PI §208) If he errs we respond, 'You didn't do the same' or 'What you did was different from what I did.' The concept of the rule and of doing the same thing are interwoven (PI §225), since the former determines what *counts* here as *the same* (cf. RPP II §408; Z §305). We cannot decide whether acting *thus* is correct (relative to a given practice) by investigating whether it is doing the same as some act known to be correct. Nor can we explain why doing *this* is incorrect simply by saying 'You did not do the same as before', for someone's wrongly taking what he did to be correct amounts to his mistakenly believing that he did do the same (PI §185). Punching keys on a computer, enclosing a written slip in an envelope, moving a piece of wood seem very different, but might all be making the same chess move. Conversely, a series of acts of writing a name on a slip of paper and putting it in a box look the same, yet might be casting a vote, spoiling a ballot, taking part in a raffle, etc. What counts as doing the same within a practice is determined from the perspective of the practice itself and is not responsible to an external reality.

There are further complexities. Consider the technique of addition. We might say that I do something different today in adding 15 to 27 than I did yesterday in working out that sum; or we might say that I did exactly the same (cf. PI §226).[3] Is adding 15 to 27 doing something different from adding 15 to 68? The numbers added to 15 are different and so are the results. But one can also say that one does the same thing to 27 as one then does to 68, viz. one adds 15 to it. And one might well say that one does the same thing to a pair of numbers in adding 15 to 68 as one does in adding 89 to 72, viz. one calculates their sum (as opposed to their difference or product). These uses of 'doing the same' are severally legitimate; they are *not* in conflict. Bewilderment arises from thinking that there must, in such cases, be a single, correct, context-free, purpose-independent answer to the question of whether *this* is doing the same as *that* (cf. PI §226).

The concepts of regularity, predictability and agreement, in respect of techniques and practices, do not make it possible to break into the circle of normative notions 'from the outside', or hold out fresh hopes for reductionism. Rather each of these concepts, applied to practices, must be grasped from the point of view of the particular practice. We might be trained, for example, in a technique of continuing patterns of numerals; here we would recognize a uniformity in '123 123 123 etc.' or in '22 22 22

[3] Consider an imaginary case: people have seven colour words and seven days in a week, and use the words in a cycle (they call 'blue' on Tuesday what they describe as 'red' on Monday). If I say on Monday that X is red, and again on Tuesday that it is red, have I said the same of it, or something different? (cf. LSD 24)

etc.'. Yet it is easy to imagine circumstances (cf. RPP II §400) in which we discerned uniformity not in these patterns, but in such patterns as '2 22 222 2222 etc.' – another kind of uniformity associated with a different technique (cf. RFM 348). 'Only through a technique can we *grasp* a regularity.' (RFM 303) Only relative to a practice of employing a particular technique can we discriminate agreement from disagreement in procedures and results. The only regularity (or agreement) internally related to a technique is regularity from the point of view of the rules of the technique (i.e. normative regularity). Someone who writes down '0, 3, 6, 9, 12, 15, . . .' writes down a fresh symbol at each step; but we perceive regularity here, viz. the production of successive multiples of 3. This determination is rooted in our mastery of arithmetical techniques and is intelligible only in the light of them. Hence Wittgenstein's remarks about regularity, uniformity and agreement give no support to any reductionist programme; nor do they suggest that someone could use the concept of *doing the same* to gain a purchase on a practice of a kind alien to him.

These considerations bear on puzzles about applying rules to new cases. In one sense, every application of a rule is a new case, i.e. a case different from any previous applications; e.g. in now adding 15 to 27, I am doing something different from what I did yesterday in adding 15 to 27. In another sense, every application of a rule is an old case, i.e. a case of doing the same as before; e.g. in now computing the sum of two numbers larger than any I have previously added, I am still doing the very same thing as I did in adding 15 to 27, viz. adding a pair of numbers. Applying a rule might be described as acting under the guise of always doing the same (cf. Exg. §223ff.). In maintaining that the rule of addition does not predetermine what counts as the correct result of adding two numbers of unprecedented size, we in effect assert that since adding these numbers is doing something *different* from any previous addition sum we cannot say that the rule of addition is applied here (in the same way!) – and this makes *no* sense (cf. PI §227).

Certain rules may be said to have not merely a large or indefinite range of applications, but a strictly infinite one (LFM 31, 141f., 255). And we are mesmerized and baffled by 'the infinite'. How can anybody intelligibly assert that our skills embrace *infinitely* many numbers? Finite minds, finite procedures of computation and finite training seem incommensurable with the task of encompassing an infinity of numbers. This leads to the thought that sufficiently large numbers must (sooner or later) expose the limits of basic arithmetical techniques (addition or multiplication). We cannot, as Turing put it (LFM 105), put infinitely many multiplications in the archives! So when we are faced with a *new* multiplication that is not 'in the archives', what then? This reasoning is confused.

First, infinity is neither mysterious, nor huge. A technique with infinite applications does not require superhuman powers to master it; schoolchildren learn the technique of writing down infinitely many natural numbers in decimal notation (LFM 31) and to compute products of infinitely many pairs of numbers (LFM 141f., 253ff.).

Secondly, it is an illusion that we cannot (although we do!) have techniques which have infinite applications *because* there is such a large number of applications that we cannot 'put them all in the archives', i.e. ratify or acknowledge each one as a rule of grammar, and hence it is an illusion that the limits of such techniques *must* peter out (although, of course, they do not!). So to think is precisely to fail to understand what an infinite technique *is*, or more generally to fail to apprehend the possibility of unlimited techniques. The fact that there are infinitely many additions or multiplications is entirely irrelevant (LFM 105f.) to the imagined difficulty. The case of measuring with a metre-rule is, *in respect of the fear that the technique, being unlimited, might peter out*, no different from the case of the techniques of multiplication, addition or counting (to a number which has never been counted to); we may measure indefinitely many kinds of objects never previously encountered, and we may arrive at lengths greater than or different from any previously measured.

Thirdly, we must not confuse applying a fixed technique, whether limited *or* infinite, to cases to which it has not been applied hitherto with extending a technique to a new domain. These two activities are in principle altogether different, though which description to apply to a given case may sometimes be unclear (LFM 155f.). Unlimited application of a fixed technique is exemplified by multiplication of pairs of natural numbers (in decimal notation). Here a computation procedure is specified whose applicability is *independent* of the size of the numbers multiplied. No natural number is stipulated to be outside the scope of this technique, and hence none is excluded, however large or 'unprecedented'. Techniques are bounded only from within and only by stipulating what their scopes are to be. Hence the range of application of a technique is *intrinsic* to it, not something to be established by experiment or observation (e.g. of human capacities or of computers). To misidentify the scope of such a technique is to misunderstand the technique itself. *Extending* a fixed technique is something very different. It is exemplified in mathematics by, for example, extending the rules of multiplication first from natural numbers to signed integers, then to rational, irrational, complex or hyper-complex numbers. Here indeed what is to count as 'the same' must be laid down afresh and is *not* predetermined in the antecedent technique. Nothing in the practice of multiplying natural numbers made it *correct* or *logically necessary* that the product of two negative numbers be positive, or that multiplication by nought yields nought.[4] Mathematicians

---

[4] One might say that if three cows are multiplied by zero, that means they have not been multiplied, and so there are still three cows! (cf. LFM 135)

have sometimes declared their adherence to 'the Principle of the Permanence of Equivalent Forms', but they have often abandoned this dogma.[5] It would be better to say that they are guided by analogies, and what is to count as an analogy is, at least in part, a matter of decision. Sometimes analogies peter out, or are overwhelmed by countervailing considerations (as in the case of quaternions). Typically in extending a technique 'there may be many techniques that we might decide to call a continuation of the old technique.' (LFM 69)

The concepts of following a rule does not 'fit' the concept of doing the same, but rather the two concepts 'belong' to each other (cf. PI §225). In the absence of understanding the relevant rule and knowing how to apply it, the command 'Do the same' would have no meaning (RPP II §408). The very same point holds for other concepts whose explanations involve identity and difference. The use of 'regular' and 'uniform' is interwoven with the use of 'same' and thereby too with the use of 'rule' (PI §208). These grammatical connections are crucial to correct understanding of remarks relating rules and techniques to regularity.

4. *Shipwrecked on the shores of grammar*

Wittgenstein linked the observation that following a rule is a practice with the comment that to think that one is following a rule is not actually to follow it (PI §202). Apparently we are meant to conclude that an agent's sincere belief that he is following a particular rule is *always* compatible with his not in fact following this rule; i.e. that his judgements are always fallible and liable to correction by others. This remark is then held to eliminate the possibility of following a rule 'privately' (PI §202). Consequently, it seems, the idea that following a rule is a practice secures the crucial distinction between appearance and reality in following rules. Hence, too, this idea seems to be the foundation of the private language argument, since that turns on showing that mental ostensive definitions or tables in the imagination do not count as rules justifying the applications of expressions in a 'private' language because this removes the possibility of distinguishing correct applications of these 'private rules' from applications which seem to be correct to the private linguist (PI §§258, 265). The concept of a practice seems to be the axis of rotation for Wittgenstein's reflections on meaning and the mind.

Apparently, on Wittgenstein's view, there is no such thing as someone's following a given rule unless there is some objective standard for

---

[5] This principle states that properties of numbers within a narrower system must be preserved in any extension; but the total ordering of real numbers does not hold for complex numbers and the commutativity of multiplication is lost for hyper-complex numbers.

whether his acts conform with it. The claim that following this rule is a practice guarantees the necessary distinction between appearance and reality in following this rule only if it is an aspect of the concept of a practice that practices provide objective criteria of correctness. It must be made clear that the *practice* of following a given rule makes acting in this way acting in accord with the rule and acting in that way acting in conflict with it. Therefore, the fundamental issue is to clarify how a practice yields objective standards for determining what is correct.

In answering this question, we might be tempted to exploit various of Wittgenstein's remarks about the *social* dimension of human activities. He suggested that someone directs himself by a signpost 'only in so far as there exists a regular use of signposts, a custom' (PI §198). By offering this as part of a clarification of the concept of going by a signpost, Wittgenstein *seems* to have built into this concept the existence of a *shared* pattern of behaviour. This impression is immediately reinforced: going by a signpost is meant to be an instance of following a rule, and following a rule itself is characterized as a custom, use or institution (PI §199). Wittgenstein harped on the importance of training, drill and exercises in inculcating techniques within groups of people (e.g. PI §§189, 208); this is part of the background to our language-games, e.g. of signalling the ability to continue an arithmetical progression (PI §179). His focus seems to be procedures for creating or perpetuating *shared* forms of behaviour. In particular, many remarks stress the social nature of a language. Identifying uttering noises as speaking a language presupposes discerning some regularities between the sounds emitted and the actions of members of a group (PI §207) – at least enough regularities to pick out such activities as commanding, questioning, telling stories, etc., which are part of the natural history, the common behaviour of mankind (PI §§25, 206). Moreover, the very possibility of a language, of a means of communication, rests on agreement among speakers in definitions and in judgements (PI §242). It is conspicuously this social dimension of languages which is totally absent from any 'private' language. Hence his proof of the incoherence of a 'private language' seems the strongest possible ground for claiming that Wittgenstein held the speaking of a language to be *essentially* social.

These two strands of thought are readily woven together. It is tempting to claim that a practice is a *shared* pattern of behaviour, the common property of a group or community of like-minded and consenting adults. On this view, calling following a rule 'a practice' is meant to highlight the essentially social nature of what we call 'following a rule': it is necessarily a custom established in the activities of a group. This seems to offer an immediate answer to the question of how a practice provides criteria of correctness for actions. The standard behaviour of the members of the group is an external measure of what each individual does. His action in any relevant circumstances is either normal or abnormal, and deciding which does not depend on what he thinks. Provided that 'correct' means the same as 'normal', 'incorrect' as 'abnormal', then the alleged *social* character of a practice *ipso facto* guarantees that every practice generates criteria of correctness. In particular, a comparison of any individual's action with the standard response of members of his community who follow the same rule in similar circumstances yields an objective verdict on whether his action really conforms with the rule. A decision turns not on what *he thinks*, but on what *others* typically *do*. Wittgenstein is thus taken to argue for a relativistic conception of objectivity in judgements about accord and conflict with a rule; the general behaviour of a group provides, as it were, the background of the fixed stars against which individual bodies can be perceived to be in motion or at rest (regular or deviant).

A corollary of this conception is that it is only in virtue of the possibility of comparing an action with the pattern of behaviour standard in a group that we can make intelligible the distinction between thinking that one is following a rule and actually following the rule. Therefore, where such comparison cannot be made, the distinction between appearance and reality vanishes. Considered in isolation, no person can be said to conform with a rule: 'It is not possible to follow a rule "privately".' (PI §202) On this view, physical isolation may not settle that someone cannot be described as following certain rules, but it is certainly a *relevant* consideration. It seems to be an open question whether it makes sense for Robinson Crusoe to keep tallies, make arithmetical computations, design a building and execute his plans, keep a log book, etc. All of these are rule-governed techniques and hence seem impossible for Crusoe on his island if it is not possible to follow rules in isolation from a community, unless we can abstract from his isolation and consider him as a member of the English-speaking peoples. Temporal isolation would raise parallel difficulties. Would the last of the Mohicans be unable to state and follow rules for the use of expressions in his language? (Would the Mohican language die before the last native Mohican-speaker died?) Or were a sole Babylonian to have survived into the twentieth century, would it make no sense for him to teach us the techniques of ancient Babylonian arithmetic? For any philosopher who takes the practice of following a rule to be essentially social, the task of accounting for discourse of living fossils and solitary desert islanders will be central. In virtue of living alone on his island, Robinson Crusoe will be transported to the centre of certain versions of the private language argument.

This interpretation of the *Investigations* is a collage of fragments garnered from Wittgenstein's text, but the result is a caricature. The pivotal point in Wittgenstein's remarks on following rules is that a rule is *internally* related to acts which accord with it. The rule and nothing but the rule determines what is correct (PI §189). This idea is incompatible with defining 'correct' in terms of what is normal or standard practice in a community. To take the behaviour of the majority to be the criterion of correctness in applying rules is to abrogate the internal relation of a rule to acts in accord with it. That philosophical thesis is multiply mistaken. We do not in fact make use of the agreement of human beings or of statistics about their behaviour in settling what accords or conflicts with a rule (cf. RFM 406) even though it is true that we settle what rules they have by reference to their behaviour; indeed, there is no such thing as a standard or criterion of correctness which has no established use in explaining, justifying or criticizing determinations of what is correct. Similarly, we do not define 'correct' in terms of what is normal in a group (RPP II §414; Z §319) and we do not acknowledge such an explanation as manifesting understanding of the term 'correct'. A parallel claim would be that 'red' means the colour that most people call 'red' and that is simply an erroneous definition of 'red' (Z §431; cf. RFM 406), although it is, of course, true that English speakers normally call red things 'red'. Both proposals distort the concept of correctness in a similar way.

There is no possibility of building consensus in behaviour (or shared dispositions) into the explanation of what 'correct' means except at the price of abandoning the insight that a rule is internally related to acts in accord with it. In fact, a rule sets a standard for the correctness of the established responses of a group just as much as for the correctness of any individual's actions. It is intelligible that an entire community at least occasionally goes wrong in applying its own rules. If a prophet were to lay down that a special ceremony should be celebrated to mark the vernal equinox, miscalculation or miscalibration of the calendar might lead to the rites being performed on the wrong day, and after many years the error might be discovered and the observances be put on the right footing. To define 'correct' in terms of what is normal or agreed within a community wrongly locates this imaginary course of events outside the bounds of sense.

Wittgenstein's reaction to the suggestion that the practice of following a rule is essentially social is not a mere matter of speculation and conjecture. He was aware of the danger that his remarks about agreement might be misinterpreted in this way. He quite explicitly took care *not* to exclude the possibility that a solitary individual could follow a rule or speak a language to himself. In unpublished manuscripts, Wittgenstein guarded against these confusions by making clear what it makes sense to say about isolated individuals and under what circumstances they can be said to follow a rule or engage in rule-governed activities. From these reflections we can see that the impossibility of someone's following a rule 'privately' (PI §202) does not make it unintelligible that Robinson Crusoe should follow rules in physical isolation. To follow a rule in private is no more to follow a rule 'privately' than to speak to oneself for one's own private purposes (or while alone) is to speak a 'private' language (cf. PI §243).

It is noteworthy that Wittgenstein explicitly discussed Robinson Crusoe. The implication of his remarks is that there is little to discuss. Having mastered such techniques as counting, calculating and measuring, someone could certainly live alone on an island and continue to apply these techniques (MS 165, 74) just as Crusoe is depicted as doing. Similarly, having learnt to speak English, Crusoe could continue to speak to himself, speculating about what might happen, posing questions to himself and answering them, or making plans (MS 165, 103f.); equally he could keep a diary or log of his activities (MS 166, 4). In this sense of 'private' there is obviously the possibility of a private language (MS 165, 103; MS 124, 221). Since all of these activities involve following rules, the intelligibility of describing Crusoe as counting, measuring, posing a question, or keeping a diary presupposes the intelligibility of his following rules in isolation from others. Hence in this sense of 'private' there can be no doubt that Wittgenstein countenanced the possibility of following rules privately. Indeed, there seems no conceptual obstacle to imagining that Crusoe might frame novel rules (in English) for his own purposes and follow them as well as following rules that he had earlier mastered in England. Why should he not invent and play a new form of patience? Or even develop a new branch of mathematics (set theory or the predicate calculus) and write a treatise on it?

Even these seemingly anodyne remarks may raise objections. Philosophers insinuate that Crusoe cannot follow any rule at all: he cannot distinguish between its merely seeming to him that an act accords with a rule and the act's really according with the rule. Whatever seems correct to him will be correct according to the rule as he understands it, and this means that there is no question of accord or conflict. If we are to distinguish between his following a rule and his merely thinking that he is, then we can do so only by comparing his behaviour with the responses of others. He cannot do this himself since he cannot observe others' behaviour, and we cannot even do this if we consider Crusoe in isolation.

This line of reasoning is specious. It builds exuberantly on a grain of truth. No one can draw a distinction between what he thinks to be correct and what is actually correct by identifying something particular as something that he mistakenly takes to be correct or that he wrongly takes to be incorrect. There is little use for the phrase 'this seems to me to be correct, but it is actually incorrect' (by contrast with the utterances 'this seemed to me to be correct, but is actually incorrect' or 'this seems to him to be correct, but is actually incorrect'). This singularity in our grammar has many parallels; in particular, no one can pinpoint a proposition as something that he now mistakenly believes to be true, or, in other words, if English has a verb meaning 'to believe falsely', it would lack a first-person singular present tense declarative form (PI p. 190). But these grammatical truisms do not expunge any distinction between appearance and reality in respect of judgements of correctness or the truth of belief. Rather, the distinction must be drawn in a different way. And of course, it is. For there is no barrier to Crusoe's saying, 'this seemed to me (yesterday) to be correct, but it is not' and there is no conceptual puzzle about supposing him to establish its truth. He might have played out a game of patience before going to sleep, thinking he had won and leaving the cards arranged on the table in the final 'winning' position. In the morning he might look over the cards and find to his disappointment that he had confused the two red knaves; so he would now conclude that he had made a mistake in applying the rules of the game although the previous night he had thought that he had really won. We could imagine similar sequences of events in connection with his counting or measuring objects, with his keeping records of his stores or of the date, etc. In all these cases Crusoe could actually find out that what he had thought to be correct was in fact incorrect, and he could often rectify earlier errors. Moreover, he needs no community aid, and comparisons of his actions with the responses of others play no role whatever in his deliberations. Is it not clear therefore that an isolated individual can distinguish between appearance and reality in following rules? A person stranded on a desert island is not, as it were, *ex officio* disqualified from following rules and applying techniques. Crusoe's island during his occupation was indeed a (fictional) remote outpost of the British Empire and part of its culture.

Having forestalled these philosophical worries, we may feel the onslaught of a second wave. Does the intelligibility of Crusoe's following rules and speaking to himself not depend on the twin facts that we share with him such basic techniques as counting, measuring, keeping records, making and executing plans, etc., and that he also speaks our language? Would matters not look altogether different if we dropped these assumptions? With some minor qualifications, Wittgenstein returned the verdict that there would be no difference in principle, though the practical task of discovering what the desert islander meant and what rules he followed would be much more difficult. If we were to discover a shipwrecked monolingual Tibetan, the task would be formidable. Not only would his utterances be initially incomprehensible, but also many of his techniques might seem bizarre and unintelligible to us.

Befehlen ist eine Technik unsrer Sprache. Wer in ein fremdes Land käme, dessen Sprache er nicht versteht, wird im allgemeinen unschwer herausfinden, wann einen Befehl gegeben wurde.

Man kann sich aber doch auch selbst etwas befehlen. Wenn wir aber einen Robinson beobachten, der sich in einer uns fremde Sprache einen Befehl gäbe, so wäre dies schon viel schwerer zu erkennen. (MS 165, 108f.)

(Giving orders is a technique of our language. Someone who comes into a foreign country whose language he does not understand will generally find no difficulty in finding out when an order has been given.
One can indeed also give oneself an order. But if we observed a Robinson who gave himself an order in a language strange to us, then this would be much more difficult to recognise.)

Nothing, however, seems to be different in principle. Of course, unless we were very patient observers and the subject under observation were very voluble, it might not in practice be feasible to learn his language and penetrate his practices, whereas, if we could lift the veil of invisibility and interact with him, our task would become far more tractable. Likewise, nothing in principle depends on the assumption that the desert islander speaks some established language to himself (e.g. Tibetan).

Man kann sich doch einen Mensch vorstellen, der allein lebt & Bilder von den Gegenständen um ihm her zeichnet (etwa an die Wande seiner Höhle) & so eine Bildersprache liesste sich leicht verstehen. (MS 165, 105)

(One can of course imagine someone who lives by himself and draws pictures of the objects around him (say on the walls of his cave), and such a picture language could be readily understood.)

Provided that his symbolism resembles paradigmatic languages closely enough (MS 165, 106f.), and provided he satisfies the conditions for speaking to himself (which is not to say that he lives by himself and speaks (MS 165, 103)), then we can discover that he is master of a language. And parallel possibilities hold for determining whether he follows other rules and applies various techniques. No genuine technique of rule-application is in principle impenetrable.

Ruminations about desert islanders seem to be attempts to raise the philosophical question of under what conditions we can intelligibly apply the concept of speaking a language. Wittgenstein argued that the solitariness or isolation of an individual is irrelevant to the question of his speaking a language. What is crucial is the *possibility* of another's mastering the 'language' that the solitary person 'speaks'. It is certainly conceivable, Wittgenstein claimed, that each person spoke only to himself, that he was acquainted only with language-games he played with himself (giving himself orders or exhortations, asking himself questions, etc.), and even that the language of such speakers had an extensive vocabulary. An explorer who studied these monologuists could grasp the thoughts they expressed and arrive at a probable translation into his own language by observing how their activities were correlated with their articulate speech. By learning their language he would be in a position to predict what they would do in so far as what they say includes predictions or decisions (MS 124, 213f.). Crusoe on his island is just such a monologuist.

Hatte ihn jemand belauscht & beobachtet, er hätte diese Sprache Robinsons lernen können. Denn die Bedeutungen der Worte zeigten sich im Verhalten Robinsons. (MS 124, 221f.)

(Had somebody spied on him and observed him, he could have learned this language of Robinson. For the meanings of the words are made manifest in Robinson's behaviour.)

Manifestly it is the monologuist's behaviour that settles whether he is speaking to himself. He must engage in some such activities as giving himself orders, making predictions, arriving at decisions, posing questions, etc. We must be able to say of him that now he is deliberating what he ought to do, now he is reaching a decision, now he is ordering himself to do something (MS 165, 116). But each of these things is a technique of human life and of our language (MS 165, 109), and the criteria for mastery of these techniques and for engaging in them lie in someone's behaviour.

We can indeed imagine a Robinson using a language for himself, but then he must *behave* in a certain way or we shouldn't say that he plays language-games with himself. (C5, 24, in English)

But there is no such thing as a 'private' language-game, no *subjective* analogue of a language-game.

Wir nennen das Ausstossen von Lauter, *worüber wir sonst nichts wissen*, nicht 'Sprache'. Und Dein 'subjektives Sprachspiel' wäre nur *das*. (MS 119, 253)

(We do not call 'language' the emission of sounds *about which we have no further knowledge*. And your 'subjective language-game' would be merely *that*.)

There must be public criteria for a person's playing a language-game. If somebody, whether living in isolation or in society, satisfies the criteria for giving orders, framing rules and applying them, asking questions, etc., then he is correctly said to play these language-games; and if he satisfies no such criteria, then he is not correctly said to apply these techniques. Not only is physical isolation irrelevant, but so too is the comparison of his behaviour with that of other people.

It is a consequence of this reasoning that it does make sense to say that an isolated individual follows a rule. Crusoe may engage in the language-games of formulating rules, following rules, criticizing his own past performances as violations of rules, describing his activities in terms of normative concepts, and deliberating about what rules require or permit him to do. His solitude is not a conceptual obstacle to his engaging in these activities, and in judging him to play these language-games we need not consider what it would be normal for us to do in his situation. What he must satisfy are simply the criteria for following a given rule. Two general conditions are obvious. First, he must have rules of the relevant kind, and he must in particular be aware of the rule that he is said to follow. This condition may be seen to be satisfied in various ways, but the most straightforward from the point of view of the observing anthropologist is that Crusoe should formulate the rule himself or employ something as a rule-formulation (e.g. decorating his walls according to a geometrical pattern found on some driftwood). The question of whether he is following a rule can be answered only if it is possible to determine whether his acts accord with the rule, and this presupposes that *both* terms of the internal relation are given (LFM 75, 108). And, in general, it makes sense for me to say that he is following a rule only if I can understand the rule (MS 165, 72). Secondly, Crusoe's behaviour must exhibit sufficient complexity that it manifests the intentions and abilities essential to his following a rule. Otherwise it would make no sense to say that he was following a rule even if he made use of something that has the appearance of a rule-formulation (e.g. a chart or a pattern). This condition must be satisfied by someone who follows a rule whether he lives alone or with others.

If one of a pair of chimpanzees once scratch the figure \ – – \ in the earth and thereupon the other the series \ – –\ \– –\ etc., the first would not have given a rule nor would the other be following it, whatever else went on at the same time in the minds of the two of them.

If however there were observed, e.g. the phenomenon of a kind of instruction, of showing how and of imitation, of lucky and misfiring attempts, of reward and punishment and the like; if at length the one who had been so trained put figures which he had never seen before one after another in a sequence as in the first example, then we should probably say that the one chimpanzee was writing rules down and the other was following them. (RFM 345)

In short, to follow a rule is to act in accord with the rule against a background of activities and abilities, i.e. to do something as part of a ramifying practice embracing many procedures and skills. It is the *circumstances* surrounding the particular act that make the difference between following and not following the rule (cf. PI §§154f.).

Wittgenstein's verdict is clear: a solitary individual can follow a rule. (Here 'can' is the hallmark of a grammatical proposition.) Consequently, calling following a rule 'a practice' (PI §202) cannot be meant to differentiate something essentially social from something individual which may be done in privacy. Rather it must be intended to distinguish genuine cases of following rules from illusory ones. Framing rules and following them is clearly a technique of human life and of our language (cf. MS 165, 109):

. . . that technique can be private, but this only means that nobody but I knows about it, in the sense in which I can have a private sewing machine. But in order to be a private sewing machine it must be an object which deserves the name sewing machine not in virtue of its privacy but in virtue of its similarity to sewing machines, private or otherwise. (MS 166, 7, in English)

Even a private technique must satisfy the criteria for being a technique and, as long as it does so, it is a sound technique despite being unshared. But not everything that gives the intellectual appearance of being a technique does satisfy these criteria, and these must be carefully identified and weeded out. Suppose, e.g. that players of a board-game are supplied with copies of a table showing the freedom of the pieces and that no player ever makes a move without first looking at his table; however, we are quite unable to predict at all what a player will or will not do on his next move.

Aber gebraucht er die Tabelle dann nicht bloss zum Schein? Warum bloss zum Schein [?] Sie ist nötig zum Fassen seiner Entschlüsse. Und nun könnte man sie eine private Tabelle nennen. Sie schaut aus wie eine Tabelle funktioniert aber nicht wie eine solche. (MS 180(a), 59)

(But does he not then merely give the appearance of using the table? Why 'merely give the appearance'? It is necessary for his reaching decisions. And so it could be called a private table. It looks like a table but it does not function as one.)

Here there is no technique, no institution of going by the rule (cf. MS 180(a), 74f.); it would be impossible for a player to tell or teach me how to apply his table (cf. MS 180(a), 75). This means that it is an illusion that a player follows a rule when he makes a move after consulting his table. What might in other circumstances count as his following a rule does not in this setting constitute his following a rule (cf. PI §§154f., 200). He simply 'goes through the motions' of following a rule. This point holds of someone who apparently makes use of a private ostensive definition or a mental colour-chart in justifying the transition from seeing something red to saying 'This is red.' His putative performance apes applying a colour-word by appeal to an ostensive definition or a colour-chart, but it is a sham.

Darum beziehen sich die Worte 'einer Regen Folgen' auf eine Praxis, der nicht durch den Schein einer Praxis ersetzt werden kann. (MS 180(a), 76)

(Hence the words 'to follow a rule' relate to a practice which cannot be replaced by the appearance of a practice.)

Only a genuine practice, not the mere appearance of one, suffices to make an action a case of following a rule.

Wittgenstein's argument turns on the concept of a technique (institution, or language-game). The intelligibility of saying that someone is (or is not) following a rule presupposes that there is a technique of following the rule, and this depends on there being something, in the practice of following the rule, which counts as accord and conflict with it. Without such criteria of correctness there is no such thing as a technique, no possibility of distinguishing someone's thinking that he is following the rule from his actually following it. But, if such criteria are stipulated, then there must be the possibility of *anybody* (with appropriate capacities) ascertaining what they are and how they are applied, i.e. of his mastering them, learning to act in conformity with them, and engaging in associated normative activities. There is no such thing as one person's exercising a technique which nobody else *could* be taught to come to master (cf. PI §§232ff.). Crusoe's language 'is a language only in so far as it *might be used* among human beings' (LSD 34). It is this straightforward conceptual point that is formulated in the claim that one cannot follow a rule 'privately' (PI §202). The private language argument introduces 'private' to signify what *cannot* in principle be explained to another person, what cannot be understood by any others (PI §243). In this sense of 'private', the phrase 'a private technique' is shown by the private language argument to be incoherent. For there is no such thing as a technique of following a 'private' rule (and hence too no such thing as a 'private' rule). But this conclusion does not exclude the possibility of following a rule in private or in physical isolation from others, although, of course, a solitary rule-follower will lack any opportunity to explain the rules he is following to anyone else. Consideration of solitary individuals is irrelevant to the intended meaning of Wittgenstein's dictum that following a rule is a practice.

5. *On not digging below bedrock*

Of course Wittgenstein stressed the importance of regularity and agreement for the application of the concept of following a rule. Indeed, this is a leitmotiv in his writings. Far from denying this, we too give it a major role in our exposition of his ideas (cf. 'Agreement in definitions, judgements and forms of life', pp. 243ff.). The issue is not whether it is important, but what its importance is. To interpret his observations as parts of a proposal to *define* 'accord with a rule' in terms of agreement is unsupported by sound textual evidence, and it conflicts with his *Grundgedanke* that accord is an internal relation of an act to a rule.

In effect misinterpreting Wittgenstein as advocating a definition of 'accord with a rule' in terms of agreement is the resultant of accepting two premises. The first is that following a rule is a practice; the second that a practice is something essentially social. We have argued that the second premise is mistaken. What he meant by 'practice' does not make the phrase 'a shared practice' pleonastic, though of course the practices that he found philosophically interesting are indeed shared ones (and so too the techniques and calculi that preoccupied him are shared ones). This point invalidates the derivation of the prevalent misinterpretation of his remarks. But it leaves unremarked a further potential danger in the first premise. There is a strong temptation to assert that he held a practice (viz. the practice of following rules) to bind a rule to acts in accord with the rule. This invites the gloss that a practice mediates between a rule and its application or that without this practice there would be no such thing as an act's according or conflicting with a rule. But this line of reasoning seems to conflict with the claim that accord is an internal relation between an act and a rule. Must we conclude that there is an unresolved tension or inconsistency in Wittgenstein's ideas even before we arrive at considerations about agreement?

The solution lies in realizing that a practice of following a rule, and of using a rule as a guide to action (in particular, as a norm for the correct use of an expression) and as an instrument in various normative activities, is not a 'third thing', an independent 'entity' mediating between the rule and acts of following it. Rather, for there to be such-and-such a rule, for there to be acts of following (applying) this rule, is not something distinct from there being a practice of following this rule. To describe this internal relation in terms of a practice of following the rule and engaging or being able to engage in the surrounding normative activities is not to explain or base the relation on something more fundamental. It is merely to redescribe it in terms of equally familiar concepts, concepts which 'belong' to the concept of following a rule, but do not 'fit' it. Familiar though they are, they are commonly overlooked. And if they are overlooked, philosophical confusions ensue.

The concept of following a rule is complex and many-faceted. This is hardly surprising in a concept so central to so many distinctively human activities. The guiding principle for attempts to clarify it is to refrain from digging beneath it in the hope of uncovering more basic concepts upon which it rests and to which it is reducible. The network of normative concepts is to be clarified by tracing its reticulations, the pattern of internal relations, not by delving beneath it in search of foundations. Following a rule is a basic concept which we use in clarifying a myriad of other important concepts ranging from metaphysics to the laws of logic, from mathematics to morals. In this respect Wittgenstein compared his treatment of rule-following with relativity theory, namely that it concentrates, as it were, on the clocks with which we compare events rather than seeks out some definition of 'absolute' clock-independent simultaneity.

Following according to a rule is FUNDAMENTAL to our language game, it characterizes what we call description. (RFM 330)

Indeed, it characterizes most intelligent uses of a language, for in speaking (giving orders, asking questions, making statements, telling stories, etc.) we are following rules of grammar. Following rules is *fundamental* precisely because the rules of grammar are the measure of all things.

Section 203

1   The 'paradox' just resolved exemplifies a general feature of philosophical problems. We do not ordinarily think that a rule cannot guide
one, that no course of action can be determined by a rule. We do not
normally think that there is a gap between a sign and its application
(AWL 90). On the contrary, writing '1002, 1004, 1006' in compliance
with the rule of the series '+ 2' is a paradigm of an action's being dictated
by a rule. (Similarly with other philosophical problems. We do not
ordinarily think that middle-sized dry goods are mental entities; on the
contrary, chairs and tables are paradigms of mind-independent objects.)
Far from thinking that anything may conform to the rule of the series,
only *this*, we (rightly) think, will. But when we examine the issue from
the wrong perspective we see things awry. We no longer know our way
about. And this is the general form of philosophical problems (PI §123).
The remedy for this conceptual disorientation is an *Übersicht*, for a maze
loses its mystery when seen from the heights. (To shed light on the
problem from one side only, W. observed, is of no use for that will only
cast long shadows on the other side.)

2   Like §§201–2, this is absent from TS 221 and PPI(I). It originates in
MS 180(a), 74, where it succeeds the remark 'Why do the rules seem to
leave me in the lurch here?'; the implication is that when we 'approach'
the rule for the use of 'red' (the ostensive definition) from the usual side,
we do not feel left in the lurch. Transcribed into MS 129, 121, it succeeds
PI §202. It is followed there by a discussion of the *special* circumstances in
which one can say that one *recognizes* a colour, for it will not do to say 'I
see the colour and recognize it as red'. So when can one speak of seeing
something *as* such-and-such?

Section 204

1   This elaborates §§199f. and 202. There it was argued that it is senseless
to suppose that following a rule might be something that only one man
did only once; and further, that an activity constitutes following such-
and-such rules, e.g. playing chess, only in certain circumstances. Here
W. concedes that, in the context of our form of life (in which playing
games has a significant role), I can invent a game that is never played by

anyone. Against this background there can be rules of this kind which no one ever follows (and I can *show* you my list of rules, perhaps even a board and pieces which I have designed, if it is a board-game). But if no games had ever been thought of, if the very notion of a game did not exist, then it would make no sense to speak of inventing a game which no one ever played. What is possible, what makes sense, against the background of one form of life will be quite senseless, empty gestures and meaningless words, against another.

2   In all earlier drafts (MS 180(a), 4; MS 124, 207; MS 129, 28f.; PPI(I) this follows directly after §200.

MS 165, 99f. makes a parallel point about orders. Orders are sometimes disobeyed. And if once, why not always? If it were to happen always, whatever that were to look like, there would not be even the appearance of ordering. The theme is resumed at p. 117: what would it look like if orders were *never* obeyed? Today, W. continues, I can invent a game which never gets played. What would it look like if games were never played but only invented? After all, I can imagine writing down rules etc. But the question is whether, in *that context*, one can subsume these actions under our concept of a game (and hence of inventing games). There is here, W. concludes with a Hegelian flourish, a 'transition from quantity to quality'.

RFM 334f. elaborates (see Exg. §199): one can only invent games in certain surroundings. These must incorporate whatever is necessary to fix what actions are to be called 'applying the rule correctly' and 'applying it incorrectly'.

RFM 346 remarks that rule-following relates to a technique, a custom. For to follow a rule is, in general, to instantiate a regularity, which one recognizes *as* a uniformity. And the uniformity thus recognized is what one calls 'following this rule'. Hence it involves mastery of a technique, namely of producing the *correct* response to a sign or operative fact. So it involves grasping an internal relation. And *this* is manifest in action.

MS 124, 189 observes that a language is an institution. It is impossible that only once in the history of mankind a sentence should be uttered and understood. And likewise for orders and rules. In parenthesis W. added 'Compare with this the train of thought about idealism and solipsism and the possibility of a private language.'

SECTION 205

1   The interlocutor raises another objection to W.'s relating the concept of a rule to that of a regularity in §§199–204. He challenges the implication of §200 that it is unintelligible that two people should, just

once in the history of a culture unacquainted with games, play chess. And he objects to the suggestion of §204 that one could not invent the game of chess, which never gets played (here the suggestion is that it might *commence*, so that the trajectory of intention seems evident, but be interrupted). For, he claims, to *intend* to play chess does not require the existence of a custom or a technique of applying rules. Such a context or setting is inessential, since I can intend to play chess quite independently of any such setting.

The objection enshrines a misconception about intention, which W. spells out at §337. Far from the intention to play chess disproving that the game of chess is a technique which is possible only within the context of certain forms of life, intending to play chess is itself only possible because chess is a custom etc. 'An intention is embedded in its situation, in human customs and institutions. If the technique of the game of chess did not exist, I could not intend to play a game of chess.' Hence also, to explain what it is to *intend to play chess* presupposes an understanding of 'to play chess', and so cannot be used to show that playing chess in particular and following rules in general are not 'customs, uses, institutions'.

Here W.'s riposte is quicker and less explicit, relying on §197. Chess is defined by its rules, it 'is the game it is in virtue of all its rules (and so on)'. So if the act of intention were, as the interlocutor suggests, independent of the existence of a custom or technique, it would have to 'contain' in some form the rules of chess. But §197 has shown that this is absurd (it is not merely that I do not, as quick as a flash, survey the rules of chess before I say 'Let's play chess', but rather that even if I did, this would not effect the connection between the expression of intention and the thing intended). The only sense in which the rules of chess are present in the mind of someone who intends to play chess is just that sense in which the pronunciation rules of English are present in the mind of someone who reads a passage of English, i.e. he knows them (but this knowing is not a 'having in mind'). For both have mastered a technique of rule-application, not performed a mental act. The rules are not 'acting at a distance', but neither are they acting contiguously in the mysterious medium of the mind. Their role is evident in the *normative activities* which surround the practice of following them (cf. 'Rules and grammar', pp. 47ff.).

2   MS 165, 41 notes the indispensability of regularity for intending itself. 'Ein Mensch kann sich nicht nur *einmal* etwas sich vornehmen, denn hier könnte man sagen: wie weiss er, *was* er vorgenommen hat?' ('A man cannot just *once* purpose to do something, for then one could say: how does he know *what* he has purposed?') But of course it is not claimed that community support is necessary for a person to intend something.

RFM 345 elaborates: if a chimpanzee scratched a pattern in the dust, and another chimpanzee who observed this proceeded to repeat and expand the pattern, this would *not* be giving and following a rule, *no matter what went on in their minds*. But if in their behaviour and interaction the chimpanzees manifested a kind of instruction, showing how, imitation, correction, reward and punishment, if the learner finally put a new pattern into a similar sequence, then one could make out a case that a rule was given and followed. (Note that a *community* of apes is *not* necessary!) But, W. objects, suppose that right from the start the chimpanzee had *intended* to repeat the procedure of copying the pattern. 'Only in a particular technique of acting, speaking, thinking can someone purpose something. (This "can" is the grammatical "can".)'

MS 165, 98ff. develops this apropos giving orders. If one says that something is only an order in the context of a certain form of life, one must meet a similar psychologistic objection. The outward signs of an order (perhaps the imperative sentence form) are necessary for the hearer to recognize that he is being ordered. But not for him who gives the order.

Du sagst: 'Der *Befehlende* könnte doch wissen dass er befiehlt.' Aber was weiss er denn, wenn er dass weiss? Gewiss es kann vorkommen dass Einer sagt: 'Ich hatte das als einen Befehl gemeint, es wurde aber nicht so aufgefasst.' Aber wie hat er denn gelernt was ein Befehl war, was es heisst, etwas als Befehl meinen? Das sind ja Worte der Sprache, Mittel der Verständigung, nicht Stöhnen oder Grunzen. (MS 165, 100f.)

(You say: 'Surely he who gives the order could know that he is ordering.' But what does he know then, when he knows this? Certainly it can happen that someone says 'I meant that as an order, but it was not taken as one.' But how did he learn what an order was, what is called 'meaning something as an order'? These are after all words of our language, means of communication, not grunts or groans.)

A few pages later, W. concludes that ordering is a technique of our language (cf. Exg. §206(2)).

Section 206

1   §§206f. probe more deeply the conceptual links between normality and regular behaviour in the context of a form of life.

The analogy between following a rule and obeying an order was exploited in §§185f. and indicated in §199. Here the point stressed is that we are trained to react to an order in a certain way just as we are trained to follow a rule. Other analogies are elsewhere spelt out: (i) Both following rules and obeying orders are practices, instantiations of regular patterns within a complex form of life, not one-off affairs. (ii) Both rules and orders are standards for the evaluation of behaviour as correct or incorrect. (iii) In both cases an explanation or interpretation sometimes mediates between the standard and its execution, but it is not possible that this should always be the case, and typically it is not. (iv) In both cases there is a grammatical relation between the standard and the actions which we call 'compliance'. (v) Both rules and commands guide action in so far as they provide reasons for acting; hence both have a role in explanations (and justifications) of action. (vi) One may understand, misunderstand or not understand a rule or order. How one understands it is shown both in the explanation of it one may give and in the action one performs in response to it. These provide the two kinds of criteria for a person's understanding a rule or order. (vii) Both rules and orders are typically formulated in a language, although in both cases more primitive phenomena (gestures, signposts, etc.) may be used. (viii) The internal relation between the standard and compliance with it is a reflection of grammatical conventions (e.g. 'The rule (command) that Xs must φ in circumstances C' = 'The rule (command) which X obeys by φing in C'). (ix) Although rules are always general with respect to occasions, and although both rules and commands are frequently general with respect to their subjects, it is possible to give oneself orders and to adopt rules for oneself alone. (x) The practices of following common rules, the custom of issuing and obeying orders occur against a context of shared primitive responses to training and teaching.

The last point underlies the two unanswered questions at the end of §206(a). What if the reactions of people to orders and training is erratic, non-uniform? W. does not answer here (but see Exg. §206, 2 below). Different kinds of cases are imaginable according to the manner in which one might vary the context and background presuppositions.

§206(b), like §200, introduces an anthropological perspective. What justifies the judgement that alien people are giving orders, understand them, obey or flout them? In (c) a schematic answer is given. The common behaviour of mankind provides the essential leverage for interpreting an unknown language.[1] This 'common behaviour' is not merely that behaviour which manifests our animal nature, our natural needs for food, drink, warmth, our sexual drives, our physical vulner-

---

[1] Hence the initially mystifying PI p. 223: 'If a lion could talk, we could not understand him' – not because he would speak unclearly, but because any 'form of life' accessible to lions, given their natural repertoire of behaviour and their behavioural dispositions, is too far removed from ours for any noises they might emit to count as speech (see Exg. §207). Of course, in fairy tales a lion may speak. But then, as in *The Wizard of Oz*, the Lion is really a human being 'in the shape of a lion' (imagine the famous film, but with a real lion in the role of the Lion). Or, as in the *Tales of Narnia*, God is a lion. But *that* is no stranger than God's being an old man with a long white beard!

ability, etc. It also includes the diverse species-specific forms which such behaviour may naturally take for human beings. It is part of the natural history of mankind that we are impressed by fundamental features of our lives (birth, death and procreation), by elemental features of the natural world (the sun and moon, the cycle of seasons, the fecundity of nature, its fury and tranquility), by the basic patterns of human relationship arising out of sexual differentiation, parenthood, the overlapping of generations. And we give expression to these in endless forms, which we can and do recognize.

MS 165, 94ff. argues that if general disagreement were not the exception but the rule, then there would be no language. W. then raises the question of how signs and actions must be linked in order for us to have a language-game at all. Did he not make things too easy for himself in Language-Game no. 2 in supposing such circumstances (constructing a building out of bricks, columns, etc.) which so resemble those of our life?

Nein, die Sprache ist ein Teil des menschlichen Lebens und was diesem ähnlich ist. Und wenn im Märchen Töpfe und Pfannen mit einander reden, so gibt das Märchen ihnen auch noch andrer menschliche Attribute. Ebenso wie ein Topf auch nicht lächeln kann, wenn er kein *Gesicht* hat. (MS 165, 95f.)

(No, language is part of human life and what resembles human life. And although in a fairy tale pots and pans talk to each other, still the fairy tale gives them also other human features. Just as a pot cannot smile if it has no *face*.)

This observation links §206 with §§281ff.

2   MS 129, 29f. contains (a) and (b). (c) occurs on p. 89 with an important preceding remark:

Wer uns die Sprache eines Volks beschreibt, beschreibt eine Gleichförmigkeit ihres Benehmens. Und wer eine Sprache beschreibt, die Einer mit sich allein spricht, der beschreibt eine Gleichförmigkeit seines Benehmens und nicht etwas, was sich *einmal* zugetrogen hat. – 'Eine Sprache sprechen' aber werde ich nur ein Verhalten nennen das unserem/ /dem unsern/ /, gleichen Namens, analog ist.

(Someone who describes for us the language of a people, describes a regularity of their behaviour. And someone who describes a language which a person speaks only to himself, describes a regularity of his behaviour, and not something which has happened only *once*. But I shall call behaviour 'speaking a language' only if it is analogous to what we call by the same name.)

Marginal notes link *both* (c) and this remark with (a) and (b) on pp. 29f. It is again noteworthy that W.'s emphasis is not on the need for a community of speakers, but rather upon regularity of behaviour. RFM 344 likewise stresses the necessity of analogy between the actions of the solitary speaker and those of speakers in a community: 'Certainly I can give myself a rule and then follow it. But is it not a rule only for this reason, that it is analogous to what is called "rule" in human dealings?'

2.1   (i) 'Following a rule is analogous to obeying an order': cf. MS 129, 79:

> Ich folge einer Regel nicht anders, als der Answeisung 'Schlage zwei Eier in eine Pfanne.' Und gehörte dieser Satz keiner Sprache an, oder einer, die ich nicht verstehe, so folgte ich diesen Worten nicht, was immer ich täte.

> (I follow a rule no differently than the instruction 'Scramble two eggs in a frying pan.' And if this sentence did not belong to any language, or if it belonged to one which I did not understand, then I should not be following these words, whatever I did.)

It is a crucial feature of W.'s conception of rule-following that the supposition that one might follow a rule the expression of which is not intelligible to one is itself unintelligible.

MS 165, 78 presses the analogy in respect of the necessity of a general practice to provide the context for the intelligibility of saying of someone that he is following a rule. The connection between a rule and its 'extension' is just that which obtains between a command and acts of compliance with it. What one does is connected with the expression of the rule (or command) only in the context of a general practice.

(ii) 'What if one person reacts in one way . . .': cf. LFM 94f.; grammatical relations are stipulated, not discovered; but only within a framework of regularities. LFM 107f. elaborates further: if, in the process of extending mathematics, half the people do it one way, half another way, who is right? Neither. A decision, not a discovery, is needed.

> Mathematical truth isn't established by their all agreeing that it's true – as if they were witnesses of it. *Because* they all agree in what they do, we lay it down as a rule, and put it in the archives. One of the main reasons for adopting this as a standard, is that it's the natural way to do it, the natural way to go – for all these people.

MS 165, 81ff. develops the idea differently:

> Aber wie, wenn nun die Handlungen verschiedener Menschen nach der// einer//Regel nicht übereinstimmen? Wer ist im Recht, wer im Unrecht? Es lassen sich verschiedene Fälle vorstellen. Der z.B., dass Einer zum Andern am Ende sagt: 'Ach *so* hast Du die Regel aufgefasst' und dass sie sich nun verständigen.
> Wie aber, wenn sie sich nicht vereinigen können? Nun, da könnte es vorkommen, dass der Eine gleichsam wie ein Farbenblinder behandelt wird; oder wie ein Schwachköpfiger. Wir würden vielleicht von ihm sagen, das mehrfache Vorkommen der gleichen Zahlzeichen in derselben Formel verwirre ihn.

(How would it be if the actions of different people following a rule did not agree? Who is in the right, who in the wrong? One can imagine different cases; e.g. that in the end one person says to the other: 'Oh, *that* is how you understood the rule', and so they come to an understanding.

But what if they cannot arrive at a reconciliation? Well, then it might be that one of them is treated, as it were, like someone colour-blind; or like someone feeble-minded. We would perhaps say of him that multiple occurrences of the same numeral in the same formula confuse him.)

And if men did not in general agree in their acts of rule-following, W. continues, and could not come to an understanding, then this would be just as if they could not come to a mutual understanding over the senses of orders or descriptions. There would be a 'confusion of tongues', and although each might accompany his actions with the production of noises, we would not characterize this as a language.

(iii) 'In what circumstances would you say . . .': cf. RFM 352, where the same situation is imagined, but the question is what justifies us in saying of a native that he is the chief. It is not that he is the most richly clad, nor is it without question the one who always gets obeyed. W. gives no answer. Indeed, there *is* no unique answer. Rather the identification of a chieftain will depend on complex customs of a community. In certain circumstances a chieftain may be virtually powerless; and the transition from a tribe with a chieftain to one without one at all may be gradual and vague. Significantly W. follows his unanswered question with another, viz. 'What is the difference between inferring and not inferring? between adding wrong and not adding?'

MS 165, 108ff. elaborates. Ordering is a technique of our language. Typically, an explorer in an alien culture will not find it difficult to determine when an order is given. One can give orders to oneself; but if one observed a Robinson Crusoe giving himself orders in an unknown language, that would be much more difficult to recognize. But again, one can imagine cultures in which the forms of language and life differ substantially, so that nothing quite corresponds to our orders. Just as there might be a people in whose form of life *greetings* play no role. In parenthesis W. added 'chieftain'. Then follows §206(c).

SECTION 207

1   A further development of §206. In what manner does the 'common behaviour of mankind' aid us in interpreting an unknown language? It enables us to establish regular connections between the sounds they make and their actions. For if such regularities are discernible, then it is plausible to see what is said as providing a reason for what is done. This

provides us with leverage for interpreting their words. But in the absence of any such discernible regularity (even though the emission of noises does not seem superfluous) we shall not say that these alien people speak a language. (In W.'s examples, *ex hypothesi*, we shall be right.)

1.1   'carried on the usual human activities' . . .: puzzling, since if it turns out that the noises they emit are not speech, then *can* they carry on the usual human activities at all? Without a language they would just be hairless apes. W.'s story is clearer in MS 165, 111ff. where he imagines a tribe which has a language of gesture and mime, which we can interpret. They have a culture, build huts, communicate, etc. *But* they accompany their actions with sounds, which superficially seem like articulate speech. However, all our attempts to learn this 'language' fail, etc.

2   MS 124, 208f. puts the following after PI §206(a):

> Ich käme zu einem fremden Stamm und einer gäbe scheinbar in der mir unbekannten Sprache eine Befehl; seine Gebärde, Stimme, und die Situation legt es mir nahe dass es ein Befehl ist. Ich höre diese Laute oder Worte von verschiedenen Menschen bei verschiedenen Gelegenheiten im gleichen Ton ausgesprochen, sehe aber keine Regelmässigkeit in den Reaktionen der Anderen, an die die Worte gerichtet werden. Werde ich sie da einen Befehl nennen?
> In den Reaktionen auf einen Befehl muss es Gleichförmigkeit geben.

> (I come to an alien people and someone apparently gives an order in the language which I do not know; his gestures, voice and the situation suggest to me that it is an order. I hear these sounds or words from different people in different circumstances expressed in the same tone of voice, but I see no regularity in the reactions of the other to whom the words are directed. Would I call these orders?
> In the reactions to an order there must be uniformity.)

This precedes a version of PI §208.

2.1   (i) 'When we try to learn their language . . .': cf. MS 165, 72. I say of someone that he is following a rule if *I* understand the rule, i.e. if I *can* follow it. And whether I understand the rule as he does is something I shall find out by whether we agree in its application.

RFM 348 elaborates: if one discerns no regularity in what initially appears to be instruction in rule-following, 'We might say: "They appear to be following a rule which escapes us", but also "Here we have a phenomenon of behaviour on the part of human beings, which we do not understand."'

It is most important to note that the publicity requirement on rules is that it be *intelligible* that another (the anthropologist) should learn the aliens' (or alien's) rule.

(ii) 'their actions fall into confusion': cf. RFM 196; the phenomenon of 'confusion of language' is not tumult and muddle in action, but rather that 'I am lost when people talk, I cannot react in agreement with them.' Here their *actions* need not be 'confused', indeed they might only become confused if they were prevented from accompanying their actions with noises. But no language-game is being played.

(iii) 'There is not enough regularity': cf. MS 165, 97f.; when the explorer comes to the foreign land,

so kann er sie [die unbekannte Sprache] nur durch den Zusammenhang mit dem übrigen Leben der Bewohner verstehen lernen. Was wir z.B. 'Unterrichte' nennen, oder 'Befehle', 'Fragen', 'Antwort', 'Beschreiben', u.s.w. ist alles mit ganz bestimmten menschlichen Handlungen verbunden und ein Befehl ist als Befehl nur kenntlich durch die Umstände die ihm vorgehen oder folgen/ /die ihn begleitet/ /.

(then he can come to understand it [the unknown language] only through its connections with the rest of the life of the natives. What we call 'instructions', for example, or 'orders', 'questions', 'answer', 'describing', etc. is all bound up with very specific human actions and an order is only distinguishable as an order by means of the circumstances preceding or following it/ /accompanying it/ /.)

SECTION 208

1   §208(a) explores the relation between language (and rule-following) and regularity. Are 'order' and 'rule' *(Regel)* being defined by means of 'regularity' *(Regelmässigkeit)*? There are indeed conceptual connections between these fundamental notions. 'Rule' and 'same' are grammatically related (PI §225). These concepts are interwoven like 'proposition' and 'true', and can be said to 'belong' to each other, but not to 'fit' each other (cf. PI §136f.). So one might characterize the concept of a rule in terms of the concepts of regularity, of uniformly doing the same, of agreement. But these are only formal *Merkmale* of a rule, and hence cannot be invoked as *independent* determinants of accord with a rule (cf. Exg. §136). W. argues:

If you give me a description of how people are trained in following a rule and how they react correctly to the training, you will yourself employ the expression of a rule in the description and will presuppose that I understand it. (RFM 393)

Later he adds:

The words 'right' and 'wrong' are used when giving instruction in proceeding according to a rule. The word 'right' makes the pupil go on, the word 'wrong' holds him back. Now could one explain these words to a pupil by saying instead: 'this agrees with the rule – that not'? Well, yes, if he has a concept of agreement. But what if this has yet to be formed? (The point is how he reacts to the word 'agree'.)

One does not learn to follow a rule by first learning the use of the word
'agreement'.
Rather, one learns the meaning of 'agreement' by learning to follow a rule.
If you want to understand what it means 'to follow a rule', you have already to
be able to follow a rule. (RFM 405)

Does this mean that 'following a rule' is indefinable? Not at all, W.
responds (RFM 321), one can define it in countless ways. But such
definitions will be of no use here, presumably because they will employ
formal *Merkmale* and hence fail to make clear how we break out of the
tightly woven circle of internally related concepts.

The predicament is altogether to be expected. Given that 'following
according to the rule is FUNDAMENTAL to our language-game'
(RFM 330), we should not expect a further set of concepts underlying
these ones, which might serve as independent determinants of them
(which might 'fit' them, rather than 'belong' to them).

(b) notes that the words 'regular', 'uniform', 'same' may be explained
to someone (e.g. a Frenchman) by translation. But if someone lacks these
concepts? Then he will be taught their use by means of examples and
exercises. Of course, we are prone to think that examples merely
exemplify something we know but do not fully state by the examples.
Examples seem only to gesture in a certain direction, in which the learner
must go by himself (but in which *we* have already gone). This fallacy is
exposed in PI §75 and §§209f.

There is no circularity in these elementary explanations by example, of
teaching by means of exercises such as bringing the *same* colour, *same*
shape, continuing a progression in the *same* way, etc. This instruction is
grounded in action. At this level of explanation we do not explain what
'same colour', 'same shape', etc. mean by citing a rule, but rather explain
a rule by exemplifying what it is that we call 'same colour', 'same shape',
etc.

(e) adds that such explanations of what it is to follow a given rule, of
what counts as 'the same', of what it is, in respect of a given rule, to
continue uniformly, must also impart an understanding of the expression
'and so on'. For when we explain what a word means by examples, we
'intend them to be taken in a particular way' (cf. §71 and Exg.), and our
'and so on' has a certain trajectory. In this way we explain family
resemblance concepts; and also such concepts as 'series of natural
numbers', viz. 'we write 2 after 1, 3 after 2, . . ., 14 after 13, . . ., 124
after 123, *and so on.*' But this is an explanation only for someone who
understands this use of the words 'and so on', i.e. its use to indicate the
indefinite recurrent application of a general technique (RFM 394, cf. 349).
If it is not understood, then it too must be explained, e.g. by a gesture.
We point at an object or place when ordering people to go over there ↗,

or to pick up that ↗ thing. Analogously, the role of 'and so on' is to signify that the examples have, as it were, a certain direction. We might also replace the 'and so on' by an arrow. In both kinds of case the symbols (and hence too the 'and so on' or the dots) indicate that the end of the series of examples does not signify an end of their application (RFM 417). Hence they are understood when the learner goes beyond what is given by the examples to further cases in the desired, correct, manner.

Of course, one must sharply distinguish two uses of 'and so on', as an abbreviation for a finite list (e.g. 'the letters of the alphabet, viz. A, B, C, D and so on') and as an indication of a technique of unlimited application. Employed as an abbreviation, 'and so on' is replaceable by an enumeration; if instead of 'and so on' we use the sign '. . .' then these dots are 'dots of laziness' (AWL 6; cf. PLP 165). But employed, e.g., in explaining the concept of the series of even numbers ('2, 4, 6, 8, 10, 12, 14, . . ., 22, 24 and so on'), the 'and so on' is not an abbreviation at all. Rather, it indicates a technique for constructing an indefinitely long series (cf. BB 95). This is rendered more explicit by 'and so on *ad infinitum*'. But one must beware of the muddled thought that an infinite development (such as π) is merely much longer than a finite one (so that as it were, God sees right to its end, but we cannot). The 'and so on' in these two kinds of case is a completely different sign.

(g) concludes that teaching the meaning of an expression that is defined by an enumeration is different from teaching the meaning of an expression by examples plus an 'and so on'. And the criterion of understanding differs between such cases. In the first case repetition of the examples (e.g. the integers from 1 to 10) will betoken understanding; in the second, the production of further, hitherto unmentioned examples (e.g. continuing the series at an arbitrary point).

§208 exemplifies W.'s observation:

What the correct following of a rule consists in cannot be described *more closely* than by describing the learning of 'proceeding according to the rule'. And this description is an everyday one, like that of cooking and sewing, for example. It presupposes as much as these. It distinguishes one thing from another, and so it informs a human being who is ignorant of something particular. (RFM 392)

1.1   (i) 'by means of examples': a cardinal point of W.'s argument is that a series of examples can themselves be employed as the expression of a rule. Cf. 'Isn't my knowledge, my concept of a game, completely expressed in the explanations that I could give? That is, in my describing examples of various kinds of games . . . and so on.' (PI §75) Cf. Exg. §208, 2.1 below.

(ii) 'durch Übung': 'and *exercises*' (cf. BB 141). *Übung* should not be conflated with *Praxis*.

(iii) 'I influence him by expressions of agreement, rejection . . .': the

effect of explanations depends on the learner's responses to encourage-
ment, pointing, etc. (cf. Exg. §145).

2.1   (i) 'by means of examples': cf. MS 165, 74: 'Wann machen A und B
"das Gleiche"? Wie kann ich das beantworten? Durch Beispiele.' ('When
do A and B do "the same"? How can I answer that? By examples.') Also
BT 188:

> Eine Regel kann ich nicht anders geben, als durch einen Ausdruck; denn auch
> Beispiele, wenn sie Beispiele sein sollen, sind ein Ausdruck für die Regel, wie
> jeder andre.

> (I cannot give a rule in any way other than by means of an expression; for even
> examples, if they are meant to be examples, are an expression for a rule like any
> other.)

(See also PG 273; RFM 320ff.) We are prone to think that a statement of a
rule plus a few examples are only an indirect way of conveying to the
pupil what the teacher has in mind. 'But the teacher also has only the rule
and examples. It is a delusion to think that you are producing the
meaning in someone's mind by indirect means, through the rule and
examples.' (AWL 132)

     (ii) 'I do not communicate less to him than I know myself': elsewhere
W. stressed this point. We are inclined to think that a rule contains its
own applications, and hence that when we understand a rule, our
understanding foresees all its applications. (Hence, when we order a
pupil to expand a segment of a series, we conceive of our meaning him to
write '1002' after '1000' etc. as an *anticipation*.) Here we confuse, *inter alia*,
a grammatical articulation which we know (*can* say or think) with a *future*
step in an unfolding process. But my knowing the meaning of 'x^2' gives
me no more reliable an insight into my own future performances than I
can have of another's. I have done many examples, I have understood
and can give appropriate explanations. 'I know about myself just what I
know about him.' (LFM 28) An ability to employ a symbol according to
a rule is not a mental container out of which my subsequent acts are
drawn; 'You yourself do not foresee the application you will make of the
rule in a particular case. If you say "and so on", you yourself do not
know more than "and so on".' (RFM 228) This is *not* a form of
scepticism, but an objection to a certain metaphysical delusion. We do not
think that if A is able to hit a bull six times in succession, then, in some
sense, he *has* already done so in advance. But we are prone to think that if
A understands the rule of the series '+2', and now knows that '1002'
succeeds '1000', '1,000,002' succeeds '1,000,000' (which he does), then *in
some sense* the sequence he is to write unfolds in his mind in advance of his
writing it. *Hence*, we think, he must be able to predict what he will do at
any stage in the application of the rule. But this is muddled, and the

muddle runs parallel to that in kinematics (cf. Exg. §193), where the use of the future tense to state *principles* of movement looks like a *prediction* of a future movement.

(iii) 'and so on': discussed at length in PG 280ff. 'And so on', or some corresponding sign such as dots, is essential if we are to indicate endlessness. This is effected not by the magical powers of the sign, but by the rules for its use. It seems, however, that the sign 'and so on' must itself occur in the rules for the sign 'and so on', e.g.

$$1, 1 + 1 \text{ and so on.} = 1, 1 + 1, 1 + 1 + 1 \text{ and so on, } \textit{and so on.}$$

But the circularity is only apparent, since the 'and so on' affixed to particular numerals refers to a bit of a series, whereas the 'and so on' affixed to the equation does not, but refers to a quite different structure (viz. one including 'and so on').

PLP 166ff. stresses the ineliminability of 'and so on' in our number calculus. It does not abbreviate a large number of numerals which, through human fraility, we cannot write down. It is an essential sign governed by its own particular (*finite*) grammar. Nor is there anything inexact or incomplete about it.

We are strongly inclined to think that 'and so on' is an abbreviation because we are inclined to see the examples together with 'and so on' as the *extension* of the series, rather than itself an expression of the rule of the series. Here we confuse the 'and so on' of 'To be or not to be, that is the question? Whether 'tis nobler in the mind . . . *and so on*' with the 'and so on' of '2, 4, 6, 8 *and so on*'.

(iv) 'We should distinguish between the "and so on" . . .': as W. himself did not do in TLP. PG 268ff. criticizes his earlier view of generality according to which quantified proposition were treated as analysable into logical sums or products.

(v) 'As mathematicians sometimes think': LFM 171 mentions Hardy as speaking as if the 'and so on' in 'The cardinals are 1, 2, 3, 4 and so on' were always an abbreviation. As if a superman (without our 'medical limitations') would write a huge series on a huge board!

PR 146: 'It isn't just impossible "for us men" to run through the natural numbers one by one; it's *impossible*, it means nothing.'

PG 285 amplifies: we are prone to see '1, 1 + 1, 1 + 1 + 1, . . .' as an inexact form of expression, the dots being like indistinct numerals tailing off into the distance. So it 'is as if we stopped writing numerals, because after all we can't write them all down, but as if they are there all right in a kind of box.' This confused vision conflates the 'dots of laziness' with the 'and so on *ad infinitum*'.

SECTION 209

1   Since we explain what 'the same' means by a series of examples (and so too explain what it is to follow a given rule), and since this teaching by means of examples *points beyond* them, it is natural to think that the understanding of 'the same' and of the rule explained must reach beyond all the examples.

This 'natural' thought is strengthened by the powerful feeling that 'and so on' (whereby we point out that the series of examples has a trajectory, that the end of the examples does not indicate the limit of their application) is essentially inexact, nebulous. We are inclined to think that the explanation of 'cardinal number' as whatever results from 1 by continued addition of 1, viz. '1, 1 + 1, 1 + 1 + 1, . . .' is imprecise. And, in a parallel way, we think of an explanation of a family resemblance term (e.g. 'game') as an *incomplete* expression of my knowledge of what a game is (PI §75). The examples together with 'and other such cases' or 'and so on' seem merely to hint at something unsaid. For, after all, if pressed I would reel off *more examples*. So I must, it seems, be reeling them off a spool upon which they are wound, and *that* is my understanding of the expression, the concept or rule.

Hence, (b) remarks, the explanation by examples seems not to be all there is. There must surely be a deeper explanation, one which will truly express what we understand. So it seems that explaining what 'game' means by a series of examples is merely a provisional explanation which awaits the discovery of an as yet unformulated definition which *will* completely express my knowledge (PI §75). Explanations of 'the same' (§208) seem similar. But if there is, at the moment, no deeper explanation, at any rate our *understanding* of the provisional explanation must be deeper than what is expressed by three or four examples and a few dots.

This, as W. has already argued, is profoundly misleading. It embodies a mistaken conception of understanding (as a 'reservoir' rather than a capacity) and a failure to understand how a series of examples functions *as the expression of a rule*. For we wrongly think of the examples *used in an explanation* as being an *application* of the explanandum, i.e. as part of the *extension* of the rule (or concept) explained, rather than as a symbol of the rule itself. But 'my knowledge is . . . completely expressed in the explanation that I could give' (PI §75), i.e. in descriptions of examples and indications of their trajectory. The sign '1, 1 + 1, 1 + 1 + 1, . . .' used to explain 'cardinal number', 'is perfectly exact; governed by definite rules which are different from those for "1, 1 + 1, 1 + 1 + 1", and not a substitute for a series "which cannot be written down".' (PG 284) *Do* I have a deeper understanding than is thus expressed? If so, I should be able to say *what* I thus understand, i.e. to give a 'deeper' explanation.

But I cannot; all I can do is give *more examples*. There is nothing that I am holding back, nothing which, as it were, I can communicate to myself but not to others.

Whence, then, the feeling that I have got more? (c) merely gestures in the direction of a pertinent simile (but see Exg. §209, 2 below). Our muddle about understanding is analogous to confusing an unlimited length with a hugely large length, as if to be unlimited in length is to have a certain length longer than any other. The analogy is clear. Our understanding of an expression explained by examples and an 'and so on' is a grasp of a *technique* of application (a possibility). But we are inclined to view it as a grasp of a hugely large ('infinite') series of applications.

2   (i) The idea that 'there must be a deeper explanation' is fostered by the belief that a series of terms plus 'and so on' is *inexact* in comparison with a general formulation, e.g. an algebraic formula for the general term of a series. PG 288 demonstrates the ineliminability of this elementary form of explanation. For we specify the general term of a series by reference to a basic series which cannot itself be described by a general term. Thus we can give the general term of the odd numbers by '$2n + 1$' when 'n' ranges over the cardinal numbers. But to specify the series of cardinal numbers we cannot give 'n' as the general term. Rather must we give a definition of the form '$1, 1 + 1, 1 + 1 + 1$, and so on'. (Of course, one would give '$1, 1 + 1 + 1, 1 + 1 + 1 + 1 + 1$, and so on' as the basic series; then the general term of the series of cardinal numbers would be '$\frac{1}{2}(n - 1)$'.)

(ii) §§208ff. focus on various sources of the idea that there is more in my understanding than in the explanation by examples that I give. PI §78 exhibited the temptation to think that certain features of experience are indescribable, so that what is known *transcends* what can be said. PI §73 examined the thought that the real understanding of a concept-word is what is revealed by a mental sample. PI §208 briefly emphasized our proneness to confuse 'and so on' with an abbreviation. Another intelligible confusion can be brought to light which rests on more solid ground.

When a series of examples is given as an explanation, understanding the examples as expressions of a general rule involves seeing them as a pattern or paradigm; indeed, it involves seeing a pattern *in* them (PI §§228f.). And this, it seems, is something *more* than just seeing them. Hence, one might be inclined to say that I do indeed have something more in my understanding than I can communicate in my explanation by example (cf. Exg. §74).

But this is muddled. It is possible that I see the examples differently from one who does not understand the explanation. Yet it would be wholly wrong to think that my understanding consists in or is a consequence of the experience of 'seeing the pattern in the examples'. On

the contrary, 'the substratum of this experience is the mastery of a
technique.' (PI p. 208) For we may say that what one perceives when one
sees a series of examples as the expression of a rule 'is not a property of
the object, but an internal relation between it and other objects' (PI p. 212).
So although understanding the examples as expressions of a rule may
involve an experiential component, this component is an aspect of grasping an internal relation, hence not a *means* of understanding. So my
understanding of the explanation is not *deeper* than the examples (hence
there is nothing incomplete or inexact about the explanations of what it is
that I understand). But to understand is to grasp the grammatical relation
between the expression of the rule by the series of examples and descriptions of acts in accord with it.

2.1   (i) 'whence the feeling': RFM 420 (MS 124, 161) linked this more explicitly with the thought in PI §§75, 78: 'But whence arises the feeling, as
if I had more than I can say?' (This addendum was deleted in MS 129, 48.)
         (ii) 'Is it like the case where I interpret what is not limited as a length
that reaches beyond every length?': RFM 420 adds '(The permission that
is not limited as a permission for something limitless.)' and MS 129, 48
added to this:

> Gewisse Vergleiche, in die Sprache//unsern Ausdruck//aufgenommen,
> erzeugen in uns geistigen Schwindel.

> (Certain similes, absorbed in the language/ /our expression/ /produce in us
> intellectual vertigo.)

         (iii) 'what is not limited as a length that reaches beyond every length';
PR 223, 'the infinitely long isn't a measure of distance.' A recurrent
theme in W.'s philosophy of mathematics is: the infinite is not enormously
large. Rather must the term 'infinite' always occur in association with
possibility (WWK 227ff.). LFM 142 jests:

> 'I bought something infinite and carried it home.' You might say, 'Good lord!
> How did you manage to carry it?' A ruler with an infinite radius of curvature.
> You might ask, 'Is there anything infinite about a small thing like a ruler?' But
> why should we not say, 'Yes, the radius of curvature'? But it's not huge at all.

SECTION 210

1   This continues §209. In explaining to another we give a series of
examples, but he has to guess their trajectory, to guess how we intend
them to be taken. This suggestion runs parallel to one made, and
rejected, in PI §71:

> One gives examples and intends them to be taken in a particular way. – I do
> not, however, mean by this that he is supposed to see in those examples that

common thing which I – for some reason – was unable to express; but that he is now to *employ* those examples in a particular way. Here giving examples is not an *indirect* means of explaining – in default of a better.

Here W. makes two moves. First, he notes that there is no *superior* explanation to the series of examples (that I keep to myself). This parallels §69 ('And do we know any more about it ourselves?'). Secondly, what can be *guessed* can also be *said*. To guess what I mean involves lighting upon an interpretation (one among various possible ones). But in that case he could ask whether I meant that interpretation, and I could answer. So nothing *needs* to be left unsaid, no aspect of what I understand is ineffable. And *guessing* cannot reach farther than what can be said.

.1   'various interpretations . . . come to his mind': it is not obvious that for someone to guess requires that he actually think of various inter-pretations, and choose one. For it arguably suffices that he be aware that different interpretations are possible and opt for the first one that comes to mind.

2   Vol. XII, 34f. examines whether an explanation of meaning is always a matter of hinting. In the end the learner must guess what I mean. But this is wrong. For one can hint at something only if one can also complete, fill out, the hint explicitly. So how would this explanation which is only a hint be filled out to make it a complete explanation, and what would this look like? If the learner has to guess the meaning, it must be possible to guess one thing or another, sometimes wrongly. So how is what he guesses manifest? What is the criterion for his having guessed one thing or another? For only this bears on the use or application of the language.

Cf. Z §§304ff.; even if the learner 'guesses' the next step, how will that help him with the following one? Or must he guess *every* step? Certainly there is nothing to guess which will carry him on automatically once he has chosen (no logical machine). But to guess the meaning of a rule, or to grasp it intuitively, *can* only mean: to guess its application. It cannot mean: to guess the *kind* of application, i.e. the rule for it. For that merely generates a vicious circle. In fact, no guessing comes in at all. One might guess what continuation will please the teacher. But 'the application of a rule can be guessed only when there is already a choice between different applications.'

SECTION 211

1   If I give someone a series of examples and tell him to go on in the same way, and if the examples are indeed a complete and exact expression of the rule he is to follow (§§208–10), then it may begin to appear a *mystery*

that he *knows* how to go on. If I instruct someone in drawing an ornamental pattern, e.g. '. . . ___ . . . ___ . . . ___' (cf. MS 129, 32), how *can* he know how to continue?

W. responds, typically, by turning the tables upon his interlocutor. How do *I* know how to continue? His response to this needs filling in. If the latter question means 'Have I reasons?', the answer is: my reasons will soon run out. W. is not implying that I have *no* reason for writing '. . . ___ . . . . . . ___'. My reason is that I was told to continue the ornamental pattern, and this *is* the continuation of the pattern. But if the question 'How do I know *how* to continue' means 'How do I know that *this is* the continuation of the pattern?', then my reasons will rapidly give out. To be sure I will insist that this '. . . ___ . . . ___ . . .' is a continuation of this '___ . . . ___ . . . ___', that going on thus is doing the same. And I will give further parallel examples. So I will be able to defend what I do up to a point. But if pushed further yet, my reasons will give out. *This* is what I (and others) *call* 'the same'. But no *grounds* support this. So I will continue the series, carry on doing the same, without grounds for conceiving of *this* as the same; as the earth carries on spinning without support. Nothing cements the internal relation between the expression of the rule '___ . . . ___ . . . ___ . . . and so on' and any part of its 'extension'. But, of course, other grammatical relations lie close at hand. Going on thus: '___ . . . ___ . . . ___' is a *criterion* for following this rule. And it is also a criterion of understanding the order to follow the rule.

1.1   'im Fortführen des Reihenornaments unterrichtest': better 'however you instruct him in continuing the ornamental pattern'. The referent of '*the* ornamental pattern' is evident in PI §208(b) (cf. MS 129, 32f.; MS 124, 211).

2   (i) Multiple layers of reflection underlie this brief remark, which is resumed in §217, without the stress on *knowledge* which determines the direction of §§212–16.

The contrast between reasons for action and causes is a recurrent theme. Relative to §211 the important contrast between reasons and causes is that the chain of causes of an event may well be endless, whereas chains of reasons come to an end at some point (which is not to say that there is some point where all chains of reasons come to an end). If R is the final reason for φing, then the request for a *reason* why R is a reason for φing will typically be rejected. Hence if 'you realize that the chain of *actual* reasons has a beginning, you will no longer be revolted by the idea of a case in which there is *no* reason for the way you obey the order.' (BB 15) So if you order me to expand the series '+ 2', and I write '. . ., 1002, 1004, 1006, . . .', and you ask me why I wrote this, I should say that I was obeying your order. My reason for writing this was that you ordered me to expand the series '+ 2'. But if you ask me why I obeyed the order *in this way*, why I took '1002, 1004, 1006, . . .' to *be* adding 2, I can give no further reason. That is what I *call* 'adding two' (and so does everyone else). And I have no *reason* for calling it so. 'The difficult thing here is not to dig down to the ground; no, it is to recognize the ground that lies before us as the ground.' (RFM 333)

(ii) Z §§300–2: When instructing a pupil I may say '*This* number is the right continuation of this series.' The point is not to direct him towards a kind of logical mechanism, but rather to teach him what is called 'right continuation', i.e. teach him a grammatical connection that is laid down (stipulated) in this language-game. I can show this only in examples. At the elementary level it would be quite pointless to invoke any expression of the 'law of the series'. For the possibility of employing expressions for a law of a series presupposes a grasp of what is called 'the right continuation'. A basic series (e.g. the series of cardinal numbers) is not taught by reference to a law of the series ('*n*' could not usefully be put forward as the general term of the series of cardinal numbers). Rather, at this elementary level, one is 'forming a substratum for the meaning of algebraic rules or what is like them'. (Compare PI §§143ff. with §185.)

Hence, at this bottom level, the learner must go on like this, e.g. . . ., 8, 9, 10, . . ., 18, 19, 20, . . ., *without a reason*. At this level, in this system,[2] there are no reasons. (Hence, too, it is absurd to think that schoolchildren would 'understand mathematics better' if only one could teach them set theory first.) And it is important that the *like this* (in 'go on like this') is signified by a number or value.

For at *this* level the expression of the rule is explained by the value, not the value by the rule.

For just where one says 'But don't you see . . .?' the rule is no use, it is what is explained, not what does the explaining. (Z §§301f.)

2.1   (i) 'im Fortführen des Reihenornaments': RFM 330 elaborates. If I am told to repeat the ornament   ⌐⌐   , how do I know what to do next? To be sure, I will continue without hesitation. And 'I shall also know how to defend what I do – that is, up to a certain point.' For I shall point at the paradigm, saying 'Look, here it goes like *this*, and so I drew it just so ↗.' ('If that does not count as a defence, then there is none.') So if you challenge me by querying why the fact that the paradigm goes *thus* means that I should continue thus, then there is no more that I can say. (Saying 'But going on *thus* is continuing the same' is not to give any *further* reason.)

---

[2] In the number calculus, reasons end here as a matter of *grammar*. In matters of practical reasoning it is not *only* grammar that determines where bedrock is hit, but the agent's voluntary decisions.

(ii) 'Have I reasons?': PG 101:

'I write the number "16" here *because* it says "x^2" there.' That is what every justification looks like. In a certain sense it takes us no further. But indeed it can't take us *further*, i.e. into the realm of metalogic.

(The difficulty here is: in not trying to justify what admits of no justification.)

SECTION 212

1   The lack of reasons connecting a rule to its application does not imply that 'anything goes'. On the contrary, it is at this point that we hit the bedrock of convention – this is what we call 'continuing the pattern'. Nor is the lack of reasons for calling it so (and hence for acting *thus* rather than otherwise) like the lack of reasons for choosing this rather than that when offered an option (a plate of fruits, for example). For there everything is undecided; so I may hesitate, wondering which to choose, if any. But here my application of a rule which I understand is certain. I do not, as it were, fumble, but rather act with complete confidence. W. illustrates this point with the case of being ordered by someone of whom I am afraid. I will continue the series immediately; I do not guess hurriedly in the hope of avoiding punishment if my guess is right, but rather act with perfect certainty.

This kind of certainty is not the certainty one has in propounding a proposition which rests firmly upon good evidence. It is rather the certainty of the mastery of a technique. In the former case doubt would be unjustified, but not senseless. A child may doubt whether the earth is round; the evidence of the visibility of the masts of a tall ship on the horizon while the hull is no longer or not yet visible may seem slight in comparison with the thought that if the earth were round the Antipodeans would fall off. So more explanation is necessary to show that these doubts are really groundless. But someone who doubts whether '1002' succeeds '1000' in the series '+ 2', or whether, given that this colour is red, it is true to say that this poppy (or ruby, etc.) is red, does not need further explanation. These doubts are *senseless*.

2   RFM 350 captures the point of §212 more explicitly.

SECTION 213

1   §213 further probes the issues of certainty. The interlocutor observes correctly that an expression of a rule by means of an initial segment of an arithmetical series can itself be variously interpreted. And *various* general terms can be produced as interpretations of the rule expressed by a segment of the series. Since I respond to the rule with certainty

(§§211–12), this surely means that I lighted upon *one* interpretation out of the various possible ones that came to mind (cf. §210). So a *choice* between the alternatives must have eliminated any doubt about how to continue.

Not so, W. replies. That a doubt is possible (i.e. not *senseless*) in certain circumstances does not mean that I doubted. Indeed, it does not even mean that in *these* circumstances I *could* (sensibly) have doubted. The fact that I can imagine circumstances in which a doubt could arise does not give me a ground for doubting in the present circumstances (cf. PI §84).

§213(b) connects with §186: if I continued the series without any doubt, yet various interpretations were possible, then I must have hit upon this interpretation by intuition. So it was intuition that removed the (potential) doubt. W.'s response is not to deny that we have any such intuitions (such a move would reduce the question to an empirical matter to be settled by psychological investigation). Instead he points out that even if we have such intuitions, they could not resolve the question. He gives two reasons.

First, if intuition were a kind of inner voice (cf. §232) then it speaks with symbols. But then how do I know how to obey its instructions? For if doubt can arise when confronted by the expression of a rule, e.g. '2, 4, 6, 8 and so on', then doubt can also arise when confronted by the whisper 'Write ten next' (Should I write '2, 4, 6, 8, ten next'?).

Secondly, how do I know that this inner voice guides me *correctly*. For not *anything* that an inner voice might suggest is the correct way to continue the series. Only one thing is correct, all else incorrect. So how can I distinguish a true inner voice from a false one. If 'to intuit' is a success-verb, i.e. if one cannot have 'false intuitions', then how do I know that the inner voice is the voice of intuition?

Consequently, to invoke intuition when *reasons* run out is to seek for grounds beneath ground on which one is already standing as firmly as can be. For one can know by intuition only if there is another way of knowing, viz. one that rests on evidence, calculation or stipulation (LFM 30). Intuition cannot establish, give grounds for, something's being the correct thing to do. Grounds must be discovered in experience, or stipulated in a calculus or rule-governed activity. Then there is room for intuitive knowledge (clear and distinct perception, the voice of conscience). But where reasons run out (as in the case of the question 'Why is "5" to be written after "4" in the series "1, 2, 3, 4 and so on"?'), intuition cannot bear the weight of rectitude. Nor does it need to, since there is no doubt (we *do not* doubt) that "5" comes after "4", "6" after "5" in developing the series of natural numbers. This sequence rests neither on reasons nor on intuitions, but *is* (not 'rests on') what we all call 'the series of natural numbers', and we are remorselessly trained to count thus. Any error is immediately corrected, no deviation is tolerated, and no reasons are either given or needed (RFM 37).

1.1   'the psychological "atmosphere"': the whole parenthesis, absent from MS 180(a), 11f. and MS 124, 212, was an addendum to MS 129, 35. What it alludes to is obscure. In general W. talks of the atmosphere of *words* to allude to the inseparable web of associations surrounding a word. Proper names, for example, are surrounded by an atmosphere of associations. We *refuse* to imagine, for example, Goethe's writing Beethoven's ninth symphony. It is too incongruous, ridiculous (PI p. 183). Understanding words has a perceptual component; there is a sense in which we 'experience the meaning of a word', and someone who did not, would suffer from a kind of 'meaning blindness'. But nevertheless, the meaning of a word is *not* the experience (the atmosphere) accompanying it (PI p. 181).

2   RFM 36f.: The expression of the rule 'Add 2' does not leave one in doubt about what to do at any given stage. One answers without hesitation. 'But just for that reason it is superfluous to suppose that this was determined earlier on. My having no doubt in face of this question does *not* mean that it has been answered in advance.' (So too, if I burn my hand in the fire once, I will not put it in the fire again. But not because of my faith in the uniformity of nature, from which I infer that . . ..)

SECTION 214

1   This pursues the objection to intuition. If you need an intuition in order to continue the series '1, 2, 3, 4, . . .' then you also need one for '2, 2, 2, 2, . . .'. The consequent, it is suggested, is absurd, so the antecedent must be false if the conditional is accepted. The argument is explicitly clarified in LFM 30. There W.'s example is the series whose general term is given by the formula '$y = x^2$'. If you need an intuition to continue this at, say, the 100th place, then you also need one to continue the series '+0', e.g. '2, 2, 2, 2, . . .'. Why? To ensure that one does not continue '3, 3, 3, 3, 4, 4, 4, 4, 5, . . .'. But this is absurd. No philosopher, mathematician or ordinary man would think that a special faculty of intuition is necessary in order to continue the series '2, 2, 2, . . .' any more than it is for the pattern ' ⌐⌐⌐⌐ '.

Yet perhaps they would be wrong. Could it not be that an intuition is thus necessary, even for the series '+0'? No! For then an intuition would be necessary at *every* application of *every* rule. A fresh intuition would be needed not only to carry me from 3 to 4, from 4 to 5, etc. in the series of natural numbers, but also from 4 to 6 and from 6 to 8 in the series of even numbers, or from 3 to 5 and from 5 to 7 in the series of odd numbers, and so on. But then intuition would *explain* nothing; just as it is powerless to distinguish correct from incorrect applications (continuations).

1.1   'If you have to have an intuition in order to develop the series 1, 2, 3, 4, . . .': It is perhaps no coincidence that W. here lights upon the series of cardinal numbers. According to mathematical Intuitionists this series is given to us by a *Grund-Intuition*. Given this basic intuition, the rest of mathematics is 'constructible'. Elsewhere W. explicitly criticizes this idea. (i) If this 'basic intuition' is, as Brouwer contends, a psychological process, how does this come into arithmetic, which, after all, is not a branch of psychology? Intuitionists have confused a primitive (undefined) element of a calculus of signs (viz. 1, ξ, ξ + 1) with a mental act or activity (PG 322). (ii) The idea of a 'basic intuition' is nonsensical (PG 322), for the series of cardinal numbers is no closer to any *truth* than a series which, for example, omitted 13 (LFM 82f.). The latter (. . ., 11, 12, 14, 15, 16, . . .) is just a *different* series, not a false one. It is not the series of cardinal numbers, but that is not because a 'basic intuition' assures us that 13 comes after 12, not 14. Rather do we define 'cardinal number' in such a way that 13 is the successor of 12. But one could imagine an 'arithmetic' without 13, only it would not be useful. The two 'series' represent not different realities, but different techniques. And the latter is an inconvenient, impractical technique relative to what we can do with the former. (iii) That 3 follows 2 in the series of cardinal numbers is no more something we *discover* by intuition than we *convince* someone that 103 follows 102 (LFM 127). This is our technique. It is what we call 'counting'. We fix, and teach, it thus. If there is any discovery here, it is that this technique is valuable (LFM 83).

SECTION 215

1   The hankering for an intermediate step between the expression of a rule and the action according to the rule is explored further. The expression of a rule does not *force* us to do *this*, for various interpretations are possible (although only one is correct). So how *do* we get from the rule to the action? Guessing what the teacher meant was excluded in §210; further reasons come to an end (§§211f.); intuition solves nothing (§§213f.). Could we not argue that we *see* that continuing the series 2, 2, 2, . . . with '2, 2, 2' is going on in the *same* way? And that continuing the series 1, 2, 3, 4, . . . with '5, 6, 7, 8' is carrying it on in the same way (viz. by adding one to the previous number)? It is not intuition that is our 'source of knowledge'; rather do we know it because we have (we think) a foolproof sample of identity present in every object. For every thing is identical with itself. Here there is no room for multiple *interpretations*; this is a fundamental law of logic, the rock upon which our thought rests firm! Self-identity provides us with an utterly unambiguous paradigm for 'the same'. And it is *because* we know what 'the same' means that we know that the way to continue the series '+ 0' is *thus*, and the way to

continue the series of natural numbers is *thus*. It is this which blocks the possibility of various interpretations, and which mediates between the rule and its application.

But this is a muddle! The identity of a thing with itself (see Exg. §216) is *not* a usable paradigm, but an altogether useless proposition. For I have to decide whether writing '5' after '4' is doing the same to '4' as is done to '3' by writing '4' after it. And how can the identity of my pen with itself help me to determine that? It makes no sense to say of *two* acts (viz. writing '4' after '3', and writing '5' after '4') that they are the *same* when they are what *one* thing is (viz. self-identical). Contemplating an object, perhaps while repeating *sotto voce* 'This is identical with itself', will not help me to determine whether *this* is the same as *that*.

But surely, one may reply, we must have *some* paradigm of 'going on the same', some sample which we consult, to determine whether doing *this* is doing the same as we did before? To which the reply is: yes, indeed. Going on '2, 2, 2' in response to the rule '2, 2, 2 and so on', or going on '4, 5, 6, 7' in response to '1, 2, 3 and so on' *are* paradigms of going on in the same way. But this is where we started! No definition, explanation, rule is *immune* from misinterpretation or misunderstanding (cf. §§28f.). And the *possibility* of misunderstanding is not warded off by *any* intermediate step between rule and action. We *do not* typically misinterpret. But that is not because we usually give ourselves the correct interpretation, on which we then act. Rather, we are taught in such-and-such ways (adumbrated in §208), and then, when given a typical rule for which this teaching was intended, we *act*.

2   (i) Vol. XV, 46f. places §§215–16 directly after versions of §§192–7.

(ii) LFM 26f. contains a longer and more explicit discussion. If in expanding the series 'x^2' a pupil who has gone on correctly up to 99, writes at the 100th place '20,000', we would say that he has not done the same to 100 as he did to 99. Suppose he insists that he has.

Now what is doing the same with 100? – One might put the point I want to make here by saying, '99 is different from 100 in any case; so how can one tell whether something we do to 99 is the same as something we do to 100?'

We might be inclined to respond: 'You don't know what "the same" is! I'll show you. This is the same as this.' But how is the 'explanation' in terms of self-identity to be applied?

SECTION 216

1   The 'law of identity' invoked in §215 is a paradigm of a useless proposition. W.'s animus to this traditional 'law of thought', one of Frege's 'basic laws of logic', goes back to TLP.

'Everything is identical with itself' is comparable with 'Everything fits into its shape.' In the latter case we involve ourselves in a degenerate case of 'fitting', in the former in a degenerate case of identity. We may say of a piece of ice that it fits into a glass (LFM 27), of a piston that it fits (perfectly!) into a cylinder (Vol. XV, 49), but not of the water in a glass that it *fits* into the glass, or of an object that it fits into its shape. The two partners to a fitting relationship must be independent (in shape)! This spot ◆ can be used *as a picture* of something's fitting into something (LFM 283), but it is nonsense (not false!) to say that *it* fits into its white surrounding. Why? Because an essential feature of an object A's fitting into another object B is that they *can* be separate, and that we can *try them out* for fit (Vol. XV, 49). Of course, if forced to decide whether the spot fits its surrounding or does not fit, we would be inclined to say that it does. That would be a more natural extension of our use of 'fit' (LFM 283). We might even say that 'Every coloured patch fits exactly into its own surrounding' is a law of thought (a specialized form of the law of identity!).

'A thing is identical with itself' is similarly degenerate. We can say that the colour of one book is the same as the colour of another book. They may have the same length, binding, etc. And a philosopher might think that if they 'coincided more and more', became 'more and more the same', they would actually merge and become one book! But this is nonsense. From the fact that two books might have the same colour, it does not follow that two books might be one book. From the fact that it makes sense to say 'The colour of this book is identical with the colour of that book' it does not follow that it makes similar sense to say 'This book is identical with that book.' No more does it make sense to say 'This book is identical with this book (itself).' (LFM 282f.)

We actually have no use for sentences of the form '$a = a$'. But we use a sentence of the form '$a = b$' as a substitution rule, licensing us generally to substitute 'b' for 'a'. And by applying this rule to the proposition $a = b$, we produce from it the useless sentence '$a = a$'. Of course, if forced to choose between '$a = a$' and '$a \neq a$', we would be inclined to opt for the former. That would be a more natural extension of our use of 'is identical with' or 'is the same as'. But it is 'perfectly stupid and useless' (LFM 283) for all that.

1.1   'wird eben nicht einfach dies Bild beschrieben': LFM 283 suggests the rendering 'we are not simply describing this picture'. If this: ◆ were a picture of, say, a black piece of wood fitting into a white wooden surrounding (as in very elementary jigsaws), we would say 'this pictures, represents, their fitting.' But when, in reply to the question 'Does this spot *"fit"* into its white surrounding?', we reply 'It fits', we are not simply describing this picture (as, when asked 'In the *School of Athens* is Plato pointing upwards' we answer truthfully 'He is', we are describing the picture). For 'to describe a picture', in this sense, is to describe what it is a picture of.

2   (i) Vol. XV, 49 continues after 'dies Bild beschrieben' in (c):

vergässe man dies aber, so könnte man leicht diesen Satz aufstellen: 'Jeder
Farbfleck passt genau in seine Umgebung' // so könnte man leicht dahin
kommen, diesen/den/Satz aufzustellen '. . .' //

(but if one were to forget this, one might easily propound this proposition:
'Every coloured patch fits exactly into its surrounding' // then one might easily
come to propound this/the/proposition: '. . .')

W. then proceeds to examine how we determine, in legitimate cases
(pistons and cylinders, etc.), whether something fits.

      (ii) BT 412: 'Der Satz der Identität z.B. schien eine fundamental
Bedeutung zu haben. Aber der Satz, dass dieser "Satz" ein Unsinn ist,
hat diese Bedeutung übernommen.' ('The Law of Identity, e.g., seems
to have a fundamental significance. But the proposition[3] that this "Law"
is a nonsense has taken over this significance.')

      (iii) RFM 404 (cf. also RFM 89) comments on Frege's insistence that
we distinguish sharply between Laws of Logic ('boundary stones set in
an eternal foundation, which our thought can overflow, but never
displace' (GA i, xvi)) and Laws of Thinking. 'Every object is identical
with itself' is, Frege claimed, a law of truth (logic), whereas the
corresponding psychological law of taking-to-be-true (thinking) is 'It is
impossible for people in the year . . . to acknowledge an object as being
different from itself'. 'Well', W. responds, 'if only I had an inkling how it
is done, – I should try at once!' It is not a law of human psychology, that
we cannot recognize an object as different from itself. Rather, 'an object
is different from itself' is nonsense, and *that* is why it is unthinkable (there
is nothing to think!). Hence too 'an object is identical with itself' is
nonsense; it says nothing, delimits reality in no way.

2.1   'A thing is identical with itself': MS 126, under 3 November 1942
suggests that this be compared with (the *obvious* nonsense): 'A thing is
very similar to itself.'

SECTION 217

1   §217 links up with §211, but rephrases the question 'How does one
know?' as 'How is one *able?*' This might be a question about causes. Even
as such it can be variously interpreted, e.g. how does it come about that I
am able (my father taught me), what skills are presupposed for the
acquisition of this ability (one must walk before one can run), or what

---

[3] 'Satz' means law, proposition and sentence. The pun is lost in translation.

neurological (or physiological) structures are involved in the exercise of this ability. But none of these questions is pertinent to W.'s *grammatical* puzzles (viz. How can a rule guide one when it is capable of being interpreted in many different ways? How does a rule determine its application? How can one possibly grasp a rule in an instant? How can an explanation explain the endless application of a rule?).

If 'How am I able to follow a rule?' is not about causes, then it is about my justification for acting *thus* ('dass ich *so* nach ihr handle'). In that case I should cite the rule which I was asked to follow as my justification for doing what I did. 'I wrote "1002" after "1000" because you asked me to follow the rule + 2!' Similarly, if you give me an ostensive definition of 'red' and later order me to paint a red patch, and then ask me why I painted just *this* colour in carrying out the order, I should point at the sample you gave me, saying 'This colour was called "red", and the patch I painted is this colour.' This *is* to give a reason or justification for my action (BB 14). But reasons run out. Have I a justification for projecting the sample as I did (it is not because the patch I painted *resembles* the sample that it is called 'red'; it *is* the colour of the sample[4])? If I am asked why, *given* that I was told to add 2, I wrote '1002' after '1000', there is little I can say. *'We need have no reason to follow the rule as we do.'* (BB 143) The chain of reasons has an end. When one has exhausted justifications, one reaches bedrock. This is what I do; and, of course, this is *what is to be done*.

The 'bedrock' is wherever justifications give out. W.'s point is not that here my action is *unjustified* (haphazard, a free choice), but rather that it has *already been justified*, and no further justification stands behind the justification that has been given (cf. RFM 330). The bedrock of justification in following rules is not a pre-normative foundation. Shared behavioural propensities (looking in the direction pointed at) and common responses to teaching and training (learning the sequences of natural numbers) are presuppositions for the possibility of having shared rules at all, not the bedrock of justification but the framework for its very possibility. The bedrock is the point at which justifications terminate, and the question 'why?' is answered simply by 'Well, that is what we call . . . .'

It would be a fallacy to conclude, however, that there is some determinate point, fixed in grammar, where justifications terminate. Rather is it claimed that for every chain of justification there is some point at which it terminates. In *some* cases this is fixed in grammar (cf. Z §301), e.g. in a calculus. In other cases it is not fixed in advance, for I *can*, and sometimes do, give interpretations of a rule. And in my ordinary practical reasoning, a reason which in one context may be the terminus of justification ('just for fun') may, in a different context, be

---

[4] Cf. Volume 1, pp. 195, 200 (MU pp. 108, 113).

underpinned by a further reason ('Well, my doctor said I should take exercise, so naturally I prefer exercise I enjoy to exercise I don't enjoy.').

The final parenthesis alludes to a feature of the pathology of the intellect. All too often, in philosophizing, we find the terminus of reasons 'revolting' (BB 15). And so we concoct bogus explanations, pseudo-justifications of a certain *form* (e.g. a 'private' ostensive definition which is supposed to fulfil a role analogous to a public one). We fail to notice the lack of genuine explanatory content. Hence a salient difficulty in philosophical investigation is 'recognizing as a solution something that looks as if it were only a preliminary to it' (Z §314). The solution lies in a description, not a further explanation (even if a further explanation is given, one will once again be facing a terminus (Z §315; cf. RFM 333)). But such a description will do its work only 'if we give it the right place in our considerations'. W.'s discussion of following rules attempts to give a description of the grammar of our concepts and to expose philosophical explanations as 'ornamental coping' supporting nothing. We are brought to see that no explanation is *needed* to provide a metaphysical connection between a rule and its application. And if it were, none would be possible!

1.1   'wir manchmal Erklärungen fordern': better 'we sometimes demand explanations.' (cf. below, Exg. §217, 2.1)

2   Earlier drafts make it clear that this section contains an answer to the question posed in §198, viz. that one connection between the expression of the rule and the action of following it lies in the fact that this is how I regularly act (and also what I call 'following this rule'). Acting thus in relation to this rule is part of my 'Praxis', something I do 'as a rule'.

MS 179, 2 places §217(a) and (b) after a draft of §198(a) with the coda:

> How can I follow a rule? How can it show me how it is to guide me? – If I interpret it in such-and-such a way, how can I hold tight to this interpretation, how can I be sure that it hasn't slipped unawares?[5]

> When justifications run out one hits the bedrock of a *normative* regularity – *this* is what I do.

MS 165, 90f. contains redraftings of the same sequence of remarks.

MS 129, 33 adds (c) to §217(a) and (b), and relocates these remarks between versions of §211 and §212.

2.1   (i) 'a question about causes': BB 15 exemplifies a causal answer. If, to the question 'Why did you paint just this colour when I told you to paint a red patch?', you answer 'I have been shown a sample of this colour, and

---

[5] The German original is quoted in Exg. §198.

the word "red" was pronounced. So whenever I hear the word "red", this colour comes to my mind', then you have given a cause for your action, not a reason.

(ii) 'If I have exhausted justifications': cf. PI §381, 'How do I know that this colour is red? – It would be an answer to say: "I have learnt English." ' But, of course, that answer is not a justification. It provides no reason for calling red 'red' (cf. BB 148f.), but merely reiterates that I *do* know, for I was taught to call this colour 'red'. The point is pursued differently in RFM 406f. When I am ordered to bring something red, what shows me that it is red? The agreement of the colour with the sample? But then what grounds do I have for saying 'That's red'? And do I have reasons for taking *this* to be 'agreement'? RFM 337 links the ordinary application of colour (and other) words and the application of rules:

> If I am drowning and I shout 'Help!', how do I know what the word Help means? Well, that's how I react in this situation. Now *that* is how I know what 'green' means as well, and also know how I have to follow the rule in the particular case.

(iii) 'Remember that we sometimes demand . . .': this appeared in MS 124, 5 in a different context.

> Der Gegenstand vor dem geistigen (innern) Sinnesorgan ist die / / unsre / / Erklärung, Schein-Erklärung, der Äusserung. Das Scheingesims, das das Auge fordert, wenn es gleich / / ob schon es / / nichts trägt / / trägt / /.
>
> Wir fordern oft eine Erklärung, weil wir die *Form der* Erklärung / / Erklärungs-form / / fordern; aber auch wenn sie nichts trägt.

> (The object before the mental (inner) sense-organ is the / / our / / explanation, pseudo-explanation, of the outer manifestation. The ornamental coping which the eye demands, even though / / despite / / it supports nothing.
>
> We often demand an explanation, because we demand the form of the explanation / / the explanatory form / /; even though it supports nothing.)

A redrafted version was copied from there into MS 129, 89 and linked by a marginal indication with §217(a) and (b). The original context gives a specific example of an 'architectural' demand for bogus explanations. The 'private object' is just such an ornamental coping.

Section 218

1   §§218–21 inaugurate a scrutiny of some of the pictures or metaphors associated with following rules. These amount to decorations on the ornamental coping on the grammar of our concepts.

We are naturally inclined to think of the beginning of a series as a

visible section of rails which invisibly stretch to infinity (cf. PI §170).
The series is unlimited, and each point on it is determined by the rule of
the series (i.e. there is only one correct answer to the question 'What is
the *n*th number in this series?'). Here the picture of the rails represents a
certain conception of a rule. And, of course, we imagine that the rails
stretch as far as the eye can see, and further[6] (only God can see the whole
track). This misunderstanding of the concept of the infinite inclines us to
think that the correspondence between a rule and rails is more than
merely 'iconographic'. But the infinite is not a very large number. It is
always to be associated with *possibility*, not actuality (WWK 228). So our
picture of 'infinitely long rails' corresponds to the unlimited application
of a rule, i.e. to the possibility of applying it without limit.

Other such correspondences, which make this analogy so powerful,
yet so misleading, are: (1) the absence of choice (§219); (ii) if one follows
a rule one *must* produce just *this*, just as if a train travels along the rails it
must pass through such-and-such a point (see below, Exg. §218, 2) (iii) a
rail guides a vehicle, a handrail guides a person (one 'experiences the
because') just as a rule guides someone who follows it (§§175–8); (iv) a
rule 'contains' its applications, even if no one applies it (e.g. the rule
'+ 2' determines what it is correct to write at any step, whether or not
anyone works it out, just as the imaginary Transcendent Railroad has
laid down track irrespective of whether a train will ever travel on it).

2   (i) MS 129, 176 prefaces this with PI §238 (without the parenthesis).
This links the application of a rule of an arithmetical series with the
application of a colour predicate (cf. Exg. §217, 2.1(ii)).

There follows:

Warum aber: 'Es liegt doch schon alles in ihr'? – Ich brauche nur noch die
Kurbel drehen, alles übrige tut die Maschine. Und die Kurbel drehen ist etwas so
einfaches: ich kann es automatisch tun.

(But why: 'Everything is already contained in it'? – I only need to turn the
crank, the machine does everything else. And turning the crank is something so
simple: I can do it automatically.)

This connects the rail metaphor with the machine metaphor (the 'logical
machine'). Both represent aspects of the same kind of fallacy, namely
mistaking grammatical connections for super-physical ones. This confusion has been exacerbated by the invention of electronic calculating
machines and computers.

(ii) MS 165, 83 brings out another correspondence:

Wenn Du den nächsten Schritt nach dieser Regel machst, musst Du dorthin

---

[6] Cf. RFM 264: it is easy enough to form this image, the question is what use is it to us.

kommen. Das heisst natürlich, dass jeder der den Schritt nach dieser Regel macht dahin kommen muss.

Das heisst, er wird sozusagen das persönliche Element ausgeschaltet. Wir folgen der Regel wie der Eisenbahnzug der Schiene; wenn er nicht entgleist.

(If you take the next step according to this rule you must come to there. That means, of course, that whoever takes this step according to this rule must come to there.

That means that the personal element is, as it were, eliminated. We follow a rule as a train follows the tracks; if it isn't derailed.)

Here the sting lies in the final clause. We are inclined to make the statement 'If you follow the rule, you must produce this', and we are prone to view this as a kind of prediction (wrongly). Hence the analogy with the rails seems potent. *Any* train, on these tracks, must go to there! But this *must* is causal, and, of course, the train may be derailed. By contrast, the *must* in 'If you follow the rule, must come to there' is not causal, and the conditional is not a prediction. 'If you follow the rules as best you can, you will . . .' is a prediction (RFM 317). But 'If you follow the rule, you must get . . .' is a confusing way of saying 'The result of this calculation is . . . .' The conditional form is misleading, as is the personal reference (cf. RFM 318). It is simply that such-and-such a result (writing '1002, 1004' in expanding the series '+ 2') is our criterion for following this rule ('the result of the operation is defined to be the criterion that this operation has been carried out' (RFM 319)). The rail metaphor is as powerful as the pictorial personification of abstractions (of time as a winged old man with an hourglass and scythe). But whereas no one takes iconographic conceits to be anything but just that, the rail and machine metaphors for following rules are apt to be taken as embodying a literal truth. The computer software, after all, *makes* the machine produce just this answer! (But what *makes* this answer the right answer?)

(iii) RFM 80 clarifies W.'s position. The laws of inference can be said to compel us, only *not* as the rails compel a locomotive. Logic will not seize me by the throat and compel me to write such-and-such. But, of course, I cannot continue a given series, make an inference, *any*how. For we would not call it 'inferring' or 'continuing the series'. This still seems too weak, for we are inclined to insist that one cannot *think* contrary to the laws of logic. But, W. responds, that does not mean that however hard one tries one cannot think thus, but only that we would not call that sort of transition 'thinking' (but a senseless jumble of associations). Compulsion does come in; at school, in the office, at the bank mistakes are corrected, carelessness punished, negligence reprimanded.

(iv) RFM 422: 'One follows a rule *mechanically*. Hence one compares it with a mechanism.' But that comparison is endlessly misleading if one does not understand what 'following a rule mechanically' means. For it does *not* mean, acting in response to an expression of the rule as the pianola acts in response to the perforated sheet.

(v) MS 161, 70f. suggests that the mathematician is inclined to conceive of a rule as an abstract mechanism that works, impersonally, on and through one. Of course, if one says this one does not mean that mathematical propositions are concerned with either psychological or physical processes. For this conception is not just stupid, but a truth encapsulated in a misunderstanding.

SECTION 219

1   'All the steps are really already taken' echoes §188 and §193. It is natural to employ this picture to emphasize that in following a rule one has no choice.[7] But we misunderstand the nature of following rules if we think that 'having no choice' in this context means that in some medium the rule traces out its own applications in advance of being applied, and *hence* one has no choice. For if something like that were the case, how would it help me to make the transition to action? If a written expression of the rule '+ 2' were accompanied by a phenomenal appearance (like an after-image perhaps) of '2, 4, 6, 8, . . .' stretching out into the distance, would that *determine* that one must write '2, 4, 6, 8, . . .' more firmly than the mere expression of the rule? Could one not, with perfect cogency, follow this phenomenal appearance by writing '3, 5, 7, 9, . . .'? One would be using a rule of transcription like this ⌄⌄⌄ , rather than like this ⌁ ⌁ ⌁ (cf. BB 124), but the 'lines traced out by the rule' do not *prevent* that interpretation (one still has a choice). And if one exclaims, 'But you wouldn't!', the reply is 'Perhaps not; but then I would write "2, 4, 6, 8, . . ." in response to the order "Expand the series + 2" *without* the rule thus tracing the lines to be followed anyway.'

Hence the description 'All the steps are really already taken' only makes sense if understood figuratively (like the wings on Father Time which symbolize time flying – figuratively!). So understood it signifies the fact that I *do* not choose. For once having understood the rule, I am bound in what I do further, not in the sense of being compelled, but 'I am bound in my *judgement* about what is in accord with the rule and what not.' (RFM 328f.) Hence, *if I want to follow the rule*, 'then only doing *this* will correspond to it' (RFM 332). So I follow the rule blindly; not like a machine, but with the blindness of complete certitude.

1.1   (i) 'symbolically': 'figuratively' or 'emblematically' would perhaps be clearer here. The coat of arms of a Rule, as it were, would be a pair of rails stretching to infinity.

---

[7] At any rate, if it is a rule which leaves no discretion, or a formula which determines a certain answer (see Exg. §189).

(ii) 'I should have said: This is how it strikes me': in following a rule it strikes me as if all the steps are really already taken; perhaps as it strikes the artist that Fortune must stand upon a wheel.

(iii) 'When I follow a rule, I do not choose': not, of course, because one is necessitated (by logic!). And as long as the teacher is not taking in the prep, I can write what I please! (Although only one answer is *correct*.) Nor is choice precluded because I have an irresistible disposition to do just *this*. On the contrary: '"As I see the rule, *this* is what it requires." It does not depend on whether I am disposed this way or that.' (RFM 332)

To understand a rule is to understand what is in accord with this rule and what is not. So if one then *wants* to follow the rule, there is no choice left (RFM 333).

(iv) 'I follow the rule blindly': a figurative remark. Here 'blindly' does not mean: like an automaton, but: with complete confidence. I do not need to open my eyes to other (or any) interpretations (LFM 226), since I *know* what to do. Cf. RFM 422:

> One follows the rule *mechanically*. Hence one compares it to a mechanism.
> 'Mechanical' – that means: without thinking. But *entirely* without thinking? Without reflecting.

Also RFM 326 (cf. 350):

> I have a definite concept of the rule. I know what I have to do in any particular case. I know, that is I am in do doubt: it is obvious to me. I say 'of course'. I can give no reason.

.1   'I follow the rule blindly': derived from MS 128, 45, where it is followed by the remark that one says that the rule determines all steps in advance to a learner who thinks the contrary, i.e. that he has, in a particular case, a *choice*. So this phrase 'the steps are determined in advance' has a use in a particular circumstance of teaching algebra.

SECTION 220

.1   'Supposed to bring into a prominence a difference between being causally determined and being logically determined': in the case of a causal process, e.g. having made a complex entry into one's pocket calculator and then pressed the button, one would not say, once the entry has been made, 'All the steps are really already taken'. For any number of accidents of fate may intervene, the battery may run out, I may drop the calculator and break it, you may, mischievously, press another button before the answer to my entry comes up, etc. But nothing can intervene between $x^2]_4$ and 16.

It is important to note the 'supposed to'. First, in an important sense there is no such thing as 'logical compulsion' (or 'logically inexorable') even though we speak of 'compelling arguments'. I am no more 'logically compelled' to write '1002, 1004' in expanding the series '+ 2', or to write 'q' given 'p' and 'if p then q' than I am compelled to move my king when in check. (But also no less!) A causally determined process fixes what will *happen*. A logical determination (which is not a kind of compulsion) fixes what is to be *called* . . .. Secondly, the 'symbolic expression' conspicuously fails to bring into prominence the difference. For it generates a picture of logical determination as a *super*-physical determination (cf. §193), as if being logically determined were like being causally determined, only even more inexorably (the rails not only stretch to infinity, but they never bend or break).

2.1   (i) MS 128, 46 places this after the early version of §219(c) and (d) (cf. Exg. §219, 2.1 (ii)). In that context it is clearer. For if a pupil wrongly thinks that at a certain point in following a rule he has a choice, we might well say 'The rule determines all the steps in advance.' This 'symbolic proposition' thus used is meant to emphasize that, although causally he is free to do as he pleases, logically he has no choice what to do *to follow the rule*. For what is called 'following the rule . . .' at this point is laid down in grammar (writing down '1002, 1004' at this point is following the rule '+ 2', and nothing else *counts* as so doing).

(ii) Z §296: it seems as if mechanical, causal, forms of guidance could misfire, but not a rule – a rule seems even more reliable than causal necessitation. But what distinguishes mechanical prevention of a movement and normative prevention? W. does not answer there. Chess affords a paradigm of rules' preventing a movement: in the opening move of the game you *cannot* move your king. Of course, you *can*; but then it won't be chess.

SECTION 221

1.1   'a mythological description of the use of a rule': as Adam's naming the beasts of the field is a mythological description of the introduction of names into a language. The truth which 'All the steps are already taken' mythologically represents is that what counts as a correct application of a rule is *internally related* to the rule itself. So it is not something to be discovered by experiment.

SECTION 222

1   This is the first of the group of sections concerned with a rule's intimating what is to be done in compliance with it. The thought is that

if nothing stands between a rule and my action, then the rule must *intimate* what I am to do (RFM 421).

The idea that the rule intimates what is to be done seems to be the correlate of the previously discussed suggestion that I *intuit* what I must do; I intuit what it intimates, a voice within me says 'This way' (cf. §§213, 232). Note also that this issue was raised in §171, where the written word was said to intimate the sound to be pronounced (or at least, so it seems, when one reads slowly, and tries to describe the 'experience').

Here W.'s immediate response is that the supposition of intimation is 'only a picture', presumably a 'mythological description' as in §221. Why? Because 'intimations' are irrelevant to determining whether one is following a rule. If I am tracing a line (or copying it), i.e. using it as a rule to go by, the line does not function as the rule by which I go because it intimates something to me. If I were asked, 'Why did you do *that?*' and were to answer 'The line intimated to me that I should', then I would not be following the line as (like) a rule (MS 164, 171). For it might intimate now this, now that, as it were, irresponsibly. So there would be no regularity, no internal relation between the line and what I draw, no pattern of always doing the same. But if I were to answer 'I simply followed the line', then I can be said to have treated it like a rule (a model or paradigm).

1.1   'The line intimates . . .': what line? RFM 414 clarifies this:

> Does a line compel me to trace it? – No; but if I have decided to use it as a model in *this* way, then it compels me. – No; then *I* compel myself to use it in this way. I as it were cleave to it. – But here it is surely important that I can form the decision with the (general) interpretation so to speak once and for all, and can hold by it, and do not interpret afresh at every step.

This implicitly contrasts the 'picture' of rails (where there is no 'interpreting afresh at every step', for 'all the steps are already taken') with the picture of intimation (where, it seems, a fresh intimation, a new intuition, is needed at each step). So these two 'pictures' clash. The 'picture' of intimating is merely a 'paraphrase' of the correct claim that the line is my final court of appeal in deciding how to trace. Just as 'the steps are already taken' may be said to 'paraphrase' the correct claim that the applications of a rule are internally related to the rule.

2   RFM 419 contrasts having a feeling of intimation when following a rule (treating the line one traces or copies *as* a paradigm) with having intimations, but *not* following a rule. In the first case, (i) the line is my last court of appeal for what I am to do; (ii) I simply follow the line; (iii) following is just *one thing*, always *the same*. In the second case, I do not know what I will do in advance, I await the voice of the line (cf. PI §223). So the feeling of intimation that may accompany following a rule is an irrelevant epiphenomenon (cf. RFM 421).

2.1   'it intimated this or that as it were irresponsibly': RFM 422 (MS 124, 165 = Z §282) clarifies; this means 'I can't teach you *how* I follow the line. I make no presumption that you will follow it as I do, even if you do follow it.' Again, mere intimation is to be *contrasted* with rule-following.

SECTION 223

1   This develops further the suggestion of §222 that an intimation might be capricious, but not a rule. When we understand a rule, we do not await its voice at every step of its application, baffled, as it were, about what to do next. On the contrary, it tells us, once and for all, what to do (we 'grasp it in a flash'). For the rule always tells us the same, and in following, we always do the same. And this is something one exhibits in training someone to follow a rule. By contrast it makes sense to say that what is *intimated* by a rule differs from case to case.

2   MS 129, 177 (cf. RFM 419) inserts between (a) and (b): 'Man könnte sagen: wir sehen was wir beim Folgen nach der Regel tun, unter dem Gesichtpunkt des *immer Gleichen* an.' ('One could say: we look at what we do when we follow the rule from the perspective of *always the same*.') (b) is followed by the remark: '(Faraday "The Chemical History of a Candle") "Water is one individual thing – it never changes."' (PI p. 54 n.; cf. Exg.) Faraday's observation exemplifies looking at something from the perspective of *always the same* (as do Goethe's observations about the leaf).

SECTION 224

1   This embroiders on §223(b). In training another to follow a rule, I encourage him to do the same thing that I do in the actual circumstances, and I may urge him to follow my example, giving him a paradigm of behaviour to imitate. If I am successful, he will do the same thing as I do; his action will *agree* with mine. And if I succeed in communicating the rule to him, I will have made him understand that I always do the same thing as well as what it is for him to do the same thing as I do; i.e. he must comprehend what it is for his acts to *agree* with mine. In this sense, the *concept* of agreement between the actions of different agents is related to the concept of following a rule. To learn what acts are in accord with a rule is to learn, *inter alia*, when two persons agree in their actions. The concept of accord with a rule is not the same as the concept of agreement in action, but the two concepts are related to one another as cousins.

This relation of these two concepts is employed in §232 to differentiate the concept of following a rule from the concept of acting on intimations or inspirations.

.1   '*Übereinstimmung* (agreement)': W. uses this term in different senses in different contexts. What does it mean here?

In some contexts, 'agreement' signifies accord of an act with a rule (e.g. RFM 405). There the issue is an act's agreeing (or disagreeing) *with a rule*, not different agents' agreeing (or disagreeing) in their actions. The same use of 'Übereinstimmung' is apparent in the paradox of PI §201.

In other contexts, however, 'agreement' signifies consensus among people, either consensus in their actions or consensus in their judgements (e.g. about what acts are in accord with a given rule). Calculation depends on agreement of ratifications (RFM 365), i.e. on consensus about procedures and results. Likewise, peaceful agreement, absence of disputes is the characteristic surrounding of the use of the word 'same' and of judgements about accord with a rule (RFM 323). Agreement in definitions and agreement in judgements are clearly forms of consensus (PI §§240ff.). This use of 'agreement' is manifest in various important remarks about the social nature of speaking a language (cf. 'Agreement in definitions, judgements and forms of life, pp. 243ff.).

In §224, 'agreement' is to be understood in the second sense. Two independent bits of evidence support this conclusion. First, W. appears to contrast being *related* to one another or being cousins with being interwoven (§225). But if 'agreement' meant 'accord' in §224, the uses of the terms 'rule' and 'agreement' would be *interwoven* just as are the uses of 'rule' and '(doing the) same', and this contrast would disappear. Secondly, and decisively, the original draft of §224 (MS 164, 122 = RFM 344) follows a discussion of consensus in action and in judgements. And the final version (MS 129, 130) succeeds the final version of PI §242. Hence 'agreement' in the progenitors of §224 certainly signified consensus among people.

It is vital to distinguish the grammatical remark that the *concept* of consensus is related to the concept of a rule from the misconception that the *fact* of widespread consensus (the *fact* that the vast majority agree in action and in judgements about following rules) is an essential feature of what it is to follow a rule. 'This is in accord with this rule' does not *mean* 'Most people act *thus* in these circumstances', or 'Most people agree that *this* is accord.' Rather such consensus belongs to the framework of our common language-games, but is not part of those games (if we did not occasionally disagree, we might never have heard of agreement). 'Our language only works, of course, when a certain agreement prevails, but the concept of agreement does not enter the language-game.' (Z §430) Agreement, absence of disputes over accord, consensus in action 'belong to the framework, out of which our language works.' (RFM 323)

1   This elaborates §223(b). For to teach someone to follow a rule is to teach him what is to *count* as 'the same' in this context. The use of 'rule' and 'same' are interwoven in a manner akin to 'proposition' and 'true' (cf. Exg. §136), i.e. they 'belong' but do not 'fit'. So one cannot use an independently given concept of doing the same thing to determine what is or is not in accord with a rule, just as one cannot use the concept of truth to determine what is or is not a proposition. *Doing the same thing* is only formally a *Merkmal* of following a rule, i.e. if what you did was following *this* rule, then *of course* what you did on a later occasion of following this rule was doing the same as what you did previously. What *counts* as the same depends on the rule. We take obtaining certain results as the *criterion* for having gone by the rule (RFM 317, 319), and hence as determining what counts as doing the same.

2   Z §305 emphasizes the futility of trying to delve beneath the rule to find a justification for following the rule *thus*. I can say to a pupil 'Do the same.' But in saying this I must point to the rule. But if the pupil is to understand what 'doing the same' here means, he must already have learnt, understood, what the application of the rule is. Otherwise the expression of the rule will have no meaning for him.

1   The two examples make clear that 'rule' and 'same' *belong* but do not *fit*, i.e. that identity and difference in what is done depends on the point of view. Understanding the rule (e.g. '+ 2') involves grasping what counts, relative to the rule, as going on the same way.
    If, in expanding the series $2x + 1$, one writes 1, 3, 5, 7, . . ., is one always doing the same? How is one to know? Since 4 is different from 3 anyway, how can we tell whether something we do to 4 is the same as something we do to 3 (cf. LFM 26)? The bare notion of *sameness* provides no leverage here:

> Cannot the one who is following a rule nevertheless also say that in a certain sense he does something different every time? Thus whether he does the same thing, or keeps on doing something different, does not determine whether he is following a rule. (RFM 416)

But, of course, to understand the rule of the series '$2x + 1$' is to know that going on thus *is* following the rule, i.e. going on in the same (rule-governed) way.

(b) gives an analogy. Whether one is saying the same thing every day or something different is wholly dependent on what we decide, in the context, to call 'the same'. One could say 'He uttered the same words, so he said the same thing.' Or one could say 'He uttered the same words, but he promised something different each day' (since on Monday he promised to come on Tuesday, on Tuesday he promised to come on Wednesday, etc.). Or one could say, 'Every day he made the same promise, viz. to come the following day.'

2   (i) RFM 415f. raises the question of whether we cannot say, of the person who acts on the intimation of the line, that he always does the same. Of course, in one sense, we can. For he always acts as the line intimates. But equally, the line may intimate now thus, now otherwise – and in each case he does something different. Hence 'only the total picture of the use of the word "same" as it is interwoven with the uses of the other words, can determine whether he does use the word as we do.' So 'always acts according to the intimation of the line' and 'always follows the rule' determine different criteria of identity.

(ii) LFM 176 provides an illuminating illustration. Suppose one is taught to move one, two or three paces forward when one, two or three fingers are held up, and at the fourth finger one is to climb on a chair. Is the latter 'going on in the same way'? One might say that climbing on the chair is not consistent with, does not accord with, pacing forward one, two or three steps. But that is just to say that it does not accord with the rule to step forward one step for each finger. Yet it *does* accord with the rule one was taught. (Just as moving one's pawn initially two squares, then only one at a time is following the rule for moving the pawn.) The fact that adding one to 98 yields a two-figure numeral, but adding one to 99 yields a three-figure numeral, does not incline us to say that the action taken is different.

Section 227

1   It would make no sense to say 'If he did something different every time he would not be following a rule.' Why? Because in one sense we could say that he is always doing the same thing though not following a rule, and because we could also say that he is following a rule though doing something different every time (RFM 414). To follow the rule is to do always the same thing, but *only from the point of view of the rule*. Sameness and difference in what is done provide no independent purchase on the concept of acting in accord with a rule.

1   'Wenn er jedesmal . . .': 'every time' (cf. RFM 416). There is no explicit reference to §226.

2   RFM 416 prefaces this remark with 'The procedure of following a rule can be described only like this: by describing in a different way what we do in the course of it.' So we give descriptions of the *different* acts (e.g. 'first write 2, then 4, then 6 . . .' – and, of course, writing '4' isn't the same as writing '6'!) which are fixed as following this rule. So, obviously, it will be a nonsense to say, if they are *different*, they can't be in accord with the rule!

SECTION 228

1   Another attempt to capture the experience one has when one follows a rule (cf. §171), coordinate with utterances examined in §219 and §222. When asked to continue the series, 1, 3, 5, 7, . . ., we do know how to go on. The explanation seems straightforward: 'We *see* it in just one way, and everything is already contained in this.' The series presents only a single aspect to us; we see something in it, like a shape in a puzzle picture (cf. Z §277), and this perception of a *Gestalt* mediates between the rule and our acts of writing down further terms of the series.
     W. criticizes this idea. How do we see the series? What *Gestalt* do we apprehend? Of course we may see it as a segment of the series of odd integers; or we may see it algebraically, i.e. as the series corresponding to the formula $2x + 1$. But it is nonsense to say that 'everything is already contained in *these* ways of seeing it'!
     On the other hand, this idea does embody an insight in a confused way: it expresses the fact that we look to the rule for instruction and act, without searching for further guidance. A *Gestalt* cannot, as it were, be prised away from the rule (the series 1, 3, 5, 7, . . .) and presented independently, unlike an interpretation!

1.1   (i) 'Eine Reihe hat für uns *ein* Gesicht': the translation misses the metaphor, 'A series presents us with *one* face.'
     (ii) 'Aber in dem liegt doch schon alles': 'but everything is already contained in it'.
     (iii) 'wir nur auf den Mund der Regel schauen : 'we merely look at the mouth of the rule' (picking up the previous metaphor).

2   Cf. Z §277 (MS 124, 186)

     I see something in it – like a shape *(Gestalt)* in a puzzle picture. And if I see that, I say 'that is all I need.' – If you find the signpost, you don't now look for further instruction – you *walk*. (And if instead of 'you walk' I were to say 'you go by it', the difference between the two expressions might be only that the second one alludes to certain psychological accompaniments.)

.1   (i) 'Eine Reihe hät fur uns *ein* Gesicht': cf. 'Z §276(b):

'I see a distinctive character in it.' – Well, presumably something that corresponds to the algebraic expression. – 'Yes, only nothing written, but positively something ethereal.' – What a queer picture. – 'Something that is not the algebraic expression, something for which this is only the *expression*!'

In MS 124, 184f. this immediately follows the original draft of PI §228.
    (ii) 'Aber in dem liegt schon alles': MS 124, 184 enlarges:

'Aber darin liegt doch schon alles!' Nun, was willst Du mehr. Das ist eben der Ausruf den diese Situation erzeugt. – Und es ist nun eine andere Frage: warum ich grade dies zu sagen geneigt bin. – Denn zur Anwendung der Regel gehört es // das // ja nicht.

('But everything is already contained in it!' Well, what more do you want. Just this is the exclamation which this circumstance produces. – And why I am inclined to say just this is a different question. – For at any rate it // this // has nothing to do with the application of the rule.)

This remark is followed by PI §218 (first sentence only), and then a further gloss identical with MS 129, 176 (quoted above, p. 212).

SECTION 229

1   This further elaborates the *Gestalt* idea of §228. The 'characteristic design' we see in the rule seems to 'give us everything', needing only a 'and so on' to be added. (This contains echoes of §§218f.)

SECTION 230

1   This links the idea of the line's *intimating* how it is to be followed (§222) with the *Gestalt* picture of §§228–9. Both 'paraphrase' the insight that in following a rule, we do not appeal to anything other than the rule.

1   '*letzte* Instanz': 'court of *last* resort' or '*final* court of appeal'.

.1   '*letzte* Instanz': the metaphor occurs in RFM 419 (MS 124, 160; Z §279):

When do we say: 'The line intimates this to me *as a rule* – always the same.' And on the other hand: 'It keeps on intimating to me what I have to do – it is not a rule.'
    In the first case the story is: I have no further court of appeal for what I have to do . . ..

SECTION 231

1   This links §§218–19 with §§228–9. We are inclined, in our explanations
to a learner, to say with exasperation, 'But surely you can see . . ..'
(cf. §185) This exclamation seems to express the thought that knowing
how to continue a series is a matter of *seeing* a pattern in it (§228), a pattern which gives us everything and thus 'compels' us to continue the
series correctly. Consequently, somebody who errs will be upbraided for
a failure to see something which is in plain view. This accusation will be
lodged by a teacher who is 'under the compulsion of the rule', who
understands that the rule leaves no room for making choices, and who
follows the rule with complete certainty because he does see the pattern
that it presents. (Of course, the phrase 'under the compulsion of a rule' is
at best metaphorical, and even then it is potentially misleading.)

2.1   (i) 'But surely you can see . . .?': W. associated this utterance with
'acceptance' of a rule, e.g. RFM 50 (Vol. XIV, 52)

> And how does it come out that the proof *compels* me? Well, in the fact that once
> I have got it I go ahead in such-and-such a way, and refuse any other path. All I
> should further say as a final argument against someone who did not want to go
> that way, would be: 'Why, don't you see . . .!' and this is no argument.

Cf. Z §§301f.:

> He must go on like this *without a reason*. Not, however because he cannot yet
> grasp the reason but because – in this system – there is no reason . . ..

> For just where one says 'But don't you *see* . . .?' the rule is no use, it is what is
> explained, not what does the explaining.

(ii) 'under the compulsion of a rule': cf. RFM 395:

> What is it that compels me? – the expression of the rule? – Yes, once I have
> been educated in this way. But can I say it compels me to follow it? Yes: if here
> one thinks of the rule, not as a line that I trace, but rather as a spell that holds us in
> thrall.

RFM 413 adds 'If a rule does not compel you then you aren't *following* a
rule'; i.e. a characteristic feature of rule-following is the *absence of any
choosing*; hence the exasperation expressed by 'Can't you see' – for there
is only *one* thing to do, only one thing that *counts* as following this rule.

SECTION 232

1   A further elaboration of §§222–3. What distinguishes acting on an intimation (or intuition) from following a rule? Here W. stresses: (i) In the case of 'inspiration' one *awaits* instruction, one does not 'know in advance'; this repeats the point of §223 – in following a rule one does *not* feel one has always got to wait upon the nod (the whisper) of the rule. (ii) One cannot teach another one's 'technique' of following the line (rule), for one really has no *technique*. A technique involves a method of projection from rule to act. Hence it can be correct or incorrect. But hearkening to an inner voice involves no technique at all (although the question of what to do in response to the inner voice remains wide open (PI §213)). So all that could be taught would be receptivity (how to 'listen quietly'), not a method of application. Consequently, one could not teach another to follow a rule as one does oneself. For 'the way I follow the line' is to listen to my inner voice. And *that* (by definition) does not speak to him. He can only listen to *his* inner voice. Of course, intuitionists would say: 'Thank God the inner voices all coincide.' (cf. §234)

2.1   (i) 'to teach anyone else my "technique"': RFM 418 adds (after §232 and §233) that the technique, the very possibility, of training someone else to follow a rule belongs to the following of a rule. For we train by examples. And the criterion for whether the pupil has understood is that what he does is the same as what the teacher does. 'Hence it is not as it is with instruction in receptivity.' For *that* does not require agreement of actions between teacher and pupil. (To teach one to be receptive to music or painting does not have as a criterion of success identity of reactions of teacher and learner.)

(ii) 'I cannot require him to follow the line in the same way as I do': RFM 422: to say 'it intimates thus' means: I can't teach you *how* I follow it. So I don't presume you'll follow it as I do, even if you do follow it.

(iii) 'These are not my experiences . . . grammatical notes': cf. PI §383: we are analysing not a phenomenon but a concept.

SECTION 233

1   An ironic aside. There could be a kind of arithmetic developed out of training in receptivity. But 'calculating' then would be a kind of composing. Agreement in results would be fortuitous. Indeed, reacting to the inner voice would no more *be* calculating than would painting a picture or composing a symphony. Calculation differs from intimation in that arriving at the correct result is *part* of carrying out a calculation;

e.g. there is no such thing as two (correct) *calculations* of 25 × 25 which produce different results.

2   RFM 365 introduces a similar point. A proof is a picture, which we employ for certain purposes. But it stands in need of ratification. This we give it when we work it over. (So it must be repeatable.) Yet what if it got ratification from one person, but not from another? What if there were no consensus over ratifications? Is it agreement of ratifications rather than ratifications that make this calculating?

> For another game could quite well be imagined, in which people were prompted by expressions (similar perhaps to general rules) to let sequences of signs come to them for particular practical purposes, i.e. *ad hoc*, and that this even proved to pay. And here the 'calculations', if we choose to call them that, do not have to agree with one another. (Here we might speak of 'intuition'.)

Agreement of ratifications, W. concludes, is the precondition of our language-game, not something affirmed in it.

Section 234

1   A further grammatical note on inspiration (intimation) and following rules, parallel to §233. It explores the possibility of reconciling following rules with responsible, non-capricious intimations (cf. §222). Could we not calculate as we do, yet *also* feel that the rules intimate what is to be done? Might we not feel amazed, awe-struck, by the fact that we all agree? And even thank God for our agreement? Presumably these questions are to be answered affirmatively.
    The implication is that the 'feeling of being guided as by a spell' is irrelevant to whether one is following a rule. And this differentiates the concept of following a rule from the concept of acting on inspiration.
    §234 parallels PI §160. If we give someone a hitherto unseen passage to read, and he reads it impeccably, but with the feeling that he has learnt it by heart, we should not deny that he was reading it. (But could the feeling that I had learnt it by heart accompany *all* my reading? Or could *all* my rule-following be accompanied by the feeling of being guided as by a spell?)

2   RFM 421: one can imagine someone multiplying correctly, but always prefacing his answers with 'I don't know – now suddenly the rule intimates *this* to me.' And we might reply: 'Of course; for you *are* going ahead in accord with the rule.'

SECTION 235

1   This certainly alludes to §§232–4, and possibly to the whole panoply of pictures explored in §§219–37 (most of which precede it in TS 228, §§596ff.).

1.1   'was alles zu der Physiognomie desjenigen gehört': 'From this you can see how much there is to the physiognomy of what we call "following a rule" in everyday life.' (cf. RFM 422)
     The term 'physiognomy' links up with the metaphor 'Eine Reihe hat für uns *ein* Gesicht' in §228. W. used the term extensively to signify features of an object which make a distinctive impression upon us; also the web of associations woven around an expression. So he speaks of a word having a particular physiognomy, as if it takes up its meaning into itself (PI p. 218). Thus, for example, we may well feel that 'incarnadine' really *could not* mean anything but redden, or that Beethoven really *could not* have been named 'Goethe'.
     It is part of the physiognomy of 'following a rule' that one is *not* surprised that others who follow it do just as one does oneself; that one does *not* feel guided *as by a spell*, even though, to an outsider, one's actions may look thus; that one draws the consequences of the rule *as a matter of course* (PI §238). What belongs to the physiognomy of following a rule is not *part of* the concept, but belongs to the impression made on us by the phenomenon.

SECTION 236

1   This contrasts cases of calculating prodigies of whom one would say that they do calculate (quick as a flash) with cases in which one would not. The point of the contrast is unclear. In MS 124, 160 (RFM 420) it follows a remark which, like PI §232, contrasts following a rule with awaiting an intimation. Is the suggestion that the former contrast illustrates the latter? Or is it that not *everyone* could be a calculating prodigy, although some people are, and we typically do say they calculate? In the case of the prodigy we are (rightly) genuinely astonished (surprised) that his answer accords with our calculation. And *he* may indeed talk of feeling an intimation or intuition. But such cases are *essentially* deviant. On these foundations no language-game can rest, just as not all calculating could be calculating in the head (PI §364, 366, 369, 385).

SECTION 237

1   This exemplifies how the physiognomy of rule-following may be manifest, even though the criteria for following a rule are not fulfilled. The example is linked with many previous observations. It runs parallel to §207: there we could discern 'no regular connection' between the apparent speech and actions, so the appearance of intelligent discourse was deceptive. Here too the man's action appears to be rule-following, but 'we see no kind of regularity' in the use of the compasses. It also exemplifies the point made in §222, that if a line 'intimated this or that as it were irresponsibly' we should not take it to be a case of rule-following. As is stressed in §173, the appearance of *carefulness* and the *exclusion of one's own volition* are 'part of the picture' of being guided by a rule. Here similarly the man 'alters the opening of the compasses, apparently with great precision, looking at the rule the whole time as if it determined what he did'. None the less, this is *not* a case of following a rule. For his apparently normative behaviour lacks any regularity characteristic of using the rule as 'his court of final appeal' (§230). And as in §232, 'we cannot learn his way of following the line from him.'

AGREEMENT IN DEFINITIONS, JUDGEMENTS AND FORMS OF LIFE

1. *Problems about agreement*

Wittgenstein employed the term 'agreement' *(Übereinstimmung)* in the discussion of three distinct but interrelated themes. First, there must be an agreement between a rule and its applications. Acts of following a rule must 'agree' with the rule, i.e. be in accord with it (RFM 405). The rule which is given in a correct explanation of meaning is a standard for the use of the expression explained. The use or application of that expression is correct only if it 'agrees' with the explanation. These grammatical statements have been fully clarified.

Secondly, the relative stability of the *world* is a background precondition for the application of concepts. If the world were different in certain specifiable ways we *would not* employ such-and-such concepts – not because they would be *incorrect*, but rather because the point of using them would be lost, and our purposes in employing them would not be served (LFM 42; LPE 306; RFM 51f.).

'It is as if our concepts involved a scaffolding of facts.'
That would presumably mean: If you imagine certain facts otherwise, describe them otherwise, than the way they are, then you can no longer imagine the application of certain concepts, because the rules for their application have no analogue in the new circumstances. (Z §350)

Thus, for example, if the colours of objects changed incessantly, so that we never saw unchanging colours, there would be little or no use for our language-games with colours (RPP II §198). Again, if putting the same object on a pair of scales gave different readings on every occasion, the point of weighing would be lost (PI §142; LPE 287). Similarly unless our clocks (sundials, pendulums, etc.) generally agreed with one another, we could not do with them what we want to do, namely what we call 'measuring time' (MS 123, 38). Agreement of clocks is a *precondition* of our techniques of time measurement. If this agreement did not obtain, our clock readings would not be *false* or *incorrect*; rather they would not *be* measurements of time at all.

These background constancies of the natural world and our inter-actions with it are *not* component elements of our concepts, i.e. not parts of the explanations of them. It is part of the framework within which our language-games are played, not part of the games themselves. (Similarly, it is not part of the rules of tennis that the gravitational field should be constant and roughly as it is on earth, as opposed to on the moon or on Jupiter.) We labour under the illusion that the conditions under which we employ concepts are written into the concepts, that the picture of our language-games includes the frame. For we are prone, for example, to analyse the colour predicate 'red' as equivalent to 'looks red to a normal observer *under normal conditions*'. And this is erroneous. It is true that we teach and explain, and pupils learn, our language-games under certain conditions and against a stable background, but that background is *not part of the explanation*. 'Red' does not mean 'appears red under such-and-such conditions'. On the contrary, normal conditions in respect of colour are those optimal conditions under which things are *visibly* as they are, in which a 'player' of the game *can* play the game (Z §§418ff.).

The point is a general one. Mastery of a language-game involves the ability to play it and also the ability to explain (if only by paradigmatic exemplification) how it is to be played. But it does not involve the ability to describe the normal circumstances under which it is played, any more than mastery of tennis requires the ability to specify the laws of physics abrogation of which would make the game pointless or impossible. On the other hand, 'If a circumstance makes the use doubtful, I can say so, and also say *how* the situation is deviant from the usual ones.' (Z §118) What holds for mastery of the technique holds also for the technique mastered. 'It is only in normal cases that the use of a word is clearly prescribed; we know, are in no doubt what to say in this or that case. The more abnormal the case, the more doubtful it becomes what we are to say.' (PI §142) The rules governing a technique in general, the explanations of word-meanings in particular, do not incorporate specifications of the normal conditions in which they apply. Nor, in general, could they. For then understanding any expression would presuppose the understanding of the expressions describing the normal conditions of its applications that are presupposed. This does not indicate a defect in the explanations of word-meaning. If in deviant (perhaps only imaginable) circumstances what we ordinarily give and accept as correct explanations of the meaning of a word do not suffice to settle whether it is applicable, then its application in those conditions is undetermined. '"This law was not given with such cases in view." Does this mean it is senseless?' (Z §120; cf. Z §350) There is nothing to be *discovered* here about what the expression really means, but rather a fresh stipulation would be necessary.

While the temptation to write normality conditions into the explanations of the meaning of concepts of secondary qualities has been particularly strong, most philosophers have failed to notice that concepts of primary qualities and of substances are no less dependent for their use, usefulness and applicability upon a stable framework. We would have no use for measurements of length if objects capriciously shrank and grew in size.

Similar considerations apply to weight (see above), and, more generally, to any substance-concepts:

> I say 'There is a chair.' What if I go up to it, meaning to fetch it, and it suddenly disappears from sight? – 'So it wasn't a chair, but some kind of illusion.' – But in a few moments we see it again and are able to touch it and so on. – 'So the chair was there after all and its disappearance was some kind of illusion.' – But suppose that after a time it disappears again – or seems to disappear. What are we to say now? (PI §80)

The conclusion to draw is *not* that our ordinary concepts are defective. Far from it; they fulfil their purposes perfectly adequately. Nor are our ordinary explanations typically incomplete. The supposition that a 'proper explanation' should incorporate specification of the normal conditions under which the explanandum has application involves a misguided ideal of explanation. The correct conclusion is rather that these concepts too have their home in language-games played within a presupposed framework.

We are also prone to think that we can at least free our more advanced and sophisticated concepts from any dependence upon conditions under which we exercise them and from the peculiarities of our nature. We conceive of science as aiming at that goal. For concepts of mass (as opposed to weight), of light wavelength (as opposed to colour), of numerically quantifiable concepts (as opposed to qualitative ones) seem to achieve this. But this is illusory. Changes in the world could throw *any* concepts whatever into total confusion. Such imaginable changes would not, of course, show the concepts to be false. (There is no such thing as a false concept.) But they would make our concepts *useless*. Even mathematics, in certain circumstances of chaos, would be robbed of its conditions of application to reality (RFM 51f., 200; LFM 41f.), and under such conditions it would be what formalists think it *is*, viz. a mere game with signs.

Is logic then constrained by the facts? In one sense this is obviously so, and far from denying it, Wittgenstein affirmed that concept-formation is causally conditioned. We do not play board-games with pieces that are too heavy to lift or too small to pick up, nor do we play games of cards with cards differentiated by markings that are not readily discriminable. If these are to be called 'constraints upon games', then there are indeed analogous constraints upon grammar. We do not use notations we cannot survey. We do not construct sentences with multiply-nested relative clauses beyond a very limited point. And so on. But such constraints are mischaracterized as constraints *upon logic*. Rather are they constraints *within which* we construct our grammars. These causal constraints do not make logic answerable to facts of nature. Nor do they constrain us to recognize something as making sense which does not in fact make sense, or conversely to exclude forms of words from use as being senseless which do in fact make sense. Causal constraints on concept-formation do not impugn the autonomy of grammar (any more than causal constraints upon the game of chess could bring it about that we accept certain moves as licit in chess which are in fact illicit or prohibit certain moves that are permissible). There is no such thing as *discovering* that contrary to what we all thought, 'such-and-such' makes sense, although of course we might *give* a sense to a form of words which previously had none or had a different sense. So too there is no such thing as something (undiscoverably) making sense in our language, even though no one knows it and is causally constrained from knowing it. For to make sense is *to have a use* in our linguistic, rule-governed activities. And, as we have argued in previous essays, there are no such things as 'hidden', unknown forms of representation (any more than there are 'hidden', unknown rules of chess).

The point of Wittgenstein's observations concerning the stable background of agreement between different applications of the same concepts to objects is not to investigate empirical hypotheses about concept-formation (PI p. 230; RPP I §46). That is not a philosophical issue, for philosophy investigates grammatical, conceptual structures, not the background preconditions that as a matter of fact make them possible, although the *distinction* between these is of utmost importance. Philosophy is concerned with the grammatical articulations of our concepts, and *that* is not a matter of hypotheses in natural science, but of the description of conventions. His purpose was to expose various fallacies, and also to show the absurdity of thinking that our concepts are, in some deep sense, *correct:*

If anyone believes that certain concepts are absolutely the correct ones, and that having different ones would mean not realizing something that we realize – then let him imagine certain very general facts of nature to be different from what we are used to, and the formation of concepts different from the usual ones will become intelligible to him. (PI p. 230)

The third theme in Wittgenstein's discussion of agreement is interpersonal consensus in behaviour of participants in shared language-games. We agree in definitions and also in judgements or applications (PI §242; LPE 306), in acceptance and ratification of proofs (RFM 50, 365), in results of calculation (RFM 193). What we call 'the truths of logic' are determined by a consensus in action (LFM 183f.); our agreement in applications of expressions rests on a consensus in our forms of life (MS 160, 51f.). Clarification of these claims is the subject of this essay. A multitude of misunderstandings surround them.

It is often noted that the agreement in the language we use is, according to Wittgenstein, an agreement in our *form of life* (PI §241). But his conception of a form of life is little understood. Two errors are common. First, agreement in form of life is conceived to *underpin* agreement in definitions and in judgements. But agreement in form of life is not separable from agreement in definitions and in judgements; one might say that it *surrounds* it rather than underpins it; for if one were to take away the surrounding context, the web of action and interaction, only empty marks and noises would remain (cf. RFM 345, 414). Secondly, some have thought that 'agreement in form of life' alludes to biological features of our species. Cats do not look in the direction we point, but at the hand; we humans look in the direction of the pointing finger. That, some argue, is the paradigm for differentiating forms of life. Our form of life is held to be characteristic of the species in general, and hence pre-conventional, 'natural', and, for us, 'inevitable'. And this misconception is sometimes invoked to suggest that Wittgenstein was no conventionalist in any sense of this term.

A further array of misunderstandings surrounds the relation between interpersonal agreement and meaning, explanation and understanding. First, agreement is sometimes thought to be a constitutive component of our rules for the use of expressions (of our language-games, hence of our concepts). Against this confusion Wittgenstein warned many times. Secondly, it is sometimes held that agreement between members of a linguistic community is a *sine qua non* of a language because objectivity in following rules is possibly only by reference to a public standard set by community consensus. It is this alone which allegedly fixes a difference between following a rule and thinking that one is following a rule and hence distinguishes between a bogus 'private language' and a genuine public one. This muddle has been examined above (see 'Following rules, mastery of techniques and practices' pp. 169ff.). Thirdly, interpersonal agreement is also invoked to *explain* why doing *this* (e.g. writing '1000, 1002, 1004, . . .') is correctly following the rule ('Add 2') while doing something else (writing '1004, 1008, . . .') is incorrect. That we all write '1000, 1002, 1004, . . .' in response to 'Add 2' is, it is held, what makes doing so *correct*. This too is definitely wrong.[1]

Such radical confusions distort Wittgenstein's arguments beyond all recognition. Indeed, in some cases they make a farce of his reflections, for they lend support to the very misunderstandings which he was striving to eradicate. We shall separate out the different strands in his discussions of agreement and then show how they are woven into the tapestry of his thought.

---

[1] See 'Accord with a rule', pp. 90f. and in more critical detail G. P. Baker and P. M. S. Hacker, *Scepticism, Rules and Language* (Blackwell, Oxford, 1984), pp. 64ff.

2. *The role of biological nature*

Parallel to Wittgenstein's stress on general facts of nature for understanding the 'arbitrary', conventional character of our conceptual structure, its being a human artefact which is not 'responsible' to reality (cf. 'Grammar and necessity', pp. 329ff.), is his emphasis upon our common biological nature. This too, is part of the framework within which we construct and engage in our language-games. This is often misunderstood, being construed as a defence of some form of 'naturalism' allegedly akin to Hume's empiricism. This not only misconstrues Hume but also commits the very error Wittgenstein constantly warned against, viz. painting the frame on to the canvas. A shared biological nature is indeed the foundation for a common form of representation. It is not, however, a *justification* for it. Nor is it a kind of causal necessitation which *makes* us 'go on' in such-and-such ways, let alone makes them 'correct'.

Three kinds of example may help illuminate Wittgenstein's arguments, namely perceptual concepts, psychological concepts and concepts of mathematics.

(i) *Perceptual concepts* Shared discriminatory capacities are a precondition for shared concepts of colour, taste, sound, smell, etc. Moreover, shared propensities for perceptual illusion are a precondition for shared concepts of perceptual *appearances* as distinct from actualities, viz. concepts of objects publicly looking thus-and-so although *not* being so. Without shared discriminatory capacities, there would be no point in using samples to provide standards of correctness for the use of expressions. For they would not then be employed in such a way as would yield agreement in definitions and in judgements. We would agree neither in our explanations of what our words mean nor in what we called 'correct uses' of those words, correct applications of the explanations. So we would not have a common language of perceptual terms. The reason is clear. To use a sample to define an expression one must be able to pick the sample out (i.e. pick out an object to serve as a sample) from among other objects which serve or could be used to serve[2] as samples for other concepts within the same *Satzsystem* or propositional system (e.g. other determinates of the same determinable). One cannot differentiate perceptual properties (e.g. red and green) by reference to samples between which one cannot discriminate; hence one cannot employ concepts defined by reference to such samples in the way they are to be used. It is evident, for example, that the colour-blind and tone-deaf cannot fully engage in our language-games with colours and notes.

---

[2] This is particularly evident in the case of optional samples; cf. Volume 1, pp. 196ff.; MU pp. 109ff.

Creatures with different perceptual discriminatory capacities might build very different conceptual structures which we could not employ. Wittgenstein imagined men who express shades of orange by means of a kind of binary decimal, e.g. 'R.LLRL'.[3] They learn to do this in kindergarten, just as we learn our colour-grammar. 'They would be related to us roughly as people with absolute pitch are to those who lack it. *They can do* what we cannot' (Z §368) and, of course, 'yellow' and 'red' in their mouths would differ somewhat in meaning from our colour-names (cf. PLP 250). Our language-game with colours, like all our language-games, 'is characterized by what we can and cannot do' (Z §345), and here we have described a language-game which we cannot learn *as they do*, and which we cannot engage in *as* they manifestly can (cf. PLP 253f.).

(ii) *Psychological concepts*   Mental ostensive definition is not the instrument whereby we explain our psychological concepts. We do not use, because there is no such thing as, mental samples to define psychological terms. Rather our concepts of the mental are explained by reference to behavioural criteria. These concepts presuppose a framework of shared primitive reactions. If we did not cry and weep when injured, laugh and smile at wit or good news, turn pale, tremble and run away when in danger, then our shared concepts of pain, amusement or delight, fear or trepidation would get no grip (PI §142). This is not to say that all the fundamental reactions must be 'animal'! If children (and adults) did not wake up and say 'Mummy, mummy, a tiger is chasing me', or 'I thought that I was . . .', then there would be nothing on to which to graft 'I dreamt that . . .' or 'He dreamt that . . ..' Nor is it to suggest that the conceptual structure erected on the foundation of shared primitive (or not so primitive) responses does not grow to heights undreamt of by creatures who have *only* the primitive responses, and not the conceptual

---

[3] Apparently, this notation is to represent each shade by locating it within a series of nested intervals in the spectrum between pure red on the left and pure yellow on the right. This can be elucidated by a diagram for the example 'R.LLRL':

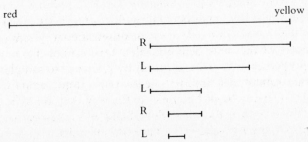

The first digit locates the shade in the right half of the spectrum of shades of orange; the second locates it in the left half of this subspectrum; the third in the left half of this next interval; etc.

structures erected thereon. My dog can want to go for a walk, but not to go to Naples before it dies. The ramifying consequences of the insight that psychological concepts rest on natural behavioural responses and reactions rather than upon what is 'given' in 'introspection' will be examined in Volume 3.

(iii) *Mathematical concepts*   Contrary to a venerable tradition in philosophy and mathematics, Wittgenstein argued that our mathematical concepts are no less influenced by our nature (or, for that matter, the nature and stability of the world we inhabit) than any other concepts. Far from our being able 'by the power of pure Reason alone' or by the aid of our 'logical faculties' to gain insight into the realm of Eternal Truths, that imaginary realm is the product of our concept-forming activities (and our natural disposition to philosophical illusion) which are themselves rooted in our natural capacities (cf. 'Grammar and necessity', pp. 318ff.). If our power to survey and take in numbers of objects and numbers of digits were different, our mathematics might be very different or non-existent. We cannot take in numerals with 250, or even 25 digits. (Large numbers are differently represented in calculations, and this difference in notation is grammatically important, not something insignificant.) But we might have been unable to take in three digits, in which case our actual mathematical notation would be useless to us. We cannot recognize 92-sided polygons without counting. But it might have been the case, as it is with many animals, that we could not distinguish a triangle from a trapezoid or even from a rectangle. Such a creature would not engage in geometry or construct an elaborate grammar for the representation of spatial relations. If our attention span were limited to a few seconds, if our ability to remember numbers were much weaker, if we always forgot what number we had 'carried', if as a consequence our 'additions' and 'multiplications' gave random results, there would be no calculations. And in the absence of calculation, there would be no mathematics: 'Die Grundlage der Mathematik ist *das Rechnen*. Gib uns ein Gift, was das Rechnen unmöglich macht, und es gibt keine Mathematik mehr.' ('The foundation of mathematics is *calculating*. Give us a poison which makes calculating impossible, and there is no more mathematics'. (Vol. XIV, 131)) For mathematics is part of human natural history, like art.

If these elementary facts of human nature[4] were to change in imaginable ways, our conceptual structures would collapse. If, one morning, poppies looked green to me, yellow to you, blue to a third person, the use of

----

[4] It is noteworthy that what belongs to *physis* and what to *nomos* is inextricably intermingled even at the highest flights of the intellect. It is, one might say, part of the natural history of the human *mind* to suffer intellectual vertigo when reflecting on concepts of the infinite, to be attracted by the uncanny or the sordid (hence part of the attraction of Freudian explanations). Similarly, although it is a vulgar fallacy to try to explain aesthetic value by reference to natural psychological reactions, our aesthetic creations and the values they exemplify or enshrine would not be as they are were our natural reactions different

colour-words would lose its *point*, for *confusion would supervene* (RFM 200). If sugar tasted sweet to one person, sour to another, salty to a third, etc., there would be 'a confusion of tastes' (Z §366; RPP II §§347ff.), and beyond a certain point we would no longer know what we once called 'a taste', what 'sweet', 'sour' and 'salty' meant. Similarly, if every time one measured the length of a room one got different results, and others got yet other results, measurement would fall into confusion. In all such cases, the *sense* (not the *truth*) of our judgements is founded on regularity, which could be disrupted by changes in our nature.

While it is important to bear such background facts in mind when reflecting on our conceptual structures, it is crucial not to misconstrue their importance. Wittgenstein pointed out a variety of tempting errors. First, although we have certain discriminatory capacities, that fact does not make our grammatical structures in respect of the properties we pick out *correct*. We form these grammatical structures, and conceive of things in this way. We say that there are four primary colours, seven colours in the spectrum, and we are prone to believe that this reflects the nature of things. But these are grammatical determinations (Z §331). Similarly children who are taught to count, and then to recite the series of even integers, will almost uniformly find it *natural* to continue '1000, 1002, 1004, . . .'. But going on thus is not *correct* because it is natural for us, in our culture. Rather, it is because we find it natural that we *make it correct* (and if we did not find it natural we would not have fixed it as 'correct'), we lay it down that *this* counts as 'doing the same', that this is to be called 'the series of even integers', that this and nothing else is 'adding two' to each successive number (see 'Grammar and necessity', pp. 334ff.)

Secondly, such facts of psychology do not force our concepts upon us. Even given these facts of human nature, these grammatical structures are not inevitable or unavoidable. Vastly different conceptual structures can be, have been, and are erected on the foundations of common human nature. The Russians distinguish two different colours where we distinguish only two shades: light blue and dark blue. We may be inclined to ask whether they do not *see* the similarity. But 'do we have a single concept everywhere where there is a similarity? The question is: Is the similarity *important* to them? And need it be so?' (cf. Z §380) Different cultures have strikingly different colour-grammars, and were the facts of nature different it might be useful to construct concepts that bear only a remote resemblance to our actual colour-concepts (e.g. if colours were

---

(e.g. our reactions to harmonies or rhythm in music, to line and perspective or colour harmony and discord in painting). Finally, one might extend these reflections to 'natural intellectual reactions', for our differentiations between what is simple and what is complex, what is puzzling and what is perspicuous, what arguments and ideas are subtle, elegant, exciting, rest upon widely shared responses common to those who have mastered such-and-such skills and techniques.

tied to different shapes, so that all and only circular objects were red, square ones green, etc.; or if colours always occurred in gradual transitions to other colours; or if *one* colour was always linked with a foul smell; and so on (RPP II §658)). We find it natural to continue the geometric series 'a^1, a^2, a^3' by 'a^4, a^5, a^6, . . .'; the Greeks did not proceed beyond a^3.

Thirdly, we must not confuse natural history with conceptual investigations. The delineation of the biological foundations of concept-formation runs the risk of just such a confusion. We might indeed claim that in a country in which everything was just one colour, people could not learn the use of colour words. And so we might say that the only reason we can use the names for colours is that things around us are of various colours. But this blurs the distinction between logical and physical possibility (RPP II §199). That distinction is important precisely because it is only logical possibility which is of concern to philosophy (cf. WWK 66f., 88f.). Although it is philosophically important and illuminating to appreciate the *framework* within which our language-games are played, philosophical investigation – the examination of conceptual structures – moves *within* the language-games. Our concern is with the rules we have and use, for it is their entanglement, our lack of an *Übersicht* of them, which is the source of philosophical questions. To be sure, if the framework set by the world and human nature were different in certain ways, we would not have these concepts ('*would* not'; not '*could* not' (Z §351); physical or psychological impossibility is philosophically irrelevant).

3. *Forms of life*

'What has to be accepted, the given, is – so one could say – forms of life.' (PI p. 226) This dark saying has occasioned considerable bafflement. And little help is given by the remarks that to imagine a language is to imagine a form of life (PI §19), and that speaking is part of a form of life (PI §23, cf. p. 174). The sole occurrence of the expression in *On Certainty* seems to shed some light. Our certainty in the truth of the kinds of proposition Moore discussed (e.g. 'This is a hand') is to be regarded as a form of life: 'I want to conceive of it as something that lies beyond being justified or unjustified; as it were, as something animal.' (C §§356f.) This is suggestive. Language is characteristic of our species and, as far as we know, only of our species. Hence, it seems to mark off the form of life of humans from that of any other animals. This idea of a unique human form of life seems to be reinforced by Wittgenstein's imagining a tribe with a very different kind of education from that human beings receive; their life would run on differently, their concepts would be alien to us. Indeed, one might say 'These people would have nothing human about them', for 'We could not possibly make ourselves understood to them. Not even as we can to a dog. We could not find our feet with them.' (Z §390)

These remarks, taken out of context and unrelated to other observations on this theme, lead to a variety of conjectual interpretations.

(i) Wittgenstein's concept of a form of life is predominantly a biological concept. There is only one *human* form of life, which characterizes our species and reflects our nature. There may be other forms of life; certainly other forms of life are imaginable, but these will characterize other biological natures (Martians, etc.).

(ii) A complementary suggestion is that other forms of life would be unintelligible to us. 'If a lion could talk, we could not understand him' (PI p. 223) – and not because he would be speaking Swahili! Humanoids who reacted in fundamentally different ways from us, e.g. who, like the cat, looked at the pointing finger rather than in the direction indicated, would be different kinds of creatures from us. We would not be able to understand them. Creatures who found it 'natural' to continue the series '2, 4, 6, 8, 10, . . .' beyond '1000, 1004, 1008, . . .' would find it impossible to enter into significant discourse with us. Their language-games would be impenetrable to us (cf. Z §390).

(iii) Although we can imagine other forms of life, and imagine their forming concepts for themselves, the concepts of another form of life would be strictly unimaginable to us. (And this is why, it is sometimes held Wittgenstein's attempted descriptions of such concepts collapse, e.g. the woodsellers' concept of quantity and value (RFM 93f.), or the concept of length possessed by the users of elastic rulers (RFM 38f.).) This too, is held to rule out the view that our concepts, our rules for the use of expressions, are conventional; allegedly, given our nature, we *could not* have significantly different ones.

(iv) The important remark that human beings agree in the language they use, not in opinions but in form of life (PI §241), may be taken to allude to our common 'natural reactions', or those elemental human practices the engaging in which makes us human. These are 'facts of human natural history' and they are prior to all *conventions*. Convention rests upon and presupposes such 'ways of going on' that are natural to us, inevitable for us. (So, again, Wittgenstein is held to have reached the conclusion that convention is a relatively superficial business. Philosophical profundity comes from delving beneath the superficial layer of convention to underlying facts of natural history that characterize our form of life.)

This cluster of interpretations and conclusions is a caricature of Wittgenstein's arguments, which in fact show it to be utterly confused.

First, what is (according to Wittgenstein) 'natural' is *not* uniformly biological (cf. 'Grammar and necessity', pp. 328, 334f.). Looking in the direction pointed at, crying out in pain, laughing when amused, etc. are biologically natural. Continuing the series of natural numbers '1001, 1002, 1003, . . . 100,001, 100,002, 100,003, . . .' is 'culturally natural' as it were. It is natural for us, but not for all people at all times and places (LFM 243). Introducing negative integers when previously only natural numbers were employed *was* certainly not 'natural', though now it is natural for us, after elementary training, to extend series involving successive subtraction beyond nought into the domain of negative numbers.

Secondly, far from other conceptual structures being *unintelligible* to us, a little *imagination* can render them *natural!*

If you believe that our concepts are the right ones, the ones suited to intelligent human beings, that anyone with different ones would not realize something that we realize, then imagine certain general facts of nature different from the way they are, and conceptual structures different from our own will appear *natural* to you. (RPP I §48; cf. PI p. 230)

'Natural', Wittgenstein emphasized, 'not "necessary"'. Here the contrast is not between what is 'natural' and what is *logically* or *metaphysically* necessary. The latter notions do not enter the domain of concept-formation, for grammar is autonomous. It *determines* logical necessity and is not its product ('Grammar and necessity', pp. 332ff.). The contrast is between what is natural (i.e. what is comfortable, dovetails smoothly with existing practices, is easy to handle, simple to teach and explain, strikes us with a salient aspect, etc.) and what is a necessary means to a certain end. For we are not mere utilitarian creatures.

Thirdly, Wittgenstein's concept of the 'natural history of man' is predominantly anthropological. What interests him will hardly be found, as it were, in the Natural History Museum (Department of Human Biology), but in the Ethnological Museum of Mankind. 'Commanding, questioning, recounting, chatting, are as much a part of our natural history as walking, eating, drinking, playing.' (PI §25) *Measuring* in all its forms is part of human natural history, and a description of its varieties will make the *concepts* of measuring, exactness, etc. intelligible to us in all their variations (RPP I §1109). One can give an ethnological account of the human institution of measuring with rulers and with the scale of feet and inches (RFM 356). Mathematics is an *anthropological* phenomenon (RFM 399). Working through proofs (hardly a feature of human *biology*) and accepting them is 'use and custom among us, or a fact of our natural history' (RFM 61). And finally, logic too belongs to the natural history of man (RFM 352f.); not to be sure, the *propositions* of logic, but rather *that we use these propositions* as we do, that we mould our concepts thus, etc. – that is a feature of our natural history. In short, the natural history of man is the history of a convention-forming, concept-exercising, language-using animal – a cultural animal. And it is important for philosophers to remember these very general facts.

Fourthly, if Wittgenstein's conception of human nature is not predominantly a biological one, then *a fortiori* his concept of a form of life is not biological, but cultural. There is no uniquely human (uniform) form of life, characteristic of the species, but rather are there multiple forms of life, characteristic of different cultures and epochs. Of course, these are *human* forms of life, resting upon human biological nature as well as upon the physical nature of the world we inhabit. These contentions can be established from careful scrutiny of the very remarks usually cited to support the opposite conclusion.

(i) *On Certainty* §§357–60 is concerned with certainty. It is the certainty of 'I know this is my foot' that is said to be 'beyond being justified or unjustified; as it were something animal'. It is true that Wittgenstein said that he wanted to regard this certainty as a form of life. But note two points: first, he added 'That is very badly expressed and probably badly thought as well'; secondly, what is said to lie beyond being justified or unjustified – to be, as it were, something animal – is this sort of certainty. Wittgenstein did indeed think that forms of life lie beyond justification, also that conceptual structures, world-pictures that are embodied in forms of life transcend justification. But does it follow that a form of life is something animal? Or is it something animal only in just that respect of transcending justification?

(ii) The source of the crucial remark 'What has to be accepted, the given is . . . forms of life' (PI p. 226) reveals it to be concerned with features of a culture. There Wittgenstein examined the familiar empiricist conception that colours are 'unanalysable'; they are something specific, which is not to be explained by anything else (this is a strange perversion of the doctrine that *individuum est ineffabile*); they are indefinable, for one cannot explain to someone what red is. Against this Wittgenstein pitted his quite different conception and philosophical method:

Instead of the unanalysable, specific, indefinable: the fact that we act in such-and-such ways, e.g. *punish* certain actions, *establish* the state of affairs thus-and-so, *give orders*, render accounts, describe colours, take an interest in others' feelings. What has to be accepted, the given – it might be said – are facts of living. (RPP I §630)

It is noteworthy that a manuscript variant of 'Tatsachen des Lebens' is 'Lebensformen'. Here the description of the activities that constitute 'the given' are manifestly cultural activities; these 'facts of living' are not something animal, biological or pre-cultural but forms of social, human, modes of intercourse, discourse and concourse.

(iii) It is true that *Zettel* §390 argues that

These men would have nothing human about them: Why? We could not possibly make ourselves understood to them. Not even as we can to a dog. We could not find our feet with them.

And yet there surely could be such beings, who in other respects were human.

However this does not confirm the interpretation that any other form of life than ours (*the* human form of life) would be unintelligible to us. First, note what is being imagined here: viz. a tribe of *men* educated to give *no expression of feeling of any kind*. Here indeed we would recoil with horror. Much that matters to us in our lives, all that is 'closest to our hearts' would be opaque, perhaps disgusting to such people. And if anything matters to them, we would not be able to understand it. Secondly, even here, in this extreme case, Wittgenstein argued 'an *education*[5] quite different from ours might also be the foundation for quite different concepts, for here life would run on differently – what interests us would not interest *them*. Here different concepts would no longer be unimaginable. In fact, this is the only way in which *essentially* different concepts are imaginable.' (Z §§387f.) So, if this *is* held to be a different form of life, it is a product of nurture not nature. Though we 'could not find our feet' with such creatures, their *concepts* are perfectly imaginable, not *opaque* to us, but useless *for us*.

Fifthly, note that Wittgenstein mentioned multiple form*s* of human life. Thus:

Ich will sagen: est ist charakteristisch für unsere Sprache, dass sie auf den Grund fester Lebensformen, regelmässiger Handlungen, emporwächst / / wächst / / dass sie auf dem Grund fester Lebensformen, regelmässiger Handlungsformen emporwächst. (Vol. XV, 148)

(I want to say: it is a feature of our language that it springs up / / it grows / / out of the foundations of forms of life, regular actions / / that it springs up from the soil of firm forms of life, regular forms of actions.)

In MS 160, 51 (cf. below, p. 258) the question: 'How is it that we agree in our applications of rules?' is answered: 'Durch Abrichtung, Drill und die Formen unsres Lebens. Es handelt sich nicht nur um einen Consens der Meinungen sondern der Lebensformen.' ('Through training, drill and the forms of our lives. This involves not only a consensus of opinions but of forms of life.)

Finally note that the remarks 'to imagine a language is to imagine a form of life' (PI §19) and 'speaking a language is part of a form of life', have as their remote ancestors the observations 'Imagine a use of language (a culture) in which . . .' and again 'imagine a language (and that means again a culture) in which . . ..' (BB 134)

---

[5] Our italics.

In short, men in different epochs, different cultures, have different forms of life. Different educations, interests and concerns, different human relations and relations to nature and the world constitute distinct forms of life. For such different cultures form different conceptual structures, adopt distinctive forms and norms of representation, limited only by the vague boundaries of the concept of a form of representation or a language. Of course, in advance of a particular question and a specific context it would be quite pointless to draw hard and fast distinctions between what counts as the same and what as a different form of life. Such distinctions depend upon the purpose and context of different kinds of investigation.

4. *Agreement: consensus of human beings and their actions*

The relation between a given rule and an act that accords with it ('agrees' with it) is internal or grammatical. Nothing mediates between a rule and its 'extension', for internal relations are not cemented by any 'third thing'. A *fortiori*, it would be absurd to hold that a condition of *this* act (e.g. writing '1002, 1004, 1006, . . .') being in accord with *this* rule (viz. the rule for the series of even integers) is that people in general agree on the application of rules or that people agree that writing *this* accords with *this* rule. Of course, if there were no agreement, there would be no common concept of addition, of adding 2, of the series of even integers. But it is an error to insert a community agreement between a rule and what accords with it. For if the rule is given, then so is its 'extension'.

Is it then to be argued that a condition for there *being any rules* is that there be general agreement on what acts accord with what rules? This is multiply confused. First, as we have seen ('Following rules, mastery of techniques and practices', pp. 169ff.), there is nothing conceptually awry about solitary rule-followers or unshared rules. Secondly, the very form of the question presupposes that rules and what accords with them, as well as understanding a rule and knowing what accords with it, are externally related.

These construals of Wittgenstein's concern with human agreement about rules, uses of language, and concept-formation correctly grasp that the concept of general consensus in definitions, judgements and actions plays an important role in his thought. But they take it at the wrong level of generality (trying to insert it between a rule and its extension), locate it wrongly (taking it to be a constituent of the concept defined by a certain rule, rather than as part of the framework within which a language-game is played) and draw incorrect conclusions from it (that an unshared language, language-game or rule is an absurdity).

It is just because unshared (as opposed to *unsharable*) concepts, rules, language-games are *not* conceptually awry that they are essentially uninteresting. Robinson Crusoe or the last Mohican make good fiction, but pose no deep philosophical problems of any kind; the only interest in these cases lies in showing just that the great (shifting) array of problems of philosophy arises out of entanglements in our understanding of the conceptual articulations of *our* languages. These are the common property of communities, nations and cultures. They are shared forms of representation, constitutive of common forms of life. They are inherited techniques, applied and exercised in countless familiar public practices and shared language-games. The problems of the philosophy of mathematics arise out of our common mathematical calculi and concepts (although a philosophy of mathematics in the fourteenth century was no less possible than it is today and no more necessary). The endless problems of philosophical logic are rooted in our shared practices of using languages, of inferring, reasoning, denying or affirming, asserting or questioning. And so on. Nothing in the previous discussions of accord with rules and following rules is intended to rob the Hegelian of his hard-won and valuable insights into the social and historical nature of man, his languages and culture. Rather was it concerned with correctly locating these important features, in particular in ensuring that they do not distort our understanding of normative concepts. Having clarified those, we can now turn to examine the issues surrounding consensus. The salient claims, against the background of previous discussions, are fairly straightforward.

There is no such thing as shared rules independently of agreement over what accords with the rules, for understanding a rule *is* knowing what accords with it. Hence having a shared understanding of a rule is to agree on its application. And since normative regularities, 'doing the same thing', are internally related to rules, it is no coincidence that

Disputes do not break out (among mathematicians, say) over the question whether a rule has been obeyed or not. People don't come to blows over it, for example. That is part of the framework on which the working of our language is based (for example, in giving descriptions). (PI §240)

Furthermore, there are no shared rules without shared patterns of normative activities, and so shared judgements about justification, criticism, explanation, description, etc. This general (but not uniform) consensus is part of the peaceful working of a common form of representation. Again, there are no shared techniques without general agreement on the results of employing the techniques, for in certain kinds of case, e.g. in calculating, *the results are part of the technique* and in other kinds of case, e.g. counting or measuring objects, constant disagreement in results would rob the technique of its *point* and so too of its *sense* (LFM 256; RFM 200), and the technique would not exist. These forms of agreement or consensus are immediate and obvious consequences of explaining what shared rules are, given the previous explanation of what rules are.

If language is to be a means of communication we must agree on the application of our rules of grammar and 'laws' of logic, otherwise we would not agree on the rules at all, i.e. nothing would be shared. 'Logic, it may be said, shows us what we understand by "proposition" and by "language".' (RFM 90) We agree that $(x)fx \rightarrow fa$; that is how we understand 'all', what we understand by 'follows'. If someone says '$(x)fx$' and another says 'So fa', we call that 'inferring correctly' or 'drawing the correct conclusion'. If someone responds 'So $\sim fa$', we say: 'He hasn't understood.' If a person says, 'No, a is $not f$', we say 'Ah, so $\sim(x)fx$.' And so on – 'it is just this that is called "thinking", "speaking", "inferring", "arguing".' (RFM 96)

Wrongly viewed, these observations may seem to lead to four predicaments which we shall first list, and subsequently resolve:

(i) Are we now arguing that *logic* (grammar in general) is a matter of consensus of opinions about the laws of logic? Is it claimed that democratic voting can determine whether *modus ponens* is a valid form of inference, whether the Laws of Excluded Middle or Non-contradiction hold? Could an Act of Parliament change the laws of logic? Wittgenstein anticipated this misunderstanding: 'What you say seems to amount to this, that logic belongs to the natural history of man. And that is not combinable with the hardness of the logical "must".' (RFM 352f.) For the adamantine laws of logic do not run: 'All men agree that $(x)fx \rightarrow fa$', or 'If everyone agrees, then $(x)fx \rightarrow fa$'; and if they did they would be neither adamantine nor laws of logic.

(ii) Wittgenstein argued that we may often explain how to apply one rule by citing another rule (a rule for applying the first rule). In such a case, the second rule seems to stand behind the first one and to justify particular applications of this rule. And this chain of reasons may continue. But it will come to an end: our reasons will soon give out (PI §211). What happens when we exhaust our justifications? We hit bedrock. And then? We can only say 'This is simply what we do!' (cf. PI §217) This situation arises with explanations of meaning as with any other rules. We may readily imagine circumstances in which *any explanation* would be open to misunderstanding and we can imagine the possibility of supplying yet another rule for applying the explanation which would remove this misunderstanding, e.g. a scheme of arrows for reading a colour-chart (PI §86) or explanations of terms used in the original explanation (PI §87). But in actual practice our explanations soon come to an end, we do not (and we do not need to) explain how to read a colour-chart or whether the sample introduced in an ostensive definition lies in the direction of the pointing finger (cf. PI §85). So it seems that following rules in general, and rules of grammar in particular, topples over the edge into mere human *habits*. What is correct seems to boil down to what is customary, to consensus of action. Where now are the adamantine laws of logic? Have we not bargained away the inexorability of conceptual, grammatical, connections? Wittgenstein anticipated this worry too:

> Darum beziehen sich die Worte 'einer Regel folgen' auf eine Praxis . . ..
> Dies scheint die Logik aufzuheben; hebt sie aber nicht auf. (MS 180(a), 76)

> (Therefore the words 'to follow a rule' signify a practice . . ..
> This seems to abolish logic, but does not do so.)

(iii) If we have a shared language we must agree in definitions, explanations of meaning, i.e. rules for the use of words. And to agree in a rule *is* to agree over what counts as its correct applications. So it follows that we must also agree in judgements about the world, or at least in a *core* of judgements about the world. And this raises further qualms:

> If language is to be a means of communication there must be agreement not only in definitions but also (queer as it may sound) in judgements. This seems to abolish logic but does not do so. (PI §242)

It does indeed sound queer, for we surely wish to take logic to be antecedent to questions of truth and falsity. To logic belongs everything that comes *before* judgements: 'That one empirical proposition is true and another false is no part of grammar. What belongs to grammar are all the conditions (the method) necessary for comparing the proposition with reality. That is, all the conditions necessary for the understanding (of the sense).' (PG 88)[6] But if so, how can the existence of a language, a method of representation, require agreement in *judgement*? Is not that like claiming that for chess to be possible there must be agreement not only over the moves (how the pieces are to be moved) but also over who is to win! But surely logic must be independent of truth, of how things are in the world, just as *truth* must be independent of human agreement.

(iv) A final objection is raised by the claim that it is essential for the phenomenon of language that we do not dispute over what counts as following a rule. But

> Wie kann Übereinstimmung Bedingung der Sprache sein? Wo wir uns Übereinstimmen denken können, können wir uns doch nicht-Übereinstimmen denken.
> Denke also es brache Nicht-Übereinstimmung über die Farbe der meisten Dinge aus.
> Wie wüssten wir dann, was wir mit der Farbwörten meinten? (MS 165, 30f.)

---

[6] This remark rides over the distinction between grammar and the framework conditions for its application.

(How can agreement be a condition of language? Where we can imagine
agreement we can also imagine disagreement.
  Imagine that disagreement over the colours of most things were to break out.
How would we then know what we meant by colour-words?)

If a certain condition is a presupposition of logic, then, it seems, its
negation should be unthinkable. For this must be incompatible with
logic (RPP II §§190f.)! But can we not imagine that there might be no
agreement? And if we cannot, how can the fact of agreement be a mere
contingent fact?
  Wittgenstein resolved each of these critical puzzles. They uniformly
rest on misunderstandings of his arguments. *First*, the consensus or
agreement that is a presupposition of logic is not an agreement in
opinions, much less in opinions on questions of logic (RFM 353). It is a
consensus in accepting a form of representation, and there is no question
of opinion here, no question of truth or falsity. But a consensus in
accepting a form of representation is a consensus in *action* (LFM 183f., cf.
107). This agreement in action manifests itself in all our deeds, which are
informed by our thoughts. It shows itself in the bustle of our lives (RPP
II §§624ff.), hence it can justly be said to be an agreement in form of life
(PI §241; MS 129, 35; MS 124, 212f.). Consequently to claim that logic
presupposes agreement is *not* to claim that the laws of logic have the form
'All men agree that . . .':

. . . the logical 'must' is a component part of the propositions of logic, and these
are not propositions of human natural history. If what a proposition of logic said
was 'Human beings agree with one another in such-and-such ways' (and that
would be the form of the natural history proposition), then its contradictory
would say that there is here a lack of agreement. Not, that there is an agreement
of another kind. (RFM 353)

But this does not mean that logic boils down into human habits or
consensus. (a) What is correct, in accord with a rule, cannot be *defined* as
what it is customary to do. That would be inconsistent with acknowledging that there is an internal relation between a rule and acting in accord
with it. (b) An interpretation of a rule does not make an act a correct
application of a particular rule; it is not the *foundation* for what accords
with the rule, and what conflicts with it. That too would represent an
interpretation as abrogating the *internal* connection between a rule and
acting in accord with it. Rather, an interpretation makes clear what is, as
it were, *already* in accord with a particular rule (in circumstances in which
misunderstandings occur or are known to be likely). Hence reaching the
end of a chain of interpretations makes no essential difference. The
applications of the original rule do not *rest* on the first interpretation or
any subsequent ones, and therefore the petering out of interpretations at

some point does not strike away props that must be replaced by invoking agreement. Agreement no more mediates between a rule and its extension than does an interpretation. On the contrary, there is no such thing as a rule which does not, by itself, constitute a standard of correctness. It is a platitude, for example, that the rule + 2 determines that writing '1002' after '1000' is correct. Why is it right to write '1002' here? – '"Well, because we all do it like that"; that will not be the reason.'[7] (Z §319; cf. RPP II §§403ff.) Agreement in action is not a surrogate for the concept of correctness because absence of interpretations generates no conceptual vacuum to be filled.

Secondly, in a certain sense we can say that following a rule is 'founded on agreement' (RFM 392). But this must be understood to refer to the *framework* within which the concept of following a rule has intelligible employment, not to the explanation of what 'following a rule' means. A framework of agreement *in behaviour* is presupposed by each of our shared language-games, but this does not 'abolish logic' or soften the 'hardness of the logical "must"', since logic belongs to the rules of the language-games we play, and the framework conditions in general and agreement in particular are not included in those rules. If there were no normal reaction to the gesture of pointing, no standard reaction in reading charts and tables, etc., our practice of explaining colour-words would fall apart. Either explanations would have to begin somewhere else (where agreement prevails) or there would be no explanations of colour-words, and hence no concept of colour at all. It is crucial that we do not have to explain to a child how to take our gesture of pointing at a sample and that we do not have to explain why he takes it as he does (PI p. 56n.). Similarly, agreement in the results of calculating is of the essence of a shared technique of calculating (RFM 193). The agreement in ratification of proofs is what puts proofs 'in the archives', for in the absence of general ratification we would not calculate with such 'proofs', we would not employ them as norms of representation. But 'the agreement of ratifications is the precondition of our language-game, it is not affirmed in it.' (RFM 365; cf. Exg. §240).

Corresponding to the fear that logic is abolished by the fact that following a rule is (in the sense explained) founded on agreement is the equally erroneous idea that logic is saved from the spectre of scepticism or of an infinite regress of 'interpretations' only by the fact of human agreement in action. The truth of the matter is that if there were no common agreement in action, there would *be* no 'logic of our language' since there would be *no* shared language at all. The grammatical relations that constitute logic are constructed within the framework of common

---

[7] But the question: 'Why is it correct to extend the series '+ 2' beyond 1000 with 1002, 1004, 1006, . . .?' can well be answered by 'That is what we do, that is what we *call* "correct".'

agreement, but that consensus in action is *not* the cement that binds together those grammatical relations.

It is a mistake to think that we can invoke agreement to break out of the circle of normative concepts to something non-normative that underlies it.

It is no use, for example, to go back to the concept of agreement, because it is no more certain that one action [*Handlung*] is in agreement with another, than that it has happened in accordance with a rule. (RFM 392)

This is clear enough, for if two people both understand a certain rule they must both call the same actions 'acting in accord with the rule'. Various acts of accord are all 'doing the same thing', viz. acting in accord with that rule. ('The use of the word "rule" and the use of the word "same" are interwoven.' (PI §225; cf. RFM 405)) If so, they will also see their several acts of following that rule as agreeing, i.e. as being the same. For one, in writing '1002, 1004, 1006, . . .', is doing the same as the other is doing (not only in writing '1002, 1004, 1006, . . .' but also in writing '768, 770, 772, . . .'), namely acting in accord with the rule + 2. ('The word "agreement" and the word "rule" are *related* to one another, they are cousins. If I teach anyone the use of the one word, he learns the use of the other with it.' (PI §224)) But if there is dispute over whether doing *this* is in accord with *this* rule, one cannot fall back on whether *this* act is the same as *that* act. For their being the same consists here in their being in accord with the rule.

Thirdly, agreement in definitions (explanations, rules for the use of expressions) does indeed require agreement in judgements, agreement in the applications of the rules, in the use of the expressions thus defined or explained. For there is a rule only if something counts in practice as correct applications of it. For there to be an agreed (shared) rule is for there to be agreement in its application; these are not two distinct things, but two sides of the same coin. Of course, this principle holds only for such cases where the truth of a judgement is not readily separable from the correct application of expressions. (This is so, for example, with perceptual judgements over a very wide range.) Otherwise there is ample room for extensive disagreement over the relevance of evidence, its weighting, probabilities, causal relations, etc. It is characteristic of judgements about feelings or suffering, for example, that there is often no unhesitant agreement over the sincerity of an emotion or the comparative intensity of pain (PI p. 227). Here there is a penumbra of indefiniteness about the application of these concepts, an indeterminacy about the concepts which is a reflection of the lack of unreflective, unhesitant agreement.

Nevertheless, it is an illusion to think that this abolishes logic by making the laws of logic dependent upon human agreement about what is true or how things are in the world. For it is not the case that if there were no agreement the laws of logic would be *false* (that a denial of the Law of Non-contradiction or of the inference-rule of *modus ponens* would be true). Rather is it that if there were not an agreed practice of using laws of logic in reasoning, arguing, inferring, of using words in accord with explanations of meaning, then there would be no laws of logic, no explanations of meaning, and no reasoning, arguing, justifying or understanding. There would be *no language*, but only a 'speaking with tongues'.[8]

The requirement of broad agreement over a core of judgements is not akin to requiring agreement over both the rules of chess and who is to win, but rather over the rules, and what counts as a legitimate move, what it is to win, and who counts, in a particular game, as having won. Wittgenstein compared the grammatical relations here involved with the special case of the relation between the determination of a method of measurement and its applications.

It is one thing to describe methods of measurement, and another to obtain and state results of measurement. But what we call 'measuring' is partly determined by a certain constancy in results of measurement. (PI §242)

Our agreement does not determine truth – that is up to the world. And our judgements do not determine our method of measurement; our methods of measurements are the norms we all follow in making measurements. But our agreement over a method of measurement (which is not an agreement in opinions – it being no 'opinion' that 12 inches is equal to 1 foot) is an agreement over the method of application, hence an agreement in the practice of measuring. If we all got wildly discordant 'results', there would be no measuring and no method of measuring.

Finally, if we argue that agreement is a condition of language, does it follow that we should not be able to imagine disagreement? The argument is analogous to *Investigations* §55 (cf. Exg. §55). In the *Tractatus* it seemed that objects must be sempiternal because, *inter alia*, it must be possible to describe a state of affairs in which everything destructible is destroyed. But this reasoning was erroneous. For it does not follow, from the possibility of such a description, that it must be possible *in that state of affairs* to describe how things are. Analogously here: given that we agree, for example, in our colour-judgements, we can describe such changes in us as would lead to disagreement in our applications (LPE 306). But, of course, beyond a certain point we could *not* say: 'They disagree in their use of colour-words', for these words would no longer *be* colour-words. They would not be used as *we* use colour-words or as the imagined

---

[8] But, again, this does not preclude the imaginary solitary speaker on his desert island.

people *used* colour-words prior to the 'chaos'. Only the shell of colour-concepts remains, for confusion has supervened (PI p. 226). But that is precisely what we should expect, given that agreement is part of the framework, the precondition or presupposition of the language-games with colour-names, i.e. not that these people would in conditions of disagreement have a different colour-grammar (that already obtains in different languages) but rather that they would have none at all (Z §351). Of course, the boundary between order and confusion is not sharp and absolute, and the dividing line between our colour-concepts and concepts sufficiently analogous to be called 'colour-concepts' is vague and purpose-relative.

Wittgenstein himself best summed up the role of agreement in his reflections:

It is of the greatest importance that a dispute hardly ever arises between people about whether the colour of this object is the same as the colour of that, the length of this rod the same as the length of that, etc. This peaceful agreement is the characteristic surrounding of the use of the word 'same'.

And one must say something analogous about proceeding according to rule.

No dispute breaks out over the question whether a proceeding was according to the rule or not. It doesn't come to blows, for example.

This belongs to the framework, out of which our language works (for example, gives a description). (RFM 323)

SECTION 238

1   It *seems* as if 'all the steps are already taken in advance' (§219); this is
how it strikes me. And this is a mythological description of the use of a
rule (§221). One gravitates towards such pictures only if one draws the
consequences oneself as a *matter of course*, if one 'follows the rule blindly'
(§219). The *immediacy* of one's action is precisely that of calling a colour
by its name; nothing mediates between a rule and its application.
    What are the criteria for something's being a matter of course for me?
That it is altogether unremarkable, unsurprising (cf. §524); hence that I
do not fumble in its application and manifest no hesitation. I await no
directions from inspiration or intimation (§232).

2   TS 228, §§336ff. links PI §238 with PI §§218, 223, and 229, presumably connecting it with the mythological pictures of following rules.

SECTION 239

1   The ramifying illusions concerning normativity grow out of the
mundane soil of unreflectively following a rule, *as* unreflectively as
calling a colour by its name (§238). The interlocutor now raises with
respect to colour a parallel question to §211 ('How can he *know* how he is
to continue the pattern . . .?') and, more generally to §198 ('How can a
rule show me what I have to do . . .?') cf. RFM 36. I call a colour by its
name as a matter of course, but how am I to *know* what colour to pick
out when I hear 'red'? To this (bogus) question the interlocutor essays a
reply: one is to take the colour whose image ('idea') occurs to one when
hearing the colour-name (cf. classical empiricism).
    The question is confused, for I have *no* reason for calling *this colour*
'red' (not: this ruby). At most I can say that I have learnt English (§381);
and that, of course, is not a reason. It merely emphasizes that I have
mastered this technique, i.e. that I can use 'red' correctly. Failing to see
this the interlocutor, rather than rejecting the request for a reason, delves
for one. Not finding a genuine reason, he assumes that there is an
explanatory mechanism that will explain how he is to know what colour
to pick out, viz. 'that the names heard, almost as readily excite certain
ideas as if the objects themselves, which are apt to produce them, did

actually affect the senses.'[1] But of course a mechanism, even if there be one, will not answer the bogus question.

W. gives two responses. First, granting, for the sake of argument, that an image does occur to one (though, of course, it usually does not), and granting that it may be the image of a colour (although the image I associate with 'red' may be of a field of poppies), how is one to know of which colour the image one has is an image? For the interlocutor certainly wants to be sure that on hearing the word 'red' we all have an image of *red*, and not of something else.[2] This impales him on the horns of a dilemma. *Either* a further criterion is necessary to identify the image-of-the-colour that occurs to one; but then what is it? *Or*, no criterion is necessary, since one 'knows immediately'; but then why was it thought that a criterion was necessary to justify one's knowing that this colour is red in the first place? The retreat into the mental then merely returns one to the point of departure, viz. ungrounded knowledge which rests on skill (training in a technique), not on evidence. Of course, W. adds parenthetically, there is such a thing as choosing the colour which occurs to one on hearing a certain word. But that presupposes mastery of the use of colour-words and does not explain it.

Secondly, if we discard the requirement that I identify the image that occurs to me as an image of red, we would be left with the stipulation that 'red' *means* the colour that occurs to me when I hear the word 'red' *whatever that may be*. But this is surely not what one wants. For not only is this not what we mean by 'red'; it is also not an explanation of the nature of designating something (in this case a colour) by a word, in particular not an explanation of how he is 'to know what colour he is to pick out when he hears "red"'; but that is what this explanation was introduced for!

The argument parallels §§198 and 201: and interpretation cannot *essentially* mediate between a rule and an action in accord with it, for correctly construed, an interpretation is merely a further rule-formulation which has to be applied. Similarly, attempting to answer the bogus question of *how* I know what colour to pick out on hearing 'red' by reference to a mechanism of mental imagery would be merely to interpose a (wrong) definition between the word heard and an action. It would therefore not explain what it is to use the word as a name of a colour.

2   (i) PG 70 (cf. Vol. VI, 61f.) contains an early draft of this in a quite different context. There it occurs in the course of arguing against the

---

[1] Locke, *An Essay Concerning Human Understanding*, III–ii–6.
[2] Cf. Locke: 'They suppose their words to be marks of the ideas in the minds also of other men, with whom they communicate: for else they should talk in vain and could not be understood, if the sounds they applied to one idea were such as by the hearer were applied to another, which is to speak two languages.' (*op. cit.* III–ii–4)

causal theory of meaning (cf. PLP ch. VI). Any causal explanation of language as a psychophysical mechanism employs a language to describe contingent phenomena. But an explanation of meaning must be normative, a part of the 'calculus'. Then follows PI §239, which is followed by an explicit repudiation of any attempt to explain what a symbol means in terms of its effect. For *which* effect is *this* effect? How do we know it is the effect meant? If the reply is, 'We compare it with our memory image', the riposte is, 'How do we know what method of comparison to use?'

(ii) Vol. XII, 37f. rephrases the final line: 'Es erklärt nicht // Keine Erklärung dessen // was das Wesen des Bedeutens ist // sei //.' ('It does not explain // It is not an explanation of what the nature of meaning is.') It continues

(Bezieht sich auf das, was Frege und gelegentlich Ramsey, vom Wiedererkennen als der // einer // Bedingung des Symbolisierens sagte. Was ist denn das Kriterium dessen // dafür //, dass ich die Farbe richtig wieder erkannt habe? Etwa, so etwas wie das Erlebnis der Freude beim Wiedererkennen?)

((This is related to what Frege and occasionally Ramsey said about recognition as the // a // requirement of symbolizing. For what is the criterion for my having recognized a colour again correctly? Perhaps something like the experience of joy at recognition?))

The reference to Frege may be an allusion to FA §62: 'If we are to use the symbol *a* to signify an object, we must have a criterion for deciding in all cases whether *b* is the same as *a* . . .' (since Frege held that an expression of the form 'The colour that occurs to me . . .' is a proper name signifying an object).

W. then observes that psychological, trivial, discussions about association always leave out what is truly remarkable, and bypass the crucial point. In this case, that any *further* explanation will leave one (philosophically) just where one *already* is, viz. at a terminus of explanation.

Section 240

1   It is a matter of course for me to apply a colour-word without grounds (§238); and if it is a matter of course, then disputes must be rare exceptions. Groundless certainty in the application of words (in following rules) within a speech-community *presupposes* a general consensus. This consensus over whether a rule has been obeyed in making empirical judgements, this 'peaceful agreement' that acting *thus* is what following such-and-such a rule consists in (this is what we call 'following this rule'), is a framework condition for the working of our language; it is 'the characteristic surrounding of the use of the word "same"' (RFM 323).

Without such peaceful agreement there would be no mutual understanding, no learning and teaching, no established patterns of explaining and justifying. The foundations of language do not lie in shared *indubitabilia*, or in given *ineffabilia*, but in the framework of agreed groundless certainty in applying rules. This is an agreement in behaviour, a possession of an array of techniques that are expressed, without dispute, in common ways of acting in certain circumstances.

1.1   '(among mathematicians, say)': this parenthesis is absent from MS 129, 127. It was added in the final TS. The point of this modification is unclear. One might speculate that it is to draw attention to a particular species of agreement in following rules, i.e. to agreement in the results of calculations. This topic is discussed in a closely parallel passage (RFM 356). But this interpretation would suggest restricting the agreement discussed in §241 to agreement about mathematical truth and falsity (or more generally to agreement in grammar), and that in turn would cut off §241 from the discussion of agreement in judgements in §242. It seems clear that the agreement considered in §240 is more general, including agreement in empirical judgements (cf. RFM 323).

2   Z §§429f. provides a parallel:

> You say '*That* is red', but how is it decided if you are right? Doesn't human agreement decide? – But do I appeal to this agreement in my judgements of colour? Then is what goes on like *this*: I get a number of people to look at an object; to each of them there occurs one of a certain group of words (what are called the 'names of colours'); if the word 'red' occurred to the majority of the spectators (I myself need not belong to this majority) the predicate 'red' belongs to the object by rights. Such a technique might have its importance.
>
> *Colour-words* are explained like *this*: 'That's red' e.g. – Our language-game only works, of course, when a certain agreement prevails, but the concept of agreement does not enter into the language-game. If agreement were universal, we might be quite unacquainted with the concept of it.

Z §429 explicitly links the issue of consensus in judgement with associative procedures similar to those specified in PI §239. And the manner in which consensus is introduced (by the wayward interlocutor) conforms to the standard empiricist conception. For mutual intelligibility is held to be contingent upon convergence of associative dispositions. But while the technique described might have a use (e.g. head-counting in respect of random associations might be given a role in decisions about the 'colour' of letters of the alphabet, or of notes of the octave), it plays no role whatever in our colour predications. We determine whether an object is red by *looking at it*, not by finding out what others say (cf. MS 123, 4f.). And if there is any room for doubt (because it is an unusual shade), then we compare the object with a standard sample.

SECTION 241

1   The interlocutor misunderstands the claim that agreement is part of the framework of giving descriptions (§240), taking it to mean that it is general agreement that decides the truth or falsity of descriptions. His question expresses the suspicion that W. has abolished the objectivity of truth. But this is mistaken. That we agree is not asserted in giving descriptions (e.g. in stating the results of measurements (§242)). It is what we *say*, the propositions that we propound in making judgements, in expressing our thoughts, that are true or false. Whether they are true or false is determined by reality, not by whether human beings agree in accepting or rejecting them. But in judging things to be true or false, we agree in the language we use, and that is an agreement in our form of life.

The remark that the agreement in language is not an agreement in *opinions* but in form of life is problematic. Is 'opinion' here equivalent to judgements about truth or falsehood or does it stand in contrast with such judgements? If the former, then this remark appears to conflict with §242 in which W. insists that for there to be a shared language there must be agreement in judgements. The two remarks might be reconciled if what is intended is that agreement in the language we use is not only agreement in opinions (i.e. judgements) but rather much more, namely an agreement in form of life which, to be sure, includes agreement in judgements. If 'opinions' stands in contrast with judgements, then there is no conflict between §241 and §242. But then it is unclear what is intended by 'opinions'. Perhaps the point is a dialectical one: if, as the interlocutor suggests, the agreement that is the framework for giving descriptions did decide truth or falsity, that would be an agreement of opinions, since objective standards of truth and falsity would be abolished. We would merely opine thus or otherwise, and agreement of our opinions would determine (as the pragmatists supposed) what is to be called true or false. But this is wrong, for the agreement in question is an agreement in our language, in our form of life. That involves a widespread agreement in judgements (§242), for which there are objective standards of truth and falsity. Such agreement in our language is presupposed in order for there to be any such thing as agreement (or disagreement) in opinions (cf. MS 164, 162; below, Exg. §241, 2.1).

.1   'in the language they use': it might be suggested that agreement in language is just agreement in grammar, i.e. in the rules of grammar (definitions, explanations of meaning, rules for the use of expressions). Then agreement in language would be distinguished from agreement in opinions as agreement in definitions in §242 is distinguished from agreement in judgements. This is wrong. Agreement in language here is agreement in form of life, and that includes both agreement in definitions and agreement in judgements (for *both* are criteria for agreement over the meanings of words, which is necessary for communication by means of language (PI §242; RFM 343)). This interpretation is borne out by RFM 342f. 'the phenomenon of language is based on regularity, on agreement in action', *both* in calling the same colours 'red', 'green', etc. *and* in a large number of judgements (cf. also MS 124, 212f.; below, Exg. §241, 2.1).

2   MS 129, 35, MS 124, 212, and MS 180(a), 12 all place this section between PI §213 and versions of §243. The sequence of sections in PPI(I) is §213, §217, §241, §243. The phrasing of MS 124, 212f. is interesting:

> So sagst Du also, dass die Übereinstimmung der Menschen bestimmt // entscheidet // was wahr // richtig // und falsch // unrichtig // ist? – Richtig und unrichtig gibt es nur im Denken, also im Ausdruck der Gedanken: und der Ausdruck der Gedanken, die Sprache, ist den Menschen gemeinsam. Er ist eine Lebensform in der sie übereinstimmen (nicht eine Meinung).

> (So you are saying that human agreement determines // decides // what is true // correct // and false // incorrect? Only in thinking do correct and incorrect exist, hence in the expression of thoughts: and the expression of thoughts, the language, is common to men. That is a form of life (not an opinion) in which they agree.)

Truth is not decided by consensus of judgement. We are not taught to determine the colour of an object by consulting a majority of viewers (Z §431). 'The same' does not mean 'what most people take to be the same', for one does not invoke majority consensus in determining identity (RFM 406).

2.1   (i) 'not agreement in opinions': this remark has many parallels in W.'s writings on logic and mathematics. There his purposes are somewhat different. LFM 183f. considers the suggestion that the truths of logic are determined by a consensus of opinions.

> Is this what I am saying? No. There is no *opinion* at all; it is not a question of *opinion*. They are determined by a consensus of *action*: a consensus of doing the same thing, reacting in the same way. There is a consensus but it is not a consensus of opinion. We all act the same way, walk the same way, count the same way.

Here agreement in opinion is contrasted with agreement in action. We might well say 'that the laws of logic show what we *do* with propositions, as opposed to expressing opinions or convictions' (LFM 232). The agreement over the laws of logic and propositions of mathematics is not an agreement of *opinions* about their *truth*, it is an agreement over norms of representation and that is an agreement in action, in applying these techniques.

(ii) '*not* agreement in opinions *but* in form of life' (our italics): MS 164 supports the suggestion that this contrast does not imply mutual exclusion. Rather, agreement in form of life includes and is presupposed by particular agreements in opinion. For it is only within an agreement in form of life (of which agreement in judgements is a part) that there is any such thing as an expression of opinion:

Ich kann ganz unabhängig was irgend jemand tut oder sagt eine Meinung haben in dem Sinne in den ich auch unabhängig von alle denn *sagen* kann:
'Ich glaube: in dieser, Flasche ist Gift.' Aber diese Lautreihe wird nur dann ein *Satz* genannt wenn sie in einem Sprachsystem steht, in einem System also des Sprechens und Handelns. Und *ebenso* wird was immer charakteristisches geschehen mag wenn ich eine Meinung habe nur dann das Charakteristikum einer Meinung sein wenn es in einem System steht. (MS 164, 162f.)

(I can, quite independently of what anyone does or says, have an opinion in the sense in which I can also, independently of everyone, *say*:
'I believe: there is poison in this bottle.' But this string of sounds will only be called a *proposition* if it stands within a language-system, hence in a system of speaking and acting. And in *just the same way* whatever may typically occur when I have an opinion will only be of the character of an opinion if it stands within a system.)

(iii) 'but in form of life': MS 160, 51:

Wie ist die Anwendung einer Regel fixiert? Meinst Du 'logisch' fixiert? Entweder durch weitere Regeln oder (gar)nicht – Oder meinst Du: wie kommt es dass wir alle sie übereinstimmend so und nicht anders anwenden? Durch Abrichtung, Drill und die Formen unsres Lebens.
Es handelt sich nicht um einen Consens der Meinungen sondern der Lebensformen.

(How is the application of a rule fixed? Do you mean 'logically' fixed? Either by means of further rules, or not at all! – Or do you mean: how is it that we agree in applying it thus and not otherwise? Through training, drill and the forms of our life.
This is a matter not of a consensus of opinions but of forms of life.)

SECTION 242

1   This clarifies the nature of agreement in language (§241) and hence the framework on which the working of our language is based (§240). W. explores what is essential to communication by language. Obviously agreement in definitions is necessary; for if two people disagreed about how to explain the words they use, then what the one meant by an utterance would not be what the other understood by it, and to this

extent communication would have broken down. But W. adds the surprising requirement that there also be agreement in judgements, and this idea is the focus of §242.

What 'agreement in judgements' means must be interpersonal consensus about the truth and falsity of a large body of empirical propositions. The phrase is clarified by an illustration. Consensus about methods of measurement (including specifications of both units and procedures of measuring lengths, weights, times, etc.) is analogous to (indeed, a case of) agreement in definitions, while consensus about the statements of results of measurements is a case of agreement in judgements. There must be a large measure of agreement about how long things are, how much they weigh, how long processes take, etc., i.e. in the truth of empirical statements. This is of course compatible with *occasional* disputes, but if these exceptions became the rule, our procedures of measuring lengths, weights, etc., would lose their point (PI §142).

Why is agreement in judgements essential for communication by language? §242 merely hints at the answer. It must run parallel to the remark that what we call 'measuring' is partly determined by a certain constancy in the results of measurement. What we call 'communication' must be partly determined by a certain consensus about what is true and what is false. Why? Because definitions (or explanations) of meanings are rules for the use of words and because the understanding of a rule is manifested in *two* ways, namely in formulating or paraphrasing it *and* in applying or following it in practice (e.g. in making empirical judgements or giving descriptions (§240)). Whether different people understand a definition in the same way is manifest in their generally reaching the same verdicts about the applicability of the defined term. Agreement in judgements is not something quite independent of agreement in definitions; rather, agreement in applying a definition is a criterion for shared understanding of the definition and hence a criterion for agreement in definitions. We follow rules of grammar in making judgements (as well as in issuing orders, asking questions, telling stories, etc.), and the correct application of these rules is the criterion of understanding them (cf. PI §146).

Failure to appreciate this role of agreement in judgements is what makes it seem paradoxical to claim that agreement in judgements is essential to communication. For then it wrongly appears that logic (grammar) is abolished. The worry that W. here addresses seems to be one that is recurrent in his reflections, harking back even to the *Tractatus*: that rules of grammar (or the logical syntax of language) might be beholden to contingent facts about the world. If agreement in judgements is part of the framework of communication by language, it seems to follow that grammatical truths are dependent upon a matter of fact, viz. whether we do or do not so agree. Hence too, it seems, grammatical propositions (e.g. that 1 foot is equal to 12 inches) would be *falsified* if the results of measurement fell into confusion. This idea is what W. rejects (cf. MS 123, 37). There is no such thing as falsifying a grammatical proposition. If confusion supervened, our techniques of measurement would indeed collapse, not because the grammar of measuring would be shown to be false, but because the language-games of measuring would lose their point (PI §142). So too with calculating, predicating colours, etc. (RFM 200). But propositions of arithmetic, colour-judgements, etc. do not assert that confusion will not supervene. Hence the requirement of agreement in judgements does not imply that rules of grammar are liable to refutation by matters of fact. In this sense logic is not abolished. Grammar is *antecedent* to the truth and falsity of empirical judgements, just as a method of measurement is antecedent to the correctness of statements of length and hence also to agreement in the results of measurement (cf. RFM 96).

Note that it would be further mistaken to assert that our concepts of length, weight, etc. *could* not exist in circumstances of confusion; rather should we say that these techniques and concepts *would* not exist (Z §351; RPP II §393).

1.1   'agreement in judgements': this is only *part* of the framework on which the working of our language is based (§240). Presumably agreement in other linguistic activities is equally essential. We must, for example, agree not only about the conditions under which orders are fulfilled or questions correctly answered, but also about the *logical* appropriateness of giving orders or asking questions, e.g. the unacceptability of ordering somebody to shut a window that is already shut. Assertion is an important activity in speaking a language, but it is not the *foundation* of all other speech-activities, and therefore agreement in assertions is not the foundation of agreement in all our activities of using words.

2   (i) LPE 301 contains early seeds of these reflections.
     (ii) RFM 342f. has a closely related sequence of remarks clarifying several important points about §242.

. . . the phenomenon of language is based on regularity, on agreement in action.
     Here it is of the greatest importance that all or the enormous majority of us agree in certain things. I can, for example, be quite sure that the colour of this object will be called 'green' by far the most of the human beings who see it. . . .
     We say that, in order to communicate, people must agree with one another about the meanings of words. But the criterion for this agreement is not just agreement with reference to definitions, e.g. ostensive definitions – but *also* an agreement in judgements. It is essential for communication that we agree in a large number of judgements.

This passage establishes that the topic of §242 is agreement about the truth of empirical judgements, that this agreement is an aspect of agreement in action (or in form of life), and that it is a *criterion* for agreement about the meanings of words and hence a *condition* for successful communication.

(iii) PI p. 225 notes that mathematicians do not in general quarrel over the result of a calculation. Disputes are rare, short, and capable of definitive resolution.

> But am I trying to say some such thing as that the certainty of mathematics is based on the reliability of ink and paper? *No*. (That would be a vicious circle) – I have not said *why* mathematicians do not quarrel, but only *that* they do not.

Here too W. rebuts the worry that grammatical truths are dependent on matters of fact.

2.1   (i) 'but also . . . in judgements': PI p. 226 has qualms over whether this can be said (i.e. is this not a grammatical truth?). For what would it be like for people not to agree, for example, in their colour-judgements? If there were chaotic conflict in judgements, with what right would we take their words 'red', 'blue', etc. to be *our* colour-words? How would they learn to use them? With what right can we characterize their activity as 'describing the colours of flowers, etc.'?

(ii) 'This seems to abolish logic': MS 180(a), 76 contains the first draft of §242, complete except for the first sentence, and it uses this phrase to point at a different problem. The context is a discussion of the transition from seeing something red to saying that it is red. Any rules for moving from a 'recognition that a visual image is red' to applying the word 'red' would leave us in the lurch and hang in the air because there would be no technique, no institution of going according to the rules. Consequently the phrase 'to follow a rule' relates to a *practice* which cannot be replaced by the mere appearance of a practice. 'This seems to abolish logic, but does not do so . . ..' (Quoted at pp. 152ff.) Here the issue is evidently what is in accord with a rule and what conflicts with it, what is correct and what is incorrect. If there is no such thing as a *practice* of acting in accord with a rule, there is held to be no accord and conflict with a rule; the 'rules' leave us in the lurch from a logical point of view. But then it seems that it is a practice, technique or institution that binds a rule to its extension. And this would abolish logic because it would amount to a denial that the accord of an act with a rule is determined by *grammar*. The dissolution of this problem involves recognizing that a practice does not stand *between* a rule and an act in accord with it, but rather surrounds this grammatical relation (cf. 'Following rules, mastery of techniques and practices', pp. 179ff.). The question of agreement in the truth and falsity of empirical judgements is not raised, and it would be relevant to this sense of 'abolishing logic' only indirectly in so far as agreement in judgements bears on the correct or incorrect application of rules of grammar.

———————————

GRAMMAR AND NECESSITY

1. *Leitmotivs*

Wittgenstein's elaborate investigation into rules and rule-following were essential for completing the argument of *Investigations* §§1–142. But they were not merely backward-looking. They yielded a harvest of seeds which, duly cultivated, produced a rich crop in distant fields, namely in philosophy of mind and philosophy of mathematics. In both directions Wittgenstein extended his investigations and produced striking results.

The laws of logic, the truths of metaphysics, the propositions of mathematics and geometry are perennial sources of philosophical bafflement. Such propositions, we think, are necessary, not contingent. Our knowledge of them is *a priori*, not empirical. They seem an especially apt subject-matter for the Queen of the Sciences. For the physical sciences investigate the empirical and contingent, what characterizes the actual world; but philosophy studies what is eternal, what could not be otherwise, the essence of any possible world. Such propositions strike us as possessing the highest degree of certitude, in comparison with which our knowledge of empirical truths seems merely highly probable. We wonder at the *source* of their necessity. Does it lie in the nature of things, or in the structure of the human mind? Or is it something that flows from the meanings of words? We puzzle how we can *recognize* their necessity. Is it by perception of the relations between universals or is it by the power of pure reason alone? Or is our recognition of necessity a special case of recognizing our own decisions and intentions? The propositions of logic, mathematics and metaphysics constitute a permanently disputed territory upon which armies of rationalists, empiricists, Platonists, formalists, Kantians, pragmatists and conventionalists clash in vehement controversy.

Wittgenstein approached the task of mapping out this terrain from a unique vantage point. His examination of the concept of following a rule provides the background for clarifying the character of mathematical statements, metaphysical propositions and the laws of logic. In the course of providing an explanation of the nature of such propositions he gave a detailed and comprehensive account of the peculiar status of these propositions, an account which explains our inclination to call them 'necessary truths'. The questions of what is the source of necessity and how we recognize it leads us astray before we have begun. The prior question is: what is it for a proposition to *be* a 'necessary proposition'? If this is answered by examining the roles of such propositions in our linguistic transactions and describing them properly, the traditional questions shrink to vanishing point. His account is as bold as it is original. Partly because his reflections on normativity have been either disregarded or misinterpreted, and partly because his analysis runs against the grain of centuries of philosophical theorizing, his arguments and conclusions have been misunderstood and distorted. The following discussion is not an essay in the philosophy of mathematics, although many themes therefrom will be touched on. It is an attempt to give at least a synoptic view of Wittgenstein's account of the various kinds of, and the corresponding roles of, 'necessary propositions'. It does not trace the historical development of his ideas on the subject, but rather adumbrates the contours of the body of his thinking that evolved, over many years, into a comprehensive *Übersicht* over this wide range of problems. On select issues the discussion will delve more deeply in order to exploit certain of Wittgenstein's insights and to elucidate their implications. Its justification is twofold. First, to have laboured to clarify his explanations of rule-following, without at least indicating its rami-fications in this domain, is to sow but to leave half the crop unharvested. Secondly, an understanding of the foregoing account of normativity is deepened by a survey of further fields.

Running through all Wittgenstein's reflections on the propositions of logic, mathematics and metaphysics is a small number of recurrent leitmotivs. Though we have by no means finished exploring these general principles, the previous discussions suffice for grasping their general import. If they are borne in mind, they will provide valuable guidelines.

(1) Necessary truths are heterogeneous. Philosophical accounts often (but not uniformly) amalgamate logical, mathematical and metaphysical propositions and offer a uniform analysis of the lot. Wittgenstein harped on the *differences* among necessary truths. Tautologies and equations are fundamentally unlike: tautologies are degenerate senseless propositions, whereas equations are rules for substituting expressions in empirical propositions. Arithmetic (like geometry) is a system of propositions that are interwoven by complex networks of proofs or calculations, and furthermore informs a wide range of techniques which are basic and pervasive features of our ways of speaking and acting. Other branches of mathematics, e.g. transfinite set theory, are very different in the latter respect. They have little or no application and unlike arithmetic and geometry could be said (cf. PI p. 232) to consist solely of methods of proof (and conceptual confusions). 'Necessary propositions of meta-physics' differ from arithmetic in both respects. Whereas arithmetic consists of rules of grammar, metaphysical propositions might more accurately be described as *hiding* rules of grammar; platitudes about the

uses of expressions are the only thing that can be refined out of this ore – otherwise it is simply worthless. Necessary propositions are as diverse as their uses.

(2) Such propositions express conceptual connections. To the extent that they are (or reflect) rules for the use and transformation of, as well as transitions between, expressions, they do not connect independent concepts, but rather are an expression of the internal relations between essentially connected, interdependent concepts. The concepts are given, in part, by each 'grammatical proposition'.

(3) To clarify the distinction between necessary and contingent propositions in an illuminating way we must focus upon the differences in their use (cf. PI §421). Use is often deceptively masked by form. Thus 'War is war', 'Boys will be boys' or 'What will be, will be' have very different uses from that suggested by their form, which is that of a logical proposition. The same sentence 'This ↗ is red' may be used to state a grammatical proposition (an ostensive definition) or to make an empirical statement (e.g. in sorting stamps). Conversely, 'This ↗ colour is red', 'This ↗ is red', and 'This ↗ is called "red"' can all be used in giving an ostensive definition (although philosophers may think that the first is a necessary truth, the second a description of an object, and the third a contingent statement about English). Whether a sentence is significant or nonsensical, and, if significant, whether it has the same sense as another sentence may depend on the circumstances of utterance. A *fortiori*, the distinction between grammatical and empirical propositions (and the finer classifications of grammatical propositions) cannot be drawn for type-sentences without regard to their particular employments.

(4) As a result of his attention to use, Wittgenstein's segregation of grammatical from empirical propositions diverges conspicuously from the traditional demarcation of necessary from contingent propositions.[1] Two related differences are striking. First, it is standard to distinguish between true and false necessary propositions. For example, '$2 + 3 = 5$' is called a true equation, '$2 + 3 = 4$' a false one; and '$2 + 3 \neq 4$' is called a true inequation, '$2 + 3 \neq 5$' a false one; all four propositions are unreflectively called propositions of arithmetic (or indeed necessary propositions). Wittgenstein argued that to be a proposition of arithmetic is to have a certain role, to function as a rule for the description of, and transformation of descriptions of, the world. But only arithmetical propositions we call 'true' have this role; the ones we call 'false' could be

---

[1] It should be noted that some propositions that were, at one time, on traditional lists, may, over time, disappear from philosophers' lists on the grounds of 'unintelligibility', e.g. 'There must be at least as much reality in a cause as in its effect'; others may be rejected as 'false', e.g. 'Every event has a cause'; and new ones may be 'discovered' and added to the list, e.g. '$\aleph_1 > \aleph_0$'. Note also that each of the reasons thus adduced for changing the list *is itself confused!*

said not to be propositions of arithmetic at all, even though they look like them (being composed of familiar arithmetical expressions in ways permitted by the arithmetical formation rules). Parallels hold for other necessary propositions. Neither contingent formulae (e.g. '$p . q \supset p . \supset . q$') nor contradictions count as 'propositions of logic'. 'The sum of the angles of a triangle is more than 180°' is not a proposition of Euclidean geometry. And 'Something can be in two places at the same time' is misconceived as a *false* necessary proposition in contradistinction to true ones. Secondly, it is also standard to identify something as a necessary proposition independently of knowing whether it is true or false. Goldbach's conjecture (every even integer is the sum of two primes) is widely held to be a necessary proposition whose truth-value is unknown. Wittgenstein thought this confused. In advance of a proof it has neither the uses of an arithmetical proposition nor any internal relations to arithmetical propositions.

(5) Philosophers often relate necessary truth to questions of evidence and knowledge; how we *recognize* necessary truths is held to be a pivotal issue. Necessity, Kant held, is a mark of a priority. Frege declared that necessity turns solely on our grounds for holding a proposition to be true (BG §4). By focusing primarily on the *uses* of expressions as norms of representation, Wittgenstein's reflections involve a major reorientation in point of view, dissolving altogether the 'epistemological problem of necessity'.

(6) The method, the only method, of philosophy is descriptive. The task of philosophy is to resolve philosophical problems by describing the uses of expressions, tabulating rules for their use and delineating their relations. Contrary to the conception of philosophy as an investigation into the necessary structure of reality, clarification of 'necessary pro-positions' is no *more* essentially philosophical than clarification of ethical propositions or propositions of natural science. And contrary to the opinion that has held sway from Plato to the present, arithmetic and geometry (and formal logic) are no more closely akin to philosophy than astronomy or physiology. 'The philosopher is not a citizen of any community of ideas. That is what makes him into a philosopher.' (Z §455)

These leitmotivs are, as it were, internal guidelines to Wittgenstein's thought on these subjects. It is, however, equally important to have external guidelines in order not to mislocate his ideas *ab initio* on the map of traditional demarcation lines. Allowing our reflections to run easily down familiar tracks, we are prone to ask whether he accepted the analytic/synthetic distinction, whether he acknowledged any synthetic *a priori* truths, or whether he recognized *a posteriori* necessary truths. The following remarks are intended to place a brake upon this drift of questioning.

Grammatical propositions and empirical statements are starkly contrasted. Grammar consists of rules for the use of expressions in empirical propositions. There is no such thing as an utterance which simultaneously expresses a rule of grammar and makes an empirical statement, just as one cannot hold a metre-stick against a platinum bar simultaneously to measure the length of the bar and to calibrate the metre-stick.

If propositions of grammar could be simply equated with necessary propositions, Wittgenstein's position could be characterized by saying that he took the terms 'empirical' and 'contingent' to be coextensive. Or one might even claim that he *assumed* that there can be no necessary empirical truths. Such comments are somewhat misleading formulations of his ideas. There was a strong tradition prior to Kant that necessary truths might be discovered in experience. This is prominent in Locke's discussion of real essences, and it has had a recent renaissance after two centuries of dormancy. This idea is certainly one for which Wittgenstein had no sympathy. Two routes lead to its repudiation. The first is the idea that any viable distinction between necessary and contingent propositions must be drawn by reference to a difference in the roles of such propositions in our practices. The supposition that there might be necessary empirical propositions is inconsistent with this requirement. It postulates a dichotomy within the category of empirical statements which cannot be correlated with any differences in how these propositions (or their constitutents) are to be explained or understood. Nothing about the actual roles of empirical propositions turns on whether they should be called 'necessary' or 'contingent'. They play related roles in giving descriptions, in framing explanations, in making predictions, etc. Hence the postulated dichotomy has no significance for the use or meaning of empirical propositions. Another way to make the same point is to observe that no intelligible explanation can be given of the term 'necessary' as applied to empirical propositions. Apparent explanations (e.g. in terms of truth in all possible worlds) are merely circular or nonsense (in spite of being dressed up sometimes in the formalism of modal logic). The second route starts from Wittgenstein's elucidation of necessary truths as rules of grammar. From this point of view, a necessary empirical truth would have to be a rule of representation which exists in nature and may be discovered by scientists but yet is (antecedently) no one's rule and is neither followed nor used by anyone to regulate behaviour. The main thrust of Wittgenstein's clarification of the concept of following a rule is to expose the incoherence of this idea. Consequently there is simply no such thing as a proposition which is both necessary and empirical.

In a parallel way, one might characterize Wittgenstein's conception of necessary truths as equating the terms '*a priori*' and '*analytic*'. One might further claim that he is committed to the tenability of the analytic/synthetic distinction and to the impossibility of synthetic *a priori* truths.

(Most members of the Vienna Circle took his account of grammatical propositions to exclude synthetic *a priori* truths.) But this too would be misleading. Wittgenstein's conception of a proposition of grammar does not mesh with the standard notion of an analytic truth. He did not argue that every proposition of grammar is a type-sentence which is either (an instance of) a law of logic or reducible to a law of logic by the substitution of definitions for certain expressions. The analytic/synthetic distinction is framed in terms of the forms and constituents of type-sentences, whereas whether an utterance expresses a grammatical pro-position depends not only on its form, but on its roles on occasions of utterance. Even if the distinction could be 'relativized to token-sentences', it would remain central to the conception of analytic truth that the truth of a sentence formulating a necessary truth be a *consequence* of the meanings (definitions) of its constituents. But it is precisely this point that Wittgenstein strove to highlight as incoherent by speaking of rules of grammar.

Whoever calls '$\sim\sim p = p$' (or again '$\sim\sim p \equiv p$') a 'necessary proposition of logic' (*not a stipulation about the method of presentation* that we adopt) also has a tendency to say that this proposition proceeds from the meaning of negation. (RFM 106; our italics)

We shall explore this matter in detail below (cf. pp. 312ff.). But it is already evident that the claim that he sought to prove all necessary truths to be analytic misrepresents his ideas on a fundamental point.

Once again there is a second route to the same conclusion. Many of the propositions which he calls propositions of grammar have no place in anybody's catalogue of analytic truths. This set includes ostensive definitions by reference to samples, which he recommended viewing as substitution-rules for replacing a word by a demonstrative, a gesture and a sample. And it is by reference to samples that he clarified the nature of such notoriously recalcitrant *a priori* truths as 'White is lighter than black.' (RFM 48) How could 'analytic' be explained to bring this proposition under the heading of analytic truths in accord with *his* account of how its meaning is to be explained? Equally problematic are explanations by examples and associated truths of grammar. Family resemblance concepts are rightly perceived to pose a threat to the analytic/synthetic distinction. And viewed from the perspective that all necessary truths are analytic, his contention that the rule formulated by '0, 2, 4, 6, 8, 10, . . .' determines '1002' as the correct number to write after '1000' (i.e. that this continuation is *internally* related to the rule) is opaque. Or, finally, his remark that ' "ABOVE" has five letters' is a truth of grammar flies in the face of modern orthodoxy which takes this to be a contingent statement about the English language. In so far as he equated necessary truths with propositions of grammar, the claim that all necessary truths are analytic manifestly fails to square with central elements of his conception. It would, however, be absurd to conclude that he deliberately left room for synthetic *a priori* truths. It would be least misleading to describe him as having thought the terms 'analytic' and 'synthetic' to be obsolete, but not for any reasons that call in doubt the dichotomy between rules of grammar and empirical statements.

It follows that we would display lack of understanding of his ideas about necessary truths if we thought that subsequent progress in philosophy had revealed new possibilities that made his reflections outmoded. We might imagine that modern scientific philosophy has discovered the possibility of empirical necessary truths or has demonstrated the distinction between contingent and necessary propositions to be indefensible. But if we do so, we should not pride ourselves in having left Wittgenstein behind; rather, we have even now not yet begun to catch up with him.

2. *Necessary propositions and norms of representation*

What philosophers have called 'necessary truths' are, in Wittgenstein's view, typically rules of grammar, norms of representation, i.e. they fix *concepts*. They are expressions of internal relations between concepts which are themselves used in stating truths about the world. Hence they license (or prohibit) transitions between concepts, i.e. transitions from one expression of an empirical proposition to another. Necessary propositions themselves are no more descriptions, either of the world or of a super-empirical reality, than are the rules of chess; 'whenever we say that something *must* be the case we are using a norm of expression.'[2] (AWL 16) The emphasis of the 'must' corresponds to the inexorability of our attitude towards our techniques of representation (cf. Z §299). Necessary propositions can be said to lie at the limits of empiricism, not because they are the limiting cases of knowledge derived from experience,[3] but rather because they are expressions of concept-formation (RFM 237), ways in which we make comparisons (RFM 387).

Wittgenstein elaborated and applied this conception to a wide range of propositions which are typically taken to describe the *language-independent essences* of things. 'To a necessity in the world', he insisted, 'there corresponds an arbitrary rule in language' (LWL 57; PI §372), '*Essence* is expressed in grammar' (PI §371) and 'the characteristic of a metaphysical question [is] that we express an unclarity about the grammar of words in the form of a scientific question.' (BB 35) His examples include 'Red is a

---

[2] A pardonable exaggeration, but correct if restricted to the subject matter of this essay.
[3] Russell, 'The Limits of Empiricism', *Proceedings of the Aristotelian Society* XXXVI (1935–6), pp. 131ff.

colour', 'What is red *must* be coloured', 'Every proposition is either true
or false', 'A proposition *must* be either true or false, there is no third
possibility', 'Every event has a cause.' Such propositions, he argued, are
normative, not descriptive; they delimit the bounds of sense. The *must*
here indicates a norm of expression (AWL 16), although, of course, its
absence does not signify that the proposition is *not* being used as the
expression of a rule of representation. If something is called red, it is
correctly characterized as coloured; to assert that it is red and deny that it
is coloured would be a misuse of language. The remark that every
proposition is either true or false looks like a description of the nature of
propositions (like 'All swans are either black or white'). But we use the
Law of Excluded Middle as a stipulation for something to be correctly
called a proposition, not as a generalization about all hitherto examined
propositions. It excludes from intelligible discourse the phrase 'a proposition which is neither true nor false'. Similarly, the Law of Causality
is a norm of explanation in a science, not a matter of experience (AWL 15f.).
So too, the proposition 'White is lighter than black' has the appearance of
a description of an essential relation between colours, but it is a grammatical proposition, a norm of description. Although it makes sense to
speak of two objects, the lighter one white and the darker black, it makes
no sense to speak of two objects, the lighter one black and the darker
white. The latter form of words is excluded from being a possible (sensible) description (RFM 48). To conceive of the grammatical ('necessary')
proposition as a *description* of the essence of black and white is in effect to
project a norm for describing coloured objects on to the objects described.
   Wittgenstein gave a similar account of formulations of logical and
'metaphysical' *impossibilities*, e.g. 'Nothing can be red and green all over'
or 'I cannot have another's pain.' Such metaphysical propositions
containing 'cannot' and 'impossible' hide grammatical rules (cf. BB 55).
'Nothing can be red and green all over' looks like a description of the
physics of colour (as 'Nothing can run faster than 80 m.p.h.' is a
description of the limits of animal locomotion). But the form of this
proposition is deceptive: we use it as a norm of representation to exclude
from currency the description of an object as being red and green all over
simultaneously, and also to license inferences of the form 'X is red, so X
is not green'. It stipulates that red and green are mutually exclusive (that
they are parallel determinates under the determinable: colour). We are
inclined to think of 'I cannot have your toothache' as the description of
an impossibility. It seems analogous to 'I cannot have your money', only
involving a more insuperable barrier than the law of property. For while
I might steal your money, there is no way in which I might have your
pain. But we are misled here by a superficial similarity of form. 'I cannot
have your toothache' is a grammatical proposition the role of which is to
exclude from intelligible discourse the attribution of one person's

sensation to another. It makes no more sense to say that I have your toothache than it makes sense to solve a chess problem by jumping a pawn with a rook. 'The rook cannot jump over pieces' excludes a move from chess. 'I cannot have your toothache' excludes a form of words from use. There is no such thing in chess as jumping a pawn with a rook, and there is no such thing as having another's pain. A logical impossibility is misconceived as something we cannot do – as if the laws of logic or metaphysics *prevented* us from doing it. Necessary propositions do not describe the limits of what is possible, fencing us in from impossible possibilities. They are norms of representation constituting the bounds of *sense*, delimiting what it makes sense to *say*. They fence us in only from the void.

In the same way, Wittgenstein argued, we misconstrue geometrical propositions if we take them to be descriptions. Rather, Euclidean geometry is the syntax of the language for describing the shapes and spatial relations among objects (WWK 38, 61ff., 162f.). Its axioms and theorems are rules of syntax (PR 216), conventions of expression and hence parts of grammar (LWL 8, 55; cf. PG 319; PLP 44). The Euclidean proposition 'The sum of the angles of a triangle is 180°' is a norm for describing things. It is a rule which specifies that if something is characterized correctly as a triangle, it is also correctly said to have angles which sum to 180°. *Pari passu*, it excludes describing an object as triangular but having angles which sum to more or less than 180°. So it expresses an internal relation between the concepts of triangularity and having three angles the sum of which is 180°, and it excludes as nonsense the words 'is a triangle the sum of whose angles is 185°'. So too the geometrical proposition 'The longest side of a triangle is opposite the largest angle' is a norm for describing spatial relations; we use it to license describing the longest side of a triangular object or array as the side opposite the largest angle and to exclude describing it as the side opposite the smallest angle.

We are prone to take arithmetical equations to describe relations between numbers in Pythagorean realms. But they are *used as norms* for describing numbers of objects in the familiar sublunary realm (cf. MS 123, 98). 'Arithmetic is the grammar of numbers.' (PR 130) In particular, equations are rules of syntax (PR 143). They are substitution-rules which are applied to the propositions of ordinary language (WWK 156; PG 347). They license transformations of empirical statements, and they exclude certain expressions as nonsense. For example, '12 × 12 = 144' legitimates transforming the statement 'There were 12 rows each with 12 soldiers on the parade ground' into 'There were 144 soldiers on the parade ground', and equally it rules out as unintelligible 'There were 12 rows each of 12 soldiers, so there were 145 soldiers on the parade ground.' Inequations have a corresponding role (PR 249). '13 > 12' is a rule that permits a characterization of a group of 13 objects as larger in number than a group of 12 objects. The argument 'There are 13 in group A and 12 in group B, so there are more Bs than As' is banned from empirical reasoning. 'What I am saying comes to this, that mathematics is *normative.*' (RFM 425)

This sketch of the drift of his thought makes clear that Wittgenstein's remarks on necessary truths are liable to arouse strong passions. The focus of attention will be his insistence on a vast and fundamental gulf between grammatical propositions and empirical statements. This idea may be greeted with enthusiasm as it was once welcomed by the Vienna Circle, who conceived of his insights as liberating them from the thrall of rationalism and 'synthetic *a priori* truths' provable by pure reason alone. Or it may be met with deep hostility because it is perceived to threaten the importance of philosophy. For did Wittgenstein not make the notions of truth, objectivity and knowledge inapplicable to all necessary propositions? Did he not thereby cut philosophy off from the possibility of giving genuine explanations, solutions to problems and real understanding? For various reasons, his apparent iconoclasm is no longer attractive, but rather repugnant.

The idea that such necessary truths are nothing but norms of representation flies in the face of a venerable tradition. From Plato onwards, truths of Reason have seemed the very bastion of certainty. Discovery of necessary truths appeared to be insight into the true essence of things, the marks in nature of the Divine Geometer. Knowledge of Eternal Truths even seemed to guarantee the sempiternality of the knower, on the grounds that the mind can know only that in the nature of which it partakes. To some philosophers such knowledge seemed to reflect innate ideas with which we are equipped, actually or virtually, from birth. To others it seemed to disclose the transcendental workings of the mind. Some features of these remarkable pictures are no longer popular. But not because we have understood the nature of necessary propositions. Rather have these pictures, in an irreligious and ostensibly anti-metaphysical age, faded away. In the place of the mysteries of metaphysics we cultivate mythologies of symbolism. But the force of the old pictures, so to speak, is still marked. The Pythagorean vision still mesmerizes us, for we are still prone to think that measurability is a mark of objectivity. We still conceive of laws of logic as certain, ineluctable, forcing themselves upon us. We think of proofs as *compelling* us to acknowledge their conclusions. We hold our mathematics to be *correct*, and inchoately think that if it were not, bridges would fall down and aeroplanes tumble from the skies. And many philosophers[4] continue to think of internal relations as discoverable in nature. As we fill in our sketch we shall show how

---

[4] Cf. Russell, 'Limits of Empiricism', p. 140; he has many followers who spin ever more sophisticated tales.

these pictures, new and old, grow from a seedbed of misunderstandings about the role and nature of 'truths of Reason'.

3. Truth, Ideal Objects and correspondence with the facts

Empirical, contingent, truths have always struck philosophers as being, in some sense, ultimately unintelligible. It is not that none can be known with certainty (though some have claimed that); nor is it that some cannot be explained (although Hume thought causal connections to be inexplicable). Rather is it that all explanation of empirical truths rests ultimately on brute contingency – *that* is how the world is! Where science comes to rest in explaining empirical facts varies from epoch to epoch, but it is in the nature of empirical explanation that it will hit the bedrock of contingency somewhere, e.g. in atomic theory in the nineteenth century or in quantum mechanics today. One feature that explains philosophers' fascination with truths of Reason is that they seem, in a deep sense, to be fully intelligible. To understand a necessary proposition is to see *why* things must be so, it is to gain an insight into the nature of things and to apprehend not only how things are, but also why they cannot be otherwise. It is striking how pervasive visual metaphors are in philosophical discussions of these issues. We *see* the universal in the particular (by Aristotelian intuitive induction); by the Light of Reason we see the essential relations of Simple Natures; mathematical truths are apprehended by Intellectual Intuition, or by *a priori* insight. Yet instead of examining the use of these arresting pictures or metaphors to discern their aptness *as pictures*, we build upon them mythological structures.

We think of necessary propositions as being *true or false*, as objective and independent of our minds or will. We conceive of them as being *about* various entities, about numbers (even about extraordinary numbers that the mind seems barely able to grasp, e.g. $\aleph_0$ (LFM 252)); or about universals, such as colours, shapes, tones; or about logical entities, such as the truth-functions or (in Frege's case) the truth-values. We naturally think of necessary propositions as *describing* the features of these entities, their essential characteristics. So we take mathematical propositions to describe mathematical objects (RFM 261). When we find that actual objects do not precisely conform with geometrical theorems, we are inclined to think of their shapes as 'imperfect'. However, we do not fault the geometrical theorem as a misdescription of the shapes of things; rather are we inclined to take it to be a description of an ideal shape. Geometers,

although they make use of the visible forms and reason about them, are thinking not of these, but of the ideals which they resemble; not of the figures which they draw, but of the absolute square and the absolute diameter . . . they are really seeking to behold the things themselves, which can be seen only with the eye of the mind.[5]

Hence investigation into the domain of necessary propositions is conceived as a process of *discovery*. Empirical scientists make discoveries about the empirical domain, uncovering contingent truths; metaphysicians, logicians and mathematicians appear to make discoveries of necessary truths about a supra-empirical domain (a 'third realm'). Mathematics seems to be the 'natural history of mathematical objects' (RFM 137), 'the physics of numbers' (LFM 139) or the 'mineralogy of numbers' (RFM 229). The mathematician, e.g. Pascal, admires the beauty of a theorem as though it were a kind of *crystal*. Numbers seem to him to have wonderful *properties*; it is as if he were confronting a beautiful natural phenomenon (CV 41). Logic seems to investigate the laws governing logical objects, 'boundary stones set in an eternal foundation which our thought can overflow, but never displace' (GA i, p. xvi). Metaphysics looks as if it is a description of the essential structure of the world (cf. TLP). Hence we think that *a reality corresponds to our (true) necessary propositions*. Our logic is correct because it corresponds to *the* laws of logic; other beings may reason according to different laws of thinking – in which case they are *wrong* (GA i, p. xvi). Our inferences, we contend, are correct when they correspond to what *really follows*, for otherwise we should come into conflict with the truth. Our rules of inference are 'responsible' to the truth-values of the relevant propositions; and upon this thought we construct metalogical validations of our logic. We think of a proof of a necessary proposition as the discovery of an antecedently existing truth. Indeed we may know the truth in advance of this proof (because it is self-evident, or because we already have an alternative proof). The proof is a *route* to a truth. The mathematician is like

a man who gazes at a distant range of mountains. . . . His object is simply to distinguish clearly and notify to others as many different peaks as he can. . . . He sees A sharply, while of B he can obtain only transitory glimpses. At last he makes out a ridge which leads from A, and following it to its end he discovers that it culminates in B. B is now fixed in his vision, and from this point he can proceed to further discoveries. . . . If he wishes someone else to see it, he *points to it*, either directly or through the chain of summits which led him to recognize it himself. When his pupil also sees it, the research, the argument, the *proof* is finished.[6]

---

[5] Plato, *The Republic* 510 d–e.
[6] G. H. Hardy, 'Mathematical Proof', *Mind* XXXVIII (1929), p. 18. Deliberately exaggerating, he goes on to claim that 'proofs are what Littlewood and I call *gas*, rhetorical flourishes designed to affect psychology, pictures on the board in the lecture, devices to stimulate the imagination of pupils.' For reasons Hardy never imagined, this remark is closer to the truth than one might think.

If we thus *find* a proof, of course it must have been there to find, i.e. it must already have been *possible* – for otherwise we could not have found it. And this possibility for us is, therefore, an actuality in the domain of mathematics (LFM 144f.), an existing route from one peak to another.

This conception is remarkable. In our eagerness to ensure the objectivity of truths of reason, their sempiternality and mind-independence, we slowly but surely transform them into truths that are no less 'brutish' than empirical, contingent truths. Why *must* being red exclude being green? To be told that this is the essential nature of red and green merely reiterates the brutish necessity. A proof in arithmetic or geometry seems to provide an explanation, but ultimately the structure of proofs rests on axioms. *Their* truth is held to be self-evident, something we apprehend by means of our faculty of intuition; we must simply *see* that they are necessarily true. 'The question why and with what right we acknowledge a law of logic to be true, logic can answer only by reducing it to another law of logic. Where that is not possible, logic can give no answer.' (GA i, p. xvii) But even if we do 'see' that '~ (*p*. ~ *p*)', do we understand *why* this *must* be so? We may analyse such ultimate truths into their constituent 'indefinables'. Yet if 'the discussion of indefinables . . . is the endeavour to see clearly, and to make others see clearly, the entities concerned, in order that the mind may have that kind of acquaintance with them which it has with redness or the taste of a pineapple' (PrM p. v), then mere intellectual vision does not penetrate the logical or metaphysical *that* to the *why* or *wherefore*. We might sympathize with Oscar Wilde's remark, 'I can stand brute force but brute reason is quite unbearable. There is something unfair about its use. It is like hitting below the intellect.' For if we construe necessary propositions as truths about logical, mathematical or metaphysical entities which describe their essential properties, then, of course, the final products of our analyses will be as impenetrable to reason as the final products of physical theorizing, such as Planck's constant.

This picture of necessary propositions is an outgrowth of deep-rooted conceptual confusions. Truths of reason must indeed be transparent to the intellect. Their intelligibility or transparency, the inchoate insight that our understanding of them is *toto caelo* different from our understanding of empirical truths, is not clarified by the idea that they are propositions of super-physics. But it is illuminated by the suggestion that they are our own norms of representation. Here indeed *verum et factum convertuntur* and *veri criterium est ipse fecisse*.[7] For rules which we *follow* (and not merely conform with) are understood by us. There is in general no such thing as following a rule which one does *not* understand,

---

[7] Giambattista Vico, *De Antiquissima Italorum Sapienta ex Linguae Latinae Originibus Eruenda*, quoted in Isaiah Berlin, *Vico and Herder* (Hogarth Press, London, 1976), pp. 13, 17.

for to know what counts as accord with it *is* to understand the rule. In so far as what are called 'necessary propositions' are actually employed as our norms of representation and are only correctly conceived as 'necessary propositions' in so far as they are thus employed (or are senseless tautologies), then our understanding of necessary truths is a special case of understanding the rules which we (collectively) have made and which we follow. And in so far as a necessary proposition is interwoven with a host of further necessary propositions by proofs, then we fully understand it in so far as we can survey the proofs, and employ the proposition as a norm of representation within a network of norms of representation whose structure is established by the proofs.

What informs the traditional picture of necessary propositions and stands in the way of even understanding, let alone accepting, Wittgenstein's conception are *(inter alia)* ramifying confusions about truth, about *being about* something, about ideal objects and correspondence with the facts. We shall elaborate in some detail Wittgenstein's moves in disentangling the knots about truth in connection with necessary propositions. Then we shall sketch his equally complex skein of arguments in respect of the other three themes.

(i) *Truth* We do, of course, say of innumerable necessary propositions that they are true (after all, we exclaim, it is not *false* that $25^2 = 625$, or that white is lighter than black!). Wittgenstein did not deny this platitude; nor did he try to persuade us to stop saying this. For 'philosophy may in no way interfere with the actual use of language . . . . It leaves everything as its is.' (PI §124) What he did, as always, was to press us to examine what we mean in saying such things, whether saying that a necessary proposition is true is like saying of an empirical proposition that it is true. The crucial question is whether we are not misled here by a superficial similarity of form that masks profound differences in use. To say that *p* is true is just to affirm or assert that *p*, for '*p*' and 'It is true that *p*' are equivalent (PI §136 and Exg.). This holds for necessary propositions and empirical ones alike. The moot question is: what differences are there between such assertions?

In the case of an empirical proposition, instead of saying '*p* is true' or '*p*', we can say 'It is a fact that *p*' or '*p* corresponds to the facts'[8] or 'Things are in reality as the proposition that *p* describes them as being.' But we should be wary of asserting that a necessary proposition corresponds to the facts or that things are in reality as it describes them as being. For then it is 'superhuman not to think' of these facts or this reality as being something similar to what corresponds to an empirical proposition (LFM 243f.). Then confusions ensue. To what facts or

---

[8] This is *not* a version of the Correspondence Theory of Truth, or of any other theory but a grammatical platitude.

reality does the tautology '$p \lor \sim p$' correspond? What would it be for '$p \lor \sim p$' to be false, i.e. not to correspond to how things are? Does saying that $25^2 = 625$ corresponds to the facts not suggest that the facts might be different? And is not the response that mathematical reality is timeless and changeless an absurd reaction to this confusion? Similarly, if the impossibility of my having another's toothache is made true by the way things are in reality, might things have been otherwise so that I could have your sensations? What is it in each such case which is *not* the case? On the model of truth for empirical propositions this requires picturing to ourselves what it would be like for 25^2 not to be 625 or for me to have your toothache. For of an empirical proposition we can say what it would be like if it were false. We can understand it without knowing whether it is true or false. And to understand an empirical proposition is also to understand its negation. None of these features characterizes paradigmatic necessary truths.

Our inclination to view the truth of necessary propositions as precisely analogous to the truth of empirical propositions originates in part in confusions about the negation of necessary truths. We explain '$\sim p$' as equivalent to 'It is false that p.' An empirical proposition which is false is the negation of an empirical proposition which is contingently true. Negating an empirical truth yields an intelligible empirical proposition which is contingently false. We are prone to make parallel moves in the case of necessary propositions. But so to do seems to require as a counterpart to each necessary truth a necessary falsehood, viz. a description of a state of affairs which happens to be impossible. This is highly problematic.

Perhaps the simplest case is logical contradictions. We consider these to be the negations of tautologies. Hence we also call tautologies the negations of contradictions. But, on the model of empirical falsehoods, to grasp the sense of a proposition of the form $\sim \phi$ is to conceive of what it would be for ϕ to be true and to understand that these circumstances are not realized. The tautology '$\sim (p. \sim p)$' is understood as the negation of the contradiction '$(p. \sim p)$'. But there is no such thing as conceiving of what it would be for '$(p. \sim p)$' to be true, and hence nothing for the initial negation in '$\sim (p. \sim p)$' to exclude. The characterization of the tautology '$\sim (p. \sim p)$' as the negation of a contradiction (or of the contradiction '$\sim (p \lor \sim p)$' as the negation of a tautology) is misleading in two ways.

First, in negating an empirical proposition one generates another empirical proposition, as it were something which belongs to the same system of propositions as the original one. But tautologies comprise what we call *the propositions of logic*; and this system of propositions does *not* include either contingent propositions or contradictions. Hence negating a tautology to produce a contradiction generates something which does *not* belong to the system of *the propositions of logic*. One might say that the system of empirical propositions is closed under the operation of negation, but the system of propositions of logic is not. This profound logical difference between contradictions and tautologies and this disanalogy with empirical propositions and their negations is obscured by calling contradictions the negations of tautologies.

Secondly, to understand 'p' and to understand '$\sim p$' in the case of an empirical proposition are two aspects of the same thing, not two independent accomplishments. What is parallel to this in the case of tautologies and contradictions is, of course, not: understanding the tautology and understanding its negation. For both are quite senseless. It is rather understanding the role of tautologies and contradictions in patterns of reasoning, or rather understanding the consequences we draw for our patterns of reasoning from the fact that a certain combination of propositions is a tautology or a contradiction. But now this is precisely disanalogous to the case of an empirical proposition and its negation. For these roles or consequences are not complementary, not two aspects of the same thing. On the contrary, tautologies and contradictions are involved respectively in two *wholly distinct* techniques. That a certain proposition is a tautology corresponds to a technique of transformation of propositions in patterns of inference. We further employ tautologies to cast all sound deductive inferences into a normal form (especially *modus ponens*). Contradictions have a completely different role in our techniques of formal reasoning, viz. in the formalization of indirect proofs in order to represent these in a unified form. This deep logical difference is likewise masked from view by calling a contradiction the negation of a tautology and conceiving of this as akin to the negation of empirical truths.

Similar considerations apply to the necessary truths of arithmetic. We say '2 and 3 do not make 4', and we naturally regard this as the negation of '2 and 3 make 4'. We might write it, it seems, either as an inequation '$2 + 3 \neq 4$' or as a negation '$\sim (2 + 3 = 4)$'. Both drag puzzles in their wake. Obviously we do not take '$\sim (2 + 3 = 4)$' as describing a possibility which is denied to obtain. So we might say 'Negation in arithmetic cannot be the same as the negation of an empirical proposition' (cf. PR 250), that it has a different meaning (cf. PR 247). But this seems unhappy, for we explain 'not' uniformly, viz. '$\sim p$' = 'It is false that p.' We say that $2 + 3 = 4$ and $2 + 3 \neq 5$ are both false, and we might express this by '$\sim (2 + 3 = 4)$' and '$\sim (2 + 3 \neq 5)$' (i.e. '$2 + 3 = 5$').

The impasse can be avoided by approaching from a different angle. We use equations to license substitutions of numerical expressions in empirical propositions. Inequations are used quite differently, to prohibit such substitutions (PR 250) and to license other transformations of empirical propositions. Hence, equations and inequations are 'different kinds of arithmetical structures' (PR 250) just as tautologies and contradictions are different logical structures. Calling inequations *the negations of equations* (or calling them *false equations*) obscures this point. One might indeed argue that an inequation such as '5 × 5 ≠ 30' ought not to be written '~ (5 × 5 = 30)' for precisely this reason. 'The denial of an equation is as like and unlike the denial of a proposition as the affirmation of an equation is like and unlike the affirmation of a proposition.' (PR 249)

One might go further and suggest that the negation of a true arithmetical equation is nonsense. This seems not only perverse but also to conflict with the way we speak about arithmetic. It seems that the only candidate for the negation of the equation '2 + 3 = 5' is the inequation '2 + 3 ≠ 5'. And this, we are inclined to say, is a false proposition of arithmetic. It is, after all, of the same form as other, true, propositions of arithmetic, e.g. '5 × 5 ≠ 30'. It contains no components other than familiar arithmetical expressions, and its negation, viz. '2 + 3 = 5', is a true proposition of arithmetic. Q.E.D. This argument is far too quick. To say that a proposition belongs to arithmetic is to characterize it as having a particular role with regard to empirical propositions. Both the equation '2 + 3 = 5' and the inequation '5 × 5 ≠ 30' have such (different) roles in licensing or prohibiting inferences or substitutions. If we read '5 × 5 ≠ 30' as 'It is false that 5 × 5 = 30', then we could say that 'true' and 'false' in arithmetic correspond to 'sense' and 'nonsense' among empirical propositions (MS 163, 93). For 'He has 2 apples in one hand and 3 in another, so he has 5' makes sense, but 'He has five sets of five stamps, so he has thirty' is nonsense. However, the 'inequation' 2 + 3 ≠ 5 has *neither* role in our practice. If construed as 5 × 5 ≠ 30 is, it would prohibit inferences that (our) arithmetic licenses, and it would stigmatize as nonsense intelligible sentences of empirical discourse. (Similarly for 'equations' such as '5 × 5 = 30'.) It does *not* have the function that its form suggests. It has *no* place in (our) arithmetic; it is not a proposition of arithmetic, just as '*p*. ~ *p*' is not a proposition of logic. But these are the diagnostic features of nonsense. Far from conflicting with the way we speak about arithmetic, it is a clarification of what is said in characterizing an arithmetical proposition as false.

Puzzles about the truth and falsity of logical and arithmetical propositions have counterparts for such 'necessary propositions' as 'Red is a colour' or 'White is lighter than black' which express grammatical rules. Their negations 'Red is not a colour', 'White is not lighter than black' are not norms of representation at all. For we do not use 'red' in such a way that something's being red licenses us to say that it is colourless. It would be best to say that the negations of such grammatical propositions are not propositions of any kind, either grammatical or empirical. Similar considerations apply to *some* so-called 'metaphysical propositions', namely to those which can be said to hide grammatical rules, e.g. 'I cannot have your pain.' The negation of such a proposition, viz. 'I can have your pain' is not a grammatical rule, but a nonsense which violates the grammar of 'pain'.

Of course, most metaphysical propositions are not misleading expressions of grammatical rules, but either nonsense or inchoate suggestions for the adoption of a different form of representation. The solipsist's 'Only my present experiences are real' is not a rule of our grammar, for we do not rule out as nonsense the attribution of an experience to someone other than the solipsist. But if we conceive of the solipsist's remark as a recommendation to adopt a different grammar, it does not concern *our* concept of 'experience', but proposes a possible rule which, if adopted, will fix an altogether different concept. But it would be misguided to dispute with the solipsist by affirming the negation of his metaphysical proposition, as if a 'false metaphysical proposition' were correctly countered by propounding a true one. The 'revisionary metaphysician' such as Berkeley presents his claims not as a recommendation to adopt a new grammar, but as a description of how things are. And philosophers who object to his idealism rush to defend the negation of Berkeley's metaphysical propositions (viz. *Esse* is not *percipi*):

> *This* is what disputes between Idealists, Solipsists and Realists look like. The one party attack the normal form of expression as if they were attacking a statement; the others defend it, as if they were stating facts recognized by every reasonable human being. (PI §402)

The upshot of this discussion is that necessary propositions and empirical propositions have very different roles and that these differences are masked by the parallel use of 'true' and 'false'. Of course, we cannot deny that $2 + 2 = 4$ is true or that $2 + 3 \neq 5$ is false, for we do use 'true' and 'false' thus. What we need to do is unmask the differences in use between true necessary propositions and true empirical ones, and the profound asymmetries between the negations of true empirical propositions and true necessary ones. What is, above all, clear is that the fact that we call such propositions as 'Either it is raining or it is not raining', '$2 + 2 = 4$', 'Red is a colour', etc. *true* tells us almost nothing about how they are used. Hence it supplies no ground whatever for challenging Wittgenstein's suggestion that the characterization 'rules of grammar' gives the most valuable *Übersicht* of the function of (at least some) necessary truths.

This conclusion is further supported by another truism. To say of *any* proposition that it is true is to affirm or assert it. But such affirmation has many forms and functions – indeed roughly as many as the roles of declarative sentences. 'It is true that . . .' may be spoken by an actor on the stage or written in a novel; it may occur in the report of a dream; it may be prefixed to a statement of a moral principle or to the formulation of a rule of chess, to an aesthetic judgement or to a religious proposition. The more one reflects upon the matter, the less there seems to be to learn from the bare fact that we say of necessary truths that they are true. Conversely, the more value there seems to be in Wittgenstein's observation that we assert mathematical truths as we affirm rules, e.g. as we assert that the Queen in chess stands on its own colour or that spades trump clubs. (Of course, this leaves open the question in what circumstances it is licit to affirm such a necessary proposition.)

(ii) *About*   In insisting that necessary propositions are typically norms of representation, Wittgenstein was not claiming that they are 'really' *about* words in English, German, or some other language, *if that means* that upon 'analysis' they are really of the form ' "F" in English is to be used . . .', i.e. that their 'depth-grammar' reveals them to be metalinguistic statements. We do say that '2 + 2 = 4' is *about* numbers; that is what we call 'a statement about numbers' (LFM 112). It is certainly not a statement about signs (marks on paper), nor is it a statement about how people use such signs (RFM 243). But, parallel to the case of 'truth', Wittgenstein challenged us to investigate whether such propositions are about numbers in the same sense in which 'Lions are carnivorous' is about lions. He suggested that we are again misled by superficial analogies of form. Statements about lions tell us facts about lions, but what we call 'statements about numbers' have the role of rules for the use of number-words or numerals. 'What I am saying is that we have given in mathematics a certain way of using signs; that the propositions of mathematics exhibit a certain technique of handling signs. That is what mathematics provides us with. Does it follow that in doing mathematics we *say* anything about these signs?' (RR 128) A sentence can be used to express a rule for the use of signs without mentioning, but rather using, the signs in question. 'This ↗ (colour) is red' expresses a rule for the use of 'red', 'A bachelor is an unmarried man' expresses a rule for the use of 'bachelor'. 'A valid will is one which . . .' tells us what a valid will is, and so gives a rule for the correct use of 'a valid will'. It is true that necessary propositions do not usually have the form we typically associate with rule-formulations, and also that we would not cite such propositions as typical examples of expressions of rules. Nevertheless, whether a form of words is a rule-formulation is not merely a question of its form (though that may tell us something) but rather of its *use* ('Rules and grammar', pp. 47ff.). Mathematical propositions are not *about* signs; nevertheless, Wittgenstein suggested, we should 'investigate whether [they] . . . are not rules of expression, paradigms – propositions dependent on experience but made independent of it. Ask whether mathematical propositions are not made paradigms or objects of comparison in this way.' (LFM 55) It is his contention that geometry gives us rules for the application of the words 'length', 'equal length', etc. (though not all the rules, since it says nothing about how lengths are to be measured or compared), and that arithmetic gives us rules for the use of number-words (LFM 256), *even though* the propositions of geometry and arithmetic are not *about* signs. Rather they show those connections of concepts we regard as rigid (RFM 243), which we treat as normative.

Because we say that arithmetical statements are about numbers, or geometrical ones about triangles or circles (we would rightly say that pages 30–52 of my geometry primer are about circles), we are readily misled into thinking that such propositions tell us truths about numbers or shapes as biological propositions tell us truths about the animal kingdom (LFM 114). This is radically mistaken, for they are not *about* numbers and shapes *in that sense*. What is about a number in the sense in which 'The sofa is blue' is about the sofa is *never* a mathematical proposition (LFM 251). A proposition about a number in *that* sense would be 'There are 2 people on the sofa'. If we fail to see the disanalogy between ' "2 + 2 = 4" is about numbers' and ' "Lions are carnivorous" is about lions', and further fail to see the analogy between ' "Lions are carnivorous" is about lions' and ' "There are 2 people on the sofa" is about 2 (as well as about people and the sofa)', we will be liable to error. For we will be prone to think that mathematical propositions, being about numbers, are about a realm of mathematical objects (LFM 114), just as propositions about lions are about the animal kingdom. We will look for a reality corresponding to mathematics in the wrong logical space, conceiving of a mathematical reality and even mathematical experience as corresponding to mathematical propositions. If we do see the analogy and disanalogy correctly, we will realize that 'being about' here means two entirely different things (LFM 251), and that 'the reality that corresponds to' mathematics is to be found in its application, i.e. in what propositions such as 'There are 2 people on the sofa' are about. For although it would be wrong to say that '2 + 2 = 4' is a proposition about numerals as ' "8" is curvilinear' is, it is a rule for the use of numerals, just as 'Bachelors are unmarried men' is a rule for the use of 'bachelor'. By contrast, 'Lions are carnivorous' is not a rule for the use of 'lion', but is an application of those rules. '2 + 2 = 4' expresses a proposition which is constitutive of the meaning of its constituent symbols and is not, in *this* sense, about numbers.

Wittgenstein applied similar reasoning to propositions such as 'Blue is more like purple than yellow' or '1 metre is 100 centimetres.' We are inclined to think of the former as being about blue and the latter about the length one metre, and of each proposition as spelling out a necessary truth concerning what it is about. This is confused. In the sense in which 'The sofa is blue' is about the sofa, then it is also about blue, i.e. the closest analogy to 'being about' for blue (or 1 metre) is just such an empirical predication (LFM 250f.). It is not *wrong* to say that 'Blue is a colour', '1 metre is 100 centimetres' or '2 + 2 = 4' are, respectively, about blue, a metre and 2, but deeply misleading in such a context. For these, unlike our paradigms of propositions about such-and-such, are grammatical propositions. They are not statements in the same sense at all, but rules preparatory for making statements about the number, lengths or colours of things. They are part of the *apparatus* of language, not *uses of the apparatus* (LFM 250).

(iii) *Ideal Objects*   Failure to differentiate these different uses of 'about' is one of the many props that support the myth that necessary propositions are about special kinds of entities, abstract objects, Ideal Objects or Universals constituting the essences of things. We think that if we assert a mathematical proposition 'about' $\aleph_0$, we are talking about one denizen of a fantastic and mysterious realm of number, 'Cantor's paradise' (as Hilbert called it). But we are not talking about a realm of anything, only giving rules for the use of ' $\aleph_0$'. When these norms of representation are specified, we can use ' $\aleph_0$' in making true or false empirical statements. And such a statement which incorporates this symbol, and which can unmisleadingly be said to be about $\aleph_0$, does not even look as if it were a report about goings-on in the paradise of transfinite cardinals. For we may say of a schoolboy that he has mastered $\aleph_0$ multiplications. Of course, this may still breed illusions: how clever of him, we may think, and in so short a time! How can a finite brain master such a large number of multiplications? But what is thereby said is altogether unmysterious, namely that the boy has mastered a certain *unlimited* technique of multiplying (LFM 252).

We are prone to think of geometry as a science about Ideal Objects. We say that a Euclidean line has no width, whereas pencilled lines all do, that a Euclidean triangle has exactly 180°, whereas all worldly triangles deviate more or less. This is a confused picture. *There is no such thing* as 'an Ideal Object' or 'an abstract object'. We should recollect that talk of Ideal Objects was initially introduced to signify things that are *not real*, that have no existence save as ideas in the imagination. To say that a certain symbol 'a' signifies an Ideal Object is to say something about the meaning, and hence the use of 'a'. In particular, it is to say that this use is in certain respects similar to that of signs which signify an object but that 'a' *does not* signify an object at all (RFM 262f.). It is sometimes held that Frege, in the *Foundations of Arithmetic*, showed that if one believes in the objectivity of mathematics, then there is no objection to thinking in terms of mathematical objects or to conceiving them as there awaiting discovery. But this is quite wrong. What Frege showed was the platitude that the occurrence in a sentence of an expression which does not stand for a perceptible or mental 'entity' does not mean that the expression is meaningless, nor does it deprive the sentence of sense. But to infer (as he did) that it (therefore) stands for an Ideal or abstract entity is precisely to draw the wrong conclusion and to fall into the snares of the Augustinian picture. Of course, one can carry on doing mathematics despite such absurd beliefs (they have always been rife among mathematicians). But then one will, in a certain sense, not know what one is doing, and when asked about it will talk much nonsense (RFM 262).

Geometry is not a science about Ideal Shapes, nor is it science about

real shapes. There is no such thing as verifying or falsifying a theorem of
Euclidean geometry by making observations about shapes or spatial
relations among objects. This mistaken idea rests on a misconception
about the applications of geometry. In surveying a building site, for
example, we apply Euclidean geometry. A surveyor does not *predict* that
the sum of the angles of a triangle formed by three boundary markers
will be 180°; rather, he rejects as meaningless the proposition that this
sum deviates from 180°, and hence he takes any apparent deviation to
show that he has made an error in observations or calculations. On the
other hand, for the purpose of terrestrial navigation of ships and planes
we do not apply Euclidean geometry, but rather plane Riemannian
geometry (and spherical trigonometry). Here the sum of the angles of a
triangle is greater than 180° by an amount that depends on the area of the
triangle. In this case it would be *nonsense* to assert that a pilot arrived back
in London by flying straight to San Francisco, turning anti-clockwise
through 60° and flying straight to Rio, turning anti-clockwise again
through 60°, flying straight back to London and intersecting his departure
path at an angle of 60°. The contrast between Euclidean and Riemannian
geometry is not a matter of which theory of space fits the facts, but what
counts as a description of a fact. Consequently it is also mistaken to
compare the difference between these two geometries with the standard
conception of the difference between Newtonian mechanics and relativity
theory, as if Euclidean geometry were an approximation to the true
Riemannian geometry of a building plot, an approximation so close to
the truth on this scale of operations that the difference is negligible. This
neglects the fact that the difference between the two geometries corresponds to a difference in discrimination of sense from nonsense, not
truth from falsity; a proposition may be nearly true, but nonsense is
nonsense even if it deviates by the merest hair's breadth from sense.
Moreover, the conception of Euclidean geometry as an approximation in
the small to the true Riemannian geometry of space in the large involves
isolating geometrical theorems from the whole system of proofs which
give them their sense, for the details of the proofs in the two cases are
entirely different.

A geometry is not a theory of space, but rather a system of rules for
describing objects in space. It sets up an *ideal of exactitude*, not by
reference to imaginary Platonic objects, but in the *form* of the statements
we make (RR 127). If a certain object is the shape of an isosceles triangle,
then the two angles at the base must be exactly equal, we say. And if they
are not, then it is not, but only approximates to such-and-such an extent
to a *grammatical* (not Platonic) ideal of isosceles triangularity (cf. Exg.
§§81, 100). 'The Ideal is your form of expression and a misunderstanding
tempts you to misapply the Ideal.' (MS 157(a), 65) If this ⟋ is exactly a
right angle and this ⟋ is precisely triangular, then the sum of the

remaining angles is 90°, and so on. In this way geometry presents us with paradigms for the transition from one description to another, a model of the way to proceed in reasoning about spatial objects and relations. 'But because mathematics presents us with paradigms of reasoning, it looks rather . . . as though it presented us with reasonings about paradigms.' (RR 127)

(iv) *A reality corresponds*   Because we think that necessary propositions express truths analogously to empirical propositions, because we think that they are about entities of various kinds, we naturally think that some sort of reality corresponds to them.[9] And we do not thereby mean merely that such propositions are true, but that, for example, 'mathematical truth is part of objective reality.'[10] Wittgenstein responded by focusing upon the use of the phrase 'a reality corresponds to'. For an empirical proposition, a reality corresponds to it if it is true (LFM 247), if things are in the world as it says they are, i.e. if it corresponds to the facts. But there is nothing properly analogous to this in the case of mathematical propositions. They no more correspond to a reality than do tautologies (although, of course, they are not tautologies). Certainly one might say that mathematical propositions, like empirical ones, are 'responsible' to something, they are not a matter of whim. But what they are 'responsible' to is not how things are in the world, but to the rest of the rules of the number calculus which give meaning to the mathematical symbols and determine what is to be called 'same number as', etc. For the 'truth' of a mathematical proposition is entirely independent of how things are in reality. And the calculus as a whole cannot be said to correspond to reality, save in the sense that it is enormously useful, has endless applications, is something which, for numerous reasons, we could not do without. This is *not* a form of pragmatism, for Wittgenstein was most emphatically denying that for a mathematical proposition to be true means that it is found to be useful. Mathematical propositions, he held, are rules of representation. They are said to be true if they are primitive propositions of the system or if they are proven. But, to be sure, the system is enormously useful. If one hankers for something in reality corresponding to a rule of representation, then it is general facts of nature which make its application possible and useful, e.g. that objects are relatively stable, that they do not coalesce or bifurcate constantly, arbitrarily, at great rapidity, do not cease to exist or spring into existence wholly unpredictably, and so on. And also general facts about *our* nature which enable us to use such rules.

[9] Wittgenstein referred to Hardy, 'Mathematical Proof', p. 4: '[Mathematical Theorems] are, in one sense or another, however elusive and sophisticated that sense may be, theorems concerning reality.' The fact that he said it, Wittgenstein added, 'does not matter; what is important is that it is a thing which lots of people would like to say.' (LFM 239)

[10] Hardy, ibid. p. 4.

We are inclined to think that 'metaphysical propositions' correspond to how things are in reality. Reality, after all, conforms with the proposition that nothing can be red and green all over, that black is darker than white, that blue and green are more similar than blue and yellow. Indeed, it seems that we can *perceive* such facts.[11] Hard-boiled empiricists may conceive of such propositions as merely very general (universal) truths about reality. Here universality is embraced without necessity, with the consequence that the universality is hypothetical (perhaps on Betelgeuse blue is more similar to yellow than to green?), and the negation of these proposition should be thinkable. Since this is absurd, we may alternatively think of these propositions as necessary, conceiving of them as descriptions of the necessary, structural features of reality. This replaces nonsense by mysteries of super-physics. For we are given no explanation of *why* nothing can be red and green all over by being told that this is the nature of colours. The resolution of these difficulties lies in the realization that these propositions are not descriptions of reality at all, but norms for describing reality. We do not perceive that black is darker than white, but that *this object* is darker than that one. If the first is black and the second white, the grammatical proposition 'Black is darker than white' licenses the description 'This object is darker than that one.' The apparent 'logical structure of the world' is merely the shadow cast by grammar. Given that such propositions are norms of representation delimiting descriptions of reality, then *of course* it will look as if 'reality conforms' with these propositions. For *we describe it so as to conform.* A form of words purporting to describe how things are in reality that contravenes such grammatical rules is *nonsense*, not false. It does not describe wrongly how things are, it violates the bounds of sense.

Similar illusions afflict us in the domain of logic. We naturally think that our rules of inference are *correct*, and that their being correct consists in their corresponding to what *really* follows. If we were to infer differently, disaster would ensue. For if we had different rules of inference, we would get into conflict with the facts. We would then infer propositions which do not really follow! Rules of inference, it seems, are responsible to the truth-values of the propositions which they allow us to link as premises and conclusion. This is confused. Rules of inference are not responsible to any reality. That picture derives from conflating

(i) The stove is smoking, so the chimney is out of order.

with

(ii) The stove is smoking.
When the stove is smoking, the chimney is out of order.
∴ The chimney is out of order. (RFM 40)

[11] Cf. Russell, 'The Limits of Empiricism', pp. 140, 148f.

In the first case we would say that the correct conclusion has been drawn if the chimney is out of order, and an incorrect conclusion has been drawn if it is not. So we might say here that the inference agrees or disagrees with reality. But the second case neither agrees nor disagrees with reality. If the chimney is *not* in fact out of order, we do not fault the inference (do not hold it responsible to reality), but one of the premises. The inference (the pattern) is merely a transformation of expressions according to a rule (below, pp. 313f.). 'Correct' here signifies accord not with reality but with a *convention*, a *use* and perhaps our practical requirements (RFM 41).

This seems hopelessly arbitrary (for we are hopelessly and helplessly captivated by the allure of a false picture). Surely we may infer only what really follows, what, as it were, the logical machine produces (and we think of model-theoretic semantics as a model of the machine!). Logic permits us to infer q from p only if q *necessarily* follows from p. But the idea of a 'logical machine' is just a metaphorical picture of a norm of reasoning. Wittgenstein compared it with the parallel notion of the Ideal Machine in kinematics, which appears to be described by the laws of kinematics but is in fact a norm of description. If an actual machine does not move thus-and-so, we fault not the laws of kinematics but rather, for example, the rigidity of the parts of the machine. The laws of kinematics no more describe an Ideal Machine than the laws of geometry describe Ideal Shapes. They are norms of description; for they license characterizing a movement thus-and-so *if* such-and-such a part moves in a certain way, and *if* the parts are rigid and . . .. The 'hardness of the logical "must" ' is precisely analogous to the 'must' of kinematics, viz. it belongs to our method of representation. If the conclusion of a logical inference is not borne out by the facts we fault the premises, as we fault the machine parts not the laws of kinematics if a certain movement does not occur (RFM 83f.).

4. *The psychology of the* a priori

Other objections to Wittgenstein's calling necessary propositions rules of grammar hurtle from a very different direction. We talk of *believing* necessary propositions, about their absolute *certainty*; we are *convinced* of their truth by a proof, and sometimes we have a *hunch* that a necessary proposition is true in advance of a proof. The mathematician *discovers* new theorems, and what he discovers is often *surprising*. A proof or valid argument *compels* our belief; if we understand it we have *no option*. Such truisms seem to war with Wittgenstein's account of necessary propositions as norms of representation. That account seems not to do justice to what might be called 'the psychology of the *a priori*'.

Wittgenstein's analysis does indeed go deeply against the grain of our most cherished *pictures* of the *a priori*. But closer scrutiny of these pictures may reveal their mythological character. Wittgenstein did not deny that we say such things, nor did he contend that it is mistaken but only that it can be deeply misleading. To conclude that necessary propositions are objects of epistemic attitudes in the sense in which empirical propositions are is to foster illusions, dreams of Reason in idleness (cf. MS 123, 117). These illusions (not falsehoods) are generated by the assumption that the transference of epistemic terms from empirical to necessary propositions involves no shift in meaning (as if one were to conclude from the fact that we talk not only of marrying a woman, but also of marrying money, that money is a special kind of woman).

(i) *Belief*   Certainly we say that we believe that $13 \times 13 = 169$.[12] But there is a *fundamental* difference, despite apparent similarities, between the roles of an arithmetical proposition and an empirical proposition. That is manifest in the different circumstances in which one says 'I believe that $13 \times 13 = 169$' as opposed to 'I believe it is going to rain', and in what characterizes those circumstances. 'What we require is a picture of the employment of mathematical propositions and of sentences beginning "I believe that . . ." where a mathematical proposition is the object of belief.' (RFM 78) Believing a mathematical proposition, Wittgenstein suggested, might be compared with believing that castling is done thus-and-so. Here one does not believe a rule of chess, but believes that a rule of chess runs like this. Is to believe that $13 \times 13 = 169$ not simply to believe that this is a proposition of arithmetic, that this formula belongs to the system of arithmetical equations? One might even say that 'mathematical proposition' signifies a role for the proposition in which believing does not occur (RFM 78). These remarks, Wittgenstein immediately conceded, may mislead, but they point to *fundamental* differences between the roles of arithmetical and empirical propositions, differences which are reflected in doxastic propositions.

Empirical propositions are (generally) bipolar; both proposition and its negation make sense. Hence too do both 'A believes that p' and 'A believes that not-p'. Belief typically has grounds that constitute evidence for what is believed (and disconfirm its negation). It is conceptually linked with actions, since a belief that p is a reason for action (in certain circumstances) and for inferring other empirical propositions. Mathematical propositions are not bipolar; their negations (e.g. '$13 \times 13 \neq 169$') are not propositions of mathematics, and can be said to be nonsense (above, pp. 276ff.). The proof of a mathematical proposition is radically

---

[12] Cf. Hardy, 'Mathematical Proof', p. 4: 'When we know a mathematical theorem, there is something, some object, which we know; when we believe one, there is something which we believe; and this is so equally whether what we believe is true or false.'

unlike the verification of an empirical one, and the calculation which yields the equation '13 × 13 = 169' and which informs our acknowledging it to belong among arithmetical equations is wholly unlike the grounds for an empirical proposition. The result of the multiplication is *part* of the calculation itself, not something external to it. Hence even if it makes sense to say 'A believes that 13 × 13 = 169', it makes none to say 'A believes that 13 × 13 ≠ 169' (or 'that 13 × 13 = 196'). For here there is, as it were, nothing to be believed. The manifestations of the 'belief' that 13 × 13 = 169 are not determinations of the truth or falsity of any empirical propositions, but the discrimination of sense from nonsense in empirical discourse. In short, the grammar of 'belief' is entirely different here. We do in fact use the proposition 'I believe that 13 × 13 = 169' typically to express hesitation about having carried out a calculation correctly (as a schoolboy may say 'I think the answer is . . .'). Here the proposition is indeed comparable to 'I believe that one castles thus.'

One might object; for surely one can believe a mathematical proposition on someone's assurance. We can ask someone what is 13 × 13, and accept his answer mechanically. But what if his reply is '196'? Do we then, after all, *believe* that 13 × 13 = 196? Wittgenstein anticipated this objection (RFM 76f.). We might say 'You can't believe that 13 × 13 = 196, because that isn't a multiplication of 13 by 13, or isn't a case of a calculation yielding a result.' To say 'A believes that 13 × 13 = 196' is nonsense, because the manifestations of belief in this 'equation' constitute criteria for his not understanding the constituent symbols. Of course, one may *say* 'I believe that 13 × 13 = 196.' But what does 'believing this' amount to? Does one attempt to arrange 196 nuts in 13 rows of 13 each? If so, how does one react to finding 27 left over? Or conversely, if one counts up nuts in a 13 by 13 array, does one say that 27 must have vanished? And if one also 'believes' that 12 × 13 = 156, does one further hold that 156 + 13 = 196? Does a person with such 'beliefs' understand what it is to multiply or to add? And if not, what is it to believe something which one does not even comprehend? Since this is absurd, this objection to Wittgenstein's clarification of the concept of mathematical belief collapses.

Similar points hold of believing other necessary truths. We may speak of believing a law of logic, e.g. the Law of Identity or of Non-contradiction. (Certainly if asked 'Which do you believe: $a \neq a$ or $a = a$?', most of us would opt for the latter!) But what is it to *believe* that ~ $(p . \sim p)$ or that $a = a$? Is '~ $(p . \sim p)$' not a tautology, i.e. *senseless*? Is there then anything to believe? What grounds are there for believing that $a = a$? If one sees a piece of chalk, does one see that it is identical with itself (PI §§215f.)? If we tell someone to leave the room and not to leave the room, and he just stands there perplexed, would we conclude 'See, the Law of Non-contradiction works' (LFM 200)? There is here an absence of symmetry even with belief in arithmetical equations. This would be restored if we focused attention instead on the expression 'to believe that "$\sim (p. \sim p)$" is a tautology' or if we took this phrase to express what is meant by 'to believe the Law of Non-contradiction'. For the statement that an expression is a tautology is the result of a *calculation*, not an experiment, and hence the proposition that '$\sim (p. \sim p)$' is a tautology is comparable to the proposition that $13 \times 13 = 169$ (though the techniques of calculation differ).

A final objection from this doxastic direction runs deep. It grows out of a failure to distinguish correctly between proofs (or calculations) and experiments, coupled with the beliefs that one can understand any proposition independently of knowing whether it is true, that a proof in mathematics is a conclusive ground for holding the conclusion to be true, and that one can believe any proposition on less then conclusive grounds. Hence one concludes that we can believe a mathematical proposition in advance of a proof. 'If Littlewood and I both believe Goldbach's theorem, then there is something, and that the same thing, in which we both believe, and that that same something will remain the same something when each of us is dead and when succeeding generations of more skilful mathematicians have proved our belief to be right or wrong.'[13] If we did not understand Goldbach's conjecture, how could we even try to prove it? And if we do understand it, surely we can believe it, even have 'inductive grounds' for our belief? Notoriously, Wittgenstein thought this conception sorely confused. A proof is not the discovery of a truth, but the determination of a new internal relation. Antecedently to the production of a proof the mathematical proposition *has* no meaning, for it is its integration into our system of mathematical propositions that gives it its meaning *as* a mathematical proposition.[14] Only then does it have a use in that vast system for the transformation of numerical expressions which is mathematics (LFM 136f.). To say that one believes it in advance of a proof can only mean either that one resolves to adopt it as a primitive proposition (rule) of the system, or that one has a hunch that the system of mathematics *will be extended* (by a proof) to incorporate this expression, 'that it will be best or most natural to extend the system in such a way that *this* will be said to be right' (LFM 137). We revert to this issue below (pp. 299f.).

The depth of the difference between empirical and *a priori* propositions with respect to 'propositional attitudes' comes out starkly in the case of wishing. Can one *wish* that 2×2 were 5 (Z §701)? No more than one can wish that one could checkmate the Queen, or that there were 36 hours in

[13] Hardy, 'Mathematical Proof', p. 24.

[14] It might, of course, be used *as an empirical proposition* – as, doubtless, 'proto-geometrical propositions' were originally. Alternatively, it might already have a proof, and a new proof might be produced. But then the new proof *changes* its meaning, weaves a new thread into the tapestry of grammatical structures.

a day! For that is merely to wish that one were playing a different game, or a different language-game. And *that*, of course, one can do. But then it is not chess, nor is it what we call 'an hour' and 'a day'.[15] And *pari passu*, it would not be what we call 'multiplying'.

(ii) *Certainty* Propositions of arithmetic and geometry, logic and metaphysics seem paradigms of truths known with absolute certainty. Here, if anywhere, the mind attains true knowledge. 'Of all those who have hitherto sought for the truth in the Sciences', Descartes wrote,[16] 'it has been the mathematicians alone who have been able to succeed in making any demonstrations, that is to say, producing reasons which are evident and certain', and the results of their thus producing reasons was the achievement of secure knowledge. Even after philosophers learned to distinguish *a priori* from empirical propositions and ceased to think of empirical science as striving after that kind of knowledge or demonstration which so mesmerized Descartes, the certainty of *a priori* truths continued to be regarded as the highest kind of certainty, the most secure form of knowledge. But Wittgenstein's claim that such propositions are correctly conceived of as being norms of representation seems inconsistent with this platitude. For surely *rules* are not certain; nor do we talk of knowing rules with certainty, but only of knowing, with certainty or otherwise, that such-and-such *is* a rule governing a certain activity. And does this not suffice to dismiss his conception?

Wittgenstein's counter-moves follow the same general pattern that we have been tracing. Of course we say, rightly, that mathematical propositions are certain. The crucial question is what this means. If we think of a proposition of mathematics as possessing the highest degree of certainty, as being more certain than any empirical truth, we are confused. It is not *more certain* that $25 \times 25 = 625$ than that this man with a broken leg is in agony, or that the sun is shining. The certainty of such necessary truths is not *greater*, but of a different *kind*, and the difference in kind is not psychological but logical, pertaining to the difference in kind between the types of proposition. 'The kind of certainty is the kind of language-game.' (PI p. 224) Having a proof is what is *called* 'establishing certainty in mathematics' – as in a court of law. But what is called 'a proof' and the role of the proof is very different! For the role of proofs in a court of law is to discriminate true empirical propositions from false ones. But the role of proofs in geometry is not to discriminate true geometrical prop-

---

[15] Yet it is extremely interesting that we *do* employ such propositions as 'If only there were 36 hours in the day!', or 'If only Sunday came after Tuesday!' For, of course, as we employ such propositions in these exclamations they do not mean 'If only 36 were 24', or 'If only Wednesday were Sunday', but 'If only I had more time!' and 'If only there were more days off!'

[16] Descartes, *Discourse on Method*, in *The Philosophical Works of Descartes*, ed. and tr. E. S. Haldane and G. T. Ross, Vol. 1 (Dover, New York, 1955), pp. 92f.

ositions from false ones but to determine the propositions of geometry, and hence to fix geometrical concepts and lay down what it makes *sense* to say in characterizing objects in space and their spatial relations. Failure to note this difference is disastrously to assimilate the proof of a mathematical proposition to the verification of an empirical one (PG 361).

We think that a proof *shows* that a proposition is certainly true, and that it is *because* of this certainty that we are secure in applying it, and are justified in so doing. The proof looks inexorable, and seems to establish what it proves as being absolutely certain. But what does its inexorability consist in? What does it force us to do? Does it compel us to acknowledge it, and if so, what is it that we acknowledge? A proof is a demonstration that such-and-such follows from so-and-so for whoever acknowledges it as a demonstration. Nothing *forces* its acknowledgement, Wittgenstein argued, but if someone does not acknowledge a well-established proof, or a proof within a well-established proof-system, 'then he has parted company with us even before anything is said' (RFM 60). But this parting of ways is not a disagreement over mathematical facts, but over mathematical concept-formation. For the proof sets up an internal relation, 'in mathematics we are convinced of *grammatical* propositions; so the expression, the result, of our being convinced is that we *accept a rule*' (RFM 162), and we take the proof as licensing us to transform symbols in such-and-such a way. To accept a proof is to elevate a proposition to the status of a norm of representation. For we thereby accept a new criterion of, for example, counting correctly, or of nothing's having been added or taken away, or of something's having the same area or volume as . . ., etc. 'We feel that mathematics stands on a pedestal – this pedestal it has because of a particular role that its propositions play in our language-games' (RFM 363), viz. as norms of representation. What is inexorable, is not the proof, but the consequences of accepting it, namely that we then apply it inexorably in empirical calculations, e.g. in physics. And we confuse the fact that we hold the proven proposition rigid (use it as a norm of representation) with the thought that it stands firm because it is certainly true – as is demonstrated by the proof!

If we think of arithmetical equations as truths on the model of empirical propositions and of their certainty as akin to the certainty of empirical propositions, we may be gripped, as Russell sometimes was, by sceptical *Angst*. It is after all possible, the sceptic in us suggests, that we are mistaken that there is a table before us, for hallucinations do occur; maybe we are dreaming; at any rate the evidence of our senses does not entail that there is a table here, so at best it is only probable. Similarly, he may reason, mistakes do occur in calculations; so perhaps we have always made a mistake in saying $12 \times 12 = 144$. But this is confused. It seems that we should be overwhelmed by fear that everything worked out this way might be wrong. 'But what does it matter? It does not matter at all! – And in that case there must be something wrong in our idea of the truth and falsity of arithmetical propositions.' (RFM 90) There is no such thing as a *wrong* or *false* method of representation. 'If we had all of us always calculated $12 \times 12 = 143$, then that would be correct – *that* would be the technique.' (LFM 97) That is, of course, not our technique – a technique of which this proposition is a part would, for us, be immensely inconvenient – but it is a possible technique. If such people almost always found that when they had a dozen groups of a dozen objects there were 144, they might thank the Gods for always giving them a gift, or they might have a theory about spontaneous generation, or they might attribute magical properties to 12 sets of a dozen. But their calculating technique would not be *wrong*. It would not be *false to the facts*, since it is not responsible to the facts. Rather is it the measure of what constitutes a fact (MS 124, 84).[17] If they are told that A has 12 sets of a dozen marbles, they say 'So he has 143 altogether', and if it turns out that A has 144 (or 142) they say 'One has been added (or subtracted).' In their system to describe a collection of items as consisting of 12 dozen objects and to describe it as consisting of 143 objects is to describe one and the same fact (just as describing something as 12 inches long is no different from describing it as one foot long in our system of measurement).

It may, however, seem that the price of rebutting such sceptical qualms is denying the 'objectivity' of mathematics. The full answer to such worries will gradually emerge, but for the moment the following points should be stressed. If 'denying the objectivity of mathematics' means affirming that mathematical propositions are a matter of whim, that each of us can decide for himself whether or not $12 \times 12 = 144$, or that it is a matter of taste, then Wittgenstein certainly did not deny the objectivity of mathematics. 'It is not at all a matter of my own will what seems to me to agree with the rule' (RFM 394), and in this sense one may well say that the rules of mathematics compel me to . . .. If affirming the objectivity of mathematics is insisting that '$2 \times 2 = 4$' does not mean the same as 'Human beings believe that $2 \times 2 = 4$', then Wittgenstein certainly affirmed the objectivity of mathematics (PI p. 226), for, of course, these two propositions have entirely different uses. Nevertheless, if everyone 'believed' that $2 \times 2 = 5$, and if this proposition were part of a system of internally related propositions, it would be a nonsense to insist that it would nevertheless still be 4, since we would be talking about a different calculus or technique (perhaps so different that we should not call it 'calculating' (PI p. 227)); but it would not be *wrong*.

Something seems to be lost in this account. One might respond that

[17] After all, when Phineas Fogg travels around the world for a full 81 days (from dawn to dawn) and yet returns to London after only 80 days, we do not fault our number theory on the grounds that 81×1 sometimes equals 80!

nevertheless 'Calculating is right as it is done'; *pace* Russell's scepticism, 'There *can* be no mistake of calculation in $12 \times 12 = 144$.' But here again we mislocate the certainty. There can be no mistake, but not because the proposition that $12 \times 12 = 144$ corresponds certainly to some truth, but rather because it belongs to, has been given a place in, our technique of representation, 'this proposition has assumed a place among the rules.' (RFM 199) Yet this too is unlikely to remove our qualms. Surely it is no coincidence that mathematicians agree over calculations; is this not a token of the certainty of the calculations? It is certainly no coincidence; but this agreement is not a consequence of all mathematicians apprehending a truth, but rather a precondition for there being any such thing as that peculiar kind of certainty we call 'mathematical certainty'. Disputes are rare, can typically be settled quickly by well-established techniques. But if that were not so, if different mathematicians constantly got different results, if when we checked our calculations they always came out differently, if figures on paper altered or seemed to alter unperceived, 'then our concept of "mathematical certainty" would not exist.' (PI p. 225) This is *not* to say that the certainty of mathematics is *based on* the reliability of ink and paper, or on mathematicians' mnemonic powers. But rather, that such facts are preconditions for having and using these techniques of representation. The 'certainty' is located, as it were, *within* the technique, and not in mathematical facts or in the empirical preconditions of the language-game.

What then is this certainty? One might claim that it is merely *analogous* to the certainty of a well-established empirical proposition.[18] For the certainty of a true mathematical proposition is not something shown by the proof in the way that incontrovertible evidence for an empirical proposition shows its certainty. It is not because the proposition is certain that we confidently apply it in counting and calculating empirical truths. If we do not doubt it, it is not because all doubt has been refuted (and our sceptical *Angst* shown to be ill founded). Rather, 'To accept [such] a proposition as unshakeably certain – I want to say – means to use it as a grammatical rule: this removes uncertainty from it.' (RFM 170) A proof forges an internal relation, and to accept a proof is to accept a rule and, accordingly, to withdraw it from doubt (RFM 363) by giving the proposition the status of a norm of representation. Doubt is not refuted, but *excluded*. For there is no such thing as doubting a norm of representation (but, at most, doubting its usefulness). The certainty of a mathematical theorem is not the *ground* for accepting it as a rule of grammar. It is not because the valid proof shows that the theorem is certain that we 'put it

---

[18] E.g. that Jupiter is closer than Neptune, that scarlet fever is caused by a streptococcus or that the Armada was defeated. With respect to propositions such as 'I have toothache', or 'The world has existed for many years', or 'My name is N.N.', there is an altogether different story to tell.

in the archives'. Rather is it that because we 'put it in the archives', accept it as a rule of grammar, that it is certain. For so to accept it is to use it as the measure, not as what is measured. It is this *role* which *excludes* any doubt, not by refutation, but by determination of the bounds of sense.

Once this is clear, it is possible to expose a widespread misconception about the application of mathematics. We conceive of the *truth* of a mathematical proposition as proven by a proof, and we then think of the proof, which shows the mathematical proposition *to be certain*, as a *guarantor* of its application in empirical propositions. It is just because proven mathematical propositions are *absolutely* certain that we can apply them with total confidence! Applying a false equation such as '2 + 3 = 4' would, we suppose, lead us into *factual error* (bridges would collapse and planes tumble from the sky). This is nonsense. '2 + 3 = 5' does not guarantee that I will find five quarts of liquid in a container into which I have just poured first two and later another three quarts; nor is it refuted by finding only four quarts in the container. The equation is a rule which fixes what makes sense, and distinguishes legitimate from incorrect inferences. It makes *no* sense to say 'I first poured in 2 quarts, later 3 quarts, and I poured only 4 quarts in all'; but if I poured first 2 and then another 3, then it follows that I poured 5, no matter how many there are now in the container. The equation licenses a transformation of a *description*, not a *prediction*. The certainty of a mathematical proposition underpins a form of description, since its proof determines an internal relation between descriptions. But the only 'guarantors' of scientific predictions are scientific theories. If our bridges fall down we may fault our physics, but it is nonsensical to attribute the fault to 'a false mathematical theory' (or to fear 'a hidden contradiction').

(iii) *Surprises and discoveries* We are often *surprised* at mathematical results. We think, for example, that things are *revealed* to us which were there all the time, such as the properties of a series. We say that we have a *hunch* that although such-and-such a proposition has not yet been proved, we will find a proof, e.g. that Goldbach's conjecture is true. So we think of the mathematician, logician, metaphysician as making *discoveries*. Do not all these features speak for necessary truths not being conventions, arbitrary rules, which could be otherwise? If they speak for it, we have not understood their language; or, better, we have mistaken their tone of voice.

We do indeed think that the properties of a series are unfolded as the series is extended, or that the properties of a number are revealed as we show that it can be produced in such-and-such ways. This is because we alternate between seeing these properties as internal and as external, as essential and non-essential (RFM 69). But, of course, they are all essential, internal properties. For mathematics is not an experiment, and its results are neither confirmed nor confuted by experiment. The results of a mathematical transformation (a calculation) are not related to the calculation as the result of an experiment is related to the experiment. Rather, in mathematics, 'process and result are equivalent.' (RFM 68) It is not a property of 100 that the 'process' of multiplying 50 by 2, 25 by 4, 10 by 10 *lead to it,* but rather 100 *is* 50 × 2, 25 × 4, 10 × 10 (RFM 69). What is 'unfolded' here is the *role* which '100' plays in our calculating system (RFM 68). The result of the transformation is incorporated into the kind of way the transforming is done (RFM 70), for obtaining this result is a criterion for having done this calculation. When, at school, we learn the properties of a series in the course of extending it, it *looks like* a discovery. For the properties of the series seem to be unfolded before us in the form of more and more unexpected features. But, in fact, we are just learning what is called 'this series', learning the array of internal properties which characterize it. For if this series did not have this-and-this property, it would not *be* this series, but another one. So what is 'unfolded' are alternative descriptions (some partial) of one and the same series, *marks of a concept, not properties of an object* (RFM 64). And even in the case of the further decimal expansion of π, we make no *discoveries,* but rather engage in a transformation of an infinite series into the repertoire of a different technique.

Certainly we are often surprised by the results of the '*a priori* sciences'. We are typically startled when we are shown that a Möbius strip has only one side (or edge), or are told, when introduced to exponentiation, that $a^0 = 1$, or that $\aleph_1 > \aleph_0$. This is not disputable. But the philosophically important question is what the surprise betokens. We are prone to think that the mathematician brings new mathematical facts to light (as it were, by means of a mathematical telescope), that he discerns new mountain ranges and new routes to them. So our surprise appears akin to surprise at the outcome of an experiment: we would never have expected iodine to sublimate, or water to *expand* as it falls below 4°C. This is a mistake. Surprise reveals lack of understanding, failure to command an *Übersicht* of a new proof, inability to grasp the change of aspect effected by a proof, i.e. a change of concepts (RFM 111f.). We are surprised if we know that $a^2 = a \times a$, $a^3 = a \times a \times a$, $a^n = a \times a \times \ldots$ (*n* times), and are then told that $a^0 = 1$. But our surprise stems from the fact that we understand the starting point of the concept of exponentiation, and do not understand how the mathematician gets from there to the 'surprising' result that $a^0 = 1$. One is not surprised at *having been led* to this result, for one is only surprised when one does not yet know the way. When one has the whole of it before one then all surprise vanishes, e.g. when one is told that 'a^m/a^n' can be abbreviated to 'a^{m-n}' because one can cancel out *n* factors in the numerator, hence that $a^m/a^m = a^{m-m} = a^0$, and hence that $a^0 = 1$ because all factors in the numerator and denominator cancel out. For nothing is hidden here (RFM 112).

This is how it is with mathematical puzzles. Their whole point is that they look surprising, produce unexpected results by a kind of wizardry – but only as long as the viewer cannot grasp the transitions! And these 'transitions' are conceptual connections or innovations. We are all surprised and amused by the Möbius strip; until we notice that the 'surprise' tacitly exploits a conflict of criteria by 'discovering' that only one criterion for 'an edge' counts, viz. that one cannot pass from a point on one edge to a point on another by moving continuously along one edge. But this manoeuvre quietly pushes aside another criterion for being an edge of a strip, viz. that if we move *across* the strip we arrive at a point on a different edge. So the *concept* of an edge was quietly redefined by reference to only one of the two customary, expected, criteria. Similar wizardry is involved in the proof that a curve may be connected, but not locally connected; or in the principle that a straight line *always* intersects a circle, sometimes in real, sometimes in complex points (BB 29). If we command a clear view of the method of transformation licensing these redescriptions, i.e. of the grammar of these expressions which is fixed by mathematical proofs and stipulations, then 'There's no mystery here!' (RFM 113) It is important to note that this is not a point about the phenomenology of surprise but rather about the status of mathematical propositions. To be surprised that p is to learn that p is true in circumstances in which one expected that not-p. But in the typical mathematical conundrum, *once the conceptual connections are clarified*, there is an obvious problem in stating coherently *what* one expected not to be the case. In the above example of $a^0 = 1$, did one *expect* $m - m$ *not* to equal 0, or that if all factors in the numerator and denominator cancel out, the quotient should *not* equal 1?

Nevertheless, it may be objected, new mathematical *discoveries* make clear existing mathematical phenomena, solve questions hitherto unsolvable, and make existing mathematical structures intelligible.[19] Waismann, in his *Lectures on the Philosophy of Mathematics*, repudiated Wittgenstein's conceptions, which he had earlier espoused in *Introduction to Mathematical Thinking*. The issues are complex and manifold, and can only be touched upon here. In 'Discovering, Creating, Inventing', Waismann argued that mathematical truths are *interdependent*, and that

---

[19] Wittgenstein examined this idea most thoroughly and subtly in connection with proofs by mathematical induction of basic laws of number theory, e.g. the associative law of addition expressed by the algebraic equation $a + (b + c) = (a + b) + c$. Mathematicians have the picture of using inductive proofs to penetrate to hidden depths concealed beneath the calculations of elementary arithmetic. It seems that new and important facts about numbers are brought to light, facts which make everyday computations fully intelligible. Wittgenstein argued in detail that this is an illusion (PG 395ff.). Rather the role of proofs by induction is to build bridges between two autonomous calculi, elementary arithmetic and algebraic expressions of generalizations about numbers (PG 423, 450). Since this case is far too complex to develop here, we have focused on a simpler example from another source.

this is incompatible with Wittgenstein's claim that they are *invented*, and essentially arbitrary, i.e. not responsible to any 'mathematical reality'. The function $1/(1 + x^2)$ may be expanded into the series '$1 - x^2 + x^4 - x^6 + \ldots$', which converges for $x < 1$, diverges for $x = 1$ (viz. $1 - 1 + 1 - 1 + \ldots$) and diverges explosively for $x > 1$ although it is everywhere 'regular'. This 'behaviour' of the function for real values is perplexing, but 'a complete explanation of such phenomena is possible only when the function is studied . . . for *complex* values of x as well.' (LPM 29) Waismann's explanation is that we can see that the series must diverge when $x = i$, because then the denominator of the fraction is nought, so the function has a point of singularity in $x = i$. Hence the series must also diverge for all values of $x \geqslant 1$, since its convergence for any such x would imply its convergence for $x = i$. What seemed so striking to Waismann is that the behaviour of the function for the reals is *fully explained* by its behaviour in the complex domain, the formula $1/(1 + x^2)$ 'behaves as if it *knew* that there are imaginary numbers' (LPM 30). So do not these surprising unanticipated interrelations *show* that 'mathematics is already *there*, arranged according to a design'?

'When it looks as if . . .', Wittgenstein remarked (RFM 137), 'we should look out.' Putting technicalities aside,[20] the moot question is whether it *makes sense* to *explain* a pattern of internal relations in one domain by reference to *the different concept of number* consequent upon the introduction of complex numbers,[21] and the internal relations involved in this new number system. Wittgenstein's answer is that it does *not*:

> The discovery of the connection between two systems wasn't in the *same* space as those two systems, and if it had been in the same space, it wouldn't have been a discovery (but just a piece of homework).

> Where a connection is now known to exist which was previously unknown, there wasn't a gap before, something incomplete which has now been filled in! –

---

[20] The technicalities are *not* apparently straightforward. Waismann contends that the explanation of the function's diverging for $x = 1$ is that it has a point of singularity in $x = i$. But we can cite infinite series which have a singularity at $x = i$, yet which nevertheless *converge* for $x = 1$ (e.g. $x - (x^3/3) + (x^5/5) - (x^7/7) + \ldots$). So the 'complete explanation' is misguided. (We are indebted to Peter Neumann for this technicality.)

[21] Complex numbers are no more adjuncts to the set of real numbers than negative numbers are an *expansion* of the set of natural numbers. Rather, just as the set of integrals (signed integers) contains a subset *corresponding* to the natural numbers (viz. positive integers), so too the set of complex numbers contains a subset corresponding to the reals (viz. numbers of which the imaginary part is nil: $0\sqrt{-1}$). Hence '$2 + 0\sqrt{-1}$' corresponds to '$1 + (1/2) + (1/4) + (1/8) + \ldots$' among the reals, which corresponds to $+2/+1$ among the rationals, which in turn corresponds to $+2$ among the integers, which itself corresponds to 2 among natural numbers. (Cf. WWK 36; IMT 60ff.; W. and M. Kneale, *The Development of Logic* (Clarendon Press, Oxford, 1962), p. 394.) When mathematicians extend the domain of number, they do not graft a new branch on a pre-existing stock, but produce a new tree, the lower branches of which are isomorphic with their previous arboreal efforts.

(at the time we weren't in a position to say 'I know this much about the matter, from here on it's unknown to me.')

That is why I have said there are no gaps in mathematics. This contradicts the usual view. (PR 187)

But by the same token, *surprise* at the homogeneity of a subset of the extended number system with the unextended number system is misplaced. For it is constructed *so as to be*, in this sense, homogeneous. Equally, it is misguided to conceive of what is found in the extended system as a *completion* of, let alone an *explanation* of, the pattern of the internal relations within the unextended system. Extensions of the number system are arbitrary in the sense that they are not accountable to a mathematical reality (cf. PG 184), but not in the sense that they are a matter of mathematicians' whim. Hence too, an 'explanation' of the behaviour of the function $1/(1 + x^2)$ in the domain of reals could not *in principle* be given by reference to its behaviour in the domain of complex numbers. Indeed, in the former domain, there is nothing more to be explained over and above the fact that the series converges for $x < 1$, diverges for $x = 1$, and diverges explosively for $x > 1$.[22]

A final objection to the argument thus far pursued is intuitively powerful. Even if we follow Wittgenstein in conceiving of the mathematician as an inventor, nevertheless *he knows what it is that he has to invent*. Mathematicians who try to confirm Goldbach's conjecture may have a hunch that it is true (or false), and surely they *understand* the proposition that they wish to prove or disprove (after all, they understand all the constituent expressions!). For if they did not understand it how could they set about proving it? And if finding a proof determined its sense, then what they successfully proved would not be what they set out to prove, since that either had a different sense or none at all! And is this not 'a monstrous perversion of the truth' (LPM 38)? A full answer to this natural objection would require a full exegesis of Wittgenstein's account of proof, in particular of proof that does not lie within what he called 'a proof-system'. A brief answer is this: a creative mathematician understands an unproven mathematical proposition only as a composer understands a theme that he has resolved to integrate into an existing composition:

Take a theme like that of Haydn's (St Antony Chorale), take the part of one of Brahm's variations corresponding to the first part of the theme, and set the task of constructing the second part of the variation in the style of its first part. That is a problem of the same kind as mathematical problems are. If the solution is found, say as Brahms gives it, then one has no doubt; – that is the solution. (RFM 370)

---

[22] We are indebted to Stuart Shanker for this argument.

The mathematician's understanding of his unproven proposition is not at all comparable to understanding an empirical proposition prior to establishing its truth or falsity. A scientist may be able to describe in the minutest detail what experimental results would disconfirm his conjectures in advance of collecting any relevant evidence, whereas a mathematician who could fully describe a proof of Goldbach's conjecture would already be in possession of a complete proof. The mathematician is not like an explorer who knows where he wants to go, can describe his goal (e.g. the North Pole (PG 373ff.)), what it will be like to arrive at it, and the route he intends to take. In the case of the 'mathematical expedition', describing the route *is* arriving at the destination. But what *looks like* a description of arriving (i.e. a description of the goal), namely the conjecture to be proved, is nothing of the sort. Take the search for the construction of a certain regular polygon (PLP 394f.) or for a method of trisecting an angle with compass and rule. If we prove these to be impossible, what is the description given by the 'conjecture' a description of? The mathematician here is not like the explorer looking for the North Pole, but not arriving, nor even like the *conquistador* looking for El Dorado but not finding it. The 'conjecture' is rather akin to describing the East Pole (LFM 64) *for which one cannot even look*. But a search in which one does not know what, if anything, one is looking for until one has found it, and in which only finding what one is looking for establishes that one was looking for something in the first place, is not a search at all. In this respect a mathematical 'conjecture' is no genuine conjecture. In advance of a proof or disproof the so-called 'conjecture' is not, as it were, a description of an object within a space (PG 365), i.e. not something that may or may not be the case. But nor is it the determination of a space. That is something effected only by a proof. For it is the proof which establishes the 'conjecture' as a proposition of mathematics, i.e. a proposition which itself determines what makes sense in the transformation of empirical propositions. A mathematical proposition is not independent of its proof; in this sense 'in mathematics process and result are equivalent.' (RFM 68f.) An 'unproven mathematical proposition' is not a proposition of mathematics; the proof makes it one. So it is the proof that gives it its significance *as* a proposition of mathematics. Hence the mathematician can be said to 'understand' it only in the sense in which he has an inkling of what kinds of techniques might be employed in its proof, a hunch as to the ways in which it might be woven into the fabric of mathematics.

Repudiation of the idea that the mathematician makes discoveries, however, needs further clarification. The dictum that the mathematician is an inventor (RFM 99, 111) is, in certain circumstances, illuminating. But, like all philosophical dicta, it is pregnant with potential misunderstandings. Wittgenstein did not contend that the mathematician is an inventor of *mathematical objects*, like an engineer who invents new gadgets, as opposed to being a discoverer of mathematical objects, a kind of Fregean Columbus. To think of the mathematician as the inventor of mathematical objects leads to confusions, for then it may seem that once the inventor has produced his creation, he must accept it as it is, and can find that it has properties which he did not anticipate and which he can now discover.

> Yes, in a way it is *we* who make the number series, yet we have *no choice* to proceed in any other way . . . . We *generate* the numbers, yet we have no choice to proceed otherwise. There is already something there that *guides* us. So we make, and do not make the numbers.
> What is so disquieting is that we can evidently not *control* the process. As with numbers, so with mathematics in general. We make, and do not make mathematics. We cannot *control* mathematics. The creation is stronger than the creator. (LPM 32f.)

Here Waismann depicted the mathematician as a Dr Frankenstein at the mercy of his creation! But this is muddled. For what the mathematician invents are not new *objects*, but new forms of representation, new extensions of the vast network of mathematics, and hence new ways of describing quantifiable phenomena in the world.[23] What he invents are new *techniques* (LFM 82); why they are *useful* and what motivates him are extra-mathematical considerations. Extending grammar does not involve creating new objects. Analogously, inventing the diatonic scale did not involve creating new entities, but using sounds, produced in such-and-such ways, as samples by reference to which a new grammar of musical description is defined, a new technique of describing sound sequences is introduced.

Of course it is not a *discovery* that 125/5 = 25; it is part of our use of these symbols. We use the mathematical proposition *as a rule*. It licenses us to make the transition from 'Jones shared out 125 marbles equally among his five children' to 'Jones gave each child 25 marbles'. But it would be equally absurd to say that 125/5 = 25 is an *invention* (LFM 101). The techniques of multiplication or division might be called inventions, but particular proofs or calculations within this technique cannot be. Even if the multiplication is one we have not carried out before, e.g. '136 × 51 = 6936', I do not *invent* the result. We learn the rules of multiplication, not the results of each multiplication. We can indeed say that we *find* that '6936' is the result (LFM 92, 101), but it would be altogether confused to assimilate finding the result of a new multiplication to a

---

[23] But there are branches of mathematics which have *no* application (as there are laws of a legal system that are never applied, perhaps because the operative facts are never instantiated). These too must be accounted for by a coherent philosophy of mathematics (cf. RFM 399).

discovery. For the result is not the outcome of an experiment, as if we asked ourselves 'Let's see what we will get this time!' For 'to find the result' is not to find what result I shall get – that *would be* an experiment; it is rather to find the *right result.* 'The result of the calculation is the proposition with which it concludes; the result of the experiment is that from these propositions, by means of these rules, I was led to this proposition.' (RFM 98) The result of the calculation is a rule, viz. that 6936 *is* (one and the same number as) 136 × 51. ('In mathematics a description (in Russell's sense [viz. 'the number got by multiplying 136 by 51']) means the same as a proper name [viz. '6936'].' (LFM 82)) It licenses us to redescribe 51 groups of 136 Fs as '6936 Fs'.

Of course, this may still mislead us. If we say that the result of every new multiplication is a new rule, we may wonder why we make multiplications at all (LFM 106) rather than laying down a new rule as we please. But this is absurd. We do not recognize a rule of multiplication *unless* it can be got in a particular way, according to a general, established technique. We do not accept the rule that 1500 × 169 = 18; *that is not what we call 'multiplying'.*

> The mathematical proposition determines a path, lays down a path for us.
>
> It is no contradiction of this that it is a rule, and not simply stipulated but produced according to a rule. (RFM 228)

The point is important, since failure to grasp it informs widespread misconceptions of Wittgenstein's philosophy of mathematics as introducing anarchism or existentialism into mathematics (as Ramsey accused Brouwer and Weyl of introducing Bolshevism into mathematics). For it is sometimes contended that according to Wittgenstein we are, at each step in our mathematical reasoning, free to accept or reject a proof as we please. He seems to some philosophers to have held that there is nothing in our formulation of axioms and rules of transformation which compels us to accept a proof that follows from them, but rather that at each step we make a fresh *decision.*

This is confused. There is indeed nothing that *forces* me to accept that 25 × 25 = 625 (except perhaps my bank manager). But if I accept anything else, e.g. that 25 × 25 = 9, then I demonstrate that I do not understand the constituent symbols. 9 *is not* the result of multiplying 25 by 25, and this is not what we call 'multiplying'. '25 × 25 = 9' does not belong to *this* technique, but to another one (or is a nonsense), and if I adopt it I shall come into conflict with my fellow men. This makes clear the absurdity of the supposition that according to Wittgenstein we can freely accept or reject any proof (including calculations) *without doing violence to the constituent concepts.* This confusion rests upon failure to draw the very distinction which he draws between new proofs (e.g. new multiplications) within an existing, established *proof-system*, and an extension of our proof-systems by an extension of mathematics (LFM 132, 134f.; RFM 313). Multiplication is a technique of transformation, and '25 × 25 = 9' fails to conform to that technique; here there are no options, save to repudiate the technique. This, however, is *toto caelo* different from extending mathematics, e.g. by introducing the system of signed integers. Here indeed acceptance of the new system involved a *decision*, and it is a striking feature in the history of European mathematics how contentious that decision was.[24] For here indeed nothing forced mathematicians to adopt the new system, and nothing in the pre-existing system of natural numbers and arithmetical operations compelled them to countenance the idea that, for example '$- a \times - b = + c$', or that $- 1/1 = 1/-1$. Between these two extreme kinds of case lies a whole spectrum of cases. Computational proof is just 'homework', and mathematical creativity is neither 'homework' nor typically the introduction of a wholly new proof system.

(iv) *Compulsion* A final array of arguments centres on the notion of compulsion. We do talk of a convincing, indeed of a *compelling argument*. We feel very strongly that a logical argument compels us to accept the conclusion. We argue that if you grant that p, and if you grant that if p then q, then you *must* grant that q – you have no option. You cannot think that if p then q, that p, and that not q! This would be 'a hitherto unknown form of madness'. Once we have grasped a rule of inference, we are surely *bound* in what we do further. We have no more freedom in the matter than does a calculating machine that has been appropriately programmed. It cannot choose to follow the rule as it pleases, nor can we! How can this feeling of compulsion, the unavoidable thought that

---

[24] In the fifteenth century Nicholas Chuquet, and in the sixteenth Michael Stifel, spoke of negative numbers as absurdities. Jerome Cardan gave negative numbers as roots of equations, but thought that these were impossible solutions, mere symbols. Descartes accepted them reluctantly and equivocally. Pascal remarked mockingly 'I have known those who could not understand that to take four from zero there remains zero.' Arnauld questioned whether $- 1/1 = 1/-1$; for -1 is less than $+1$, so how can the smaller stand to the greater as the greater to the smaller? John Wallis accepted negative numbers, but thought that division by a negative number must yield a ratio greater than infinity since the denominator is less than 0. Difficulties plagued mathematicians well into the nineteenth century (William Frend, Lazare Carnot, De Morgan). William Rowan Hamilton summed up the 'absurdities' involved in accepting negative (and complex) numbers in 1837:

But it requires no peculiar scepticism to doubt or even to disbelieve, the doctrine of Negatives and Imaginaries, when set forth (as it has commonly been) with principles like these: that a *greater magnitude may be subtracted from a less*, and that the remainder is *less than nothing*; that *two negative numbers*, or numbers denoting magnitudes each less than nothing, may be *multiplied* the one by the other, and that the product will be a *positive* number, or a number denoting a magnitude greater than nothing; and that although the *square* of a number, or the product obtained by multiplying that number by itself, is therefore *always positive*, whether the number be positive or negative, yet that numbers, called *imaginary*, can be found or conceived or determined, and operated on by all the rules of positive and negative numbers, as if they were subject to those rules, *although they have negative squares*, and must therefore be supposed to be themselves neither positives nor negative, nor yet null numbers, so that the magnitudes which they are supposed to denote can be neither greater than nothing, nor less than nothing, nor even equal to nothing. It must be hard to found a SCIENCE on such grounds as these. . . .

'Necessità 'l c'induce, e non diletto',[25] be reconciled with the suggestion that all we are concerned with are *grammatical conventions*?

Wittgenstein treated this argument as a nightmare of Reason, a fit subject for philosophical therapy by analysis. Certainly we say, 'If you really follow the rule in multiplying, you *must* all get the same result.' If this is not 'the somewhat hysterical way of putting things that you get in university talk' (RFM 430) then it merely says that getting *this* result is our criterion for having correctly followed the rule: rule and result are internally related. To say that you *must* get this result is not to say that you *will* 'inevitably' get this result, but rather that if you do not, you have *not* followed the rule (cf. RFM 239).

Clearly the laws of inference do not compel us like the rails of a locomotive, i.e. causally (RFM 80). For if I think that *p* and that if *p* then *q*, do I *have* to infer anything? I can do what I like! Hence the comparison with the calculating machine rests on confusion, for it (like the locomotive) *is* causally determined – by its circuitry. Indeed a calculating machine does *not* calculate in the sense in which we do. It does not *follow rules* at all, it cannot *justify* anything by reference to rules, it does not *use* rules. It

---

The issue is amusingly discussed in M. Kline, *Mathematics, the Loss of Certainty* (Oxford University Press, New York, 1980), and supplies an effective antidote to the idea that the Peano axioms together with the basic operations compel our assent to the body arithmetical. In fact, the difficulties are not only amusing, but also philosophically illuminating. On the one hand, calculations with negative integers were often castigated as mere manipulation of symbols, whereas computations with positive integers were held to have genuine content. Controversy focused on whether any reality corresponded to negative integers, whether negative numbers could be clearly conceived, and what was revealed by the fact that successful predictions in mechanics could be derived from calculations involving negative numbers. What should have been scrutinized instead was what it means to claim that computations with positive integers are not mere manipulations of symbols or that some reality corresponds to positive integers. On the other hand, mathematical qualms about negative integers reflected misconceptions about the applications of arithmetic coupled with a dim apprehension of the conceptual connection between mathematical and non-mathematical statements. We are inclined to take the primary application of elementary arithmetic of the integers to be to *counting* things. Hence we explain subtraction of integers in terms of taking away a subset from a set of objects or of excluding a subset and counting the remainder. Thus $12 - 7 = 5$ seems to express a principle governing counting in the same way that $12 + 7 = 19$ does. But from this point of view, $5 - 7 = -2$ is unintelligible! Of course it makes no sense to construe $0 - 4 = -4$ as saying how many things are left if four are taken away from none, and it would betray grotesque confusion to conclude that our acceptance of the use of negative integers reveals that, contrary to Pascal's blinkered view, this question can be answered by saying 'minus four'. Rather, what should be scrutinized is what the *full* range of applications of arithmetical equations is and whether equations between *negative* integers do not share *other* applications with equations between positive quantities. What now seems silly in controversies about negative integers in fact was derived from important but limited insights. And modern discussion of the history of mathematics would itself be silly if it failed to do justice to these insights or if it derided earlier mathematicians for their philosophical qualms in the belief that further mathematical developments have resolved these (e.g. the definition of negative integers as ordered pairs of integers). Philosophical qualms can only be resolved by philosophical elucidation, not by technical sophistication, which serves merely to conceal them.

[25] Dante, *Inferno*, Canto xii, line 87.

merely passes electric current along predetermined circuits[26] and displays figures on its display screen. Indeed, if a calculating machine fell among baboons (or even ancient Babylonians) and they punched the buttons, thus producing a display, would *they* have calculated? Would the machine have calculated? If the figures' appearance on the screen amused them, primitive people might play games with the calculating machine, but would what they did be mathematics (RFM 257ff.)? Of course not, for without an application mathematics is just a game (of sorts) with signs. And the apparent 'inexorability' of mathematics *is our inexorability* in employing it as a system of representation. Analogous considerations apply, as we shall see, to the 'adamantine' laws of logic.

One might concede that 'I can do what I like!', but object that I cannot *if I wish to remain in accord with the rules*. But, Wittgenstein responded, who says what 'accord' is (RFM 79)? Yet if we call *that* (e.g. going on '1000, 1004, 1008, . . .' in expanding the series + 2) 'accord', we have changed the meaning of 'accord'! To which Wittgenstein responded again: who says what 'change' and 'remain the same' means here? 'However many rules you give me – I give a rule which justifies *my* employment of your rules.' (RFM 79) What this shows is *not* that it is *untrue* that if I wish to remain in accord with these rules, then I must infer thus-and-so, but rather that the 'must' here is not the anankastic 'must', but rather the 'must' of *convention*. If I do not infer thus-and-so, then 'we shan't call it "continuing that series" and also presumably not "inference".' (RFM 80) Somebody may insist that he is following our rules, that going on thus is doing the same or is what he calls 'accord'; in short, he 'may reply like a rational person and yet not be playing our game.' (RFM 80)

We do indeed say that once one has understood a rule one is *bound* in what one does further. But this does not indicate a special form of compulsion, which applies with equal force to us and to our calculating machines. Rather it 'only means that I am bound in my *judgement* about what is in accord with the rule and what not.' (RFM 328f.) The rules of inference do not compel me to *do* anything. But to understand the rule is to know what *counts*, in the practice of employing it, as being in accord with it.

One can even say that a person cannot *think* that both *p* and not-*p*, cannot *think* that the series '+ 2' continues '1000, 1004, 1008, . . .'. But this does not mean that he is *prevented* from so doing, that the Laws of Thought *force* him not to do so, *compel* him to think that $\sim (p. \sim p)$, or to continue '1000, 1002, 1004, . . .'; it does not mean that no matter how hard he tries, he will never succeed. It means that such-and-such transitions in reasoning are definitive of what we *call* 'inferring', 'think-

---

[26] Of course, one can build in randomizers! But will *that* transform causally determined operations into intentionalist rule-following ones?

ing'; that going on '1000, 1002, 1004, . . .' is definitive of the series '+ 2' so that anyone who, with eyes open, as it were, continues otherwise is not expanding *this* series – and if he insists that he is, then he does not understand the rule of the series and hence does *not think* that *this* series continues thus, for he does not know what *this* series is.[27] We cannot even *try* to think contrary to the laws of logic; but not because they compel us to think thus-and-so, but because what is 'contrary to the laws of logic' is nonsense, and there is no such thing as *thinking* nonsense (any more than there is such a thing as check-mating a rook).

Of course, Wittgenstein conceded, there is an innocuous sense in which laws of inference can be said to compel. One gets punished at school if one infers wrongly; the bank clerk will be dismissed if he does not calculate thus-and-so (RFM 81). Again, we do say 'If you grant *this* and *this*, then you must also grant *this*!' We compel people to admit something thus,[28] just as we compel someone to go over there with an imperious gesture. Equally, if my teacher orders me to expand a series according to a rule, and, being frightened of him, I write down a segment of the series, I can be said to be compelled. But here the rule, e.g. '+ 2', compels me neither more nor less than the order 'Shut the door!' (RFM 333) Finally, just as we can contrast an order which compels a given outcome (a categorical order) with one which leaves open an option (a disjunctive order), so too one can contrast a rule which determines a result (e.g. $y = x^2$) with one which leaves open various possibilities (e.g. $y \neq x^2$). But the latter distinction is not one between forms of compulsion, or between compulsion and lack of compulsion. It is between kinds of orders, and kinds of rules or formulae (PI §189; RFM 81).

It may appear as if Wittgenstein was arguing that 'what seems to be a logical compulsion is in reality only a psychological one.' (RFM 82) But this is not so at all. The coercive pressures of bandits, of the sanctions of the law, of the threats of punishment by teachers, are severally species of compulsion. Wittgenstein was not assimilating logical compulsion to psychological compulsion, but showing us that what we try to capture by our talk of logical compulsion is not, in the same sense, a species of compulsion at all. It is no more a kind of super-compulsion than the 'inexorability of the Law' is a kind of super-inexorability (which, unlike the human judges who are sometimes merciful, always punishes transgressors (RFM 82)).

---

[27] Of course, one must budget for mistakes and for partial understanding. Further, 'The line between what we include in "thinking" and what we no longer include in "thinking" is no more a hard and fast one than the line between what is still and what is no longer called "regularity".' (RFM 80)

[28] But, of course, they might – stubbornly – refuse to admit it (RFM 57); to which we might respond: 'Well, if they *think*, they must admit it!'; the reply to *this* has been spelled out above.

Our talk of compulsion here is a distorted reflection of our inexorably cleaving to our method of representation. 'What compels us to proceed according to a rule, to conceive something as a rule? What compels us to talk to ourselves in the forms of the languages we have learnt? For the word "must" surely expresses our inability to depart from *this* concept. (Or ought I to say "refusal"?)' (RFM 238) But this 'inability' or 'refusal' is not a form of compulsion but is rather our cleaving to our language-games. These are the rules we use, our norms of representation. 'I don't want to say, either, that the rule compels me to act like this, but that it makes it possible for me to hold by it and let it compel me.' (RFM 429) The 'must' merely expresses the fact that these rules are concept-forming (cf. RFM 430). 'And concepts help us to comprehend things. They correspond to a particular way of dealing with situations.' (RFM 431) These ways of dealing with situations are features of our form of life. It is, therefore, an illusion that 'logical' or 'mathematical' compulsion is a metaphysical correlate of physical or psychological compulsion, let alone a form of psychological compulsion. For while coercion forecloses possible courses of action by making them less eligible (the gunman will shoot me if I act thus-and-so), revulsion or terror lead one not to take advantage of opportunities for acting, and physical constraint makes an intelligible action physically impossible in the circumstances, what seems like a form of compulsion in the nightmares of Reason forecloses nothing – save nonsense.

The upshot of these considerations pertaining to the psychology of the *a priori* is that our natural use of standard psychological expressions and idioms in connection with propositions of mathematics and logic both feeds on and fosters conceptual confusions. We overlook crucial differences between the uses of these expressions in empirical discourse and in the *a priori* domain. Consequently we distort and misconstrue the nature of (the grammar of) 'necessary propositions'.

5. *Propositions of logic and laws of thought*

What are variously called the propositions of logic, the principles of inference (or deduction), the laws of truth, of thought or of logic have always struck philosophers as the very paradigms of necessary truths. They seem adamantine, 'fashioned from the hardest of materials, a hundred times stronger than concrete or steel'.[29] A venerable Catholic tradition stemming from Augustine identified these eternal truths with archetypes in the divine mind. The nature and status of these propositions has always aroused puzzlement.

---

[29] J. Łukasiewicz, quoted in C. Coope, P. Geach, T. Potts and R. White, *A Wittgenstein Workbook* (Blackwell, Oxford, 1970), p. 22.

Unclarity runs deep. Indeed, it is exposed by raising the question what count as laws of logic or laws of thought. The range of answers is wide:

(i) Contemporary philosophers distinguish sharply between inferences or arguments and propositions or statements and withhold the predicates 'true' and 'false' from the former, and the predicates 'sound', 'unsound', 'valid', etc. from the latter. Hence they distinguish valid rules of inference from logically true propositions. But this is a modern innovation. Earlier logicians would list among the laws of thought *both* the *dictum de omni* ('whatever is true of *all* is true of each') *and* the principle of the syllogism

> All As are Bs
> All Bs are Cs
> ———————————
> So all As are Cs.

Modern logicians, following Russell's practice, take the Law of Excluded Middle to be expressed by the (tautologous) formula '$p \lor \sim p$'; but Frege (GA ii, §56) identified it with the principle that every proposition is either true or false (now often called the Law of Bivalence). From the modern point of view, the phrases 'laws of logic' or 'laws of thought' are equivocal.

(ii) A sound inference has traditionally been characterized as one in which the conclusion is already *contained in* the premises; the conclusion *adds nothing to* the premises. Moreover, laws of thought (and indeed, logically true or analytic propositions) have often been cast in the role of exhibiting inferences in normal forms; e.g. the principle

$$a = b.\, b = c.\, \supset .\, a = c$$

might be used to exhibit the inference

$$a = b,\, b = c,\, \text{so } a = c$$

in the form of *modus ponens*. Hence the laws of thought have themselves often been called *empty* or *trifling*; they add nothing to the premises of any argument. But this idea sits uncomfortably with the widespread notion that one law of logic may be justified by deriving it from others. In this context different laws of thought must be held to have genuine and different content, to say different things. Pulled both ways, Frege remarked that laws of logic are 'almost without content'![30] Do they really say both something and nothing?

(iii) Philosophers have always striven to present the laws of logic in axiomatic systems modelled on Euclidean geometry. This conception informed the systematization of syllogistic reasoning, the logical algebras of Boole, Venn, Schröder, etc., and the functional logic developed by

---

[30] G. Frege, 'Compound Thoughts', reprinted in *Essays on Frege*, ed. E. D. Klemke (University of Illinois Press, Illinois, 1963), p. 556.

Frege and in *Principia*. Only by laying down a set of axioms which potentially contain all of the boundless laws of logic can one hope to survey the totality (BG §13) and thereby satisfy the condition required for a full understanding of logical truths (FA, p. 5). Linked with this axiomatic conception of logic is another ambiguity in 'laws of thought'; sometimes it is reserved for the fundamental laws of a logical system (the Law of Identity ('Everything is identical with itself' (or '$a = a$'), the Law of Non-contradiction ('$\sim (p. \sim p)$' in *Principia*), etc.), whereas sometimes it is applied to the theorems as well. This equivocation is trivial, but the background to it is important.

(iv) The relation of the laws of thought to thinking, reasoning, or inferring is unclear. Two distinct conceptions have been prominent, namely Platonism and psychologism. On the first view, typified in modern logic by Frege, the laws of logic are *about* logical entities just as the laws of physics are laws about physical entities. These laws of logic were also held to be or to give rise to laws of thought, norms of correct thinking (hence logic is a 'normative science'). They are laws of thought in so far as they *prescribe* how we ought to think if we are to attain truth in reasoning and avoid drawing a false conclusion from true premises. Their normative status, therefore, is akin to that of technical norms that presuppose causal connections in nature. Patterns of valid reasoning presuppose logical connections in a 'third realm' that are *described* by the laws of logic. We need not reason according to the laws of thought, but we *should* if we wish our arguments to be correct.

Psychologism, exemplified in pre-modern logic by Boole and Erdmann, conceived of the laws of logic as laws of human thinking – not prescriptions for how we ought to think but descriptive laws of how we do think. We *cannot* think contrary to the Law of Identity or Non-contradiction, for *we* are so constrained by the empirical (or, according to some neo-Kantians, the transcendental) nature of our minds. 'We cannot help assenting to them – such is the nature of our presentation and thinking. They are universally valid, provided our thinking remains the same. They are necessary, since to think means for us to presuppose them, as long, that is, as they express the essence of our thinking.'[31] The laws of logic are the laws according to which *we* think, but, of course, there might be creatures who think according to different laws of thought.

Wittgenstein's philosophical work *began* (in 1912) from questions concerning the nature and status of the laws of logic. His early reflections were in part responses to deep-rooted confusions which he discerned in the writings of Frege and Russell. The first fruits of his labours are in the *Tractatus*, a book which marks a watershed in the philosophy of logic.

---

[31] B. Erdmann, *Logik*, quoted by Husserl, *Logical Investigations*, Vol. 1, tr. J. N. Findlay (Routledge and Kegan Paul, London, 1970), p. 162.

Light had dawned for him with the realization that the logical constants are not representatives (TLP 4.0312), i.e. that they do not stand for logical objects or functions, but rather signify *operations* (TLP 5.2ff., 5.4). The landscape had been illuminated for him by the invention of the T/F symbolism, the explanation of the logical constants by truth-tables, and the realization that 'The propositions of logic are tautologies.' (TLP 6.1) This was amplified in the striking claim that 'It is the peculiar mark of logical propositions that one can recognise that they are true from the symbol alone, and this fact contains the whole philosophy of logic.' (TLP 6.113) Tautologies, unlike significant propositions, are *senseless*; they say nothing (TLP 6.11; cf. AWL 137; PG 298), and they so combine propositions that all information cancels out (cf. TLP 6.121).

This conception of the propositions of logic has revolutionary consequences. It exposes a confusion of form with generality marked in Russell's identification of logical forms or propositions with completely general propositions (TLP 5.525, 6.1231ff.; cf. PM i, p. 93). It shows that the laws of logic are not generalizations about propositions or descriptions of relations between logical objects or functions. These laws have no 'subject-matter' (TLP 6.124); hence both Platonism and psychologism are nonsensical. Appealing to self-evidence in justifying the fundamental laws of logic (TLP 5.4731, 6.1271; cf. GA ii, Appendix) is not merely unnecessary, but rather inconsistent with the realization that one can *calculate* whether a proposition belongs to logic from the properties of the *symbol* (TLP 6.126). Wittgenstein sharply distinguished propositions of logic from valid inferences. That q follows from (or can be inferred from) p expresses an internal relation between these two propositions (TLP 5.131); this cannot be expressed by any proposition, in particular not by the proposition $p \supset q$. Rather, *that $p \supset q$ is a tautology* makes it clear that q follows from p (NB 107). This in turn shows how to differentiate laws of thought despite the fact that all tautologies say the same thing, viz. nothing. Although both $p \vee p. \supset .p$ and $p. \, p \supset q. \supset .q$ are empty tautologies, the statement that $p \vee p. \supset .p$ is a tautology is manifestly *different* from the statement that $p. \, p \supset q. \supset .q$ is a tautology (NB 113); that is, to say that p follows from $p \vee p$ is not the same as saying that q follows from $p. \, p \supset q$. The idea that the 'laws of thought' say nothing and so might collapse into a single (empty!) law arises from identifying them with tautologies rather than with rules of inference. A remedy which Wittgenstein later advocated is to say that a logical formula is not a law of thought, but rather *that it is a tautology* is a law of thought (AWL 137ff.; LFM 277ff.). Russell invited multiple confusions by writing the Law of Excluded Middle[32] as '$p \vee \sim p$'; a better notation would be '$p \vee \sim p = $ Taut.' (LFM 277f.)

[32] Note how misleading is its traditional title 'Law of Excluded Middle' (AWL 140). What is it that it excludes? 'Every proposition is either true or false' sounds like 'These objects are either red or green, there is no third possibility.' But what third possibility is

Wittgenstein's conception undermines the intelligibility of an axiomatic unification of the propositions of logic. That one proposition follows from another is an internal relation between these propositions; it manifests a relation between the truth-conditions of the two propositions (TLP 5.11ff.). According to this explanation, a tautology follows from any proposition whatever because it has no truth-conditions, being unconditionally true (TLP 4.46f.). This is a *reductio ad absurdum* of the idea that a derivation of one proposition of logic from another in Frege's or Russell's system achieves something by proving that one *follows* from the other. *Any* of the theorems follows from *any* of the axioms of these systems, and indeed *any* of the axioms from *any* of the theorems! Hence the propositions of logic are all of equal status; none is essentially primitive (an axiom), none essentially derived (a theorem). Finally, 'It is clear from the start that a logical proof of a proposition that has sense and a proof *in* logic must be two entirely different things.' (TLP 6.1263; cf. NB 108) The proof of a logical proposition is not a demonstration that it follows from other logical propositions, but rather a procedure for producing a further tautology by successively applying certain operations to some initial tautologies (NB 108; TLP 6.126). Such procedures are not essential to identifying the propositions of logic, but amount merely to a mechanical expedient to facilitate the recognition of tautologies in complicated cases (TLP 6.126, 6.1262). Against the whole tradition of the philosophy of logic, Wittgenstein argued that the propositions of logic are flat.

The conception of the propositions of logic in the *Tractatus* was, in broad outline, a permanent feature of Wittgenstein's thought. He continued to emphasize that the propositions of logic are not *about* anything (PG 52f.; AWL 138f.; LFM 277, 279). He warned against thinking that tautologies are useless because they convey no information (AWL 137f.; RFM 231). In a tautology expressions are expressly so combined that the result *should* say nothing; a tautology is, as it were, a balance on which the lever does not move (LFM 281). But, of course, it is the use of the logical operators in propositions that *do* convey information that gives significance to the fact that in the propositions of logic they are so combined that all information cancels out.

One of the points that did change in Wittgenstein's later discussion was the *Tractatus* allocation of the truth-table explanations of the logical constants to logical *syntax* on the grounds that they do not specify meanings by correlating signs with objects. Wittgenstein abandoned this misconception about meaning after 1929. Thenceforth he accepted truth-

---

excluded by the Law of Excluded Middle? – that a proposition should be neither true nor false? That just means that *there is no such thing as* a proposition which is neither true nor false. In this language-game we do not recognize something as a proposition if it is neither true nor false. As Wittgenstein noted already in 1915, 'The expression "tertium non datur" is really a piece of nonsense. (For no third thing is in question in '$p \lor \sim p$'.)' (NB 57) tables as explanations of *meanings* of propositional connectives. From the point of view of his account of tautologies, this is primarily a mere terminological change. But it also represented a deepening and purification of the notion of the autonomy of the propositions of logic. For it removed the metaphysical constraints on them, viz. that they reflect the logical properties of language and the world (TLP 6.12). The propositions of logic are now perspicuously autonomous. This aspect of Wittgenstein's thought has not been widely understood, largely because modern logicians have employed the truth-table method of the *Tractatus* to support a philosophy of logic at loggerheads with Wittgenstein's later conception of logic. What is illuminating for one person may bedazzle another who faces in the wrong direction!

The seemingly insignificant claim that the tautology '$\sim \sim p \equiv p$' can be deduced from the truth-table explanation of '$\sim$' is in fact the focal point of a clash of *Weltanschauungen*. Wittgenstein castigated this idea as a mythology of symbolism (PG 53). It is as if one took the truth-table to determine a meaning-body, an invisible solid attached to the symbol '$\sim$' whose shape prevents the combination '$\sim \sim p$' from being equivalent to '$\sim p$' and ensures its equivalence to 'p' (cf. PG 54; LFM 282). More generally, he argued that the notion that the propositions of logic can be derived as *consequences* of the meanings (or explanations of meaning) of the logical operators is nonsense. This criticism is rejected by all modern logicians, for they take the development of model theory or logical semantics to be *the* major achievement of twentieth-century logic. The guiding idea of this science is that the truth of a truth of logic can be rigorously demonstrated from the semantic definitions of the logical constants. The simplest case is the proof that a well-formed formula is a tautology, a proof which proceeds from the truth-tables for the relevant connectives. More generally, the programme is to show how the semantic value (T or F) of any well-formed formula in a given model is uniquely determined by its structure together with the semantic value of its constituents in this model; logical truths are then identified as those formulae which take the value T for *any* admissible interpretation. The apparatus of logical semantics allegedly gives a precise, scientific sense to the claim that the truths of logic can be deduced from the meanings of the logical operators.

Wittgenstein's opposition to this conception is central to his thought, exemplifying an important aspect of his conception of grammar. The truth-tables, like other explanations of meaning, are rules of grammar. So too are rules of inference such as the rule that p follows from $\sim \sim p$. This rule is not happily expressed by the tautology '$p \equiv \sim \sim p$' but '$p \equiv \sim \sim p$ is a tautology' does express the rule of inference (law of thought). To say that $p \equiv \sim \sim p$ is a tautology *is* to say that p follows from $\sim \sim p$ (LFM 277f.). Propositions of this form, e.g. '$p \vee \sim p = $ Taut.',

'~ $(p. \sim p)$ = Taut.', are propositions of grammar, rules for the use of 'proposition'; each partly defines what a proposition is (AWL 140), specifying that the concepts 'true' and 'false' *belong* to our concept of a proposition, but do not *fit* it (PI §136; cf. AWL 140). 'If a logic is made up in which the Law of Excluded Middle does not hold, there is no reason for calling the substituted expressions propositions.' (AWL 140; PG 367f.) So Brouwer, far from having discovered that this law does not hold for certain kinds of propositions, has merely 'discovered' that one can so conjoin symbols that the result looks like the expression of a proposition but is *not* one. The 'law of thought' that $p \lor \sim p$ = Taut. partly determines the language-game with 'proposition'. Similarly '$\sim \sim p \equiv p$ = Taut.' and '$p. p \supset q. \supset . q$ = Taut.' are rules which partly define what is to be called 'an inference'; they determine the concept of an inference by reference to specific patterns for transforming expressions, viz. patterns in which all information cancels out (LFM 277ff.; cf. RFM 39).

In saying that it is a *rule of grammar* that $\sim \sim p \equiv p$ is a 'necessary proposition of logic' Wittgenstein was emphasizing that it does not *proceed* from the meaning of '~' (RFM 106; cf. AWL 3f.), but rather partly *constitutes* its meaning, i.e. it is one of the rules for the use of '~' which jointly make up its meaning (AWL 4). Failure to apprehend this point is the cardinal sin of logical semantics. One source of confusion which we have already touched on tangentially is the use of the phrase 'propositions of logic'. A proof in logical semantics is held to certify that what a given well-formed formula expresses is a logical truth. So the role of logical semantics seems to be to single out *true* propositions of logic from the totality of propositions of logic. But this is misleading. For propositions of logic, of course, include such formulae as '$p \lor \sim p$'; but this must be understood as a schema exemplified by 'Either it is raining or it is not raining.' Hence we must conceive of logical semantics as singling out logical truths from the totality of all propositions whatever. So what a proof in logical semantics establishes is not the truth of a logical proposition, but rather *that* an expression *is* a logical proposition (NB 108; TLP 6.126; LFM 278). We converge on the same conclusion by noting (above, pp. 277f.) that it is misleading to call contradictions 'false logical propositions', since contradictions do not have the same role in the formalization of inferences that tautologies do. Hence it is misleading to conceive of a proof in logical semantics as a way of calculating whether an expression is a *true* proposition of logic (a tautology) as opposed to a false one (a contradiction). It is best to regard 'false logical proposition' as nonsense and hence to divorce proofs in logical semantics from the idea of establishing something *to be true*.

Similar confusions arise from the idea that logical semantics establishes the validity or soundness of rules of inference, for we fail to notice different uses of 'infer'. Philosophers use 'q can be inferred from p' and

'q follows from p' interchangeably. Accordingly one can say that someone has inferred 'q' from 'p. $p \supset q$' (but not 'q' from 'p. $q \supset p$', for that would not be a 'logical inference'). We also call 'The chimney is smoking; so it must be blocked' (RFM 40) or 'The wheelbarrow won't push; so the axle needs cleaning' (RFM 397) an inference. And we acknowledge that such a 'non-logical' inference may prove wrong (e.g. the axle may be bent, not clogged up). But, we think, a *logical* inference cannot be wrong, 'at least if it is made according to correct rules of inference' (RFM 398). It may then seem that the task of logical semantics is precisely to *validate* rules of inference, to pick out the correct from the incorrect ones. But this again is confused, conflating different uses of 'infer'. A proof of soundness in logical semantics is a calculation *that* a pattern of propositions *expresses a rule of inference* (TLP 6.1221, 6.126; LFM 278); that an implication is a tautology shows that the transformation of its antecedent into its consequent *is* a rule of inference.

The other source of confusion is to conflate a calculation in logical semantics with the deduction of one empirical proposition from another, thus confusing a move within a calculus with an application of the calculus. We are inclined to represent the truth-table definition of '$\sim$' as an 'analytic truth': '$\sim p$' is true if and only if 'p' is false. And we think of the T/F calculation as *verifying* the proposition that $\sim \sim p \equiv p$ is a tautology. It then seems that the procedures of the T/F calculus prove that this proposition *follows from* the truth-table definition of '$\sim$'. But the truth-table definitions are rules for the use of symbols, not truths about functions. If we view them as rules for transforming formulae of the propositional calculus (e.g. '$\sim \sim p \equiv p$') into another notation (the T/F notation of the *Tractatus* (TLP 5.101),[33] it will be obvious that the proof that '$\sim \sim p \equiv p$' is a tautology is simply a rule-governed derivation of one symbol from another (AWL 135ff.). There is here no question of *inferring* one proposition from another, or of showing that the Law of Double Negation *follows from* anything. What is done is rather to calculate that a certain expression is a tautology.

Wittgenstein's earlier criticism of Frege's and Russell's conception that proofs within their axiomatic systems establish that one proposition of logic *follows from* other propositions of logic reappears in the form of the principle that the use of a rule of inference in a logical system in the

---

[33] 'We could do away with *negation, disjunction, conjunction*, etc. and use *true* and *false*, making up a notation containing only the words "true" and "false". I once did that, with the notation for truth-functions.' Conversely, 'The words "true" and "false" are two words on which philosophy has turned, and it is very important to see that philosophy always turns upon nonsensical questions. Discussion of these words is made easier once it is realized that the words "true" and "false" can be done away with altogether. Instead of saying "p is true" we shall say "p", and instead of "p is false", "not-p". That is, instead of the notions of *truth* and *falsity*, we use *proposition* and *negation*. That we can do this is a useful hint, but it does not do away with the puzzles connected with truth and falsity.' (AWL 106)

transformation of one logical proposition into another is altogether different from the use of a rule to make an inference from one empirical proposition to another (AWL 138). We must not confuse the idea that one empirical proposition follows from others in accord with a schema that we call 'a law of logic' with the altogether different (and misleading) idea that one logical proposition follows from another. It is a deep-seated illusion that proofs in grammar ground necessary truths in more primitive necessary truths. It is equally misguided to think that rules of inference can be *justified* by reference to the meanings of their constituent logical operators or by reference to some transcendent logical reality that stands behind the rules that constitute our form of representation.

Is logical inference correct when it has been made according to rules; or when it is made according to *correct* rules? Would it be wrong, for example, if it were said that p should always be inferred from $\sim p$? But why should one not rather say: such a rule would not give the signs '$\sim p$' and 'p' their usual meaning?

We can conceive the rules of inference – I want to say – as giving the signs their meaning, because they are rules for the use of these signs. So that the rules of inference are involved in the determination of the meaning of the signs. In this sense rules of inference cannot be right or wrong. (RFM 398)

This point about the autonomy of grammar is expressed in the negative dicta that there is no metalogic, no metamathematics (PG 296ff.), nothing behind logic or mathematics, no logical machinery, no foundations of arithmetic (PG 244; LFM 194ff., 260ff., 271f.; RFM 83, 249). There are formal calculi called 'metalogic', 'metamathematics', 'foundations of arithmetic', but they do not have the *philosophical* significance they claim. It is nonsense to suppose that logic or arithmetic has foundations as chemistry has (in quantum mechanics). Metalogic and metamathematics are simply further calculi that stand beside the calculi of logic and arithmetic, but they do not support anything, any more than the painted rock is the support of a painted tower (RFM 378; PG 297).

We can now see why Wittgenstein called it a mythology of symbolism to imagine that the truth table for '$\sim$' contains the rule of double-negation elimination. One could not argue that it would be self-contradictory to combine with the explanation

p	$^{\star}p$
T	F
F	T

the stipulation that $^{\star}\,^{\star}\,p \equiv\,^{\star}\,p$ is a tautology[34] (cf. RFM 102ff.). Of course, in arguing '$^{\star}\,^{\star}$ it is raining, so * it is raining', one would be

---

[34] The asterisk is not used as '$\sim$' is used in the calculus, but as negation in 'I ain't done nuffink.' We might say: that really means that he has done something. But, Wittgenstein suggested, consider what this 'really' means (RFM 106).

applying the truth-table differently than one applies the isomorphic truth-table for '∼' in arguing '∼ ∼ it is raining, so it is raining.' That is trivial, for to arrive at a different *correct* result just *is* to apply it differently. The symbol

$$
\begin{array}{c|c}
p & \\
\hline
T & F \\
F & T
\end{array}
$$

does not *constrain* us to apply it one way rather than another. But only this absurd idea makes sense of the claim that the rule of inference '∼ ∼ p, so p' is *contained* in the truth-table.

The meaning-body conception is not as absurd as it seems. First, it presents a platitude slightly askew. We think that '⋆ ⋆ p ≡ ⋆ p' is a tautology and that '∼ ∼ p ≡ p' is a different tautology *because* '⋆' and '∼' differ in meaning (hence we are loathe to entertain the idea that they might have the same truth-tabular explanation!) But '⋆' and '∼' differ in meaning *because* '⋆ ⋆ p ≡ ⋆ p' and '∼ ∼ p ≡ p' are both tautologies (LFM 192; RFM 107). The meaning-body picture puts this back to front. It is as if we explained that a pound can be exchanged for ten francs *because* the pound has a value ten times that of a franc, whereas what it is for the pound to have a value ten times that of a franc just *is* that one pound can be exchanged for ten francs. Secondly, it reflects an important conceptual connection, albeit distortedly. For we would judge someone who refused to acknowledge the inference '∼ ∼ p, so p' as not understanding '∼' (PG 52); and we also describe the truth-table for '∼' as a correct and *complete* explanation of '∼' (PG 55). This seems to imply that the rule of inference *follows* from the truth-table. But this illusion must be shattered without denying either of the truisms on which it rests. Since the truth-table is an expression of what '∼' means, understanding '∼' and understanding its truth-table are the same thing. Somebody who is taught the use of '∼' by the truth-table explanation and then argues '∼ ∼ it is raining, so it is raining' manifests his understanding of '∼' *and also* of its truth-tabular explanation, while refusal to acknowledge this inference would manifest misunderstanding of *both* (cf. PI §29). In the case of '⋆', arguing '⋆ ⋆ it is raining, so ⋆ it is raining' would manifest understanding of '⋆' *and* of its similar truth-tabular explanation. The point misrepresented by the meaning-body conception is that there is no such thing as combining the truth-table explanation of '∼' *as we understand it* (cf. PI §201) with the denial that ∼ ∼ p ≡ p is a tautology, not because some adamantine machinery produces the tautology from the truth-table, but simply because denying that this is a tautology is what we call *misunderstanding* the truth-table explanation! We fancy that in the absence of something *behind* the laws of thought, things will fall apart and the centre will not hold. But everything is held together by connections of concepts expressed within grammar, in particular by overlapping criteria of understanding. The metalogical principles or meaning-bodies imagined to discharge this role are shadows cast by the concept of understanding.

Finally, we should review the two traditional pictures of the foundations of logic, Platonism and psychologism. Wittgenstein thought that both views were confused. Frege was right to insist against Erdmann that '$a \neq a$' is nonsense, and that it is absurd to suggest that '$p. \sim p$' might be a basic law of an alternative logic. But he was misguided in grounding these insights in the essential natures of propositions, or of functions allegedly named by the logical constants, or of the True and the False. The laws of logic *define* what counts as a proposition, inference, proof or deduction. Frege was further confused in his conception of the relation between laws of logic (the propositions of logic) and 'laws of human thinking'. It is *not* a 'law of human thinking' that we cannot recognize an object as different from itself (GA i, p. xvii). If it were, one could try – as one can try to run a mile in three minutes. But nothing *counts* as trying (RFM 89f.). It is no more a law of thinking than is the fact that human thinking cannot recognize checkmate in draughts; i.e. there is no such thing (cf. Z §134). Hence, there is no such thing as thinking that *a* is different from itself, not because it is too difficult for us to think it, but because *there is nothing to think*. One cannot think a nonsense, only burble. Finally, Frege was mistaken to conceive of the 'normative' laws of thought as technical norms grounded on anankastic connections in a third realm that are described by the laws of logic. The laws of thought are not instrumental for, but constitutive of, thinking and reasoning; as the rules of chess can be said to be constitutive of playing chess (PLP 373).

Psychologism likewise was confused, but not, perhaps, as much as might appear. 'Die Meinung, dass die logischen Gesetze Ausdruck von "Denkgewohnheiten" sind ist nicht *so* absurd, als sie ausschaut.' ('The opinion that the laws of logic are the expression of "thinking-habits" is not as absurd as it seems.' (Vol. XIV, 12)) There are conceptual connections between thinking, reasoning, inferring, etc. and the laws of thought. But it is mistaken to relate the laws of thought to the nature of human *thinking*, as if angels, demons or computers might *think* and *reason* in accord with different laws of thought, or as if the laws of logic might become obsolete (and different laws of logic become valid) were the nature of human thinking to undergo a change. Erdmann was wrong to think that, *though it is unintelligible to us*, there might be beings who reasoned according to a rule of affirming the consequent or who rejected the Law of Identity. Frege was wrong to concede this ('This impossibility of our rejecting the law in question hinders us not at all in supposing beings who do reject it'), and equally wrong to suppose that if there are such beings, then we know that they are wrong and we are right. Both philosophers failed to appreciate that the laws of thought partly *define* what counts as thinking, reasoning, inferring, etc. (cf. LFM 230; RFM 80). One cannot mean what we mean by 'not', 'if . . . then', 'the same' and also repudiate the Law of Non-contradiction or of Identity, or have affirming the consequent as a rule of inference. Psychologism fails to do justice to the internal relations between rules of inference (laws of thought) and thinking, inferring or reasoning, in part because it misconstrues the latter as interior mental activities (RFM 39). Nevertheless, it was not so far from a truth as it seems:

> The laws of logic are indeed the expression of 'thinking habits', but also of the habit of *thinking*. That is to say they can be said to show: how human beings think, and also *what* human beings call 'thinking'. . . .
> The propositions of logic are 'laws of thought', 'because they bring out the essence of human thinking' – to put it more correctly: because they bring out, or show, the essence, the technique, of thinking. They show what thinking is and also show kinds of thinking. (RFM 89f.)

Alternative forms of thought are conceivable – up to a point. We would surely not deny that a system without our negation but with '*' was a language. And different calculi are not only conceivable, but have been invented (though they are not calculi with what we call 'propositions'). What circumscribes 'alternative forms of thought' are the *indeterminate* limits of what we call 'thinking', 'calculating', 'inferring': 'The line between what we include in "thinking" and what we no longer include in "thinking" is no more a hard and fast one than the line between what is still and what is no longer called "regularity".' But that is not to say that 'thinking', and 'inferring' (or 'counting') are bounded by an *arbitrary*, i.e. capricious definition, but rather 'by natural limits corresponding to the body of what can be called the role of thinking and inferring in our life' (RFM 80).

6. *Alternative forms of representation*

'Necessary truths' are norms or reflections of norms of representation and of reasoning which form the network of concepts and transitions between concepts and propositions in terms of which we describe the world. A form of representation is the product of human activity throughout history. It is moulded by the nature of the world around us, conditioned by human nature, focused and directed by human, historically determined, interests and concerns. Consequently we can envisage different forms of representation, limited only by what we call 'a language', 'a proposition', 'an inference', etc.

It might be imagined that some propositions,[35] of the form of empirical propositions, were hardened and functioned as channels for such empirical propositions as were not hardened but fluid; and that this relation altered with time, in that fluid propositions hardened, and hard ones became fluid. . . . But I distinguish between the movement of the waters on the river-bed and the shift of the bed itself; though there is not a sharp division of the one from the other. . . .

And the bank of that river consists partly of hard rock, subject to no alteration or only to an imperceptible one, partly of sand, which now in one place now in another gets washed away, or deposited. (C §§96–9)

This (Spenglerian) conception is elaborated throughout Wittgenstein's writings on the philosophy of mathematics, and numerous fragmentary examples of alternative forms of representation with respect to counting, calculating, measuring, colour-geometries, etc. are given. It has, however, been received with almost complete incomprehension. His examples have been held to be 'thin and unconvincing', even 'wholly inept' or 'seriously confused'. It has been argued that they are thin and unconvincing perforce, in as much as they *are* examples of alternative forms of representation, and these are in principle 'something that is unimaginable or inconceivable'. Are these criticisms justified, and is this interpretation correct? To answer these questions we must first sketch a few of Wittgenstein's examples.

(i) We can not only imagine, but even find, tribes who employ different techniques of counting from ours, who count '1, 2, 3, 4, 5, many' (AWL 117; PLP 250). But note that '3' in this technique does not mean the same as in ours, but only corresponds to our '3' (and similarly for the other symbols). For in this primitive system, if these people 'add' then 3 + 4 = 3 + 5, since both equal 'many'. And if they do not have an operation corresponding to our addition, then a *fortiori* their numbers differ from ours, since they are not embedded in that dense network of internal relations characteristic of our system of arithmetic, and which is definitive of our number concepts.

(ii) Our practices of measuring are quite useless to us if our rulers are unstable, if they themselves expand or contract significantly. But we can imagine circumstances in which rulers with *very* high coefficients of expansion would be very useful (RFM 91; LFM 83), or even in which it was reasonable to measure things with an *elastic* ruler[36] (RFM 38; LFM 83; RR 121f.)!

(iii) We can readily imagine people selling wood on the grounds of a

---

[35] Wittgenstein was concerned here primarily with propositions of the *Weltbild* that are a central theme of *On Certainty*. But it is evident that this simile applies to propositions of logic and mathematics too. The 'hard rock' of the river bank may be considered as the fundamental propositions of logic that are partly definitive of thinking, reasoning and inferring.

[36] His example is derived from an Eddie Cantor film *Strike me Pink* (RR 121).

calculation, e.g. they measure the length, breadth and height of a pile, calculate the product and the result is the price in pence. We would say (but they do not) that they sell wood by the cubic measure (not by weight, labour calculated in a certain way, or time taken to grow the timber). This may seem odd, but not unintelligible. But what if they sold wood at a price proportionate to the *area* covered by a pile irrespective of the height of the pile? They might even justify this by saying 'Of course, if you buy more timber, you must pay more.' This too, Wittgenstein insisted, is a method of calculating price, a system of payment (RFM 93f.; LFM 201f.).

These, and many other examples, are meant to show that there is nothing sacrosanct about our concepts and our methods of representation. They are not *true* or *correct*. They do not *correspond to the facts*, to the 'logical form of the world', to something that lies 'deep in the nature of things' (as Frege thought). Rather, they are useful; and, above all, *they are used*. There could be *analogous* concepts, which are yet very different. They would be no less 'correct'. For they would be perfectly good, not for us, but for others with different interests and purposes, in different circumstances.

Why does this seem so difficult to grasp? It is because we think that internal relations flow from the natures of the related terms, rather than constituting their natures. (Here the influence of the Augustinian *Urbild* and the accompanying *Bedeutungskörper* conception of meaning is pervasive, subtle and powerful, steering philosophers' sophisticated theories into elaborate mythologies of symbolism.) Thus we are prone to take cases of simpler, more 'primitive', conceptual structures than ours (for example, a technique of counting antecedent to techniques of adding and subtracting) to contain a *necessary* directional growth, as a seed 'contains' the plant which will spring from it (cf. FA §88). So we think that a primitive system of counting just is an undeveloped form of *ours*, i.e. of the one and only *correct* system. It lies in the nature of numbers that $5 + 7 = 12$, and people who count as we do are *committed*, whether they know it or not, to these arithmetical truths. After all, we may argue, we can produce inexorable *proofs* taking us from the primitive system to the more evolved one!

A much discussed example strengthens this picture. We can imagine someone who employs a technique of counting and has the concept of more and less, but no technique of addition and subtraction (hence the questions 'How many more?' and 'How many less?' have no intelligible answer save 'More' and 'Less'). Such a person may count 5 boys in a room and 7 girls; when asked how many children are in the classroom, he counts again and answers '12'. But the next day, he might count 5 boys, 7 girls and 13 children! We would say that he had made a mistake; but, it is argued, there must also be something in what he did, which, if he had noticed it, he would have allowed as showing that he had miscounted. And *this* shows that the concept of addition is already implicit in the concepts of number and of counting that he has. So if we were now to introduce him to the concept of addition, we would not merely be getting him to adopt a new criterion for miscounting (expressed by '5 + 7 = 12'), but rather showing him something to which he is committed if he wishes to 'remain faithful' to the concepts he *already* has!

But this is confused. Why has he miscounted if he counted 5 boys, 7 girls and then counted up 13 children? After all, maybe while he was counting the group another child came in. Let us say that no one came in; and he counts 5, 7 and then 13. Does he have any reason for thinking that he made a mistake? No, not yet. But if he counted the class yesterday and found 12 children, and he remembers this and also sees no new faces, then he does have a reason. 'Funny', he may say, 'there were 12 of you yesterday, and yet there are no new faces. So I must have miscounted.' Here '5 + 7' is irrelevant (in fact, for him, meaningless). It is at best an empirical truth that when one counts first 5 and then 7, and then counts up the group, one will *usually* count 12 – but not always! For sometimes one gets added in the interim, or one goes away, or . . . .. But if he counts 12 children, and then, being unsure of himself, recounts and gets 13, and observes that no one goes out or comes in, then he has a criterion for having miscounted. For there cannot be both 12 and also 13 children in this same group. So he will count a third time to make sure. We, however, have an additional criterion, *a mathematical criterion*, for his having miscounted. We take '7 + 5 = 12' to provide a criterion for nothing's having been added or subtracted; i.e. if there are 5 boys and 7 girls, then there *are* 12 children (to say this, for us, is merely an alternative description). If there are in fact more or less than 12, we say 'Some must have come in (or gone out)', or, if we can exclude that, 'We must have miscounted.' Hence also, by introducing the technique of addition, we introduce a new criterion for miscounting. His criterion for nothing being added or subtracted is perceptual, or getting the same result on successive recounts and *not* having miscounted. And, correspondingly, his criterion for miscounting is: getting first 12 and then 13, *given* that nothing was added or subtracted. To get him to accept our technique of addition is indeed not simply to be described as persuading him to adopt a new criterion for having miscounted, for it is also to get him to adopt a new criterion for: something's having been added or taken away (AWL 160).

This new criterion was not implicit in the simple counting practice. It is a mathematical criterion. But *he has no mathematics*. Counting may well be said to be the foundations of arithmetic, but it is not yet arithmetic. Whether there are 12 in the class or 13 is an empirical question. The results of counting are, for him, the results of an 'experiment', not of a calculation. Only when calculation is introduced do we have a primitive arithmetic. His number concepts are *not* the same as ours, for it is not part of what he means by '12' that that very number is also '7 + 5', '8 + 4', '9 + 3', etc. Adding the arithmetical operations changes the concept of number no less than introducing signed integers to someone who employs only natural numbers changes the concept of number. It was no more implicit in his concepts of 7, 5 and 12 that $7 + 5 = 12$, than it was implicit that $7 - 12 = -5$! For him, for his number concepts, 12 is not one and the same number as $7 + 5$, since *there is no such thing*, in his system, as $7 + 5$ (just as Pascal held that there was no such thing as $0 - 4$). And this is correct – there is no such thing until these symbols are integrated into a technique and given a use. We argue wrongly if we argue that if he means the same by '5', '7', '12', etc. as we do, then, *whether he knows it or not*, $5 + 7 = 12$. Rather, his meaning the same as we do is manifest in his agreeing that $5 + 7 = 12$ and his using this proposition as a rule of representation. His meaning the same is not something independent of his acknowledging that $5 + 7 = 12$. The latter is not something that *follows* from his primitive practice of counting.

We turn now to Wittgenstein's measuring examples. Are his sketchy illustrations *really* measuring? They may well seem not to be. For, we may argue, it is a feature of the concept of measuring that an accurately measured object will yield distinct measurements at different times only if *it* changes; it is essential that the measure should not change. Measuring, after all, is supposed to increase accuracy over mere observation, but if rulers expand and contract, it will not. Indeed, in Wittgenstein's 'absurd story', two objects measured to be the *same* length may turn out *different* when placed alongside each other. Moreover, measuring is used for *fitting*, viz. if I have to fill a three-foot gap, and I measure three blocks of one foot each, I can be sure that they will fit. But not with a measure that stretches! So the practical purposes of measuring will not be served in Wittgenstein's story. Finally, different yardsticks will themselves differ in length. Surely what Wittgenstein described is not *measuring* at all, although it may superficially look like it. Why should we describe the activities of such people as measuring? Only, it seems, if, when they are made to confront the variability of their results, they abandon their practice of measuring with expanding or elastic rulers, and adopt *our correct* practice of measuring with rigid rulers. The woodsellers, it seems, can only rightly be said to be calculating the value of the wood if, when we point out to them that there is more wood in a higher pile and maybe less wood in a pile with greater area but lesser height, they immediately abandon their practice in favour of calculating value by quantity. In short, they can only be said to be employing concepts similar to our concepts of measurement if, when we confront them with the facts, they can be brought to accept the superiority of our techniques.

Such a response is singularly parochial and unimaginative, smacking of nineteenth-century British clergymen in 'darkest Africa'. To imagine alternative forms of representation, alternative conventions, is, of course, to imagine different concepts, different techniques, different language-games. You can play chess, but you need not; you can play football instead. But, for our purposes, we must imagine practices that are *analogous* to ours, because Wittgenstein was trying to shake the grip of that preconception which holds that concepts are 'responsible' to reality, and, what is more, that our concepts are right! So the contrasts we are interested in are not like that between chess and football, but between chess and its variants, e.g. losing-chess. *Of course*, the variant forms of (language-)games that concern us will involve different rules, different networks of internal relations, different determinations of what counts as the same and what as different. To be sure, if Wittgenstein is to call his imagined activities 'measuring', there must be sufficient similarity in the techniques to count as measuring at all. But 'sufficient' may not be very much. (Is a number system consisting of '1, 2, 3, 4, 5, many' *not* a number system?)

In order to disturb this sadly parochial vision, let us attend briefly to Gulliver's fifth voyage (about which, alas, Swift never learnt). He travelled, so it is said, to the lands beyond the sunset. And when, after countless hardships and incredible adventures, he returned to England, he recounted his experiences. Among his many tales, he related how the strange inhabitants of this unknown land measured time. The Esenapajs, as he called them, made excellent and beautiful clocks. At noon their clocks strike nine, although they do not say that it is nine o'clock. They say that it is the hour of the Horse. The next time the clock strikes, it strikes one. This signifies that half an hour has passed. The next hour, the clock strikes eight, and this the Esenapajs call the hour of the Sheep. But now, most strange to say, the clock strikes two, to signify that a half an hour has passed! The hour of the Monkey is signified by seven chimes, and the subsequent half hour is struck only once. Strange to say, Gulliver continues, the hour of the *Cock* is at sunset (although cocks crow at dawn) and is signalled by six bells. For only three hours separate noon from sunset. At this point, something most strange occurs. A rumbling occurs in the machine, and it starts ticking at *a different rate*, sometimes faster than before, sometimes slower. The half hour is struck twice, and the hour of the Dog (five chimes) is followed (after a single chime) by the hour of the Boar (four chimes). Midnight strikes nine, however, and subsequent hours are struck eight (the Ox), seven (the Tiger), six (the Hare), which signals sunrise. At this point, again, the clocks change their rate, moving slower or faster. It is altogether curious, Gulliver observed, that the daytime hours are hardly ever the same length as the night-time hours, sometimes being twice as long, and at other times only half as long! Worse, the length of a daytime hour differs every fortnight, and so too does the length of a night-time hour. So the time it takes to walk from Gulliver's dwelling to the Emperor's palace 10 miles away may be one hour today, but two hours tonight, or half an hour one day yet an hour and a half in six months' time, even though one walks at the same speed (which, brave man, he carefully measured using his own pocket watch!).

To those who have not yet fathomed what is happening this may seem fantastic. It is surely not a method of measuring *time*! With variable rates, fluctuating hours at day and night, hours of different length every fortnight, it is wayward, inept, thin and unconvincing. And seriously confused! Perhaps; but what we have described is the Japanese method of measuring time which persisted until 1873. Daytime was divided into six units or 'hours', and night-time into six units.[37] The clocks struck nine chimes down to four chimes;[38] the hours were designated not by numbers but by zodiacal names. Half hours were struck alternately one and two, to enable one to estimate between *which* hours the time was (which would be easy enough during the day). When introduced to the early European mechanical clock, they quickly adapted it by building in *two* separate foliot balances with separate verges, each verge being linked to its own escape wheel, both of which were mounted back to back upon a common arbor. Each escapement could be engaged with or disengaged from the going train by means of a cam actuated automatically by the locking plate at dawn and dusk. The weights on each foliot were adjusted fortnightly to reproduce the rate required for the day and night hours of the current time of year.

Of course, they could not usefully tell one *in general* how many hours it takes to walk to the palace from the temple, except by saying 'Just as long as it takes to eat a four-course meal (or plough an acre).' No doubt they avoided replying to such questions by 'It takes longer on winter days than on summer days, and longer on summer nights than on summer days!'[39] It would be a feeble joke to tell someone that if he wants

---

[37] But note that though our division of the day into 24 units is ancient, going back at least to the ancient Egyptians, it was originally and throughout the classical period of Greece and Rome a division of *daytime* into 12 units and of night-time into 12 units, the day and night units varying with the seasons, as with the Japanese. In Rome, at the winter solstice a day hour was 44 minutes (in *our* terms) and a night hour 76 minutes; at the summer solstice the inverse ratio obtained. The equitemporal-hour 24 hour clock was not introduced until the late thirteenth or early fourteenth century.

[38] If this seems odd, reflect that the first European mechanical clocks struck four (at first light) then three, two, one (noon), two, three, four (at nightfall) and then were silent throughout the night. These were the monastic clocks (which had no dial at all, being genuine 'clocks' (from *Glocke*) i.e. chimers (not 'watches'), used to sound the canonical hours which divided daylight into seven seasonally variable units from matins to compline.

[39] But it is noteworthy to find that the Romans, using similarly seasonally variable hours, specified that their troops were drilled (during the reign of Valentian I (364–75)) to march at the rate of 20 miles in five *summer hours* (i.e. 5/12 of the summer daylight time).

to plough a field really quickly he should do it on the summer solstice. It would be very odd (but not impossible!) with such a technique of time measurement to pay by *time*. Rather would one pay by products, results or tasks performed. The idea of a fixed hourly wage would be ridiculous (though not unintelligible). Doubtless there are hundreds of things we say and do which we would neither say nor do with such a technique of time measurement. Possibly such clocks were initially used primarily to mark times for prayer (as were the European church clocks) or meal times, or to indicate what fraction of daytime or night-time is left, or whether A took just as long as B to carry out a given task *on the same day*. But there is no doubt that they were measuring time.

Furthermore there is also no doubt that the Japanese were not immediately 'brought to accept the superiority of our techniques'. On the contrary, they adapted our mechanical clocks to *their* techniques. For their method of measuring time served their purposes admirably. Only when Japan industrialized, threw over the old order of the Tokugawa shogunate, adopted wholly different forms of organization of labour, methods of production and payment, etc. was their old technique manifestly inadequate.

Wittgenstein's examples could, with a little imagination, be similarly elaborated. Rulers with a very high coefficient of expansion might be very useful if they were used only for measuring objects made of the same material which we moved from one location to another, given that the different locations enjoy different fixed temperatures (LFM 83; RR 121). 'It can be said: what is here called "measuring" and "length" and "equal length", is something different from what we call those things. The use of these words is different from ours; but it is akin to it; and we too use these words in a variety of ways.' (RFM 39) Similarly, to make sense of measuring with elastic rulers[40] merely requires a reasonably imaginative context and a plausible circumscription of the practice. We might suppose that these stretchable rulers are used only for selling cloth and that the merchant 'cheats' the customer, as we would say, by selling 'short measure'; people in this society are not *interested* in measuring anything else (after all, weights were presumably originally used only for selling merchandise). Perhaps, further, it takes a very strong man to stretch a measure. And people might accept this with equanimity. Of course, they will use the terms 'same length' and 'different length' in ways different from ours. But, they may insist, strong men *should* earn more money. Is

---

Greeks and Romans used clepsydras (water clocks) as 'timers', e.g. to limit time for pleading in court. Court clocks measured approximately six minutes (hence our phrase 'time is running out').

[40] It is striking to find the following sentence in a description of time measurement in non-equitemporal units by means of sundials in the ancient world: 'The sundial was an elastic yardstick', D. J. Boorstin, *The Discoverers* (Random House, New York, 1983), p. 28.

this incoherent? We measure the value of work with a monetary measure. It 'shrinks' and 'expands' according to who is working. For we pay doctors and lawyers more than dustmen and milkmen, even though they do 'the same amount' of work! Someone from a different society might think that 'unintelligible'.

Wittgenstein insisted not only that units of measurement and methods of measurement are conventional, responsible not to how things are in the world but only to our practical requirements (RFM 40f.), but also that the *conversion* of one unit of measurement into another (e.g. 1 inch = 2.54 centimetres) is merely a convention. Here again our prejudices may get in the way of a sound understanding. For, we may object, it was surely a matter of *discovery* that the units of the imperial system and the metric system correspond thus? So the rule of conversion is responsible to the results of accurate measurement in both systems! Certainly it *was* a 'discovery' that a 1 in piece of wood is 2.54 cm long, but that was an empirical proposition, the result of an 'experiment'. We have, however, 'hardened it into a rule'. We *use* it as a *rule* of conversion, which is not subject to falsification by experiment or experience. If we make a widget 3 in long and send it to a customer in Toulouse who writes back complaining that it is 7.65 cm long, we do not conclude that centimetres in Toulouse are 2.55 to the inch; we conclude that the widget expanded. We do not need to travel around the continent to check whether perhaps 1 in does not equal 2.5399 cm on Mont Blanc, or 2.5401 cm in the Pyrenees. Rather we hold the proposition '1 in = 2.54 cm' rigid. If we need a metre-rule and do not have one, we can calibrate one by reference to a yardstick. But we might have done things differently. After all, we allow our currency to fluctuate against the French franc. Today £1 = 8.2 francs, tomorrow it could be 9.1 francs! But if we *never* travelled to France, and bought from France *only* lengths of cloth, wholesale purchasers might find it more useful to keep our currency constant and allow the 'exchange rate' 1 in = 2.54 cm to fluctuate!

We think that different though analogous conceptual structures are impossible because they will lead to contradictions. 3 + 2 *must* yield 5, for if it is 6 or 4, then it is not 3 + 2! This is correct. But it does not mean that there could not be an arithmetic in which 3 + 2 = 6 (this does *not* mean that '6' means 5). Rather, that would be a different calculus. That 3 + 2 = 5 in our calculus is not an arithmetical truth that flows from the meanings of these signs. Rather the meanings of these signs is given by the arithmetic for them (RR 114). That the addition of 2 to 3 yields 5 is an internal property of 3. In a calculus in which 3 + 2 = 6 the signs will have different meanings, since they have a different arithmetic, a different pattern of internal relations. It would not be useful for us, with our purposes. But circumstances can be envisaged in which this technique might be useful for people with somewhat different purposes than ours.

They would no more 'come into conflict with the facts' than we do. (After all, when we pour 3 quarts into a bucket and then another 2, so that we have poured 5 quarts in all, and then we find only 4 quarts in the bucket, do we say that our arithmetic is in conflict with the facts?)

It is natural, though confused, to respond to Wittgenstein's arguments by protesting that it is unintelligible that we could 'adopt the convention' that writing down '996, 998, 1000, 1004, . . .' is going on in the same way. It is even more confused to suggest that it is inconceivable for us because we *find it natural* to extend the series of even integers thus and not otherwise, that it is a contingent but avoidable fact about us that we continue thus, not a convention to which there are alternatives among which we might choose. It will then seem that all Wittgenstein showed, and all he *could* show, is that it is intelligible that different kinds of people might have different concepts, but not that such different concepts are intelligible. So to argue is to revive the confused psychologism of the nineteenth century discussed above. Erdmann too held that

We cannot help admitting that all the propositions whose contradictions we cannot envisage in thought are only necessary if we presuppose the character of our thought, as definitely given in our experience: they are not absolutely necessary, or necessary in all possible conditions. On this view our logical principles retain their necessity for our thinking, but this necessity *is not seen as absolute, but as hypothetical.* We cannot help assenting to them – such is the nature of our presentation and thinking.[41]

What is so wrong with such 'naturalist' conceptions?

First, we have adumbrated an example which is not merely hypothetical, but actual. And many others might be produced by examination of the history and anthropology of arithmetic and techniques of measurement. Secondly, there is nothing unintelligible about modifying, or having different techniques of, counting, calculating or measuring.[42] What is unintelligible is having a different technique while adhering to the present concepts of number, arithmetical operation, sameness and difference of measurement. For the technique defines what it *means* to 'go on in the same way', to 'add 2', 'the series of even integers'. It *is* inconceivable that *our* rule '+ 2' should be followed differently, since the rule and what counts as its extension are internally related. But a different calculus which resembled ours in many respects might proceed differently. Of course, it would not involve our concepts of two and of addition. Thirdly, Wittgenstein's observations about what is *natural* to us are

---

[41] Erdmann, *Logik*, p. 162.
[42] Is it *wrong* to measure winning margins in horse-races by 'a nose', 'a short neck' or 'half a length'? And could we not imagine a tribe who were *only* interested in measuring margins of winning in horse-races? And need it matter to them that one horse's short neck may be another horse's nose?

grossly misconstrued here. That it is natural for us, in our culture, to continue the pattern '2, 4, 6, 8, 10, 12, 14, . . .' as we do, that this needs little training, that the progression is readily surveyable and not typically confusing, etc., is *not what makes it correct*. Rather that we find it natural is what makes it reasonable *to make it correct*. What is natural to most of us is the *foundation* for a technique. 'Before the calculation was invented or the technique fixed, there was no right or wrong result.' (LFM 95) Is it equally 'natural' and 'inevitable' for us to extend the series '− 2' according to the formula $a_0 = 1000$; $a_{n+1} = a_n − 2$ beyond 0 (viz. + 2, 0, − 2, − 4, . . .)? One might indeed say that it is; our schoolchildren have no difficulty in doing so. But Descartes, Arnauld, Pascal, Bernoulli found it most 'unnatural'. What is, in this sense, natural today may have been altogether unnatural in other times or in other cultures.[43]

Finally, we turn to Wittgenstein's notorious example of the woodsellers. Are they really *calculating* the price? There might be all sorts of ways of calculating the price of timber: by volume, by weight, by labour measured by the age and strength of the woodsman. But does it make sense to calculate the price of a pile of wood irrespective of its height? Or is this 'a hitherto unknown kind of madness'? We might be inclined to think so. For their activities look like selling wood, they seem to be calculating the price, but then we notice a staggering discrepancy between what they do and what we would do. And we can no longer see any *point* in their activity, and pronounce it a form of madness, or at any rate, not an activity to be called 'calculating the price'. But care is needed. Not every feature of our activities needs a point (does every feature of a coronation ceremony have a point?). We may find, if we fill in a context with sufficient imagination, that it would be altogether natural to say that the woodsellers are indeed estimating the price by a calculation, but not as we would do. Of course, if they say, as the area increases and the volume decreases, 'Yes, now it is a lot of wood and costs more', then they do not mean the same by 'a lot of wood' as we do (RFM 94). But suppose they do not live only by selling wood, and so it does not *much* matter what they got for it. And suppose further that long ago a king told them to calculate the price of wood by area, keeping the height constant. But over the centuries they ceased to worry about the height of the heaps (LFM 204). Is there anything *wrong* with this? They do a

---

[43] It is sometimes argued that Wittgenstein's examples of different number-systems are too thin to be convincing, and the challenge is laid down to invent something that is obviously a number-system, yet distinctively different from ours, involving different patterns of internal relations. The simplest way to meet the challenge is to draw attention to the fact that for people with an arithmetic consisting only of the natural numbers and the four elementary operations, *our* developed number system would be in many respects altogether unintelligible (cf. fn. 24 for a discussion of responses to the introduction of negative numbers). For them it is senseless to have *less* than zero, or to divide 1 by 2, to multiply 4 by − 1, or to raise a number to the power of zero.

calculation, and charge a price accordingly. It is rather pointless, from our point of view, and *we* could ruthlessly take advantage of them. But 'they get along all right. What more do you want?' The difficulty we have in envisaging the woodsellers' activity as calculating the price stems from its detachment from economic motivation. If the sellers maximized area and minimized height we would understand them easily; if the buyers bought piles with maximum height and minimal area, their behaviour would be readily intelligible. But we do not find it unintelligible that *we* sometimes buy the more expensive of a pair of apparently similar items (e.g. if it is more prestigious to buy one in Bond Street rather than Portobello Road). We find Wittgenstein's woodsellers difficult to understand on the assumption that wood is sold in the marketplace where one witnesses the reorganizing of the piles into different shapes, and in which many different piles are simultaneously available. But they are less difficult to fathom if woodsellers rather infrequently sell single large quantities of wood, in separate locations (in the place of felling perhaps), without advertisement or dissemination of information about bargains struck. And so on. The plausibility of Wittgenstein's imaginary practice depends on how the background is filled in. It is crude only when served up raw.

7. *Arbitrariness and the autonomy of grammar*

Consider: 'The only correlate in language to an intrinsic necessity is an arbitrary rule. It is the only thing which one can milk out of this intrinsic necessity into a proposition.' (PI §372)[44]

Philosophers have indeed considered this suggestion, and found it both baffling and unconvincing. Yet Wittgenstein insisted that rules of grammar, and hence 'necessary propositions', are arbitrary. 'Grammar is not accountable to any reality. It is grammatical rules that determine meaning (constitute it) and so they themselves are not answerable to any meaning and to that extent are arbitrary.' (PG 184) This may seem objectionable. We associate the arbitrary with the *capricious*, as when we complain that a person's judgements or verdicts are entirely arbitrary. We say that the decision by Parliament that barges but not lightships qualify for salvage money is arbitrary, i.e. *discretionary*. But surely grammatical rules are not a matter of caprice, and necessary propositions, far from being discretionary, are absolutely inexorable, the hardest of the hard! This is, in one sense, correct, and Wittgenstein did not deny it. Nor need grammatical rules be arbitrary in the sense of being *unimportant* (as

[44] Cf. PG 184; in the MS source Wittgenstein added 'Perhaps apropos of the paradox that mathematics consists of rules.'

we might say that in a certain game it is quite arbitrary who moves first –
it does not affect the outcome). In the sense in which a system of rules *can*
be said to be arbitrary this does *not* mean that they are unimportant: 'To a
man who invented chess, everything in it may have been very important
– no more arbitrary than a poem is arbitrary. ("Not a comma to be
changed.")' (LFM 143) Rules of grammar are not arbitrary in the sense of
being a matter of individual *choice* or *decision*.[45] On the contrary, we are
remorsely drilled and trained to use the expressions of our language and
our arithmetic correctly, in accord with the accepted use; and we are not
free to decide that $2 + 2 = 9$, or that white can be darker than black. A
form of representation, e.g. of measuring, is not arbitrary if that suggests
that a quite different system would do just as well for the same purpose.
On the contrary; earlier Japanese methods of measuring time would be
useless in a modern industrial society. It is no coincidence that we do not
measure rooms in microns (MS 166, 12f.) or distances between cities in
banana lengths. Nor is it an arbitrary matter that we use the decimal
system rather than the Babylonian (base 60), or that we do our
calculations with Arabic notation rather than Roman. Not only do
different grammatical structures serve certain purposes better, worse or
not at all, but further, different forms make certain purposes *possible* (the
ancient Romans could barely even have *wanted* to calculate rates of
change of deceleration). Finally, if what is arbitrary is what is *easily*
dispensable or alterable, then, of course, our rules of grammar (and our
necessary propositions) are far from arbitrary. 'Compare a concept with
a style of painting. For is even our style of painting arbitrary? Can we
choose one at pleasure? (The Egyptian, for instance.) Is it a mere question
of pleasing and ugly?' (PI p. 230)

The claim that rules of grammar are arbitrary is aimed at a different
target, namely that our grammar, our rules for the use of words, our
rules of inference or of mathematics are answerable to some kind of
reality. We are prone to think that 'red is darker than yellow' or that
'there are only four[46] primary colours' is *made true* by the nature of
colours. Even if we are persuaded by Wittgenstein that we employ such
sentences as norms of representation, we are inclined to claim that, at any
rate, they are *correct* rules. For they express how things are, *necessarily*, in
the world. We think that $\sim \sim p$ follows from p, because that is the nature
of negation. And we conceive of advances in mathematics as progressive
discoveries of the nature of numbers. It is against these mesmerizing

---

[45] Of course, introduction of neologisms and new technical terminology may be a matter
of individual choice.

[46] It is striking, and amusing, that there is disagreement over this. What is the nature of
this disagreement? And how would it be settled? Not by experiment! Or rather, if by
experiment, then we have changed the meaning of 'primary colour' and it is an empirical
truth that could be otherwise, and on Betelgeuse may be so.

pictures that Wittgenstein warred. His insistence that grammar is arbitrary is one and the same with his insistence that *grammar is autonomous*.

> One is tempted to justify rules of grammar by sentences like 'But there really are four primary colours.' And the saying that the rules of grammar are arbitrary is directed against the possibility of this justification, which is constructed on the model of justifying a sentence by pointing to what verifies it.[47] (Z §331; cf. PG 185f.)

Our colour-grammar, with its complex geometry, does not reside in the nature of colours (Z §357). On the contrary, it is our rules for the use of colour-words which create what we call 'the nature (the essence) of colour'. But, of course, if we had *very* different rules, they would not determine a concept of colour, but some other more or less remotely related concept. So too with the misguided conception of a *Bedeutungskörper* underlying our use of 'not', which makes certain inferences correct:

> There cannot be a question whether these or other rules are the correct ones for the use of 'not'. (I mean, whether they accord with its meaning.) For without these rules the word has as yet no meaning; and if we change the rules, it now has another meaning (or none), and in that case we may just as well change the word too. (PI p. 147n.; cf. PG 184)

Similarly, it would be an illusion to think that the colour-octahedron penetrates the nature of colour, rather than constituting a rather special expression of the grammar of colour-words (PR 51f.).

> Die grammatischen Regeln sind willkürlich heisst: ihr *Zweck* ist nicht (z.B.) dem Wesen der Negation oder der Farbe zu entsprechen – sondern der Zweck der Negation und des Farbebegriffs. Wie der Zweck der Schachregeln nicht ist dem Wesen des Schach zu entsprechen aber dem Zweck des Schachspiels.
> Oder: – Die Schachregeln sollen nicht dem Wessen // der Natur // des Schachkönigs entsprechen denn sie *geben* ihm dieses Wesen, wohl aber sollen die Regel des Kochens und Braten der Natur des Fleisches entsprechen. – Dies ist natürlich eine grammatische Bemerkung. (MS 160, 6)

> (The rules of grammar are arbitrary means: their *purpose* is not (e.g.) to correspond to the essence of negation or colour – but is the purpose of negation and of the concept of colour. As the purpose of the rules of chess is not to correspond to the essence of chess but to the purpose of the game of chess.
> Or: – the rules of chess are not to correspond to the essence // the nature // of the chess king for they *give* it this essence, but the rules of cooking and roasting should indeed correspond to the nature of meat. – This is, of course, a grammatical remark.)

---

[47] Of course, it is similarly confused to assimilate a mathematical proof to a verification (PG 361).

The rules of cooking are *not* arbitrary (autonomous) because cooking is defined by its goal, i.e. production of tasty food, which is conceptually independent of the rules of cooking (but causally dependent on the activity of cooking). If one does not follow the rules of cooking one cooks badly, produces poor dishes. The rules 'correspond' to the nature of the foodstuff (beef takes longer to roast than lamb) and to our nature. But the concept of language is not defined by the purposes of language (PG 184, 190), for the purposes of language are not independent of the concept of language.[48] If one follows deviant grammatical rules it does not mean that one is saying something wrong (we are not concerned with a *mistake* in English, where one intends to follow the rules of English, but errs). Rather is one speaking of something else (which one may have to explain), just as if one follows rules other than those of chess one is playing another game (PG 185).

Grammatical rules are arbitrary, autonomous. There is no such thing as justifying grammar by reference to reality. For grammar determines the bounds of sense, what it makes sense to say. Hence it determines what is to be called 'a description of reality' (whether that description is true or false is another matter, which is settled by reality).

> If I could describe the point of grammatical conventions by saying they are made necessary by certain properties of the colours (say), then that would make the conventions superfluous, since in that case I would be able to say precisely that which the conventions exclude my saying. Conversely, if the conventions were necessary, i.e. if certain combinations of words had to be excluded as nonsensical, then for that very reason I cannot cite a property of colours that makes the conventions necessary, since it would then be conceivable that the colours should not have this property, and I could only express that by violating the conventions. (PR 53; cf. 55)

But it does not follow, however, that there is, underlying our system of grammar, an ineffable metaphysical necessity that inexpressibly justifies it.

---

[48] One might object: surely the purpose of language is to *communicate*! But this is like 'the purpose of chess is to checkmate.' Without a telephone we could not speak from Europe to America; and without a mouth we could not communicate with each other as we do. But we cannot similarly say that without a language we could not communicate, for 'the concept of language *is contained in* the concept of communication.' (PG 193) For the same reasons it is muddled to hold that the purpose of language is to communicate or to express *thoughts*, as a Fregean might hold. 'So presumably the purpose of every sentence is to express a thought. Then what thought is expressed, for example, by the sentence "It's raining"?' (PI §501) The naïve response that is invited is 'Why, the thought that it is raining'; to which the reply is 'Precisely!' For it is 'of the essence' of the thought that it is raining that we express it by saying 'It's raining.' The thought and its expression are internally, hence not instrumentally, related.

Of course, this does not imply that a dog cannot communicate its desire to go for a walk by pawing the door. Nor that it cannot think that its master is outside. But it can think and want only what it can express. So too with us; without a language the only thoughts *to express* are limited to thoughts expressible without a language!

Alternative grammars are conceivable (indeed, exist and have existed). But, of course, alternative grammars will determine alternative concepts, not the same concepts. Wittgenstein conceded the potentially misleading character of the suggestion that grammar is arbitrary. To call mathematics arbitrary 'is certainly misleading and very dangerous in a way' (LFM 143). Some of the ways in which it is misleading have been clarified, but a crucial point remains. The arbitrary rules of chess are often contrasted with the 'theory of chess', e.g. that one cannot mate with only a king and a knight. That follows *necessarily*. If you prove that one cannot mate thus, then it is a fact – and so not arbitrary (LFM 143). This is still confused. We must distinguish the arbitrariness (or necessity) *of* a system from the arbitrariness (or necessity) *within* a system (LFM 241f.). In saying that within a certain calculus a given conclusion follows necessarily from the axioms and premises, either we are contrasting two kinds of case within the calculus (viz. where a unique answer is yielded as opposed to the case in which it is left open what follows (LFM 242)) or we are speaking pleonastically. For to say that within this system this result follows *necessarily* is just to say that within this system, this result *follows*, i.e. this is what we call 'a correct result' within the system. But if we say that the system as a whole, e.g. arithmetic, geometry or colour-grammar (or even each of its constitutent parts, such as the axioms of geometry) is necessary, we are confused. For how things are in reality does not make this grammar correct, let alone *necessary*. Grammar is only 'responsible to reality' in the sense that were the world different in specifiable ways, certain features of our form of representation would no longer be useful. So too, if human nature were different, parts of our grammar might no longer be usable. And if we had a different grammar we would say and do quite different things (cf. 'Agreement in definitions, judgements and forms of life', pp. 234ff.). Nevertheless, that we have the grammatical structures that we have tells us something about the world we describe in terms of this form of representation:

In a way . . . you might say that the choice of the units [of measurement] is arbitrary. But in a most important sense it is not. It has a most important reason lying both in the size and in the irregularity of shape and in the use we make of a room that we don't measure its dimensions in microns or even in millimetres. That is to say not only the proposition which tells us the result of measurement but also the description of the method and unit of measurement tells us something about the world in which this measurement takes place.

And in this way, the technique of use of a word gives us an idea of *very* general truths about the world in which it is used; of truths in fact which are so general that they don't strike people (and I'm sorry to say philosophers too). (MS 166, 12ff. (in English))

This idea, of course, harks back to the *Tractatus* account of the most fundamental principles of natural science (TLP 6.32ff.) as *a priori* insights

about the forms in which the propositions of science can be cast.
Newtonian mechanics, for example, imposes a unified form on the
description of the world:

The possibility of describing the world by means of Newtonian mechanics tells
us nothing about the world: but what does tell us something about it is the
precise *way* in which it is possible to describe it by these means. (TLP 6.342)

Consequently, there is something further that is potentially misleading
about the claim that grammar is arbitrary. For it suggests that *nothing at
all* speaks in favour of one form of representation (a colour-system or a
system of calculating) rather than another. It would be wiser to say that
'It is akin both to what is arbitrary and to what is non-arbitrary.' (Z §358)
The kinship to what is non-arbitrary is evident from reflection upon the
determinants of concept-formation.

   For our forms of representation to be usable by us, we must,
tautologically, be able to use them. So there will be natural limits to our
symbolisms and their rules of transformation that reflect our powers of
surveying, our mnemonic capacities and our perceptual discriminatory
powers. What we find natural, i.e. easily memorized, readily recognized,
simple to repeat, provides a *foundation* for concept-formation. Because
we find it natural to manipulate signs thus-and-so, it is reasonable for
certain purposes to construct a technique in which it is *correct* to do so.
But even at very basic levels what is 'natural' is not, or not necessarily,
what is untutored (cf. 'Agreement in definitions, judgements and forms
of life', pp. 239ff.). 'It is unnatural for us, though not for everyone in the
world, to count: "one, two, three, four, five, many". We just don't go
on in that way.' (LFM 243) *A fortiori*, at more advanced levels of concept-
formation, the fact that a certain procedure strikes us as 'natural' (that we
feel 'comfortable' with it) will depend more and more upon our training,
education and existing practices. Furthermore, one can always ask
'natural *for what*?' and 'natural, in what circumstances?' (LFM 137)
Consequently, one should neither overestimate the importance of considerations of naturalness in concept-formation, nor mislocate its importance.

   Three errors merit attention. First, we might argue that given that we
find one procedure natural, we will therefore find any other unintelligible.
This is quite wrong. (i) That we find certain patterns natural does not by
itself render anything correct or even intelligible. Only after a technique
is fixed can we talk of correctness and intelligibility (sense and nonsense).
(ii) That something strikes us as natural does not force us to adopt *any*
technique; and often different techniques can be constructed. (Was the
development of non-Euclidean geometries by Gauss, Lobachevski,
Bolyai and Riemann unnatural? – Only to someone too deeply and
confusedly enmeshed in Euclidean geometry!) (iii) What makes different

techniques *appear* unintelligible is not that they are 'unnatural' (i.e. difficult to survey, unmemorable, complex, etc.) but that they are different *techniques*. They determine different *concepts*, which do not mesh with ours.[49] Considerations of naturalness arise when it comes to *extending* our techniques. (Does the new extension dovetail smoothly? Are its forms of operation analogous to pre-existing ones? Are its calculations readily surveyable?) They are marginal for clarifying alternative systems, whether imaginary, or in other cultures.

Secondly, it might be thought that Wittgenstein's emphasis upon what we find natural was meant to show that what we hold to be a correct employment of our symbols is not a matter of convention or decision, for there are no alternatives for us between which we can choose. If *this* is natural for us, then we can do no other! This too is confused. (i) What is unnatural here today for us may be natural elsewhere at another time for others. (ii) Certainly, given that we have inherited and use our methods of representation, it is extremely difficult, and perhaps for some of us impossible, to jettison them and adopt very different ones. For a form of representation involves a form of life, and a radical change in form of life is neither trivial nor easy. (iii) Changing even a feature of a form of representation is not a decision akin to a decision to go to London tomorrow, or a convention like wearing a tie. But to accept the introduction of, for example, negative integers, irrationals or infinitesimals is the adoption of conventions, of norms of representation. And nothing *forced* mathematicians to do so, save, in the course of time, the contempt of other mathematicians and the increasingly obvious utility and power of the new systems.

Thirdly, many extensions of concepts are not justified by 'naturalness', whether tutored or untutored. Wittgenstein discussed this issue in connection with our methods for counting roots of quadratic equations. Is it 'most natural' to count a quadratic equation as having two roots? What of such equations as '$x^2 + 2x + 1 = 0$' (the solution of which is '$x_1 = -1; x_2 = -1$')? It can hardly be 'natural' to say that the equation has two roots rather than one, only they are identical! In so far as 'How many roots does a quadratic equation have?' means 'What values of the variable will satisfy the equation?', then it will be most natural to say that most quadratics have two roots, but this one has only one, viz. -1. But once the general formula for solving quadratic equations of the form $ax^2 + bx + c = 0$ is invented, then the number of roots is *stipulated* to be two, viz.

---

[49] One might say that the *more* different they are, the more readily intelligible they are. And conversely the more they resemble ours, while differing, the *less* intelligible. For then they raise expectations of identical conceptual articulations and purposes, which, when dashed, incline us to think that what is occurring is unintelligible, i.e. a violation of (our) system of conceptual connections.

$$x_1 = \frac{-b + \sqrt{(b^2 - 4ac)}}{2a}$$

$$x_2 = \frac{-b - \sqrt{(b^2 - 4ac)}}{2a}$$

Now the reasons for counting $(-1, -1)$ as two roots are overwhelming (LFM 154), for the proof of the general formula makes a new connection between coefficients and roots. 'By means of what we call the proof of being roots to an equation we really know what proposition has been proved, and we know the answer to the question . . .. The answer here has much more in it than the question did. Normally it is not like this.' (AWL 197)

It would, therefore, be ludicrous to think that what is natural for us is the sole relevant consideration in concept-formation, either in its social evolution or in deliberate introduction of concepts (e.g. by mathematicians). It would be equally misguided to suppose that the claim that grammar is arbitrary is intended to suggest that there are no *reasons* for using the concepts we use, let alone that concept-formation is always blind. Grammar is autonomous, but many reasons guide our concept-formation, e.g. in mathematics, and many reasons can be given why certain concepts are *useful*. But such reasons will not have the form 'Because there really are . . .'.

(i) *The promptings of experience* We noted Wittgenstein's emphasis upon the fact that were the world and our experience of it different in specifiable ways, our present concepts might be useless to us, and others might be both natural and fruitful. Given the multicoloured character of the world (and our perceptual capacities), our colour-grammars are usable and useful. A colour-grammar that distinguished six colours over what we call the red–orange range and only one over the rest of the spectrum would strike us as very odd and far less useful for our purposes. But in a world consisting primarily of multishaded red–orange objects, in which other colours are extremely rare, it might be natural and useful (cf. RPP II §658). Of course, with such a grammar, people would look at things in a very different way from the way we do (cf. PI §401). They would discern differences and similarities where we notice none. Similarly, if material objects did not persist in regular ways, retaining their spatial forms and identity, our counting and calculating might be very different (RR 123). Inhabitants of a liquid world would have a quite different arithmetic (or none at all). To this extent experience *prompts* us, although it does not make our grammars true. Babylonian and Egyptian calculations of areas, volumes, diagonals, etc. began as empirical observations. Indeed, the literal meaning of the Greek word *geometria* (viz. land measurement) betrays the origins of this subject. Geometry proper only began when such observations were hardened into a system of rules, when 'experiments' became norms of representation.

(ii) *Practical needs* Our requirements are commonly an important stimulus to conceptual innovation (RFM 99). Negative numbers were invented by the Hindus as a notation for registering and calculating debts (but that does not mean that one can acquire the concept of a negative number by running up debts (Z §332)). Infinitesimals were invented in response to needs in physics, viz. to represent rates of change of velocity. It is, however, noteworthy that some branches of mathematics evolve without external stimuli, and only later, if at all, find applications.

(iii) *Theoretical needs* An elaborate mathematical system may generate requirements of its own, as it were. New notations may increase surveyability within the system. It is a fundamental error to conceive of new notations as mere abbreviatory conveniences of no conceptual importance (RFM 181). Introduction of the Arabic notation was not merely *more convenient* than the system of Roman numerals. Simplification of calculations was the primary purpose of Napier's invention of logarithms (despite the fact that irrationals were a conceptual stumbling block). The desire to systematize mathematics provides a further array of guiding reasons (RR 124). For mathematicians have often been guided by the Principle of the Permanence of Equivalent Forms, and they typically seek to maximize symmetry or uniformity in their extensions of mathematics.

(iv) *Aesthetic considerations* This factor is prominent when mathematicians endeavour to achieve greater 'elegance' within a mathematical system (RR 132) or are fascinated by the possibility of inventing new symmetries, e.g. the principle of duality in projective geometry.

These kinds of factors guide mathematicians to lay down new paths in certain ways. To be sure, most of us do not *agree*, we are taught at school, and that's an end to it! It is up to the community of mathematicians to accept or reject these conceptual innovations. It is a cardinal argument of Wittgenstein's philosophy of mathematics that a new proof does *not* force the mathematician to accept it (we are not concerned here with 'homework', i.e. proofs or calculations within a proof-system). Rather, it persuades him to adopt a new norm of representation, a new articulation within mathematics, or a new mathematical system. It persuades him that this is the best way to go on from here; that, given the existing calculus, this is the most natural way to extend it. It persuades him by its extensive analogies with the body of mathematics, by its dovetailing smoothly with the existing calculus. The subject of proof is a large and important one, which we shall not pursue further here. It is crucial, however, to realize that in denying that proofs can compel us to accept something, Wittgenstein was not advocating mathematical

Existentialism. 'There could be no mathematical investigations if there were nothing by which our procedure is guided, and nothing by which our results could be checked.' (RR 115)

5. Conventionalism

To the limited extent to which philosophical illumination can be derived from pigeon-holing global philosophical conceptions, it seems plausible to claim that Wittgenstein espoused *conventionalism* in his account of propositions of logic, mathematics and metaphysics. How else could one classify his calling diverse kinds of necessary propositions 'rules of grammar' or 'norms of representation'? Plausible though this is, it carries with it immense dangers of distortion for two related reasons. First, preprepared pigeon-holes tend to accommodate only prepackaged ideas; and secondly, the prepackaged versions of conventionalism familiar to the philosophical community are those produced by the Vienna Circle. Their defence of logical empiricism called for the elimination of synthetic *a priori* knowledge. They argued that all *a priori* truths are analytic; such propositions are 'true by convention' or 'true in virtue of the meanings of their constituent words'; they are, some held, rules or conventions, or at any rate consequences of rules for using words (i.e. definitions). In matters of detail there was persistent controversy, but consensus reigned that any genuine necessary proposition must somehow be demonstrably analytic. Labelling Wittgenstein's reflections, 'conventionalism' associates his ideas with those of the logical positivists.

Indeed, there is more than mere association. We noted substantial continuity between Wittgenstein's later conception of logical propositions and the account he had given in the *Tractatus*. The *Tractatus* played a pivotal role in the development of the Circle's conventionalism. In their view the insight into the tautological nature of logic and that all sound deductive inference consists of tautological transformations of symbols was Wittgenstein's signal achievement. It was he who inaugurated 'The conception that the truth of logical statements is based only on their logical structure and on the meaning of the terms.'[50] This made the *Tractatus* the turning point in philosophy,[51] since it made possible a definitive formulation of consistent empiricism. The historical influence of the *Tractatus* apparently cements Wittgenstein's later account of necessary propositions to the positivists' conventionalism.

---

[50] R. Carnap, 'Intellectual Autobiography', in *The Philosophy of Rudolf Carnap*, ed. P. A. Schilpp (Open Court, Illinois, 1963), p. 25.

[51] M. Schlick, 'Die Wende der Philosophie', Erkenntnis I (1930/1); translated by D. Rynin and reprinted in A. J. Ayer (ed.), *Logical Positivism* (George Allen and Unwin, London, 1959).

This initial classification of Wittgenstein's ideas has important implications: it affects the evaluation of his position. Classical conventionalism,
if we may so call it, is argued to be irremediably incoherent.[52] Truth by
convention cannot give a general explanation of the source of necessary
truths and of the grounds of their knowledge. Two counter-arguments
are prominent. First, definitions are substitution-rules for expressions,
hence the proof that a proposition is analytic must start from an instance
of a proposition of logic (as Frege noted). Consequently, the isolation of
logical truths is presupposed by the definition of analytic truth and in the
formulation of any linguistic conventions. So logical truths (in the object
language) cannot be merely the products of convention. Secondly,
necessary truths (even of logic) cannot be exhausted by enumeration;
consequently, if they are made true by conventions, there must be
substantial reasoning (in the meta-language), e.g. the principle of universal instantiation, which is indispensable for specifying what the
consequences of the conventions are; but since these logical principles fall
outside the scope of conventions (in the meta-language), the notion of
truth by convention effects a less fundamental simplification for philosophy than it seems to promise.[53] This argument purports to disclose a
lacuna in conventionalism on the ground that exhibiting every necessary
truth in the object-language as true by convention presupposes further
necessary truths in the meta-language whose necessity remains unexplained.[54] This second argument is now considered to be decisive.
Indeed, standard conventionalism is condemned as entirely superficial; in
accepting that necessary statements are typically not direct registers of
conventions, but rather more or less remote *consequences* of conventions,
it leaves entirely unexplained the status of the assertion that if we adopt
certain conventions as axioms, together with others registered as principles of inference, then we *must* adhere to the convention embodied in
the theorem. Conventions must, it seems, be dismissed as a general
explanation of the source of necessary truth.

The upshot of this reasoning is that any form of conventionalism
stands condemned unless it differs radically from the conventionalism of
the Vienna Circle. In fact, it must make no use of the concept of logical
consequence in clarifying the concept of truth by convention. Instead, it
must explain each one of the infinitely many propositions of logic or
mathematics to be true by convention *independently* of the truth of any

[52] Also obsolete, for under Quine's influence the notion that there *is* a logical difference
between analytic and synthetic propositions is commonly rejected in favour of a pragmatic
distinction in the degree of entrenchment of beliefs.

[53] W. V. Quine, 'Truth by Convention' (1936), reprinted in *Philosophy of Mathematics,
Selected Readings*, 2nd edn, ed. P. Benacerraf and H. Putnam (Cambridge University Press,
Cambridge, 1983).

[54] *Ibid.*; see also A. Pap, *Semantics and Necessary Truth*, ch. 7 (Yale University Press, New
Haven, 1958).

other necessary proposition, since otherwise logical consequence would again hold sway in the realm of conventions. Precisely such a 'full-blooded' or 'radical' conventionalism is commonly extracted from Wittgenstein's later philosophy of mathematics. According to this view,

the logical necessity of any statement is always the *direct* expression of a linguistic convention. That a given statement is necessary consists always in our having expressly decided to treat that very statement as unassailable; it cannot rest on our having adopted certain other conventions which are found to involve our treating it so.[55]

That Wittgenstein subscribed to this conception of the mutual independence of the rules of grammar seems evident in his notorious claims that in a mathematical proof or calculation we win through to a new decision and put the conclusion 'in the archives' as something unassailable. It also seems supported by interpreting his discussion of following a rule as *denying* that a rule determines what counts as acting in accord with it, e.g. that the rule '+2' does *not* determine '1002' as the correct number to write after '1000'. With this denial he is held to have coupled the positive claim that each fresh application of a rule of inference in a mathematical proof or computation is a new decision, the registering of a fresh convention.

But this 'full-blooded' conventionalism is difficult to accept, being irreconcilable with the conviction that a mathematical proof drives us along willy-nilly until we arrive at the conclusion. We do say that the Pythagorean theorem follows necessarily from the axioms; geometrical proofs provide paradigms of logical consequence. Moreover, it is inconsistent with saying that one proposition follows from another that acknowledging the truth of the second leaves open the question of acknowledging the truth of the first; there is no room for exercising choice or making an arbitrary decision.

If Wittgenstein advanced a form of conventionalism then he is faced by a destructive dilemma. If conventionalism exploits the concept of logical consequence in specifying what is true by convention, it is bankrupt as a general explanation of necessary truth. If it does not, it makes nonsense of the deductive structure and compelling force of mathematical and logical systems. Both 'moderate' and 'full-blooded' conventionalism are absurd, and if these exhaust the possibilities, conventionalism *tout court* is absurd.

Two immediate strategies might be invoked in Wittgenstein's defence. First, one might rightly distinguish his ideas from those of the positivists, and show that objections to their position leave his intact. The

[55] M. A. E. Dummett, 'Wittgenstein's Philosophy of Mathematics', *The Philosophical Review* LXVIII (1959), p. 329.

differences are numerous and deep.[56] For example, most members of the Circle advocated logicism, assimilating equations to tautologies and hoping that technical improvements[57] would eliminate objections to Russell's analysis of numbers. Wittgenstein, by contrast, always stressed significant differences between equations and tautologies, and criticized logicism as philosophically incoherent, not as technically defective (TLP 6.2ff., and for later elaboration, e.g. WWK 218ff.: AWL 146ff.: LFM 284ff.). Members of the Circle thought that the necessary truths of geometry were the theorems of an uninterpreted calculus the axioms of which implicitly define the primitive uninterpreted symbols. Given a physical interpretation, the theorems of 'physical geometry' are contingent propositions of an empirical theory of space open to empirical confirmation or refutation. By contrast, Wittgenstein thought that geometry gave the *grammar* of space and spatial concepts. Euclidean and Riemannian geometries *with their physical interpretation* constitute different grammars, not different theories. They define different *concepts* of space and spatial relations, determining what it makes sense to say rather than hypothesizing truths about space. Positivists were prone to argue that the necessary propositions of logic are *made true* by convention. But by Wittgenstein's lights, this must be confused. For how can a convention *make* such a proposition true? On the model of what 'makes' an empirical proposition true, the only proposition a convention can 'make true' is a proposition such as 'There is a convention that . . .'. We can hold a proposition rigid, immune from falsification. This is precisely to transform it into a norm of representation. But the 'truth' of a norm of representation is *toto caelo* different from the truth of an empirical proposition. And *both* are different from the degenerate truth of propositions of logic. The positivists argued that logical truths are *consequences* of linguistic conventions, that their truth *follows from* the meanings of their constituent expressions as laid down by conventions or rules (definitions or axioms conceived as implicit definitions). This is precisely the *Bedeutungskörper* conception which Wittgenstein criticized. As we have seen, he held it misguided to think that a necessary proposition *follows* from the meanings of its constituent expressions; rather it is partly *constitutive* of their meanings.

Having noted such differences (and there are many others!) we might

---

[56] There were also substantial differences among the positivists and considerable evolution in their views. Our sketch ignores most of these complications.

[57] In their 1929 Manifesto *The Scientific Conception of the World: The Vienna Circle*, (Reidel, Holland, 1973), p. 13, they surmised that the essential features of logicism, formalism and intuitionism 'will come closer in the course of future development and probably, using the far-reaching ideas of Wittgenstein, will be united in the ultimate solution'. This betokens complete incomprehension of Wittgenstein's mathematical reflections even in 1929.

show how objections to the Circle's conventionalism carry no force against Wittgenstein's position. Thus, for example, many standard counter-arguments (cf. Quine and Pap) depend upon details of Carnap's explication of necessary truth in terms of the technical meta-linguistic concept of 'L-truth'. But neither Wittgenstein's explanation of truths of logic as tautologies nor his explanation of the nature of mathematical propositions as rules of representation are in this target area (irrespective of whether these criticisms of Carnap are correct). Similarly, it is evident that standard objections to the contention that necessary propositions are rules[58] are deflected by Wittgenstein's own arguments. It was argued that if necessary propositions are rules for the use of expressions, then, it *seems*, (i) they are not genuine propositions at all; (ii) they are neither true nor false; (iii) far from being necessary, they are contingent, or more accurately, arbitrary, since there are no necessary *rules*, for rules are optional, and we can choose what rules we wish; (iv) we delude ourselves in thinking that we *know* any necessary truths, and *a fortiori* that we discover, in our logical and mathematical investigations, new ones, for rules are not objects of knowledge (but only that there is such-and-such a rule), let alone objects of discovery (save in the sense in which an anthropologist 'discovers' rules); (v) such rules must be rules *about* something, presumably about the use of signs; but that is puzzling, since tautologies say nothing (and surely a rule should say something) and other necessary propositions say nothing about *signs*.

It should be evident from the previous discussion that these criticisms, however effective they may be against formulations of a conventionalist view by Schlick, Hahn and others, fail to undermine Wittgenstein's position. A brief riposte to each point may help to clarify matters further. First, Wittgenstein did not contend that everything that philosophers call 'a necessary proposition' is a rule. In particular, tautologies are not. Secondly, to say that '$25^2 = 625$' expresses a rule is not incompatible with

---

[58] Such objections impressed A. J. Ayer. In the preface to the second edition (1946) of *Language, Truth and Logic*, he wrote: 'I now think it is a mistake to say that [*a priori* propositions] are themselves linguistic rules. For apart from the fact that they can properly be said to be true, which linguistic rules cannot, they are distinguished also by being necessary, whereas linguistic rules are arbitrary. At the same time, if they are necessary, it is only because the relevant linguistic rules are presupposed. Thus, it is a contingent empirical fact that the word 'earlier' is used in English to mean earlier, it is an arbitrary, though convenient, rule of language that words that stand for temporal relations are to be used transitively; but, given this rule, the proposition that, if A is earlier than B and B is earlier than C, A is earlier than C becomes a necessary truth.' Two confusions are evident immediately. First, necessary truths do not become or cease to be. Rather, certain signs become used or ceased to be used in such-and-such ways. Secondly, it is not an arbitrary rule of language that words *that stand for temporal relations* are used transitively. It is an arbitrary rule that the English word 'earlier' is used to mean earlier. But given that it is so used it is wholly non-arbitrary that it is used transitively. For if it were not so used, it would not mean *earlier* at all, but something else. Its being so used *defines* the concept of being earlier than.

its propositional status. This is what we call 'a mathematical proposition' (just as we call 'It is better to suffer evil than to do evil' an ethical proposition). But we must come to see that such propositions are used as norms of representation. Thirdly, he did not deny that we say that it is *true* that $25^2 = 625$ (just as we say that it is true that cruelty is evil), nor did he suggest that we should refrain from this. He only insisted that we observe the differences between saying of a mathematical or grammatical proposition that it is true, and saying this of an ordinary empirical proposition. Fourthly, and along precisely parallel lines, he did not suggest that those propositions which we are inclined to call 'necessary' and which he suggested are rules, should not be said to be necessary. Rather he urged that we should investigate what this means. Of course, a rule is not illuminatingly said to be necessary (or contingent), but rather, in the sense explained, arbitrary. That we say of 'Nothing can be red and green all over' that it is a necessary proposition does not mean that this norm of representation is necessary, since there is no such thing as *a necessary norm of representation*. Rather it means that this proposition *expresses a norm of representation*; hence its adamantine appearance. Fifthly, to say that necessary propositions are rules does not preclude knowledge of them. We do rightly distinguish one who knows mathematics from one who is innumerate. But that distinction is altogether different from that between one who knows physics and one who is ignorant of truths of physics. And the growth of the body mathematical is not an accumulation of discovered truths about numbers but rather an extension of a network of rules of representation. Finally, if some kinds of necessary propositions are rules, then, of course, they are rules for the use of signs. But only confusion makes one insist that they should *mention* rather than *use* those signs.

A second strategy to avoid the horns of the destructive dilemma that seems to threaten Wittgenstein's account of necessary propositions is to distinguish his ideas from the theses of the *notional* doctrines of 'full-blooded' conventionalism. In one respect this has already been definitively done. It is a travesty of his explanation of rule-following and of what it is for an act to accord with a rule to suggest that he *denied* that a rule (e.g. '+2') determines what accords with it. On the contrary, he argued that there is an internal relation between a rule and its 'extension' and proceeded to explain what this means. In other respects, detailed examination of his conception of proof and calculation would be necessary. Full-blooded conventionalism denies that a geometrical proof or an arithmetical computation ever settles the status of an expression as a proposition of mathematics; at best it prompts us to make a decision and treat the conclusion as a new norm of representation, but we are free to go another way. This idea is indeed plausible for proofs that extend mathematics as opposed to proofs *within* a proof-system (e.g. elementary

computations and 'homework'), though in what way the concept of
decision fits even these cases would required detailed examination of
such proofs. Otherwise talk of choice or decision is at best a confused
formulation of a negative insight. As Wittgenstein stressed (TLP 6.1263)
and others have often noted, entailment cannot have the same meaning
when applied to necessary propositions as it has when applied to
contingent ones; in particular, it cannot be given the standard definition
in terms of relations among the truth-conditions of propositions. It is
tempting to frame this point by denying that any geometrical theorem
follows from the axioms, that $(\exists x)(y) Rxy \supset (y)(\exists x) Rxy$ *follows
from* the logical axioms of *Principia*, etc.; and this point may in turn
be rephrased by the claim that every two geometrical (logical, etc.)
propositions are *independent* of each other.[1] This (misleading) reasoning
perhaps explains Wittgenstein's own occasional (and relatively early)
claims that the rules of grammar are all mutually independent (e.g.
AWL 3) as well as some of his (typically qualified) claims that proofs
result in decisions. It is just as confusing to wrap up the correct
observation about a difference in the conception of entailment in the
terms 'independent' and 'decision' as it would be to paraphrase the
remark that 'I know that I have a toothache' is nonsense into the statement 'I never know whether I have a toothache'! Certainly Wittgenstein
connected the concepts of decision and choice with an explicit awareness
of alternatives which are *absent* in making computations. Great caution
must be exercised in interpreting his remarks that in a proof one wins
through to a decision, and his distinction between proofs within a proof
system and proofs that extend mathematics needs careful investigation.
There is no reason to suppose that he ever adopted, let alone continued to
cleave to, an extreme and wholly general form of logical or mathematical
existentialism.

We do speak of proof and deductive inference in respect of necessary truths; we say that a theorem follows from the axioms of
geometry. Wittgenstein did not deny this, but only the picture that lies
behind saying that it follows *necessarily*. If it does not follow, it is not *this*
calculus, but a different one or none at all (RFM 38ff.). For in calculi,
process and result are equivalent (RFM 68f.). We do not speak of making
fresh decisions or of laying down novel conventions in arriving at
arithmetical equations by elementary computations. On the contrary, as
Wittgenstein emphasized, we derive these rules in accord with the rules
of computation. 'The mathematical proposition determines a path, lays
down a path for us. It is no contradiction of this that it is a rule, and not
simply stipulated but produced according to rules' (RFM 228). But it is
crucial to note that the expression 'to follow from' does not have the
same grammar when applied *within* a system of necessary propositions as
it does when applied to the transformation of empirical propositions *in*

accord with the rules constituted by a given system of representation. This use of 'follows from' must be clarified, not taken to be self-explanatory. For to carry over features from the latter case to the former yields grotesque conceptual confusions. We transform empirical propositions in accord with paradigms that define what we call 'valid inference'. Given *this* and *this*, we argue, *this* proposition *must* be the case. The 'must' marks a norm of representation. But if we transpose this picture of 'following from' or 'follows necessarily' onto the network of norms of representation we generate the illusion that behind them stands a logical or mathematical reality to which they are responsible, or that there is a system of super-norms of representation that determines the 'follows from' *within* our system of norms of representation – a metalogic that justifies our logic. But so-called 'metalogic' or 'metamathematics' is only 'another calculus, just like any other one' (WWK 121); it is just more logic and mathematics 'in disguise' (WWK 136). To insist upon the autonomy of grammar is not to embrace the confusions of 'full-blooded conventionalism'.

Wittgenstein's account of the propositions philosophers call 'necessary' is not a form of 'moderate' conventionalism, nor is it a form of 'full-blooded' conventionalism. (Similarly, his philosophy of mathematics does not defend a form of 'strict finitism', depsychologized 'intuitionism' or 'constructivism'.[59] His purpose was not to take sides in the debates between rival schools of mathematicians, but rather to question the presuppositions which provided the framework for their debates.) He aimed at a complete reorientation of viewpoint – a fact which partly explains why his reflections are so difficult to comprehend and why they have been so extensively misunderstood by those who have attempted to locate his philosophy of mathematics and logic on existing philosophical maps.

If 'moderate conventionalism' and 'full-blooded conventionalism' exhaust the possible forms of conventionalism, then there can be no doubt that Wittgenstein's explanations of the character of necessary propositions should *not* be pigeon-holed as 'conventionalism'. Indeed,

---

[59] The issue is a large and complex one. Briefly, Wittgenstein did not object to the employment of indirect proofs (WWK 179ff., 207f., PG 304f.). He did not repudiate the Law of Excluded Middle (PR 176; PG 367f.), on the contrary, he conceived it as definitive of what is called 'a proposition' in *our* logical and mathematical calculi (but one can invent other calculi). He did not think that there are undecidable mathematical propositions (e.g. that there are three consecutive sevens in the expansion of π), but rather that such expressions are strictly senseless (PR 210ff.; AWL 196ff.). He did not conceive of a proof as akin to the verification of a truth, or to the 'construction' of a 'mathematical object', but rather as the construction of a rule of grammar the *meaning* of which is given by the proof (PG 359ff.; RFM *passim*). He did not repudiate the existence of transfinite numbers (although he divorced this concept from the 'actual infinite'), but rather questioned mathematicians' interpretation of what they had *invented* (WWK 227f.; PR ch. XII).

there are even deeper reasons for this *if* we take the classical conventionalism of the Circle as the defining paradigm or paradigms of the doctrine.
For both in its first phase, in which its primary inspiration was Hilbert's
Foundations of Geometry and the *Tractatus* (extensively misconstrued), and
in its second post-Tarskian phase, in which logical semantics significantly transformed it, it was rooted firmly in two misconceptions the
diagnosis of which is the leitmotiv of Wittgenstein's later philosophy.

First, the *Grundgedanke* of these forms of conventionalism is the idea
that what it is for something to be a necessary truth can be characterized
solely by reference to the *forms* of expressions. Wittgenstein, in diametric
contrast, held that necessary propositions must be characterized in terms
of their roles in our method of representation and patterns of reasoning.
What elevates a proposition to the dignity of a necessary proposition is
the function it fulfils – as a norm of representation, a rule for the
transformation of propositions, a correlate of a rule of inference, an
explanation of meaning, etc. This conception, worked out in detail for
the *various* kinds of necessary propositions, clarifies the very matters left
wholly unexamined in the classical conventionalism of the Circle. One
might say that they had no idea, or no adequate idea, of what it is for a
proposition to express a norm of representation.

Secondly, these forms of conventionalism were conspicuously caught
within the field of force of the Augustinian picture of language. The
original claim that the axioms of geometry, the Peano postulates and the
primitive propositions of *Principia* are conventions, and the claim that the
theorems of geometry and arithmetic, as well as the truths of logic,
follow from conventions rested on the principle that they could be
understood independently of correlating words with reality; this was
interpreted to imply that they were independent of the *meanings* assigned
to the primitive terms. Tarski's invention of logical semantics, which
was crucial for the development of Carnap's philosophy, did not challenge this primitive concept of meaning. On the contrary, it entrenched
it by apparently bringing the 'correlation of symbols with reality' within
the pale of rational 'scientific' discourse. But the resultant conceptions of
necessary propositions as 'true independently of meaning' or as 'true
under every possible interpretation (i.e. assignment of meaning)' are
irredemiably flawed by the misconception of meaning involved. To put
it crudely, necessary propositions are neither true independently of
meanings nor true in virtue of meanings, but rather constitutive of
meanings.

Unlike the conventionalism developed by members of the Vienna
Circle, Wittgenstein did not hold that 'analytic propositions' (e.g. 'Red is
a colour', 'A bachelor is an unmarried man') were 'true in virtue of the
meanings of words', but rather that they express rules for the use of
words. He did not argue that tautologies are true in virtue of the

meanings of their constituent logical expressions. He denied that mathematical propositions are tautologies, and repudiated the compositionalist idea that they are true in virtue of the axioms, definitions and rules of the number system. He objected to the supposition that our need to prove mathematical theorems stemmed from the limitations upon our intellectual powers, as if, were our intellect more powerful, we would see at a glance the totality of mathematical 'truths'. He did not hold that apparently synthetic *a priori* propositions such as 'Nothing can be both green and red all over' are tautologies (though he experimented with that idea in 1929) or analytic truths. They are, he held, norms of representation.

Nevertheless, if, after grasping the ways in which his analysis differs from the forms of conventionalism propounded in the 1930s and 1940s, we wish to classify it, there is surely some justice in saying that it is a conventionalist account. However, if we do so we must deny classical conventionalism the status of a defining paradigm of the doctrine, and repudiate the assumption that 'moderate' and 'full-blooded' conventionalism are exhaustive. If Wittgenstein's account is to be called conventionalist, it is deeply different from the classical varieties and from the 'full-blooded' version, and must be examined and evaluated in its own terms. It would be foolish to try to summarize his conception in a simple dictum; 'these things are finer spun than crude hands have any inkling of' (RFM 420), and the richness and diversity of the tapestry he wove defies compression into a slogan. What must be done is to trace each thread, and observe in detail how it is interwoven with the others. In this essay we have traced a few of these threads along a part of their length. Many crucial issues have been only touched upon (e.g. the nature of mathematical proof), others have been barely mentioned (e.g. consistency proofs and the fear of 'hidden contradictions' in a calculus). To explore these properly would involve a lengthy volume in its own right. Our purpose has been to show how Wittgenstein's reflections on 'necessary propositions' are related to his discussions of following rules that lie at the heart of the *Philosophical Investigations*. And also to demonstrate that current debates about Wittgenstein's philosophy of logic and mathematics extensively misinterpret his work, partly through failure to grasp this relation and also through misunderstandings of his remarks on rule-following.

INDEX

(Since the exegetical part of this book corresponds exactly to PI, this index should be used in conjunction with the original text and its index.)